# The Premier

# WORD PUZZLE

# Dictionary

This dictionary is designed for the thousands of people who derive pleasure from the solving and compiling of Word Puzzles.

In this book over 45,000 words are grouped alphabetically under their respective headings of one, two, three, four, five, six, seven and eight letters.

For the compiler and solver of Word Puzzles, this book is an invaluable aid, lessening considerably the task of discovering words for introduction into a puzzle.

Published by

Grandreams Limited
Jadwin House, 205/211 Kentish Town Road, London NW5 2JU.

Printed in England

ISBN 0 86227 637 3

WD1

# The Premier
# Word Puzzle Dictionary

## One-Letter

A | I | I | O

## Two-Letter Words

| A | B | F | I | L | N | P | T | V |
|---|---|---|---|---|---|---|---|---|
|    | Be | Fa | Id | La | Na | Pa | Ta | Va |
| Ab | Bo | Fy | If | Li | Ne | Pi | Ti | Vo |
| Ae | By |    | In | Lo | No |    | To |    |
| Ah |    |    | Io |    |    |    |    |    |
| Ai | **D** | **G** | Is |    | **O** | **R** |    | **W** |
| Am |    | Go | It |    |    | Ra |    | We |
| An | Do |    |    |    | Od | Re |    | Wo |
| As |    |    | **J** | **M** | Of |    | **U** |    |
| At | **E** | **H** | Jo | Ma | Oh |    | Ug |    |
| Au |    | Ha | Me | On |    | Up |    |    |
| Ax | Ee | He | **K** | Mi | Or |    | Ur | **Y** |
| Ay | Eh | Hi | Ka | Mo | Os | **S** | Us | Ye |
|    | Em | Ho | Ky | My | Ox | Si | Ut | Yo |
|    | En |    |    |    |    | So |    |    |

## Three-Letter Words

| A | | | B | | C | | D | | E |
|---|---|---|---|---|---|---|---|---|---|
|       | Ait | Art | Bah | Bon | Car | Cud | Did | Dug |     |
| **A** | Ake | Ary | Bam | Boo | Cat | Cue | Die | Dun |     |
| Aam   | Ala | Ash | Ban | Bot | Caw | Cup | Dig | Duo |     |
| Aba   | Alb | Ask | Bap | Bow | Cay | Cur | Dim | Dup |     |
| Abb   | Ale | Asp | Bar | Box | Cid | Cut | Din | Dux |     |
| Abc   | All | Ass | Bat | Boy | Cit |     | Dip | Dye |     |
| Abu   | Alp | Ate | Bay | Bub | Cly | **D** | Dis | **E** |   |
| Aby   | Als | Auf | Bed | Bud | Cob | Dab | Dit | Ean |     |
| Ace   | Alt | Auk | Bee | Bug | Cod | Dad | Div | Ear |     |
| Act   | Ama | Ava | Beg | Bun | Cog | Dag | Dod | Eat |     |
| Add   | Ana | Ave | Ben | Bur | Col | Dah | Doe | Eau |     |
| Ado   | And | Awe | Bet | Bus | Con | Dak | Dog | Ebb |     |
| Adz   | Ane | Awl | Bey | But | Coo | Dam | Dom | Ecu |     |
| Aft   | Ann | Awn | Bib | Buy | Cop | Dan | Don | Ee  |     |
| Aga   | Ant | Axe | Bid | Bye | Cor | Dap | Dop | Eft |     |
| Age   | Any | Aye | Big |     | Cos | Daw | Dor | Egg |     |
| Ago   | Ape |     | Bin | **C** | Cot | Day | Dot | Ego |   |
| Aha   | Apt | **B** | Bis | Cab | Cow | Dee | Dow | Eke |   |
| Aid   | Arc | Baa | Bit | Cad | Coy | Den | Dry | Eld |     |
| Ail   | Are | Bac | Boa | Cam | Coz | Dew | Dub | Elf |     |
| Aim   | Ark | Bad | Bob | Can | Cry | Dey | Dud |     |     |
| Air   | Arm | Bag | Bog | Cap | Cub | Dib | Due |     |     |

### THREE-LETTER WORDS—*continued*

Elk
Ell
Elm
Eme
Emu
End
Ene
Ens
Eon
Era
Ere
Erf
Erg
Err
Ess
Eve
Ewe
Eye

**F**

Fad
Fag
Fam
Fan
Fap
Far
Fat
Faw
Fay
Fed
Fee
Fen
Fet
Feu
Few
Fey
Fez
Fib
Fid
Fie
Fig
Fin
Fir
Fit
Fix
Flu
Fly
Fob
Foe
Fog
Foh
Fon
Foo
Fop
For
Fou
Fox

Foy
Fro
Fry
Fub
Fud
Fum
Fun
Fur

**G**

Gab
Gad
Gae
Gag
Gal
Gam
Gap
Gar
Gas
Gat
Gay
Ged
Gee
Gem
Gen
Geo
Get
Gey
Gib
Gid
Gie
Gif
Gig
Gim
Gin
Gio
Gip
Gnu
Gob
God
Gog
Got
Gue
Gum
Gun
Gut
Guy
Gym
Gyp

**H**

Had
Hae
Hag
Hah
Ham
Han
Hap

Has
Hat
Haw
Hay
Hel
Hem
Hen
Hep
Her
Hew
Hey
Hic
Hid
Hie
Him
Hin
Hip
His
Hit
Hoa
Hob
Hod
Hoe
Hog
Hop
Hot
How
Hox
Hoy
Hub
Hue
Hug
Huh
Hum
Hun
Hup
Hut
Hux
Hyp

**I**

Ice
Ich
Icy
Ide
Ido
Ilk
Ill
Imp
Ink
Inn
Ion
Ire
Irk
Ish
Ism
Its
Ivy

**J**

Jab
Jag
Jah
Jak
Jam
Jap
Jar
Jaw
Jay
Jet
Jew
Jib
Jig
Job
Joe
Jog
Jot
Jow
Joy
Jud
Jug
Jur
Jus
Jut

**K**

Kae
Kam
Kat
Kaw
Kay
Kea
Keb
Keg
Ken
Kep
Ket
Kex
Key
Kid
Kin
Kip
Kit
Koa
Kob
Kye

**L**

Lac
Lad
Lag
Lam
Lap
Lar
Lat
Lav

Law
Lax
Lay
Lea
Led
Lee
Leg
Leo
Let
Leu
Lev
Lew
Ley
Lib
Lid
Lie
Lig
Lin
Lip
Lis
Lit
Lob
Log
Loo
Lop
Lot
Low
Loy
Lud
Lue
Lug
Lum
Luz
Lye
Lym

**M**

Mab
Mac
Mad
Mag
Man
Map
Mar
Mat
Maw
Max
May
Men
Met
Mew
Mho
Mid
Mil
Mim
Mir
Mix

Moa
Mob
Mod
Moe
Mog
Moo
Mop
Mot
Mow
Mud
Mug
Mum
Mun
Mux
Mya

**N**

Nab
Nag
Nam
Nap
Nas
Nay
Neb
Nee
Nef
Nep
Net
New
Nib
Nil
Nim
Nip
Nis
Nit
Nix
Nob
Nod
Nog
Nom
Non
Nor
Not
Now
Noy
Nub
Nun
Nur
Nut
Nux
Nye
Nys
Nyx

**O**

Oaf
Oak
Oar

Oat
Obi
Oca
Odd
Ode
Oes
Off
Oft
Ohm
Oho
Oil
Oke
Old
One
Oof
Ope
Opt
Orb
Orc
Ord
Ore
Ort
Our
Out
Ova
Owe
Owl
Own

**P**

Pad
Pah
Pal
Pam
Pan
Pap
Par
Pas
Pat
Paw
Pax
Pay
Pea
Ped
Peg
Pen
Pep
Per
Pet
Pew
Pia
Pie
Pig
Pin
Pip
Pit
Piu
Pix

Ply
Poa
Pod
Poe
Poh
Pom
Pop
Pos
Pot
Pox
Poy
Pro
Pry
Pub
Pud
Pug
Pun
Pup
Pur
Pus
Put
Puy
Pye
Pyx

**Q**

Qua

**R**

Rad
Rag
Rai
Raj
Ram
Ran
Rap
Ras
Rat
Raw
Rax
Ray
Red
Ree
Reh
Rei
Ren
Rep
Res
Ret
Rew
Rex
Rib
Rid
Rie
Rig
Rim

Rio
Rip
Rit
Rob
Roc
Rod
Roe
Rog
Rok
Rom
Rot
Row
Roy
Rub
Ruc
Rud
Rue
Rug
Rum
Run
Rut
Rye

**S**

Sab
Sac
Sad
Sae
Sag
Sai
Sal
Sam
Sap
Sat
Saw
Sax
Say
Sea
Sec
Sed
See
Seg
Sel
Sen
Sep
Set
Sew
Sex
She
Shy
Sib
Sic
Sil
Sim
Sin
Sip
Sir

THREE-LETTER WORDS—*continued*

Sis, Sit, Six, Ski, Sky, Sly, Sny, Sob, Soc, Sod, Sog, Sol, Son, Sop, Sot, Sou, Sow, Sox, Soy, Spa, Spy, Sty, Sub, Sue, Sug, Sum, Sun, Sup, Syb

**T**
Tab, Tad, Tag, Tai, Taj, Tan, Tap, Tar, Tat, Tau, Taw, Tax, Tea, Ted, Tee, Teg, Ten, Ter, Tew, The, Tho, Thy, Tib, Tic, Tid, Tie, Tig, Tin, Tip, Tir, Tit, Tod, Toe, Tog, Tol, Tom, Ton, Too, Top, Tor, Tot, Tow, Toy, Try, Tub, Tug, Tui, Tun, Tup, Tut, Twa, Two, Tye, Tyr

**U**
Ugh, Ule, Una, Ure, Urf, Urg, Urn, Use, Uta, Uva

**V**
Vae, Vag, Van, Vas, Vat, Vet, Vex, Via, Vie, Vim, Vis, Viz, Vly, Voe, Vol, Vow, Vox, Vug, Vum

**W**
Wad, Wae, Wag, Wan, Wap, War, Was, Wat, Wax, Way, Web, Wed, Wee, Wen, Wet, Wey, Who, Why, Wig, Win, Wis, Wit, Woe, Won, Woo, Wop, Wot, Wow, Wox, Wry, Wye

**Y**
Yah, Yak, Yam, Yap, Yaw, Yea, Yen, Yes, Yet, Yew, Yex, Yid, Yon, You

**Z**
Zax, Zea, Zed, Zel, Zip, Zoo, Zuz

# Four-Letter Words

| | | | | | | | |
|---|---|---|---|---|---|---|---|
| **A** | Agio | Amen | Aril | Babe | Bawl | Bike | Bode |
|  | Agog | Amia | Arms | Babu | Bawn | Bile | Body |
| Abba | Agua | Amic | Army | Baby | Baye | Bilk | Boer |
| Abbé | Ague | Amid | Arow | Back | Bays | Bill | Bogy |
| Abed | Ahem | Amin | 'Arry | Bade | Bead | Bind | Boil |
| Aber | Ahoy | Amir | Arum | Baff | Beak | Bing | Bold |
| Abet | Aile | Amma | Asar | Baft | Beam | Bink | Bole |
| Abib | Aire | Amok | Asci | Bail | Bean | Bird | Boll |
| Able | Airt | Amyl | Ashy | Bait | Bear | Birk | Bolo |
| Ably | Airy | Anas | Atom | Bake | Beat | Birl | Bolt |
| Abut | Ajar | Anew | Atop | Bald | Beau | Birr | Bomb |
| Abye | Ajee | Anil | Aula | Bale | Beck | Birt | Bond |
| Acer | Ajog | Anna | Auld | Balk | Bede | Bise | Bone |
| Ache | Akee | Anoa | Aunt | Ball | Beef | Bisk | Bony |
| Acid | Akin | Anon | Aura | Balm | Been | Bite | Boob |
| Acme | Alar | Ansa | Aval | Band | Beer | Bitt | Booh |
| Acne | Alas | Anta | Avel | Bane | Beet | Blab | Book |
| Acop | Albe | Apay | Aver | Bang | Bein | Blae | Boom |
| Acoy | Alca | Aper | Aves | Bank | Bell | Blay | Boon |
| Acre | Alee | Apex | Avid | Barb | Belt | Blea | Boor |
| Acta | Alew | Apis | Avis | Bard | Bema | Bleb | Boot |
| Adam | Alfa | Apod | Avow | Bare | Bend | Bled | Bora |
| Adar | Alla | Apse | Away | Bark | Bene | Blee | Bord |
| Ades | Ally | Aqua | Awny | Barm | Bent | Blet | Bore |
| Adit | Alma | Arab | Awry | Barn | Bere | Blew | Born |
| Adry | Alme | Araf | Axil | Baru | Berg | Bley | Bort |
| Adze | Alms | Arar | Axis | Base | Berm | Blin | Bosa |
| Aeon | Alod | Arba | Axle | Bash | Best | Blob | Bosh |
| Aery | Aloe | Arca | Ayah | Bask | Bete | Blot | Bosk |
| Afar | Alow | Arch | Ayme | Bass | Bevy | Blow | Boss |
| Affy | Also | Area | Ayry | Bast | Bias | Blue | Bote |
| Aged | Alto | Aret | **B** | Bate | Bice | Blur | Both |
| Agee | Alum | Arew | Baal | Bath | Bide | Boad | Bots |
| Agen | Ambe | Aria | Baba | Bauk | Bier | Boar | Boud |
| Agha | Ambo | Arid |  | Bawd | Bigg | Boat | Boun |

**FOUR-LETTER WORDS—*continued***

| | | | | | | | |
|---|---|---|---|---|---|---|---|
| Bout | Cade | Chew | Cold | Cuca | Daze | Dive | Duad |
| Bowl | Cadi | Chic | Cole | Cuff | Dead | Doab | Dual |
| Bows | Café | Chid | Coll | Cull | Deaf | Doat | Duan |
| Brad | Cage | Chig | Colt | Culm | Deal | Dock | Duce |
| Brae | Cain | Chin | Coma | Cult | Dean | Dodd | Duck |
| Brag | Cake | Chip | Comb | Curb | Dear | Dodo | Duct |
| Bran | Calf | Chit | Come | Curd | Deaw | Doer | Dude |
| Brat | Calk | Chop | Coms | Cure | Debt | Doff | Duds |
| Bray | Call | Chou | Cond | Curl | Deck | Doge | Duel |
| Bred | Calm | Chow | Cone | Curr | Deed | Dohl | Duet |
| Bree | Calp | Chub | Conk | Curt | Deem | Doit | Duff |
| Bren | Calx | Chum | Conn | Cusk | Deep | Doke | Duke |
| Brer | Came | Chut | Cony | Cusp | Deer | Dole | Dule |
| Bret | Camp | Ciel | Coof | Cuss | Deft | Doll | Dull |
| Brew | Cane | Cima | Cook | Cute | Defy | Dolt | Duly |
| Brig | Cang | Circ | Cool | Cyar | Deil | Dome | Duma |
| Brim | Cant | Cirl | Coom | Cyma | Dele | Done | Dumb |
| Brin | Cany | Cist | Coon | Cyme | Delf | Doob | Dump |
| Brio | Capa | Cite | Coop | Cyst | Dell | Dood | Dune |
| Brit | Cape | City | Coot | Czar | Deme | Dook | Dunt |
| Brob | Card | Cive | Cope | | Demy | Dool | Dupe |
| Brog | Care | Clad | Copt | **D** | Dene | Doom | Dura |
| Broo | Cark | Clag | Copy | | Dent | Door | Dure |
| Brow | Carl | Clam | Corb | Dace | Deny | Dope | Durn |
| Bubo | Carp | Clan | Cord | Dade | Derm | Dora | Duse |
| Buck | Carr | Clap | Core | Dado | Dern | Dorn | Dush |
| Buff | Cart | Claw | Corf | Daff | Desk | Dorp | Dusk |
| Buhl | Case | Clay | Cork | Daft | Devi | Dorr | Dust |
| Bulb | Cash | Clef | Corm | Dago | Dewy | Dory | Duty |
| Bulk | Cask | Cleg | Corn | Dais | Dhak | Dose | Dyad |
| Bull | Cast | Clem | Cose | Dale | Dhow | Doss | Dyak |
| Bump | Cate | Clew | Cosh | Dali | Dial | Dote | Dyer |
| Bung | Cauf | Clio | Coss | Dall | Dibs | Douc | Dyke |
| Bunk | Cauk | Clip | Cost | Dalt | Dice | Doum | Dyne |
| Bunt | Caul | Clod | Cosy | Dame | Dick | Dour | |
| Buoy | Cave | Clog | Cote | Damn | Dido | Dout | **E** |
| Burd | Cavy | Clot | Cott | Damp | Dieb | Dove | |
| Burg | Cawk | Cloy | Coup | Dane | Diet | Dowf | Each |
| Burk | Cede | Club | Cove | Dang | Dika | Down | Earl |
| Burl | Ceil | Clue | Cowl | Dank | Dike | Doxy | Earn |
| Burn | Cell | Coak | Coxa | Dare | Dill | Doze | Ease |
| Burr | Celo | Coal | Coze | Darg | Dime | Dozy | East |
| Burt | Celt | Coat | Cozy | Dari | Dine | Drab | Easy |
| Bury | Cent | Coax | Crab | Dark | Ding | Drad | Eath |
| Bush | Cere | Coca | Crag | Darn | Dink | Drag | Ebon |
| Busk | Cern | Coch | Cram | Dart | Dint | Dram | Ecce |
| Buss | Cess | Cock | Cran | Dash | Dire | Drat | Eche |
| Bust | Cest | Coco | Craw | Data | Dirk | Draw | Echo |
| Busy | Chad | Coda | Crax | Date | Dirl | Dray | Ecru |
| Butt | Chai | Code | Cree | Daub | Dirt | Dree | Edam |
| Buzz | Chal | Coff | Crew | Daud | Disa | Drey | Edda |
| Byde | Cham | Coft | Crib | Dauk | Disc | Drib | Eddy |
| Byre | Chap | Coif | Crop | Daur | Dish | Drip | Eden |
| | Char | Coil | Crow | Dauw | Disk | Drop | Edge |
| | Chat | Coin | Crup | Davy | Diss | Drow | Edgy |
| **C** | Chaw | Coir | Crut | Dawd | Dite | Drub | Edit |
| | Chay | Coix | Crux | Dawk | Diva | Drug | Eery |
| Caba | Chef | Coke | Cube | Dawm | | Drum | Egad |
| Cack | | | | Dawn | | | Egal |

## FOUR-LETTER WORDS—*continued*

| | | | | | | | |
|---|---|---|---|---|---|---|---|
| Eger | Faba | Find | Fowl | Gasp | Gleg | Grum | Hask |
| Egis | Face | Fine | Foxy | Gast | Glen | Guan | Hasp |
| Egma | Fact | Finn | Fozy | Gate | Gley | Guhr | Hast |
| Eigh | Fade | Fire | Frab | Gaub | Glib | Gula | Hate |
| Eild | Faik | Firk | Frap | Gaud | Glim | Gulf | Hath |
| Eine | Fail | Firm | Frau | Gaul | Glit | Gull | Haul |
| Ejoo | Fain | Firn | Fray | Gaum | Glow | Gulp | Haum |
| Elan | Fair | Fisc | Free | Gaun | Glue | Guly | Have |
| Elmy | Faix | Fish | Fret | Gaup | Glum | Guru | Hawk |
| Else | Fake | Fist | Frit | Gaur | Glut | Gush | Hawm |
| Elul | Fala | Fitt | Friz | Gave | Gnar | Gust | Haze |
| Emeu | Fall | Five | Frog | Gawd | Gnat | Gyal | Hazy |
| Emir | Falx | Fizz | From | Gawk | Gnaw | Gybe | Head |
| Emit | Fama | Flag | Frow | Gawn | Goad | Gyle | Heal |
| Emys | Fame | Flam | Fuar | Gawp | Goaf | Gyra | Heam |
| Enew | Fand | Flap | Fuel | Gaze | Goal | Gyre | Heap |
| Enow | Fane | Flat | Fuff | Gazy | Goat | Gyte | Hear |
| Ente | Fang | Flaw | Fugh | Geal | Goby | Gyve | Heat |
| Envy | Fard | Flax | Full | Gean | Goel | | Hebe |
| Eoan | Fare | Flay | Fume | Gear | Goer | | Hech |
| Epic | Farl | Flea | Fumy | Geat | Goff | **H** | Heck |
| Epos | Farm | Fled | Fund | Geck | Gola | | Heed |
| Ergo | Faro | Flee | Fung | Gedd | Gold | Haaf | Heel |
| Eric | Fash | Flex | Funk | Geed | Golf | Haar | Heft |
| Erin | Fast | Fley | Furl | Gees | Gome | Hack | Heir |
| Erne | Fate | Flip | Fury | Geez | Gone | Hade | Held |
| Erse | Faun | Flit | Fuse | Gegg | Gong | Hadj | Hele |
| Ersh | Fawn | Flix | Fuss | Geld | Good | Haet | Hell |
| Erst | Feal | Floe | Fust | Gelt | Goor | Haft | Helm |
| Esox | Fear | Flog | Fuze | Gena | Gore | Haha | Help |
| Espy | Feat | Flop | Fuzz | Gens | Gorm | Haik | Hemp |
| Esse | Feck | Flot | Fyke | Gent | Gory | Hail | Hend |
| Etch | Feed | Flow | Fyrd | Germ | Goss | Hain | Hent |
| Ethe | Feel | Flue | | Gern | Goth | Hair | Herb |
| Etna | Feer | Flux | | Gest | Gouk | Hait | Herd |
| Etui | Feet | Foal | **G** | Geum | Goul | Hajj | Here |
| Euge | Fell | Foam | Gaby | Ghat | Gout | Hake | Hern |
| Even | Felt | Fogy | Gael | Ghee | Gowd | Hald | Hero |
| Ever | Feme | Foil | Gaff | Gibe | Gowf | Hale | Herr |
| Evet | Fend | Foin | Gage | Gibs | Gowk | Half | Hers |
| Evil | Fent | Fold | Gain | Gift | Gown | Hall | Hery |
| Ewer | Feod | Folk | Gair | Gild | Grab | Halm | Hest |
| Ewft | Fere | Fond | Gait | Gill | Graf | Halo | Hewn |
| Ewry | Ferm | Fone | Gala | Gilt | Gram | Halt | Hide |
| Exit | Fern | Font | Gale | Gimp | Gray | Hame | High |
| Exon | Fess | Food | Gall | Ging | Gree | Hand | Hill |
| Exul | Fête | Fool | Galt | Ginn | Grey | Hang | Hilt |
| Eyas | Feud | Foot | Gamb | Gird | Grid | Hank | Hind |
| Eyer | Fiar | Ford | Game | Girl | Grig | Hard | Hink |
| Eyne | Fiat | Fore | Gamp | Girn | Grim | Hare | Hint |
| Eyot | Fico | Fork | Gamy | Girr | Grin | Hark | Hire |
| Eyra | Fief | Form | Gang | Girt | Grip | Harl | Hish |
| Eyre | Fife | Fors | Gant | Gist | Grit | Harm | Hisk |
| Eyry | Fike | Fort | Gaol | Gite | Grog | Harn | Hiss |
| | Fiky | Foss | Gape | Give | Gros | Haro | Hist |
| **F** | File | Foud | Garb | Gizz | Grot | Harp | Hive |
| Faam | Fill | Foul | Gare | Glad | Grow | Harr | Hizz |
| Faap | Film | Four | Gash | Glee | Grub | Hart | Hoar |

**FOUR-LETTER WORDS**—*continued*

| | | | | | | | |
|---|---|---|---|---|---|---|---|
| Hoax | Icon | Jimp | Keir | Koul | Leer | Loge | Mace |
| Hobo | Icos | Jink | Kelk | Kris | Lees | Loin | Made |
| Hock | Idea | Jinn | Kell | Kroo | Leet | Loki | Mage |
| Hogg | Idem | Joey | Kelp | Ksar | Left | Loll | Magi |
| Hoit | Ides | John | Kelt | Kudu | Lend | Loma | Maid |
| Hold | Idle | Join | Kemb | Kurd | Leno | Lomp | Maik |
| Holm | Idly | Joke | Kemp | Kyle | Lens | Lone | Mail |
| Holp | Idol | Jole | Kent | | Lent | Long | Maim |
| Holt | Idyl | Joll | Kepi | | Lere | Loof | Main |
| Holy | Ilex | Jolt | Kept | **L** | Less | Look | Make |
| Home | Ilka | Jook | Kerb | | Lest | Loom | Male |
| Hone | Imam | Josh | Kerf | Lace | Lett | Loon | Mall |
| Hong | Impi | Joss | Kern | Lack | Levy | Loop | Malm |
| Honk | Inby | Jouk | Khan | Lade | Lewd | Loos | Malt |
| Hood | Inca | Jove | Khel | Lady | Liar | Loot | Mama |
| Hoof | Inch | Jowl | Khud | Laic | Lias | Lope | Mane |
| Hook | Inia | Juba | Kibe | Laid | Lice | Lord | Manx |
| Hoop | Inky | Jube | Kiby | Lain | Lich | Lore | Many |
| Hoot | Inly | Judo | Kick | Lair | Lick | Lorn | Marc |
| Hope | Inro | Judy | Kier | Lakh | Lied | Lory | Mare |
| Horn | Into | Juga | Kill | Lake | Lief | Lose | Mark |
| Hors | Iota | Juju | Kiln | Laky | Lien | Loss | Marl |
| Hose | Irid | Juke | Kilo | Lama | Lieu | Lost | Marm |
| Host | Iris | July | Kilp | Lamb | Life | Lote | Mars |
| Hour | Iron | Jump | Kilt | Lame | Lift | Loth | Mart |
| Hova | Isca | June | Kind | Lamp | Like | Loud | Mash |
| Hove | Isis | Junk | Kine | Lana | Lill | Loup | Mask |
| Howe | Isle | Juno | King | Land | Lilt | Lour | Mass |
| Howk | Itch | Jupe | Kink | Lane | Lily | Lout | Mast |
| Howl | Item | Jury | Kino | Lang | Limb | Love | Mate |
| Huck | Itis | Just | Kipe | Lank | Lime | Lown | Math |
| Hued | Iwis | Jute | Kirk | Lanx | Limn | Luce | Matt |
| Huel | | | Kiss | Lapp | Limp | Luck | Maud |
| Huer | | | Kist | Lard | Limy | Ludo | Maul |
| Huff | **J** | **K** | Kite | Lare | Line | Lues | Mawk |
| Huge | Jack | Kadi | Kith | Lark | Ling | Luff | Maya |
| Huia | Jade | Kago | Kive | Lash | Link | Lull | Maze |
| Hulk | Jail | Kagu | Kiwi | Lass | Linn | Lump | Mazy |
| Hull | Jain | Kaif | Knab | Last | Lint | Lune | Mead |
| Hump | Jamb | Kail | Knag | Late | Liny | Lung | Meal |
| Hung | Jane | Kain | Knap | Lath | Lion | Lunt | Mean |
| Hunk | Jann | Kaka | Knar | Laud | Lipp | Lure | Mear |
| Hunt | Jant | Kaki | Knee | Lava | Lira | Lurk | Meat |
| Hurl | Jape | Kala | Knew | Lave | Lire | Lush | Meed |
| Hurt | Jarl | Kale | Knit | Lawk | Lirk | Lusk | Meek |
| Hush | Jaup | Kali | Knob | Lawn | Lisp | Lust | Meer |
| Husk | Jawy | Kama | Knop | Laze | List | Lute | Meet |
| Huso | Jazz | Kame | Knot | Lazy | Lith | Lyam | Mell |
| Hyen | Jean | Kami | Know | Lead | Live | Lyme | Melt |
| Hyke | Jeer | Kana | Knub | Leaf | Load | Lynx | Memo |
| Hymn | Jeff | Kang | Knur | Leak | Loaf | Lyon | Mend |
| Hypo | Jehu | Kans | Knut | Leal | Loam | Lyra | Ment |
| | Jerk | Kava | Koba | Leam | Loan | Lyre | Menu |
| | Jess | Keck | Koff | Lean | Lobe | | Mere |
| **I** | Jest | Keek | Kohl | Leap | Loch | **M** | Meri |
| Ibex | Jibe | Keel | Kola | Lear | Lock | | Merk |
| Ibid | Jill | Keen | Koth | Leat | Lode | Ma'am | Mesa |
| Ibis | Jilt | Keep | Koto | Leef | Loft | Maar | Mesh |
| | | | | Leek | | | |

## FOUR-LETTER WORDS—*continued*

| | | | | | | | |
|---|---|---|---|---|---|---|---|
| Mess | Moop | Naze | Nurl | Oval | Peak | Plap | Prim |
| Meta | Moor | Neaf | Nyas | Oven | Peal | Plat | Proa |
| Mete | Moot | Neal |  | Over | Pean | Play | Prod |
| Meum | Mope | Neap | **O** | Ovum | Pear | Plea | Prog |
| Mewl | Mops | Near | Oaks | Ower | Peas | Pled | Prop |
| Miau | Mora | Neat | Oaky | Owre | Peat | Plim | Prow |
| Mica | More | Neck | Oast | Owse | Peba | Plod | Prys |
| Mice | Morn | Need | Oath | Oxen | Pech | Plop | Puce |
| Mich | Mort | Neem | Obex | Oxer | Peck | Plot | Puck |
| Mico | Mose | Neep | Obey | Oyer | Peek | Plow | Pudu |
| Mida | Moss | Neif | Obit | Oyes | Peel | Ploy | Puff |
| Mien | Most | Nemo | Oboe | Oyez | Peen | Plug | Pugh |
| Miff | Mote | Neon | Obol |  | Peep | Plum | Puke |
| Mike | Moth | Nepe | Obus | **P** | Peer | Plus | Pule |
| Mild | Moue | Nero | Odal | Paca | Pela | Pnyx | Pull |
| Mile | Move | Nesh | Odds | Pace | Pelf | Pock | Pulp |
| Milk | Moxa | Ness | Odic | Pack | Pell | Poco | Pulu |
| Mill | Moya | Nest | Odin | Paco | Pelt | Poem | Puma |
| Milt | Moze | Nett | Ogam | Pact | Pend | Poet | Pump |
| Mime | Much | Neum | Ogee | Paff | Pent | Poke | Pumy |
| Mina | Muck | News | Ogle | Page | Peon | Poky | Puna |
| Mind | Muff | Newt | Ogre | Paid | Pepo | Pole | Punk |
| Mine | Muid | Next | Oily | Paik | Peri | Polk | Punt |
| Ming | Muir | Nias | Okra | Pail | Perk | Poll | Puny |
| Mink | Mule | Nice | Olio | Pain | Pern | Polo | Pupa |
| Mino | Mull | Nick | Olla | Pair | Pert | Polt | Pure |
| Mint | Mult | Nide | Olpe | Pais | Peso | Pome | Purl |
| Minx | Mumm | Nigh | Omen | Pala | Pest | Pomp | Purr |
| Miny | Mump | Nike | Omer | Pale | Phew | Pond | Push |
| Mire | Mure | Nill | Omit | Pali | Phiz | Pone | Puss |
| Mirk | Murk | Nine | Once | Pall | Phut | Ponk | Putt |
| Miry | Musa | Nisi | Ondy | Palm | Pica | Pons | Puxi |
| Mise | Muse | Nizy | Oner | Palp | Pice | Pony | Pyre |
| Miss | Mush | Nock | Only | Palt | Pick | Pood |  |
| Mist | Musk | Node | Onst | Paly | Pict | Pooh | **Q** |
| Misy | Muss | Noel | Onto | Pand | Pied | Pool | Quab |
| Mite | Must | Noll | Onus | Pane | Pier | Poon | Quad |
| Mity | Mute | Nome | Onym | Pang | Piet | Poop | Quag |
| Mixt | Muxy | None | Onyx | Pant | Pike | Poor | Quat |
| Moan | Myna | Nook | Oofy | Papa | Pila | Pope | Quay |
| Moat | Myth | Noon | Ooze | Para | Pile | Pore | Quey |
| Mock |  | Norm | Oozy | Pard | Pill | Pork | Quib |
| Moco |  | Norn | Opah | Pare | Pine | Port | Quid |
| Mode | **N** | Nose | Opal | Park | Ping | Pory | Quin |
| Modi | Nabk | Nosy | Open | Parr | Pink | Pose | Quip |
| Moff | Naga | Note | Opus | Part | Pint | Posh | Quit |
| Mohr | Naib | Noul | Oral | Pash | Piny | Post | Quiz |
| Moil | Naif | Noun | Orgy | Pass | Pipe | Posy | Quod |
| Moke | Naik | Nous | Orle | Past | Pipi | Pour | Quop |
| Mold | Nail | Nout | Orra | Pate | Pipy | Pout |  |
| Mole | Name | Nowl | Oryx | Path | Pirn | Prad | **R** |
| Moll | Naos | Nowt | Otic | Paul | Pise | Pram | Rabi |
| Moly | Nape | Nowy | Otto | Pave | Pish | Pray | Raca |
| Mome | Nard | Nude | Ouch | Pavo | Pith | Pree | Race |
| Monk | Nary | Null | Ourn | Pawl | Pity | Prep | Rach |
| Mood | Nave | Numb | Ours | Pawn | Pixy | Prex | Rack |
| Mool | Navy | Nung | Ouse | Peag | Pize | Prey | Racy |
| Moon |  |  | Oust |  | Plan | Prig |  |

## FOUR-LETTER WORDS—*continued*

| | | | | | | | |
|---|---|---|---|---|---|---|---|
| Rade | Rest | Roon | Sair | Seil | Silt | Slur | Sour |
| Raff | Rete | Roop | Sake | Seld | Sind | Slut | Sous |
| Raft | Reus | Root | Saki | Self | Sine | Smee | Sout |
| Rage | Reve | Rope | Sale | Sell | Sing | Smew | Sowl |
| Ragg | Rhea | Ropy | Salt | Seme | Sink | Smit | Sown |
| Ragi | Rhus | Rose | Same | Send | Sipe | Smug | Soya |
| Rahu | Rial | Ross | Samp | Sens | Sire | Smur | Spae |
| Raid | Rice | Rosy | Sand | Sent | Sist | Smut | Span |
| Rail | Rich | Rota | Sane | Seps | Site | 'Snag | Spar |
| Rain | Rick | Rote | Sang | Sept | Sith | Snap | Spat |
| Raja | Ride | Rotl | Sank | Sera | Sium | Snar | Spay |
| Rake | Riem | Roue | Sans | Serb | Siva | Sneb | Sped |
| Raki | Rife | Roum | Sapo | Sere | Size | Sned | Sper |
| Rale | Rift | Roup | Sard | Serf | Sizy | Snee | Spet |
| Rama | Rile | Rout | Sari | Serr | Skat | Snib | Spew |
| Ramp | Rill | Roux | Sark | Sess | Skaw | Snig | Spie |
| Rana | Rima | Rove | Sarn | Seta | Skee | Snip | Spin |
| Rand | Rime | Ruby | Sash | Sett | Skeg | Snob | Spit |
| Rane | Rimy | Ruck | Sass | Sewn | Skep | Snod | Spot |
| Rang | Rind | Rudd | Sate | Sext | Skew | Snot | Spry |
| Rani | Rine | Rude | Sati | Shad | Skid | Snow | Spud |
| Rank | Ring | Ruff | Saul | Shag | Skim | Snub | Spue |
| Rant | Rink | Ruga | Saut | Shah | Skin | Snug | Spun |
| Rape | Rino | Ruin | Save | Sham | Skio | Soak | Spur |
| Rapt | Riot | Rule | Sawn | Shan | Skip | Soap | Stab |
| Rare | Ripe | Rump | Saxe | Shaw | Skit | Soar | Stag |
| Rase | Ript | Rune | Scab | Shay | Skua | Sock | Stam |
| Rash | Rise | Rung | Scad | Shea | Skue | Soda | Star |
| Rasp | Risk | Runn | Scan | Shed | Skug | Sofa | Staw |
| Rata | Risp | Runt | Scar | Shet | Skye | Sofi | Stay |
| Rate | Rite | Rusa | Scat | Shew | Skyr | Soft | Stem |
| Rath | Riva | Ruse | Scot | Shim | Slab | Soho | Step |
| Rave | Rive | Rush | Scow | Shin | Slae | Soil | Stet |
| Raze | Rivo | Rusk | Scry | Ship | Slag | Soke | Stew |
| Read | Rixy | Russ | Scud | Shod | Slam | Sola | Stie |
| Reak | Road | Rust | Scug | Shoe | Slap | Sold | Stir |
| Real | Roam | Ruta | Scum | Shog | Slat | Sole | Stoa |
| Ream | Roan | Ruth | Scun | Shoo | Slav | Soli | Stob |
| Rean | Roar | Ryal | Scup | Shop | Slaw | Solo | Stog |
| Reap | Robe | Ryfe | Scur | Shot | Slay | Soma | Stop |
| Rear | Rock | Ryke | Scut | Show | Sled | Some | Stot |
| Reck | Rode | Rynd | Scye | Shug | Slew | Song | Stow |
| Redd | Roil | Ryot | Seah | Shun | Sley | Soon | Stub |
| Rede | Roin | Rype | Seal | Shut | Slid | Soop | Stud |
| Reed | Roke | Ryve | Seam | Sice | Slim | Soot | Stug |
| Reef | Roky |  | Sean | Sich | Slip | Soph | Stum |
| Reek | Role | **S** | Sear | Sick | Slit | Sora | Stun |
| Reel | Roll | Sack | Seat | Sida | Slob | Sorb | Stye |
| Reem | Rome | Sadr | Seax | Side | Sloe | Sord | Styx |
| Reft | Romp | Safe | Sect | Sift | Slog | Sore | Subx |
| Reim | Rone | Saga | Seed | Sigh | Slop | Sorn | Such |
| Rein | Rong | Sage | Seek | Sign | Slot | Sort | Suck |
| Reis | Ront | Sago | Seel | Sike | Slow | Sory | Sudd |
| Rely | Rood | Sagy | Seem | Sikh | Slub | So-so | Suds |
| Rend | Roof | Saic | Seen | Sile | Slud | Soss | Sued |
| Rent | Rook | Said | Seep | Silk | Slue | Soul | Suet |
| Repp | Rool | Sail | Seer | Sill | Slug | Soum | Suit |
| Resp | Room | Sain | Sego | Silo | Slum | Soup | Sulk |

**FOUR-LETTER WORDS—*continued***

| | | | | | | | |
|---|---|---|---|---|---|---|---|
| Sump | Tarn | Tidy | Tour | **U** | Vena | Wane | Whit |
| Sung | Taro | Tier | Tout | | Vend | Wang | Whiz |
| Sunk | Tart | Tiff | Town | Udal | Vent | Want | Whoa |
| Sunn | Tash | Tige | Towy | Ugly | Verb | Wapp | Whom |
| Supe | Task | Tike | Toze | Ulex | Vert | Ward | Whop |
| Sura | Tass | Tile | Tram | Ulna | Very | Ware | Whot |
| Surd | Tata | Till | Trap | Umbo | Vest | Wark | Whur |
| Sure | Tate | Tilt | Tray | Unau | Veto | Warm | Wick |
| Surf | Tath | Time | Tree | Unbe | Vial | Warn | Wide |
| Swab | Taut | Tind | Trek | Unco | Vice | Warp | Wife |
| Swad | Taws | Tine | Tret | Undo | Vide | Wart | Wild |
| Swag | Taxi | Ting | Trey | Unio | View | Wary | Wile |
| Swam | Tayo | Tink | Trez | Unit | Vild | Wase | Will |
| Swan | Tead | Tint | Trig | Unto | Vile | Wash | Wilt |
| Swap | Teak | Tiny | Trim | Upas | Vill | Wasp | Wily |
| Swat | Teal | Tire | Trio | Upby | Vina | Wast | Wind |
| Sway | Team | Tirl | Trip | Upon | Vine | Watt | Wine |
| Swig | Tean | Tiro | Trod | Urao | Vint | Waul | Wing |
| Swim | Tear | Tirr | Tron | Urde | Viny | Wave | Wink |
| Swop | Tede | Titi | Trot | Urdu | Viol | Wavy | Winy |
| Swot | Teed | Tivy | Trow | Urea | Vire | Wawe | Wipe |
| Swum | Teem | Toad | True | Urge | Visa | Wawl | Wire |
| Sybo | Teen | Toby | Trug | Uria | Vise | Waxy | Wiry |
| Syce | Teer | Toco | Tsar | Urim | Viva | Weak | Wise |
| Syke | Teff | Todo | Tsun | Urry | Vive | Weal | Wish |
| | Teil | Tody | Tuba | Ursa | Vivo | Wean | Wisp |
| | Tela | Toff | Tube | Urus | Vlei | Wear | Wist |
| | Teld | Toft | Tuck | Urva | Voce | Weed | Wite |
| **T** | Tell | Toga | Tufa | User | Void | Week | With |
| | Tend | Toho | Tuff | Utas | Vola | Weel | Wive |
| Taal | Tent | Toil | Tuft | Uvea | Vole | Wecm | Woad |
| Tabu | Term | Toit | Tump | | Volt | Ween | Woke |
| Tace | Tern | Tola | Tuna | **V** | Vote | Weep | Wold |
| Tack | Test | Told | Tune | | Voya | Weet | Wolf |
| Tact | Tete | Tole | Turf | Vade | | Weft | Wont |
| Tael | Tett | Toll | Turk | Vail | | Weir | Wood |
| Taft | Text | Tolt | Turm | Vain | **W** | Weld | Woof |
| Taha | Than | Tolu | Turn | Vair | | Welk | Wool |
| Tahr | Thar | Tomb | Turr | Vake | Waac | Well | Woom |
| Taic | That | Tome | Tush | Vale | Wadd | Welt | Woon |
| Tail | Thaw | Tone | Tusk | Vamp | Wade | Wend | Word |
| Tain | Thea | Tong | Tucu | Vane | Wadi | Went | Wore |
| Tait | Thee | Tony | Tuum | Vang | Wady | Wept | Work |
| Take | Them | Took | Tuza | Vara | Waff | Were | Worm |
| Talc | Then | Tool | Tuzz | Vare | Waft | Wert | Worn |
| Tale | Thew | Toom | Twal | Vari | Wage | West | Wort |
| Talk | They | Toon | Tway | Vary | Waid | Whap | Wove |
| Tall | Thig | Toot | Twig | Vase | Waif | What | Wowf |
| Tame | Thin | Tope | Twin | Vast | Wail | When | Wrap |
| Tamp | This | Tore | Twit | Vaut | Wain | Whet | Wren |
| Tana | Thor | Torn | Tyke | Veal | Wair | Whew | Writ |
| Tane | Thou | Tort | Tymp | Veda | Wait | Whey | Wull |
| Tang | Thud | Tory | Tyne | Veer | Wake | Whid | Wynd |
| Tank | Thug | Tose | Type | Vega | Wale | Whig | |
| Tant | Thus | Tosh | Tyre | Veil | Walk | Whim | |
| Tapa | Tice | Toss | Tyro | Vein | Wall | Whin | **X** |
| Tape | Tick | Tost | Tzar | Veld | Walt | Whip | |
| Tapu | Tide | Tote | | Vele | Waly | Whir | Xema |
| Tare | | | | Vell | Wame | | Xyst |
| | | | | | Wand | | |

## FOUR-LETTER WORDS—*continued*

| Y | | | | | Z | | |
|---|---|---|---|---|---|---|---|
| **Y** | Yarr | Yede | Yill | Yowl | Zarf | Zeus | Zone |
| | Yate | Yeen | Yite | Yuck | Zati | Zimb | Zoom |
| Yaff | Yaud | Yeld | Yoga | Yuga | Zeal | Zinc | Zoon |
| Yald | Yaup | Yelk | Yoke | Yule | Zebu | Zion | Zulu |
| Yama | Yawl | Yell | Yolk | Yunx | Zein | Zobo | Zuna |
| Yank | Yawn | Yelp | Yond | Yurt | Zend | Zoea | Zuni |
| Yapp | Yaws | Yerk | Yoni | **Z** | Zero | Zoic | Zupa |
| Yard | Yead | Yest | Yoop | | Zest | Zoll | Zurf |
| Yare | Yean | Yett | Yore | Zaim | Zeta | Zona | Zyme |
| Yarn | Year | Yeve | Your | Zany | | | |

# Five-Letter Words

| **A** | Acton | Agave | Algum | Ambit | Ankus | Ardeb |
|---|---|---|---|---|---|---|
| | Actor | Agaze | Alias | Amble | Annal | Aread |
| Abaca | Acute | Agent | Alibi | Ambon | Annat | Areal |
| Aback | Adage | Agile | Alien | Ambry | Annet | Arear |
| Abaft | Adapt | Agist | Alife | Ameer | Annex | Areca |
| Aband | Adays | Aglee | Align | Amend | Annoy | Arede |
| Abase | Addax | Aglet | Alike | Ament | Annul | Arefy |
| Abash | Adder | Agley | Aline | Amere | Anode | Arena |
| Abask | Addle | Aglow | Alish | Amice | Anona | Areng |
| Abate | Adeps | Agnel | Alive | Amict | Antic | Arete |
| Abbey | Adept | Agnus | Allah | Amide | Antre | Argal |
| Abbot | Adieu | Agone | Allay | Amine | Anura | Argil |
| Abcee | Admit | Agony | Alley | Amiss | Anvil | Argol |
| Abeam | Admix | Agood | Allis | Amity | Anzac | Argon |
| Abear | Adobe | Agora | Allod | Among | Aorta | Argot |
| Abele | Adopt | Agree | Allot | Amort | Apace | Argue |
| Abhal | Adore | Agrin | Allow | Amour | Apart | Argus |
| Abhor | Adorn | Agrom | Alloy | Amove | Apeak | Arian |
| Abide | Adown | Agued | Allyl | Ample | Apeek | Ariel |
| Abies | Adrad | Ahead | Almah | Amply | Apert | Aries |
| Ablen | Adult | Aheap | Almeh | Ampul | Apery | Ariot |
| Abode | Adust | Ahigh | Almry | Amsel | Aphid | Arise |
| Aboil | Aeger | Ahold | Almug | Amuck | Aphis | Arles |
| Aboma | Aegis | Ahull | Aloed | Amuse | Apian | Armed |
| Abord | Aerie | Aider | Aloes | Amzel | Apish | Armet |
| Abort | Afear | Aiery | Aloft | Anana | Apism | Arnot |
| About | Affix | Aigre | Aloin | Ancle | Apium | Aroba |
| Above | Afire | Aisle | Alone | Ancon | Apoop | Aroid |
| Abray | Aflat | Aitch | Along | Aneal | Aport | Aroma |
| Abuse | Afoam | Ajuga | Aloof | Anear | Appal | Arose |
| Abuzz | Afoot | Alack | Aloud | Anele | Appay | Arrah |
| Abysm | Afore | Aland | Alpen | Anent | Apple | Arras |
| Abyss | Afoul | Alant | Alpha | Angel | Apply | Array |
| Accoy | Afric | Alarm | Altar | Anger | Appui | Arret |
| Acera | Afrit | Alary | Alter | Angle | Appuy | Arris |
| Acerb | After | Alate | Alula | Angor | April | Arrow |
| Achor | Again | Album | Alure | Angry | Apron | Arsis |
| Acini | Agama | Alder | Aluta | Anigh | Apsis | Arson |
| Aclis | Agami | Aleft | Alway | Anile | Aptly | Artel |
| Acock | Agant | Alert | Amain | Anime | Araba | Aryan |
| Acold | Agape | Algae | Amass | Anise | Araby | Ascus |
| Acorn | Agast | Algid | Amate | Aniso | Arack | Ashen |
| Acred | Agate | Algin | Amaze | Anker | Arbor | Ashes |
| Acrid | Agaty | Algor | Amber | Ankle | Ardea | Ashet |

### FIVE-LETTER WORDS—*continued*

| | | | | | | |
|---|---|---|---|---|---|---|
| Asian | Awful | Baron | Being | Billy | Blush | Bousy |
| Aside | Awned | Barry | Bejan | Bingo | Board | Bowed |
| Asker | Awner | Basal | Bekah | Binny | Boast | Bowel |
| Askew | Awoke | Basel | Belay | Biped | Bobby | Bower |
| Asoak | Awork | Basic | Belch | Birch | Bocal | Bowet |
| Aspen | Axial | Basil | Belee | Birle | Boche | Bowne |
| Asper | Axile | Basin | Belie | Birse | Bodge | Bowse |
| Aspic | Axiom | Basis | Belle | Birsy | Bodle | Boxen |
| Assai | Axite | Bason | Belly | Birth | Bogey | Boxer |
| Assay | Axled | Bassa | Below | Bison | Boggy | Boyar |
| Asser | Axoid | Basse | Bemad | Bitch | Bogie | Boyau |
| Asset | Ayelp | Basso | Bench | Biter | Bogle | Boyer |
| Assot | Azoic | Basta | Bendy | Bitts | Bogus | Brace |
| Astay | Azote | Baste | Benet | Bixin | Bohea | Brach |
| Astel | Azoth | Basto | Benjy | Black | Boiar | Bract |
| Aster | Aztec | Batch | Benty | Blade | Bolas | Braid |
| Astir | Azure | Bated | Bepat | Blain | Bolin | Brail |
| Aston | Azurn | Bathe | Beret | Blame | Bolus | Brain |
| Asway | Azury | Baton | Berob | Bland | Boned | Brait |
| Aswim | Azyme | Batta | Beroe | Blank | Bones | Brake |
| Ataxy | | Bauge | Berry | Blare | Bonne | Braky |
| Atilt | **B** | Baulk | Berth | Blasé | Bonny | Brame |
| Atlas | | Bavin | Beryl | Blash | Bonus | Brand |
| Atoll | Babel | Bawdy | Beryx | Blast | Bonze | Brank |
| Atomy | Baboo | Bayed | Besee | Blate | Booby | Brant |
| Atone | Bacca | Bayou | Beset | Blaze | Boody | Brash |
| Atony | Bacco | Bayze | Besit | Bleak | Boops | Brass |
| Atrip | Baccy | Bazar | Besom | Blear | Boord | Brast |
| Attar | Bacon | Beach | Besot | Bleat | Boort | Braul |
| Attic | Badge | Beads | Betel | Bleck | Boose | Brave |
| Aubin | Badly | Beady | Beton | Bleed | Boost | Bravo |
| Audit | Baffy | Beamy | Betso | Blend | Boosy | Brawl |
| Auger | Baggy | Beano | Betty | Blent | Booth | Brawn |
| Auget | Bahar | Beard | Bevel | Bless | Boots | Braxy |
| Aught | Bairn | Beast | Bever | Blest | Booty | Braze |
| Augur | Baize | Beath | Bewet | Blimp | Booze | Bread |
| Aulae | Bajan | Beche | Bewig | Blind | Borax | Break |
| Aulic | Baker | Bedad | Bewit | Blink | Boree | Bream |
| Aumil | Balas | Bedel | Bezan | Blirt | Borer | Brede |
| Aural | Baler | Bedew | Bezel | Bliss | Boric | Breed |
| Auric | Balky | Bedim | Bezil | Blist | Borne | Breem |
| Aurum | Balmy | Bedye | Bhang | Blite | Boron | Breer |
| Avail | Balsa | Beech | Bibbs | Blive | Bosky | Brere |
| Avant | Banal | Beefy | Bible | Bloat | Bosom | Brest |
| Avast | Banat | Beele | Biddy | Block | Boson | Breve |
| Avens | Banco | Beery | Bidet | Bloke | Bossy | Briar |
| Avert | Bandy | Befit | Bidon | Blond | Botch | Bribe |
| Avian | Banjo | Befog | Bidri | Blont | Bothy | Brick |
| Aviso | Banns | Befur | Bield | Blood | Botts | Bride |
| Avoid | Banny | Begad | Bifid | Bloom | Bouge | Brief |
| Await | Bantu | Began | Bight | Blore | Bough | Brier |
| Awake | Barbe | Begem | Bigly | Blote | Boule | Brill |
| Award | Baret | Beget | Bigot | Blowy | Boult | Brine |
| Aware | Barge | Begin | Bijou | Blues | Bound | Bring |
| Awarn | Baria | Begum | Bilbo | Bluff | Bourd | Brink |
| Awash | Baric | Begun | Bilge | Blunt | Bourg | Briny |
| Awave | Barky | Behot | Bilgy | Blurb | Bourn | Brisk |
| Aweek | Barmy | Beige | Bilin | Blurt | Bouse | |

## FIVE-LETTER WORDS—*continued*

| | | | | | | |
|---|---|---|---|---|---|---|
| Brite | Bursa | Canoe | Cetic | Chirt | Cleat | Colza |
| Briza | Burse | Canon | Cetyl | Chive | Cleek | Combe |
| Brize | Burst | Canto | Chace | Chivy | Cleft | Comer |
| Broad | Busby | Canty | Chack | Chock | Clepe | Comet |
| Broch | Bushy | Caper | Chaco | Chode | Clerk | Comic |
| Brock | Busky | Caple | Chafe | Choir | Cleve | Comma |
| Brode | Butte | Capoc | Chaff | Choke | Clevy | Compo |
| Brogh | Butts | Capon | Chaft | Choky | Click | Compt |
| Broil | Butty | Capot | Chain | Chord | Cliff | Comus |
| Broke | Butyl | Capra | Chair | Chore | Clift | Conch |
| Broma | Buxom | Capul | Chalk | Chose | Climb | Cones |
| Brond | Buyer | Caput | Chama | Chout | Clime | Coney |
| Brood | Buzzy | Carat | Champ | Chubb | Cling | Conge |
| Brook | Byard | Caret | Chank | Chuck | Clink | Congo |
| Brool | By-end | Carex | Chant | Chuet | Clint | Conia |
| Broom | By-law | Cargo | Chaos | Chuff | Cloak | Conic |
| Brose | Byous | Carib | Chape | Chump | Cloam | Conin |
| Broth | By-way | Carle | Chard | Chunk | Clock | Conne |
| Brown | | Carny | Chare | Churl | Cloff | Conto |
| Bruin | **C** | Carob | Chark | Churn | Cloke | Cooee |
| Bruit | Caaba | Carol | Charm | Churr | Cloop | Cooey |
| Brume | Cabal | Carom | Charr | Chuse | Cloot | Cooky |
| Brunt | Cabas | Carry | Chart | Chute | Close | Cooly |
| Brush | Cabby | Carse | Chary | Chyle | Closh | Coomb |
| Brust | Caber | Carte | Chase | Chyme | Cloth | Co-opt |
| Brute | Cabin | Carus | Chasm | Chynd | Cloud | Coost |
| Bucco | Cabir | Carve | Cheap | Cibol | Clour | Copal |
| Buddy | Cable | Carvy | Cheat | Cicer | Clout | Copec |
| Budge | Cabob | Casal | Check | Cider | Clove | Coper |
| Buffo | Cacao | Casco | Cheek | Cigar | Clown | Copos |
| Buffs | Cache | Caste | Cheep | Cilia | Cluck | Copra |
| Buffy | Caddy | Catch | Cheer | Cimar | Clump | Copse |
| Buggy | Cadet | Cater | Chela | Cimex | Clung | Copsy |
| Bugle | Cadge | Cates | Cheng | Cinch | Clunk | Coral |
| Build | Cadgy | Catty | Chert | Circa | Cnida | Corbe |
| Built | Cadre | Cauld | Chess | Circe | Coach | Corky |
| Buist | Cagot | Caulk | Chest | Cisco | Coact | Corno |
| Bulby | Ca-ira | Cause | Chevy | Cital | Co-aid | Cornu |
| Bulge | Caird | Cavie | Chian | Civet | Coaly | Corny |
| Bulgy | Cairn | Cavil | Chica | Civic | Coarb | Corps |
| Bulky | Caked | Cavin | Chich | Civil | Coast | Corse |
| Bulla | Calid | Cawky | Chick | Clack | Coati | Cosey |
| Bully | Calif | Caxon | Chide | Claes | Cobby | Cotta |
| Bulse | Calin | Cease | Chief | Claik | Coble | Couch |
| Bumbo | Calix | Cebus | Chiel | Claim | Cobra | Cough |
| Bumpy | Calla | Cedar | Child | Clamp | Cocky | Could |
| Bunce | Calmy | Cedry | Chili | Clams | Cocoa | Count |
| Bunch | Calpa | Cella | Chill | Clang | Cocus | Coupé |
| Bunco | Calve | Cello | Chimb | Clank | Codex | Courb |
| Bunko | Calyx | Cense | Chime | Clare | Codle | Coure |
| Bunny | Camel | Cento | China | Clary | Cogie | Court |
| Bunty | Cameo | Ceorl | Chine | Clash | Cogue | Couth |
| Burgh | Camis | Ceres | Chink | Clasp | Coign | Coven |
| Burin | Canal | Cerge | Chirk | Class | Colic | Cover |
| Burly | Candy | Ceric | Chirl | Clats | Colin | Covet |
| Burnt | Caneh | Cerin | Chirm | Claut | Colly | Covey |
| Burro | Canna | Certy | Chirp | Clean | Colon | Covin |
| Burry | Canny | Cesse | Chirr | Clear | Color | Cowan |

FIVE-LETTER WORDS—*continued*

| | | | | | | |
|---|---|---|---|---|---|---|
| Cower | Croon | Cynic | Dempt | Dobby | Draft | Dungy |
| Cowry | Crope | Czech | Demur | Doddy | Drail | Dunne |
| Coyly | Crore | **D** | Denay | Dodge | Drain | Dunny |
| Coypu | Cross | | Denim | Dodgy | Drake | Duper |
| Cozen | Croud | Dadda | Dense | Dogal | Drama | Duple |
| Crack | Croup | Daddy | Depot | Doggo | Drant | Durga |
| Craft | Crout | Dagge | Depth | Doggy | Drape | Durgy |
| Craig | Crowd | Dagon | Derby | Dogma | Drawl | Durio |
| Crake | Crown | Daily | Derma | Doilt | Drawn | Duroy |
| Crame | Croze | Daint | Derth | Doily | Dread | Durra |
| Cramp | Crude | Dairy | Desse | Dolce | Dream | Dusky |
| Crane | Cruel | Daisy | Deter | Dolly | Drear | Dusty |
| Crank | Cruet | Daker | Deuce | Domal | Dregs | Dutch |
| Crape | Crumb | Dally | Devil | Domed | Drent | Duvet |
| Crapy | Crump | Daman | Dewan | Donah | Dress | Dwale |
| Crare | Crunt | Damar | Dhobi | Donat | Dreul | Dwalm |
| Crase | Cruor | Dampy | Dhole | Donee | Drier | Dwang |
| Crash | Cruse | Dance | Dhoti | Donet | Drift | Dwarf |
| Crass | Crush | Dandy | Diana | Donga | Drill | Dwaum |
| Crate | Crust | Darby | Diary | Donna | Drily | Dwell |
| Crave | Crusy | Daric | Diced | Donor | Drink | Dwine |
| Crawl | Crwth | Darky | Dicer | Donya | Drive | Dyaks |
| Craze | Crypt | Daroo | Dicht | Doole | Droil | Dynam |
| Crazy | Cuban | Datum | Dicky | Dooly | Droit | |
| Creak | Cubeb | Dauby | Dicta | Doree | Droll | **E** |
| Cream | Cubic | Daunt | Didst | Doric | Drome | |
| Creck | Cubit | Davit | Didus | Dormy | Drone | Eager |
| Credo | Cuddy | Dayak | Dight | Dorse | Drony | Eagle |
| Creed | Cufic | Deads | Digit | Dorso | Drook | Eagre |
| Creek | Cuish | Dearn | Dilli | Dorty | Drool | Eared |
| Creel | Culch | Deary | Dilly | Doseh | Droop | Early |
| Creep | Culet | Death | Dimly | Dosel | Dross | Earst |
| Crena | Culex | Deave | Dinar | Doser | Drouk | Earth |
| Crêpe | Cully | Debar | Diner | Dotal | Drove | Easel |
| Crept | Cumin | Debel | Dingo | Doter | Drown | Easle |
| Cress | Cupel | Debit | Dingy | Dotes | Druid | Eater |
| Crest | Cupid | Debut | Dinic | Dotty | Drunk | Eaves |
| Creux | Curch | Decad | Dinky | Douar | Drupe | Eblis |
| Crewe | Curdy | Decay | Diode | Douay | Druse | Ebony |
| Crick | Curer | Decem | Diota | Doubt | Drusy | Eclat |
| Crier | Curia | Decoy | Dipus | Dough | Druxy | Ectad |
| Crime | Curio | Decry | Dirge | Doura | Dryad | Ectal |
| Crimp | Curly | Dedal | Dirty | Douse | Dryer | Edder |
| Crine | Curre | Deedy | Disme | Dover | Dryly | Edict |
| Crisp | Curry | Defer | Dital | Dowar | Dsomo | Edify |
| Crith | Curse | Deify | Ditch | Dowdy | Ducal | Edile |
| Croak | Curst | Deign | Ditto | Dowel | Ducat | Educe |
| Croat | Curve | Deism | Ditty | Dower | Duchy | Educt |
| Crock | Cushy | Deist | Divan | Dowie | Duddy | Eerie |
| Croft | Cutch | Deity | Diver | Dowle | Dulch | Egest |
| Croma | Cutis | Dekle | Dives | Downy | Dulia | Eggar |
| Cromb | Cutto | Delay | Divet | Dowry | Dully | Egger |
| Crome | Cutty | Delph | Divot | Dowse | Dulse | Egret |
| Crone | Cycad | Delta | Dixie | Doyen | Dummy | Eidam |
| Crony | Cycle | Delve | Dizen | Dozen | Dumps | Eider |
| Crook | Cyder | Demit | Dizzy | Dozer | Dumpy | Eight |
| Crool | Cymar | Demon | Djinn | Draco | Dunce | Eigne |
| Croom | Cymry | Demos | Do-all | Draff | Dunch | Eikon |

FIVE-LETTER WORDS—*continued*

| | | | | | | |
|---|---|---|---|---|---|---|
| Eirie | Enrol | Evict | Favus | Finos | Floss | Foyer |
| Eisel | Ensew | Evite | Feast | Fiord | Flota | Frack |
| Eject | Ensky | Evoke | Feaze | Firer | Flour | Frail |
| Eking | Ensue | Ewest | Fecal | First | Flout | Frame |
| Elain | Ental | Ewhow | Feces | Firth | Flown | Franc |
| Eland | Enter | Exact | Fecit | Fishy | Fluey | Frank |
| Elaps | Entry | Exalt | Feeze | Fisty | Fluff | Frate |
| Elate | Enure | Excel | Feign | Fitch | Fluid | Fraud |
| Elbow | Envoi | Exeat | Feint | Fitly | Fluke | Freak |
| Elchi | Envoy | Exeme | Felid | Fitte | Fluky | Freck |
| Elder | Enzym | Exert | Felis | Fiver | Flume | Freer |
| Elect | Eolic | Exies | Felly | Fives | Flump | Freet |
| Elegy | Eosin | Exile | Felon | Fixed | Flung | Freit |
| Elemi | Epact | Exist | Femur | Fixer | Fluor | Fremd |
| Eleot | Ephah | Exode | Fence | Fizzy | Flush | Fresh |
| Elève | Ephod | Expel | Fenks | Fjord | Flute | Frett |
| Elfin | Ephor | Extol | Fenny | Flack | Fluty | Friar |
| Elide | Epoch | Extra | Feoff | Flaff | Flyer | Fried |
| Elite | Epode | Exude | Ferae | Flail | Flyte | Frier |
| Elmen | Epopt | Exult | Feral | Flair | Foamy | Frill |
| Eloge | Epsom | Eyrie | Ferly | Flake | Focal | Frisk |
| Elogy | Epure | | Ferny | Flaky | Focus | Frith |
| Eloin | Equal | **F** | Ferry | Flame | Foehn | Frizz |
| Elope | Eques | | Fesse | Flamy | Fogey | Frock |
| Elsin | Equip | Faard | Fetal | Flang | Foggy | Frond |
| Elude | Equus | Fable | Fetch | Flank | Fogle | Frons |
| Elvan | Erase | Faced | Fêted | Flare | Foist | Front |
| Elver | Erato | Facer | Fetid | Flary | Folio | Frore |
| Embar | Erect | Facet | Fetor | Flash | Folly | Frory |
| Embay | Ergot | Facia | Fetus | Flask | Fomes | Frost |
| Embed | Erica | Faddy | Fetwa | Flawn | Fondu | Froth |
| Ember | Erode | Fadge | Feuar | Flawy | Foots | Frown |
| Embog | Erose | Faery | Fever | Flaxy | Footy | Frowy |
| Embow | Error | Fagin | Fiars | Fleak | Foray | Froze |
| Embox | Eruca | Fagot | Fiaun | Fleam | For-by | Fruit |
| Embus | Erupt | Faint | Fibre | Fleck | Force | Frump |
| Emend | Ervum | Fairy | Fichu | Fleer | Fordo | Frush |
| Emery | Escot | Faith | Ficus | Fleet | Forel | Fryer |
| Emmet | Eskar | Faker | Fidge | Flesh | Foret | Fubby |
| Emmew | Esker | Fakir | Field | Flews | Forge | Fubsy |
| Emong | Essay | False | Fiend | Flick | Forgo | Fucus |
| Empty | Ester | Famed | Fiery | Flier | Forky | Fudge |
| Emure | Estoc | Fanal | Fifer | Flies | Forme | Fudgy |
| Enact | Estop | Fanam | Fifth | Flimp | Forte | Fuero |
| Enate | Etern | Fancy | Fifty | Fling | Forth | Fuffy |
| Ender | Ethal | Fanon | Fight | Flint | Forty | Fugal |
| Endew | Ether | Farad | Filar | Flipe | Forum | Fugle |
| Endon | Ethic | Farce | Filch | Flirt | Fossa | Fugue |
| Endue | Ethos | Farcy | Filer | Flisk | Fosse | Fully |
| Eneid | Ethyl | Farle | Filly | Flite | Fouat | Fumet |
| Enema | Ettle | Farse | Filmy | Float | Foule | Fumid |
| Enemy | Etude | Fasti | Filth | Flock | Foult | Fundi |
| Engle | Etwee | Fatal | Final | Flong | Found | Fungi |
| Enjoy | Eurus | Fated | Finch | Flood | Fount | Funis |
| Enmew | Evade | Fatly | Finer | Flook | Fouth | Funky |
| Ennui | Event | Fatty | Finis | Floor | Fovea | Funny |
| Enode | Evert | Faugh | Finks | Flora | Fowth | Furor |
| Enorm | Every | Fault | Finny | Flory | Foxed | Furry |
| | | Fauna | | | | |

## FIVE-LETTER WORDS—*continued*

| | | | | | | |
|---|---|---|---|---|---|---|
| Furze | Geest | Glean | Graff | Guard | Hanse | Hiems |
| Furzy | Geist | Glebe | Graft | Guava | Haply | Hight |
| Fusee | Gelid | Gleby | Grail | Guelf | Happy | Hilar |
| Fusil | Gemel | Glede | Grain | Guess | Hards | Hilch |
| Fussy | Gemma | Gleed | Graip | Guest | Hardy | Hillo |
| Fusty | Gemmy | Gleek | Grama | Gueux | Harem | Hilly |
| Fusus | Gemot | Gleet | Grame | Guide | Harns | Hilum |
| Fuzee | Genet | Glene | Grand | Guild | Harpy | Hindi |
| Fuzzy | Genie | Glide | Grant | Guile | Harry | Hindu |
| Fytte | Genii | Gliff | Grape | Guilt | Harsh | Hinge |
| | Genio | Glint | Graph | Guise | Haste | Hinny |
| **G** | Genre | Glisk | Grapy | Gular | Hasty | Hirer |
| Gabel | Genro | Glist | Grasp | Gulch | Hatch | Hitch |
| Gable | Genty | Gloam | Grass | Gules | Hater | Hithe |
| Gadge | Genus | Gloat | Grate | Gulfy | Haugh | Hiver |
| Gadus | Geode | Globe | Grave | Gully | Haulm | Hoard |
| Gager | Gerah | Globy | Gravy | Gumbo | Hault | Hoary |
| Gaily | Gerbe | Glode | Graze | Gummy | Haunt | Hoast |
| Galah | Gesso | Glome | Great | Gunny | Haurl | Hobby |
| Galea | Get-up | Gloom | Grebe | Gurge | Haven | Hobit |
| Gally | Ghast | Glory | Grece | Gurly | Haver | Hocus |
| Galop | Ghaut | Gloss | Greed | Gurry | Havoc | Hodge |
| Gamba | Ghazi | Glout | Greek | Gushy | Hawse | Hoise |
| Gamic | Ghost | Glove | Green | Gusto | Hazel | Hoist |
| Gamin | Ghoul | Gloze | Greet | Gusty | Hazer | Holey |
| Gamma | Ghyll | Gluer | Greit | Gutta | Heady | Holla |
| Gamut | Giant | Gluey | Grese | Gutty | Heald | Hollo |
| Ganch | Gibbe | Glume | Greve | Gyall | Heapy | Holly |
| Ganil | Gibel | Glyph | Grice | Gygis | Heard | Homed |
| Ganja | Giber | Gnarl | Gride | Gypsy | Heart | Homer |
| Ganza | Gibus | Gnarr | Grief | Gyral | Heast | Honey |
| Gaper | Giddy | Gnash | Grill | Gyron | Heath | Hooch |
| Gappy | Gigot | Gnome | Grime | Gyrus | Heave | Hooka |
| Garth | Gigue | Gobbo | Grimy | Gyves | Heavy | Hooky |
| Garum | Gilly | Godly | Grind | | Heben | Hooly |
| Gassy | Gilpy | Goety | Gripe | **H** | Hecht | Hoosh |
| Gated | Gipsy | Gofer | Grise | Habit | Hedge | Hoove |
| Gaucy | Girth | Going | Grist | Hable | Heeze | Hoppo |
| Gaudy | Giust | Golly | Grize | Hades | Hefty | Hoppy |
| Gauge | Given | Gonad | Groan | Hadji | Heigh | Horal |
| Gault | Giver | Goner | Groat | Hadst | Helix | Horde |
| Gaumy | Glacé | Goods | Groin | Hafiz | Hello | Horny |
| Gaunt | Glade | Goody | Groom | Haikh | Helot | Horse |
| Gauze | Glaik | Goose | Grope | Haily | Helve | Horsy |
| Gauzy | Glair | Goral | Gross | Haint | Hemal | Hotel |
| Gavel | Gland | Gorge | Group | Hairy | Hempy | Hotly |
| Gawcy | Glans | Gorse | Grout | Haith | Hence | Houff |
| Gawky | Glare | Gorsy | Grove | Hajji | Henna | Hough |
| Gawsy | Glary | Gotha | Growl | Hakim | Henry | Hound |
| Gayal | Glass | Gouda | Grown | Halfa | Hepar | Houri |
| Gayly | Glaum | Gouge | Gruel | Hallo | Herby | House |
| Gazel | Glaur | Goura | Gruff | Halma | Heron | Hovel |
| Gazer | Glaux | Gourd | Grume | Halse | Herry | Hover |
| Gazon | Glave | Gouty | Grunt | Halve | Herse | Howbe |
| Geach | Glaze | Gowan | Gryde | Hanap | Heugh | Howdy |
| Gebur | Glazy | Graal | Grype | Hance | Hevea | Howff |
| Gecko | Glead | Grace | Guaco | Hanch | Hewer | Howso |
| Geese | Gleam | Grade | Guano | Handy | Hider | Hubby |

**FIVE-LETTER WORDS**—*continued*

| | | | | | | |
|---|---|---|---|---|---|---|
| Huffy | Imbar | Irony | Jonah | Kerve | Kutch | Leach |
| Hullo | Imbed | Isiac | Joram | Kesar | Kvass | Leady |
| Hully | Imber | Islam | Jorum | Ketch | Kyley | Leafy |
| Human | Imbow | Islet | Jotun | Kevel | Kylin | Leaky |
| Humet | Imbue | Issue | Jougs | Keyed | Kylix | Learn |
| Humic | Immit | Istle | Joule | Khaki | Kyloe | Leary |
| Humid | Immix | Itchy | Joust | Kheda | Kypoo | Lease |
| Humph | Impel | Ivied | Judas | Kibed | Kyrie | Leash |
| Humpy | Impen | Ivory | Judge | Kiddy | Kythe | Least |
| Humus | Imply | Ivyed | Jugal | Kidel | | Leave |
| Hunch | Imput | Ixion | Juice | Kidge | **L** | Leavy |
| Hunks | Inaja | Ixtle | Juicy | Kiley | Label | Ledge |
| Hurds | Inane | Izard | Julap | Kimbo | Labis | Ledgy |
| Hurly | Inapt | | Julep | Kinic | Lacet | Ledum |
| Hurra | Inarm | **J** | Julis | Kinky | Laden | Leech |
| Hurry | Inbye | Jabot | Julus | Kinsh | Ladin | Leery |
| Hurst | Incog. | Jadoo | Jumbo | Kiosk | Ladle | Leese |
| Husky | Incur | Jager | Jumpy | Kitty | Lagan | Leeze |
| Hussy | Incus | Jaggy | Junco | Klang | Lager | Legal |
| Hutch | Incut | Jakes | Junta | Klick | Laird | Leger |
| Hutia | Index | Jalap | Junto | Kloof | Laity | Leggy |
| Huzza | Indra | Jambe | Jupon | Knack | Laker | Leman |
| Hyads | Indri | Jambu | Jural | Knarl | Lakin | Lemma |
| Hydra | Indue | Jammy | Jurat | Knave | Lamia | Lemon |
| Hydro | Indus | Jantu | Juror | Knead | Lammy | Lemur |
| Hyena | Inept | Janty | Jussi | Kneed | Lance | Lento |
| Hyleg | Inerm | Janus | Jutes | Kneel | Lanch | Leper |
| Hylic | Inert | Japan | Jutty | Knell | Lande | Lepid |
| Hymen | Ineye | Jarde | | Knife | Lanky | Lepis |
| Hyoid | Infer | Jasey | **K** | Knock | Lapel | Lepra |
| Hypha | Infix | Jaspe | Kaaba | Knoll | Lapis | Letch |
| Hyrax | Infra | Jaunt | Kaama | Knoop | Lapse | Lethe |
| Hyson | Ingle | Javel | Kafir | Knosp | Larch | Levee |
| Hythe | Ingot | Jawed | Kaiak | Knote | Lardy | Level |
| | Inion | Jedge | Kalif | Knoud | Lares | Leven |
| | Inkle | Jehad | Kalpa | Knout | Large | Lever |
| **I** | Inlaw | Jelly | Kames | Known | Largo | Levin |
| Ichor | Inlay | Jemmy | Kamis | Knubs | Larky | Lewis |
| Icily | Inlet | Jenny | Kandy | Knurl | Larry | Liana |
| Icing | Inner | Jerid | Kaneh | Knurr | Larum | Liang |
| Ictic | Inorb | Jerky | Kapok | Koala | Larus | Liard |
| Ictus | Input | Jerry | Karma | Koban | Larva | Liart |
| Ideal | Inset | Jesse | Karob | Kobil | Laser | Libel |
| Idiom | Inter | Jetty | Karoo | Kodak | Lasso | Liber |
| Idiot | Intil | Jewel | Kassu | Kokob | Latch | Libra |
| Idler | Inure | Jewry | Kauri | Kokra | Later | Licit |
| Idris | Inurn | Jiffy | Kayak | Koord | Latex | Liege |
| Idyll | Inuus | Jimmy | Kayle | Kopje | Lathe | Lifer |
| Igloo | Invar | Jimpy | Kecks | Koran | Lathy | Ligan |
| Ileac | Inwit | Jingo | Kecky | Ko-tow | Latin | Light |
| Ileum | Iodal | Jinks | Kedge | Kraal | Laugh | Liken |
| Ileus | Iodic | Jippo | Kedgy | Krait | Laund | Lilac |
| Iliac | Ionic | Jocko | Keesh | Krang | Laura | Limbo |
| Iliad | Irade | Jodel | Keeve | Kreng | Lautu | Limit |
| Ilium | Irate | Joint | Kelpy | Krone | Laver | Limma |
| Image | Irian | Joist | Kelty | Kudos | Laxly | Linch |
| Imago | Irish | Joker | Kemps | Kufic | Layer | Linen |
| Imaum | Irite | Jolly | Kerne | Kukri | Lazar | Liner |

FIVE-LETTER WORDS—*continued*

| | | | | | | |
|---|---|---|---|---|---|---|
| Lingo | Lucid | Mammy | Melon | Modal | Mower | Nacre |
| Lingy | Lucky | Maneh | Mercy | Model | Mpret | Nadir |
| Links | Lucre | Manet | Merge | Moder | Mucic | Naeve |
| Linny | Luffa | Manga | Merit | Modus | Mucid | Naggy |
| Lippy | Lumpy | Mange | Merle | Mogul | Mucky | Nagor |
| Lisse | Lunar | Mango | Merry | Mohur | Mucor | Naiad |
| Litas | Lunch | Mangy | Mesal | Moire | Mucro | Naïve |
| Lithe | Lunge | Mania | Meshy | Moist | Mucus | Naked |
| Lithy | Lupin | Manis | Mesne | Molar | Mudar | Naker |
| Litre | Luppa | Manly | Messy | Molla | Muddy | Namer |
| Lived | Lupus | Manna | Metal | Molto | Mudir | Nandu |
| Liven | Lurch | Manor | Meter | Momus | Mufti | Nanny |
| Liver | Lurid | Manse | Metic | Monad | Muggy | Nappy |
| Livid | Lurry | Manta | Metif | Monal | Mugil | Nares |
| Livre | Lushy | Manus | Metis | Monas | Mulch | Naris |
| Llama | Lusty | Maori | Metra | Monde | Mulct | Narre |
| Llano | Lusus | Maple | Metre | Moner | Muley | Nasal |
| Loach | Luter | Maqui | Meute | Money | Mulga | Nasty |
| Loamy | Lyart | Marah | Mezzo | Monox | Mulla | Natal |
| Loath | Lying | Maray | Miaul | Monte | Mulse | Natch |
| Lobar | Lymph | March | Miche | Month | Mulsh | Natte |
| Lobby | Lynch | Marge | Micky | Mooch | Mummy | Natty |
| Lobed | Lyric | Marly | Midas | Moody | Mumps | Naval |
| Local | Lyrid | Marry | Middy | Moola | Munch | Navel |
| Loche | Lyrie | Marsh | Midge | Mooly | Mungo | Navew |
| Locus | Lysis | Mashy | Mid-on | Moony | Mural | Navvy |
| Lodge | Lyssa | Mason | Midst | Moory | Muray | Nawab |
| Loess | Lythe | Massa | Might | Moose | Murex | Nazir |
| Lofty | Lytta | Masse | Milch | Moppy | Murky | Neath |
| Logan | | Massy | Miler | Mopsy | Murra | Nebel |
| Logge | **M** | Masty | Milky | Mopus | Murre | Neddy |
| Logia | Macaw | Match | Mimic | Moral | Murry | Needs |
| Logic | Macer | Mater | Minar | Morat | Musca | Needy |
| Logos | Macle | Matin | Mince | Moray | Musci | Neese |
| Lolly | Macon | Matte | Miner | Morel | Muser | Neeze |
| Lolog | Madam | Maund | Minim | Moril | Muset | Negro |
| Longe | Madge | Mauve | Minor | Mormo | Mushy | Negus |
| Looby | Madia | Mavis | Minus | Morne | Music | Neigh |
| Loofa | Madid | Maxim | Mirth | Morse | Musky | Neist |
| Loord | Madly | May-be | Mirza | Morus | Mussy | Neive |
| Loose | Magar | Mayor | Misdo | Mosey | Musty | Nempt |
| Lorel | Magic | Mayst | Miser | Mossy | Mutch | Nerve |
| Loris | Magma | Mazda | Misgo | Motet | Muzzy | Nervy |
| Lorry | Magot | Mazer | Misle | Mothy | Myall | Neski |
| Losel | Mahdi | Mealy | Misly | Motif | Myoid | Netty |
| Loser | Mahwa | Meant | Missy | Motor | Myoma | Neume |
| Lotah | Maize | Mease | Misty | Motto | Myope | Never |
| Lotto | Major | Meath | Mitra | Motty | Myops | Nevel |
| Lotus | Maker | Meaty | Mitre | Mouch | Myopy | Newel |
| Lough | Makwa | Mecca | Mitts | Mould | Myrrh | Newly |
| Louis | Malar | Medal | Mixen | Moult | Mysis | Newsy |
| Louse | Malay | Media | Mixer | Mound | Myxon | Nexus |
| Lover | Malic | Medic | Mizen | Mount | | Niche |
| Lower | Malta | Medoc | Mizzy | Mourn | **N** | Nicol |
| Lowly | Malty | Meiny | Mobby | Mouse | Nabee | Nidge |
| Loxia | Mamba | Melée | Moble | Mousy | Nabit | Nidor |
| Loyal | Mamey | Meles | Mocha | Mouth | Nabob | Nidus |
| Lubra | Mamma | Melic | Moche | Mover | | Niece |

## FIVE-LETTER WORDS—*continued*

| | | | | | | |
|---|---|---|---|---|---|---|
| Nifty | Nyula | Optic | Oxeye | Pashm | Perse | Pipit |
| Night | Nymph | Orach | Ox-fly | Passe | Pesky | Pipul |
| Nihil | | Orale | Oxide | Paste | Petal | Pique |
| Ninny | **O** | Orang | Oxlip | Pasty | Petar | Piste |
| Ninth | Oaken | Orant | Oxter | Patch | Peter | Pitch |
| Niobe | Oaker | Orate | Ozena | Pated | Petit | Pithy |
| Nippy | Oakum | Orbed | Ozone | Patée | Petre | Pitri |
| Nirls | Oasis | Orbit | | Paten | Petto | Pivot |
| Nisan | Oaten | Orcin | **P** | Patin | Petty | Pixie |
| Nisus | Obang | Order | Paced | Patio | Pewet | Place |
| Nitid | Obeah | Oread | Pacer | Patly | Pewit | Plack |
| Nitre | Obese | Orgal | Pacha | Patte | Phare | Plaid |
| Nival | Obole | Organ | Padar | Patty | Pharo | Plain |
| Nixie | Occur | Oriel | Paddy | Pause | Phase | Plait |
| Nizam | Ocean | Orion | Padma | Pavan | Pheer | Plane |
| Nobby | Ocher | Orlop | Padra | Paven | Pheon | Plank |
| Noble | Ochre | Ormer | Padre | Paver | Phial | Plant |
| Nobly | Ochry | Ornis | Paean | Pavin | Phlox | Plash |
| Nodal | Ocrea | Orpin | Paeon | Pavid | Phoca | Plasm |
| Noddy | Octad | Orris | Pagan | Pavon | Phone | Plate |
| Nodus | Octet | Ortyx | Pagle | Pawed | Photo | Platt |
| Nohow | Octyl | Orval | Pagus | Pawky | Phren | Plead |
| Noils | Ocuba | Oscan | Paint | Payee | Phyle | Pleat |
| Noint | Oddly | Oshac | Paird | Payer | Phyma | Plebs |
| Noise | Odeon | Osier | Palas | Payne | Piano | Plesh |
| Noisy | Odeum | Osmic | Palay | Payse | Picea | Plica |
| Nokes | Odium | Otary | Palea | Peace | Picot | Pluck |
| Nomad | Odour | Other | Pales | Peach | Picra | Pluff |
| Nomen | Odyle | Ottar | Palki | Peaky | Picul | Plumb |
| Nomic | Ofbit | Otter | Palmy | Pearl | Picus | Plume |
| Nomos | Offal | Oubit | Palpi | Peart | Piece | Plump |
| Nonce | Offer | Ought | Palsy | Pease | Piend | Plumy |
| Nones | Often | Ounce | Panax | Peaty | Pieno | Plush |
| Nonet | Ogham | Oundy | Panch | Pecan | Pieta | Pluto |
| Nonny | Ogive | Ouphe | Panda | Pecht | Piety | Plyer |
| Noops | Ogler | Ourie | Pandy | Pecul | Pight | Poach |
| Noose | Oiler | Ousel | Paned | Pedal | Pigmy | Pocky |
| Nopal | Okapi | Outby | Panel | Pedum | Piked | Podge |
| Noria | Olden | Outdo | Panic | Peece | Piker | Podgy |
| Norma | Oleic | Outer | Pansy | Peery | Pilar | Poesy |
| Norna | Olein | Outgo | Pants | Peggy | Pilau | Pogge |
| Norse | Olent | Outré | Papal | Peine | Pilaw | Poind |
| North | Oleon | Ouzel | Papaw | Peise | Pilch | Point |
| Nosed | Olive | Ovary | Paper | Pekan | Piler | Poise |
| Nosey | Ollam | Ovate | Pappy | Pekoe | Piles | Pokal |
| Notch | Ology | Overt | Parch | Pelma | Pilot | Poker |
| Notum | Ombre | Ovine | Pardi | Pelta | Pilum | Polar |
| Notus | Omega | Ovoid | Pardy | Penal | Pilus | Poley |
| Nould | Omlah | Ovolo | Parer | Pence | Pinch | Polka |
| Novel | Oncer | Ovule | Parka | Penna | Piney | Polly |
| Novum | Onion | Owche | Parle | Penny | Pinic | Polyp |
| Nowed | Onset | Owler | Parol | Peony | Pinky | Pongo |
| Nowel | Onymy | Owlet | Parry | Perch | Pinna | Pooja |
| Noyau | Oopak | Owner | Parse | Perdu | Pinny | Poppy |
| Nucha | Oorie | Owsen | Parsi | Perdy | Piony | Poral |
| Nudge | Opera | Owser | Party | Peril | Pious | Porch |
| Nurse | Opine | Oxbot | Pasch | Perky | Pipal | Porer |
| Nutty | Opium | Oxbow | Pasha | Perry | Piper | Porgy |

**FIVE-LETTER WORDS**—*continued*

| | | | | | | |
|---|---|---|---|---|---|---|
| Porte | Prune | Quake | Rainy | Redan | Rhine | Ronde |
| Poser | Pryan | Quaky | Raise | Redia | Rhino | Rondo |
| Posit | Pryer | Qualm | Rajah | Redif | Rhomb | Ronin |
| Posse | Pryse | Quant | Rakee | Redly | Rhumb | Roody |
| Potch | Psalm | Quarl | Raker | Redub | Rhyme | Roofy |
| Potin | Pshaw | Quart | Rally | Redux | Rhyne | Rooky |
| Potto | Psoas | Quash | Ralph | Re-dye | Riant | Roomy |
| Potty | Psora | Quasi | Ramal | Reedy | Riata | Roopy |
| Pouch | Ptere | Quass | Ramed | Reefy | Ribes | Roose |
| Poulp | Pubis | Quayd | Ramee | Reeky | Rider | Roost |
| Poult | Pucka | Quean | Ramie | Reesk | Ridge | Rooty |
| Pound | Pudgy | Queen | Rammy | Reest | Ridgy | Roper |
| Powan | Pudic | Queer | Ramus | Reeve | Rieve | Roque |
| Power | Puffy | Queet | Rance | Refel | Rifle | Roral |
| Poyou | Pugil | Quell | Ranch | Refer | Rigel | Roric |
| Praam | Puker | Queme | Randy | Refit | Right | Rorty |
| Prank | Pukka | Querk | Ranee | Regal | Rigid | Roset |
| Prase | Pulas | Querl | Range | Reget | Rigol | Rosin |
| Prate | Puler | Quern | Ranty | Régie | Rigor | Rotal |
| Prawn | Pulex | Query | Raphe | Regma | Rimer | Rotor |
| Predy | Pulka | Quest | Rapid | Reign | Ringe | Rouge |
| Preen | Pulpy | Queue | Raspy | Reins | Rinse | Rough |
| Press | Pulse | Quhat | Rasse | Reist | Ripen | Roule |
| Prest | Pumps | Quick | Ratal | Reive | Ripon | Round |
| Prexy | Punch | Quiet | Ratan | Relax | Risel | Roupy |
| Price | Punic | Quihi | Ratch | Relay | Risen | Rouse |
| Prick | Punka | Quill | Ratel | Relet | Riser | Roust |
| Pride | Punto | Quilt | Rater | Relic | Rishi | Rousy |
| Prief | Punty | Quina | Rathe | Reman | Risky | Route |
| Prier | Pupal | Quink | Ratio | Remex | Rissa | Routh |
| Prill | Pupil | Quint | Ratty | Remit | Risus | Rover |
| Prima | Puppy | Quipo | Ravel | Renal | Rithe | Rowan |
| Prime | Purée | Quipu | Raven | Renes | Rival | Rowdy |
| Primo | Purge | Quire | Raver | Renew | Rivel | Rowel |
| Primp | Purim | Quirk | Ravin | Renne | Riven | Rowen |
| Primy | Purre | Quirt | Rawly | Rente | River | Rower |
| Prink | Purse | Quite | Rayah | Repay | Rivet | Rowme |
| Print | Pursy | Quits | Rayed | Repel | Rizom | Royal |
| Prior | Pussy | Quoad | Rayle | Repet | Roach | Royle |
| Prise | Putid | Quoif | Rayne | Reply | Roast | Royne |
| Prism | Putoo | Quoin | Rayon | Repot | Robin | Rubia |
| Privy | Putty | Quoit | Razee | Resaw | Roble | Rubin |
| Prize | Put-up | Quota | Razor | Reset | Robot | Ruble |
| Probe | Pygal | Quote | Reach | Resin | Rocky | Rubus |
| Proem | Pygmy | Quoth | React | Resow | Rocta | Ruche |
| Proin | Pylon | Quran | Ready | Resty | Rodeo | Rudas |
| Proll | Pyoid | | Realm | Retch | Rodge | Ruddy |
| Prone | Pyral | **R** | Reame | Retex | Roger | Rudge |
| Prong | Pyrus | Rabat | Rearm | Retry | Rogue | Ruffe |
| Proof | Pyxis | Rabbi | Reata | Reune | Roguy | Rugby |
| Prore | | Rabid | Reave | Revel | Rohan | Ruler |
| Prose | **Q** | Rabot | Rebec | Revet | Roist | Rumal |
| Prosy | Q-boat | Racer | Rebel | Revue | Rokee | Rumbo |
| Proud | Quack | Radge | Rebus | Rewet | Roker | Rumen |
| Prove | Quaff | Radio | Rebut | Rewin | Romal | Rumex |
| Prowl | Quaid | Radix | Recta | Rheic | Roman | Rummy |
| Proxy | Quail | Raffe | Recto | Rhein | Romic | Runch |
| Prude | Quair | Rafty | Recur | Rheum | Rompu | Runer |

### FIVE-LETTER WORDS—*continued*

| | | | | | | |
|---|---|---|---|---|---|---|
| Runic | Sandy | Scion | Seise | Shank | Shred | Skelp |
| Rupee | Sansa | Scoat | Seity | Shape | Shrew | Skene |
| Rupia | Sapan | Scobs | Seize | Shard | Shrof | Skied |
| Rural | Sapid | Scoby | Sekos | Share | Shrow | Skier |
| Rushy | Sapor | Scoff | Selah | Shark | Shrub | Skiey |
| Rusma | Sappy | Scold | Semis | Sharn | Shrug | Skiff |
| Rusty | Sarda | Scomm | Senal | Sharp | Shuck | Skill |
| Rutal | Saroh | Scone | Sence | Shave | Shunt | Skimp |
| Rutic | Saros | Scoon | Sench | Shawl | Shyly | Skink |
| Rutty | Sarse | Scoop | Senex | Shawm | Sibbe | Skirl |
| Ruvid | Sasia | Scoot | Senna | Sheaf | Sibyl | Skirr |
| | Sasin | Scopa | Sense | Sheal | Sicca | Skirt |
| S | Sasse | Scope | Senvy | Shear | Sided | Skite |
| | Satan | Scops | Senza | Sheen | Sider | Skive |
| Sabal | Satin | Score | Sepal | Sheep | Sidle | Skoal |
| Saber | Satyr | Scorn | Sepia | Sheer | Siege | Skran |
| Sable | Sauce | Scots | Sepic | Sheet | Sield | Skulk |
| Sabot | Sauch | Scoup | Sepoy | Sheik | Sieve | Skull |
| Sabre | Saugh | Scour | Serac | Shelf | Sight | Skunk |
| Sacra | Sault | Scout | Serai | Shell | Sigil | Skyey |
| Sacre | Saunt | Scove | Serge | Shend | Sigma | Skyte |
| Sadda | Saury | Scovy | Seric | Sheol | Silex | Slack |
| Sadly | Saute | Scowl | Serif | Sherd | Silky | Slade |
| Saffo | Saver | Scrag | Serin | Sheth | Silly | Slaie |
| Sagan | Savin | Scrap | Seron | Sheva | Silva | Slain |
| Sagra | Savor | Scrat | Serow | Shiel | Simar | Slake |
| Sagum | Savoy | Scraw | Serra | Shier | Simia | Slang |
| Sahib | Savvy | Scray | Serry | Shift | Since | Slank |
| Saiga | Sawny | Scree | Serum | Shiko | Sinew | Slant |
| Saily | Saxin | Screw | Serve | Shine | Singe | Slash |
| Saint | Saxon | Scrim | Sesha | Shiny | Sinic | Slate |
| Saith | Sayer | Scrip | Sesia | Shire | Sinto | Slatt |
| Saiva | Sayon | Scrod | Sessa | Shirk | Sinus | Slaty |
| Sajou | Scaff | Scrog | Seton | Shirl | Sioux | Slave |
| Saker | Scala | Scrub | Set-to | Shirr | Siren | Sleek |
| Sakia | Scald | Scrum | Seven | Shirt | Sirih | Sleep |
| Salad | Scale | Scudo | Sever | Shist | Sirup | Sleet |
| Salam | Scall | Scuff | Sewel | Shive | Sisal | Slice |
| Salda | Scalp | Scuft | Sewen | Shoad | Sison | Slick |
| Salep | Scaly | Sculk | Sewer | Shoal | Sissy | Slide |
| Salic | Scamp | Scull | Sexte | Shoat | Sitar | Slily |
| Salin | Scand | Sculp | Sexto | Shock | Sithe | Slime |
| Salix | Scant | Scurf | Shack | Shoer | Sitta | Slimy |
| Salle | Scape | Scuse | Shade | Shole | Sivan | Sling |
| Sally | Scard | Scute | Shady | Shone | Sixth | Slink |
| Salmi | Scare | Seamy | Shaft | Shook | Sixty | Slipe |
| Salmo | Scarf | Sea-ox | Shahi | Shoon | Sizar | Slish |
| Salon | Scarp | Sease | Shake | Shoot | Sized | Slive |
| Salop | Scart | Seave | Shako | Shore | Sizel | Sloam |
| Salpa | Scath | Sebat | Shaky | Shorl | Sizer | Sloat |
| Salse | Scatt | Secco | Shale | Shorn | Skail | Sloid |
| Salts | Scaup | Sedan | Shall | Short | Skain | Sloom |
| Salty | Scaur | Sedge | Shalm | Shout | Skald | Sloop |
| Salve | Scelp | Sedgy | Shalt | Shove | Skate | Slope |
| Salvo | Scend | Sedum | Shaly | Shown | Skean | Slops |
| Sambo | Scene | Seedy | Shama | Shows | Skeel | Slopy |
| Samia | | Segno | Shame | Showy | Skeet | Slosh |
| Sammy | | Seine | Shand | Shrab | Skein | Sloth |
| Sampi | Scent | | | | | |

FIVE-LETTER WORDS—*continued*

| | | | | | | |
|---|---|---|---|---|---|---|
| Sloyd | Snort | Sowse | Spirt | Stall | Stole | Sudak |
| Slump | Snouk | Sowth | Spiry | Stamp | Stoma | Sudra |
| Slung | Snout | Soyle | Spite | Stand | Stond | Suede |
| Slunk | Snowy | Space | Spitz | Stang | Stone | Suety |
| Slush | Snuff | Spade | Spiza | Stank | Stony | Sufic |
| Slyly | Soapy | Spado | Splay | Stare | Stood | Sugar |
| Slyne | Soave | Spaer | Split | Stark | Stook | Suint |
| Slype | Sober | Spahi | Spode | Starr | Stool | Suist |
| Smack | Sobol | Spail | Spoil | Start | Stoom | Suite |
| Small | Socle | Spait | Spoke | State | Stoop | Sujee |
| Smalt | Soddy | Spake | Spole | Stave | Stoor | Sulks |
| Smart | Softa | Spald | Spoof | Stead | Stope | Sulky |
| Smash | Softy | Spale | Spook | Steak | Store | Sully |
| Smear | Soger | Spall | Spool | Steal | Stork | Sumac |
| Smell | Soggy | Spalt | Spoom | Steam | Storm | Sumph |
| Smelt | Soken | Spane | Spoon | Stean | Story | Sunna |
| Smift | Solah | Spang | Spoor | Steed | Stosh | Sunni |
| Smile | Solar | Spank | Spore | Steek | Stouk | Sunny |
| Smirk | Soldo | Spare | Sport | Steel | Stoup | Sun-up |
| Smite | Solen | Spark | Sposh | Steem | Stour | Super |
| Smith | Sol-fa | Spasm | Spout | Steen | Stout | Supra |
| Smitt | Solid | Spate | Sprad | Steep | Stove | Surah |
| Smock | Solon | Spave | Sprag | Steer | Strae | Sural |
| Smoke | Solum | Spawl | Sprat | Stela | Strap | Surfy |
| Smoky | Solus | Spawn | Spray | Stele | Straw | Surge |
| Smolt | Solve | Speak | Spred | Stell | Stray | Surgy |
| Smoot | Somaj | Spean | Spree | Steme | Strew | Surly |
| Smore | Soncy | Spear | Sprig | Stend | Stria | Surya |
| Smout | Sonny | Speck | Sprit | Stent | Strig | Sutor |
| Smowt | Sonsy | Specs | Sprod | Stere | Strip | Sutra |
| Smuck | Sonty | Speed | Sprue | Stern | Strix | Swack |
| Snack | Sooja | Speer | Sprug | Steve | Strob | Swage |
| Snail | Soote | Speir | Spume | Stica | Strop | Swain |
| Snake | Sooth | Speld | Spumy | Stich | Strow | Swale |
| Snaky | Sooty | Spelk | Spunk | Stick | Stroy | Swamp |
| Snape | Sopha | Spell | Spurn | Stiff | Strub | Swang |
| Snare | Sophi | Spelt | Spurs | Stile | Strum | Swank |
| Snarl | Sopor | Spend | Spurt | Still | Strut | Swape |
| Snary | Soppy | Speos | Spyre | Stilp | Stuck | Sward |
| Snash | Sopra | Sperm | Squab | Stilt | Study | Sware |
| Snath | Sorbo | Spewy | Squad | Stime | Stufa | Swarf |
| Snead | Sorda | Sphex | Squat | Stimy | Stuff | Swarm |
| Sneak | Sordo | Spial | Squaw | Sting | Stull | Swart |
| Sneap | Soree | Spica | Squib | Stink | Stulm | Swash |
| Sneck | Sorel | Spice | Squid | Stint | Stulp | Swath |
| Sneer | Sorex | Spick | Sruti | Stipa | Stump | Swats |
| Snell | Sorry | Spicy | Stack | Stipe | Stung | Sweal |
| Snick | Sorus | Spiff | Stade | Stirk | Stunk | Swear |
| Snide | Sough | Spike | Staff | Stirp | Stunt | Sweat |
| Sniff | Sound | Spiky | Stage | Stive | Stupa | Swede |
| Snift | Soupy | Spile | Stagy | Stivy | Stupe | Sweep |
| Snipe | Souse | Spill | Staid | Stoak | Sturt | Sweer |
| Snirt | South | Spilt | Staig | Stoat | Styca | Sweet |
| Snood | Sowar | Spina | Stain | Stock | Style | Sweir |
| Snook | Sower | Spine | Stair | Stoep | Styme | Swell |
| Snool | Sowle | Spink | Stake | Stoic | Suage | Swelt |
| Snoop | Sownd | Spiny | Stale | Stoke | Suave | Swept |
| Snore | Sowne | Spire | Stalk | Stola | Subah | Swift |

**FIVE-LETTER WORDS**—*continued*

| | | | | | | |
|---|---|---|---|---|---|---|
| Swill | Tamil | Telic | Thirl | Toady | Trait | Tsuba |
| Swine | Tamin | Temed | Thoft | Toast | Tramp | Tuath |
| Swing | Tamis | Tempo | Thole | Tobas | Trank | Tubal |
| Swink | Tammy | Tempt | Thong | Tobit | Trant | Tubar |
| Swipe | Tamus | Temse | Thorn | To-day | Trapa | Tubby |
| Swire | Tango | Tench | Thorp | Todde | Trape | Tuber |
| Swirl | Tangy | Tenet | Those | Toddy | Trash | Tucan |
| Swish | Tanna | Tenne | Thoth | Toged | Trass | Tucum |
| Swiss | Tanka | Tenon | Thous | Togue | Trave | Tudor |
| Swith | Tansy | Tenor | Thowl | Toile | Trawl | Tufty |
| Swoln | Tanto | Tense | Thrap | Toise | Tread | Tuism |
| Swoon | Tanty | Tenth | Thraw | Tokay | Treat | Tulip |
| Swoop | Taper | Tenty | Three | Token | Treen | Tulle |
| Sword | Tapet | Tepal | Threw | Toman | Trend | Tumid |
| Swore | Tapir | Tepee | Thrid | Tomin | Tress | Tumpy |
| Sworn | Tapis | Tepid | Throb | Tommy | Trest | Tuner |
| Swote | Tappa | Tepor | Throe | Tonal | Trews | Tunic |
| Swung | Tardo | Terce | Throw | Toned | Triad | Tunny |
| Sycee | Tardy | Terek | Thrum | Tonga | Trial | Tupik |
| Syker | Targe | Teres | Thule | Tongs | Trias | Tuque |
| Sylph | Tarin | Terma | Thumb | Tonic | Tribe | Turbo |
| Sylva | Taroc | Terne | Thump | Tooth | Trice | Turco |
| Synod | Tarot | Terra | Thurl | Topau | Trick | Turfy |
| Syren | Tarre | Terry | Thyme | Topaz | Tride | Turps |
| Syrup | Tarry | Terse | Thymy | Topee | Trier | Tusky |
| Sythe | Tarse | Tervy | Tiara | Toper | Trild | Tutor |
| | Tarsi | Testa | Tibet | Topet | Trill | Tutti |
| **T** | Tarve | Testy | Tibia | Topia | Trine | Tutty |
| | Tasse | Teuch | Tidal | Topic | Trior | Tuzzy |
| Tabby | Taste | Teugh | Tiddy | Toque | Tripe | Twain |
| Taber | Tasty | Tewel | Tiger | Torah | Trist | Twait |
| Tabes | Tatar | Thack | Tight | Toran | Trite | Twang |
| Tabic | Tater | Thane | Tikul | Torch | Troad | Twank |
| Tabid | Tatie | Thank | Tilde | Torse | Troat | Tweak |
| Table | Tatta | Tharm | Tiled | Torsk | Troco | Tweed |
| Taboo | Tatty | Thawy | Tiler | Torso | Trode | Tweel |
| Tabor | Taube | Theca | Tilia | Torus | Troic | Tween |
| Tacca | Taunt | Theft | Tilka | Tossy | Troke | Tweer |
| Tacet | Tawer | Thegn | Tilth | Total | Troll | Twice |
| Tache | Tawie | Theic | Timid | Totem | Tromp | Twier |
| Tacit | Tawny | Their | Timon | Touch | Trona | Twill |
| Tacky | Tawse | Thema | Tinea | Tough | Trone | Twilt |
| Taffy | Taxel | Theme | Tined | Touse | Troop | Twine |
| Tafia | Taxer | There | Tinge | Tousy | Trope | Twink |
| Tahli | Taxin | Therm | Tingi | Towel | Troth | Twire |
| Taint | Taxis | These | Tinny | Tower | Trout | Twirk |
| Taken | Taxus | Theta | Tinty | Towny | Trove | Twirl |
| Taker | Tazza | Thews | Tipsy | Toxic | Truce | Twist |
| Tales | Teach | Thewy | Tiraz | Toxin | Truck | Twite |
| Tally | Tease | Thick | Tired | Toyer | Trull | Twyer |
| Talma | Techy | Thief | Tisic | Toyle | Truly | Tyche |
| Talon | Teens | Thigh | T-iron | Trace | Trump | Tyler |
| Talpa | Teeny | Thilk | Tisri | Track | Trunk | Tynde |
| Taluk | Teeth | Thill | Titan | Tract | Truss | Typal |
| Talus | Tehee | Thine | Tithe | Trade | Trust | Typha |
| Tamal | Teian | Thing | Title | Traik | Truth | Typic |
| Tambu | Teint | Think | Tiver | Trail | Tryma | Tyran |
| Tamer | Telar | Third | Tizzy | Train | Tryst | Tythe |

FIVE-LETTER WORDS—*continued*

| | | | | | | |
|---|---|---|---|---|---|---|
| **U** | Unpay | Valet | Virgo | Waive | Whelp | Wordy |
| | Unpeg | Valid | Virid | Waken | Where | World |
| U-boat | Unpen | Value | Virtu | Waker | Which | Wormy |
| Udder | Unpin | Valva | Virus | Waled | Whiff | Worry |
| Ugric | Unred | Valve | Visie | Waler | Whift | Worse |
| Uhlan | Unrig | Vapid | Visit | Walie | While | Worst |
| Ukase | Unrip | Vapor | Vison | Walla | Whilk | Worth |
| Ulcer | Unsay | Varec | Visor | Walty | Whine | Would |
| Ulema | Unset | Varix | Vista | Waltz | Whipt | Wound |
| Ulmic | Unsex | Varus | Vital | Wandy | Whirl | Woven |
| Ulmin | Unson | Vasal | Vitex | Wanly | Whirr | Woxen |
| Ulmus | Untax | Vasty | Vitis | Wanty | Whisk | Wrack |
| Ulnad | Untie | Vatic | Vitta | Warre | Whist | Wrang |
| Ulnar | Until | Vault | Viure | Warth | White | Wrath |
| Ultra | Untin | Vaunt | Vivat | Warty | Whity | Wraul |
| Umbel | Unweb | Vauty | Vivda | Washy | Whizz | Wrawl |
| Umber | Unwed | Vealy | Vives | Waste | Whole | Wreak |
| Umbra | Upbar | Vedic | Vivid | Watch | Whoot | Wreck |
| Umbre | Uplay | Veery | Vixen | Water | Whorl | Wrest |
| Umiak | Upper | Veiny | Vizir | Waugh | Whort | Wrick |
| Unapt | Uprun | Veldt | Vizor | Waved | Whose | Wring |
| Unarm | Upsee | Velia | Vlach | Waver | Whoso | Wrist |
| Unbag | Upset | Velum | Vocal | Wavey | Whurt | Write |
| Unbar | Uptie | Venal | Vodka | Waxen | Wicky | Wroke |
| Unbay | Upupa | Venew | Vogie | Wazir | Widdy | Wrong |
| Unbed | Urate | Veney | Vogle | Weald | Widen | Wrote |
| Unbid | Urban | Venge | Vogue | Weard | Widow | Wroth |
| Unbit | Uredo | Venom | Voice | Weary | Width | Wrout |
| Uncap | Urena | Venue | Volar | Weave | Wield | Wrung |
| Uncle | Urger | Venus | Volee | Webby | Wiery | Wryly |
| Uncus | Urial | Verge | Volet | Wecht | Wigan | |
| Uncut | Urile | Verre | Volta | Wedge | Wight | **X** |
| Undam | Urite | Verse | Volte | Weedy | Willy | |
| Under | Urman | Verso | Volti | Weely | Wince | Xebec |
| Undid | Urnal | Verst | Volve | Wefte | Winch | Xenon |
| Undue | Urson | Vertu | Vomer | Weigh | Windy | X-rays |
| Unfed | Ursus | Verve | Vomic | Weird | Wingy | Xylem |
| Unfit | Urubu | Vespa | Vomit | Weism | Winna | Xylol |
| Unfix | Urved | Vesta | Voter | Welch | Winze | |
| Unget | Usage | Vetch | Vouch | Welsh | Wiper | **Y** |
| Ungum | Ushas | Vexer | Vowel | Wench | Wispy | |
| Unhat | Usher | Vexil | Vower | Wenny | Witan | Yacca |
| Uniat | Usual | Vezir | Vuggy | Wersh | Witch | Yacht |
| Unify | Usure | Viand | Vulva | Whack | Withe | Yager |
| Union | Usurp | Vibex | | Whale | Withy | Yahoo |
| Unite | Usury | Vicar | **W** | Whall | Witty | Yakut |
| Unity | Utter | Viewy | | Whame | Wives | Yamun |
| Unked | Uvula | Vifda | Wacke | Whang | Wizen | Yapok |
| Unkid | Uzbeg | Vigia | Waddy | Whare | Woden | Yapon |
| Unlap | | Vigil | Wader | Wharf | Woful | Yasht |
| Unlaw | **V** | Villa | Wafer | Whaup | Woman | Yauld |
| Unlay | Vague | Villi | Wager | Wheal | Women | Yawey |
| Unled | Vagus | Vimen | Wages | Wheat | Woody | Yclad |
| Unman | Vails | Vinca | Wagon | Wheel | Wooer | Ydrad |
| Unmew | Vaire | Vinic | Wahoo | Wheen | Woofy | Yearn |
| Unnun | Vairy | Viola | Waide | Wheft | Woold | Yeast |
| Unode | Vakil | Viper | Waift | Whelk | Woont | Yesty |
| Unoil | Vales | Vireo | Waist | Whelm | Wootz | Yewen |
| | | | Waits | | | Yield |
| | | | | | | Y-moth |

**FIVE-LETTER WORDS**—*continued*

| | | | | | | |
|---|---|---|---|---|---|---|
| Yodel | Yucca | Zamia | Zibet | Zoaea | Zoist | Zoril |
| Yogin | Yucky | Zayat | Zimbi | Zocco | Zonal | Zorra |
| Yoick | Yufts | Zebec | Zinco | Zocle | Zonda | Zorro |
| Yojan | Yulan | Zebra | Zinke | Zoeal | Zonic | Zupan |
| Yokel | | Zebub | Zinky | Zofra | Zooid | Zygal |
| Young | **Z** | Zeine | Zizel | Zohar | Zooks | Zygon |
| Yours | Zabra | Zerda | Zloty | Zoism | Zoppo | Zymic |
| Youth | Zambo | Zhobo | | | | |

# Six-Letter Words

| A | Accept | Adonis | Agamic | Aldern | Amende | Annona |
|---|---|---|---|---|---|---|
| | Access | Adoors | Agaric | Aldine | Amends | Annual |
| Abacot | Accite | Adorer | Agazed | Alegar | Amened | Anoint |
| Abacus | Accloy | Adread | Agency | Aleger | Amerce | Anolis |
| Abater | Accoil | Adrift | Agenda | Alegge | Amidin | Anonym |
| Abatis | Accord | Adroit | Aghast | Alerce | Amidst | Anotto |
| Abbacy | Accost | Advene | Agnail | Alette | Amnion | Anoura |
| Abbate | Accrew | Advent | Agname | Ale-vat | Amoeba | Answer |
| Abbaye | Accrue | Adverb | Agnate | Alexin | Amomum | Ant-cow |
| Abbess | Accuse | Advert | Agnise | Algate | Amoral | Anthax |
| Abdals | Aceric | Advice | Agoing | Algoid | Amoret | Anthem |
| Abdest | Acetic | Adview | Agonic | Algous | Amount | Anther |
| Abdiel | Achene | Advise | Agouta | Alight | Ampère | Antiar |
| Abduce | Acidic | Adviso | Agouti | Aliped | Amrita | Antler |
| Abduct | Acknow | Adytum | Agrail | Alisma | Amulet | Antlia |
| Abider | Acopic | Aedile | Agrise | Alkali | Amurca | Antrum |
| Abject | Acorus | Aeneid | Aguise | Allege | Amylic | Anubis |
| Abjure | Acquit | Aeolic | Aguish | Allice | Anabas | Anyhow |
| Abkari | Acrisy | Aerate | Aidant | Allies | Anadem | Anyway |
| Abkary | Acrita | Aerial | Aidful | Allude | Ananas | Aonian |
| Ablaut | Across | Aerify | Aiglet | Allure | Anarch | Aorist |
| Ablaze | Acting | Aerose | Aigret | Almain | Anatta | Aortal |
| Abloom | Action | Aether | Air-bed | Almner | Anatto | Aortic |
| Ablush | Active | Afeard | Air-gas | Almoin | Anbury | Apache |
| Aboard | Actual | Affair | Air-gun | Almond | Anchor | Apathy |
| Aboral | Acuity | Affear | Airily | Almost | Ancome | Apedom |
| Abound | Acumen | Affect | Airing | Almuce | Andean | Apepsy |
| Abrade | Adagio | Affeer | Airman | Alnage | Angary | Apercu |
| Abrayd | Adamic | Affine | Airsac | Alpaca | Angina | Aphony |
| Abroad | Addeem | Affirm | Airway | Alphos | Angled | Aphtha |
| Abrook | Addict | Afflux | Aisled | Alphus | Angler | Apiary |
| Abrupt | Addled | Afford | Akimbo | Alpine | Angles | Apical |
| Absent | Addoom | Affrap | Alalia | Alpist | Angola | Apices |
| Absorb | Adduce | Affray | Alarum | Alsike | Angora | Apiece |
| Absurd | Adhere | Affret | Alated | Altern | Anhima | Apinch |
| Abuser | Adieus | Affuse | Albata | Aludel | Anicut | Aplomb |
| Acacia | Adieux | Afghan | Albeit | Alumna | Anight | Aplome |
| Acacio | Adipic | Afield | Albert | Alvine | Animal | Apnoea |
| Acadia | Adject | Aflame | Albino | Always | Animus | Apodal |
| Acajou | Adjoin | Afloat | Albion | Amadou | Ankled | Apogee |
| Acarus | Adjure | Afraid | Albite | Amatol | Anklet | Aporia |
| Acater | Adjust | Afreet | Albugo | Amazon | Anlace | Apozem |
| Acates | Admire | Afresh | Alcaic | Ambage | Annals | Appeal |
| Accede | Adnate | Afront | Alcaid | Ambler | Annate | Appear |
| Accend | Adnoun | Agalma | Alcedo | Ambury | Anneal | Append |
| Accent | Adonic | Agamae | Alcove | Ambush | Annexe | Appose |

SIX-LETTER WORDS—*continued*

| | | | | | | |
|---|---|---|---|---|---|---|
| Apulse | Arrest | Astral | Averse | Bailer | Barret | Became |
| Aptera | Arride | Astray | Aviary | Bailey | Barrow | Becket |
| Aptote | Arrive | Astrut | Aviate | Bailie | Barter | Beckon |
| Arabic | Arroba | Astute | Avidly | Bairam | Barton | Become |
| Arabin | Arrowy | Aswarm | Avised | Bajree | Baryta | Becurl |
| Arable | Arroyo | Aswing | Avital | Bakery | Basalt | Bedash |
| Araise | Arshin | Aswoon | Avocat | Baking | Basely | Bedaub |
| Arango | Arsine | Asylum | Avocet | Balaam | Bashaw | Bed-bug |
| Arbour | Artery | Atabal | Avoset | Balata | Basial | Bedell |
| Arbute | Artful | Ataman | Avouch | Baldly | Basify | Bedder |
| Arcade | Artist | Ataxia | Avoure | Baleen | Basket | Bedeck |
| Arcady | Arundo | Ataxic | Avowal | Balize | Basnet | Bedkey |
| Arched | Ascend | Athrob | Avowee | Balker | Basque | Bedlam |
| Archer | Ascent | Atkins | Avowry | Ballad | Basset | Bedral |
| Archil | Ascian | Atomic | Avulse | Ballet | Baston | Bedrid |
| Archly | Aseity | Atoner | Awaken | Ballot | Basyle | Bedrop |
| Archon | Asgard | Atonic | Awaste | Balsam | Batata | Beduck |
| Arctic | Ashake | Atrium | Awatch | Bamboo | Bateau | Beduin |
| Ardent | Ashame | Attach | Aweary | Banana | Bather | Bedust |
| Ardour | Ashery | Attack | Aweigh | Banate | Bathos | Beenah |
| Areola | Ash-fly | Attain | Awhape | Bandit | Bating | Beetle |
| Areole | Ashlar | Attask | Awhile | Bandle | Batlet | Beeves |
| Arette | Ashler | Attend | Awning | Bandog | Batman | Befall |
| Argala | Ashore | Attent | Awrack | Banged | Batoon | Befana |
| Argali | Ash-pan | Attest | Awrong | Bangle | Battel | Befoam |
| Argand | Ash-pit | Attire | Awsome | Bangue | Batten | Befogs |
| Argema | Asitia | Attorn | Axicle | Bangup | Batter | Befool |
| Argent | Askant | Attrap | Axilla | Banian | Battle | Before |
| Argive | Aslake | Attune | Axunge | Banish | Battue | Befoul |
| Argosy | Aslant | Atwain | Aye-aye | Banker | Baubee | Begaum |
| Arguer | Asleep | Atween | Azalea | Banket | Bauble | Beggar |
| Argufy | Aslope | Atwixt | Azarin | Bannat | Bawbee | Begift |
| Argute | Asnort | Atypic | Azonic | Banner | Bawble | Begild |
| Aridas | Aspect | Aubade | Azotic | Bantam | Bawdry | Begilt |
| Aright | Aspick | Auburn | Azrael | Banter | Bawler | Begird |
| Arioso | Aspire | Augean | Azured | Banyan | Bawley | Begnaw |
| Arista | Asport | Augite | Azurin | Banzai | Bawsin | Begone |
| Arkite | Aspout | Augury | | Baobab | Bawsin | Behalf |
| Armada | Asquat | August | **B** | Barbed | Baxter | Behave |
| Armful | Assail | Aumail | Baaing | Barbel | Bayard | Behead |
| Armlet | Assart | Aumbry | Baalim | Barber | Bayrum | Beheld |
| Armory | Assent | Aumuce | Babble | Barbet | Bazaar | Behest |
| Armour | Assert | Aurate | Babish | Bardic | Beachy | Behind |
| Armpit | Assess | Aureat | Bablah | Barege | Beacon | Behold |
| Arnaut | Assets | Aureus | Baboon | Barely | Beaded | Behoof |
| Arnica | Assign | Aurist | Backed | Bargee | Beadle | Behone |
| Aroint | Assist | Aurora | Backer | Barish | Beagle | Behove |
| Around | Assize | Aurous | Backet | Barium | Beaked | Behowl |
| Aroura | Assoil | Auspex | Badger | Barken | Beaker | Behung |
| Arouse | Assort | Auster | Baffle | Barker | Beamed | Bejade |
| Aroint | Assume | Author | Baftas | Barley | Bearer | Bejant |
| Aroynt | Assure | Autumn | Bagful | Barman | Beaten | Bejuco |
| Arpent | Astare | Avatar | Bagged | Barney | Beater | Bekiss |
| Arrach | Astart | Avaunt | Baggit | Barony | Beaune | Belace |
| Arrack | Astern | Avener | Bagman | Barque | Beauty | Belamy |
| Arrant | Astert | Avenge | Bagnio | Barras | Beaver | Belate |
| Arrear | Asthma | Avenor | Bagwig | Barrel | Becall | Belaud |
| Arrect | Astony | Avenue | Bailee | Barren | Becalm | Beldam |

## SIX-LETTER WORDS—*continued*

| | | | | | | |
|---|---|---|---|---|---|---|
| Belfry | Bestud | Billow | Bluffy | Boreas | Branky | Browse |
| Belgic | Betail | Bimana | Bluish | Boring | Branny | Browst |
| Belial | Betake | Binary | Bluism | Borley | Brasen | Bruise |
| Belief | Beteem | Binate | Blunge | Borrel | Brasil | Brumal |
| Belike | Bethel | Binder | Bobbin | Borrow | Brashy | Brunch |
| Belive | Betide | Binous | Bobble | Borzoi | Brasse | Brushy |
| Bellis | Betime | Biotic | Bobwig | Bosket | Brassy | Brutal |
| Bellon | Betise | Bipont | Bocage | Bossed | Brawly | Brutus |
| Bellow | Betony | Birder | Bodega | Boston | Brawny | Bryony |
| Belock | Betook | Bireme | Bodger | Botany | Brayer | Bubble |
| Belone | Betorn | Birkin | Bodice | Botchy | Brayle | Bubbly |
| Belong | Betoss | Birler | Bodied | Bot-fly | Brayer | Buccal |
| Belted | Betrap | Birsle | Bodily | Bother | Brazen | Buccan |
| Beluga | Betray | Bisect | Boding | Bothie | Brazil | Bucket |
| Bemask | Betrim | Bishop | Bodkin | Botone | Breach | Buckie |
| Bemaul | Better | Bisley | Boggle | Bo-tree | Breare | Buckle |
| Bembex | Bettor | Bismar | Boglet | Bottle | Breast | Buckra |
| Bemire | Bevile | Bisque | Bog-oak | Bottom | Breath | Buddha |
| Bemoan | Beware | Bisson | Bog-ore | Bouffe | Breech | Buddle |
| Bemock | Beweep | Bistre | Boiler | Bought | Breeks | Budger |
| Bemoil | Bewept | Bister | Bolary | Bougie | Breese | Budget |
| Bemuse | Bewrap | Biting | Bolden | Boulet | Breeze | Budlet |
| Bender | Bewray | Bitter | Boldly | Bounce | Breezy | Buffel |
| Bengal | Bewter | Bittle | Bolero | Bounds | Bregma | Buffer |
| Benign | Beylik | Bittor | Bolide | Bounty | Brehon | Buffet |
| Bennet | Beyond | Bizard | Bolled | Bourne | Breton | Bugler |
| Ben-nut | Bezant | Bladed | Bollen | Bourse | Brevet | Buglet |
| Benote | Bezoar | Blague | Bolter | Bovine | Brewer | Bugong |
| Benshi | Bezzle | Blanch | Bombax | Bowboy | Briber | Bukshi |
| Benumb | Biacìd | Blashy | Bomber | Bow-dye | Bricky | Bulbar |
| Benzol | Biased | Blatta | Bombic | Bowels | Bridal | Bulbed |
| Bepelt | Biaxal | Blazer | Bombyx | Bowery | Bridge | Bulbul |
| Bepity | Bibber | Blazon | Bonbon | Bowess | Bridle | Bulbus |
| Bepuff | Biblus | Bleach | Bonded | Bowfin | Briery | Bulgar |
| Berate | Biceps | Bleaky | Bonder | Bow-leg | Bright | Bulger |
| Berber | Bicker | Blebby | Bonito | Bowler | Brigue | Bulimy |
| Berean | Bicorn | Blench | Bonmot | Bowman | Brills | Bulker |
| Bereft | Bidale | Blende | Bonnet | Bow-net | Briony | Buller |
| Berkie | Bidder | Blenny | Bonten | Bow-oar | Brisky | Bullet |
| Berlin | Bident | Blewit | Bon-ton | Bow-pen | Briton | Bumkin |
| Bertha | Biding | Bleyme | Bonxie | Bow-saw | Broach | Bummed |
| Besant | Biffin | Blight | Boodle | Bowsie | Brogan | Bummel |
| Beseem | Biflex | Blinds | Boohoo | Bow-wow | Brogue | Bummer |
| Beseen | Bifoil | Blinks | Booked | Bowyer | Broken | Bummle |
| Beside | Bifold | Blinky | Bookie | Box-bed | Broker | Bumper |
| Besigh | Biform | Blithe | Boomer | Box-day | Brolly | Bunchy |
| Besing | Bigamy | Blonde | Boopic | Boxing | Bromal | Bundle |
| Besmut | Biggen | Bloody | Booted | Boyish | Bromic | Bungle |
| Besoil | Biggin | Bloomy | Bootee | Bracer | Bronco | Bunion |
| Besort | Bigwig | Blosme | Bootes | Bragly | Bronze | Bunker |
| Bespat | Bilged | Blotch | Bopeep | Brahma | Bronzy | Bunkum |
| Besped | Bilker | Blouse | Borage | Brainy | Brooch | Bunsen |
| Bespew | Bilied | Blower | Borate | Braird | Broody | Bunted |
| Bespit | Billet | Blowse | Borcer | Braise | Brooky | Bunter |
| Bespot | Billie | Blowth | Bordar | Braize | Broomy | Bunyip |
| Bested | Billon | Blowze | Bordel | Branch | Broose | Burble |
| Bestir | Billot | Blowzy | Border | Brandy | Brough | Burbot |
| Bestow | | Bluely | Boreal | Branks | Browny | Burden |

## SIX-LETTER WORDS—*continued*

| | | | | | | |
|---|---|---|---|---|---|---|
| **Bureau** | Cabble | Camise | Carina | Caviar | Chancy | Chitin |
| Burgee | Cabeca | Camiso | Carlot | Caving | Change | Chiton |
| Burgle | Cabiri | Camlet | Carman | Cavity | Chanty | Chitty |
| Burgoo | Cablet | Canada | Carnal | Cavort | Chapel | Choice |
| Burial | Cabman | Canard | Carney | Cawker | Chappy | Choker |
| Burlap | Cabril | Canary | Carpal | Caxton | Charet | Chokey |
| Burler | Cabrit | Cancan | Carpel | Cayman | Charge | Choler |
| Burman | Caburn | Cancel | Carper | Cayuse | Charon | Cholic |
| Burner | Cachet | Cancer | Carpet | Cecils | Charry | Choose |
| Burnet | Cachou | Candid | Carpus | Cecity | Chaser | Chopin |
| Burrel | Cackle | Candie | Carrat | Cedarn | Chasmy | Choppy |
| Burrow | Cacoon | Candle | Carrel | Cedary | Chasse | Choral |
| Bursae | Cactus | Cangue | Carrot | Cedrat | Chaste | Chorea |
| Bursal | Caddie | Canine | Cartel | Cedula | Chaton | Choree |
| Bursar | Caddis | Caning | Carter | Celery | Chatta | Choria |
| Bursch | Cadeau | Canker | Carton | Celiac | Chatty | Choric |
| Burton | Cadene | Cannel | Carvel | Cellar | Chaufe | Chorus |
| Buscon | Cadent | Cannon | Carven | Celled | Chauff | Chosen |
| Bushel | Cadger | Cannot | Carver | Celtic | Checky | Chough |
| Busily | Cadmia | Canopy | Caseic | Cement | Cheeky | Chouse |
| Busked | Caecal | Cantab | Casein | Censer | Cheery | Chowry |
| Busket | Caecum | Cantar | Casern | Censor | Cheese | Chrism |
| Buskin | Caesar | Canter | Cashew | Census | Cheesy | Christ |
| Bustle | Caffre | Canthi | Cashoo | Cental | Chegre | Chrome |
| Butend | Caftan | Cantle | Casing | Center | Chekoa | Chubby |
| Butler | Cagmag | Canton | Casino | Centre | Cheque | Chuffy |
| Butter | Cahier | Cantor | Casket | Cepola | Cherry | Chummy |
| Button | Cahoot | Cantus | Casque | Cerago | Cherty | Chunam |
| Buxine | Caiman | Canuck | Cassia | Cerate | Cherub | Church |
| Buzzer | Caique | Canvas | Caster | Cereal | Cherup | Churly |
| By-blow | Cajole | Canyon | Castle | Cereus | Chesil | Chutny |
| Bye-bye | Calade | Capful | Castor | Cerine | Cheval | Chylde |
| Bye-law | Calash | Capias | Casual | Ceriph | Cheven | Chymic |
| By-form | Calcar | Capite | Casula | Cerise | Chevet | Cicada |
| Bygone | Calced | Capivi | Catchy | Cerite | Chevin | Cicala |
| By-lane | Calcic | Caplin | Catena | Cerium | Chewet | Cicely |
| By-name | Calico | Capote | Catgut | Ceroon | Chiasm | Cicero |
| By-pass | Caligo | Capric | Catkin | Cerris | Chiaus | Cicuta |
| By-past | Caliph | Caprid | Catlap | Certes | Chicha | Cierge |
| Bypath | Calker | Caprin | Catlog | Certie | Chicle | Cilery |
| By-play | Calkin | Captor | Catnip | Ceruse | Chider | Cilice |
| By-plot | Caller | Carack | Catsup | Cervus | Chield | Cimbia |
| By-road | Callet | Caract | Cattle | Cessio | Chigoe | Cimier |
| Byrlaw | Callid | Carafe | Caucus | Cestui | Chigre | Cinder |
| Byroom | Callow | Caranx | Caudal | Cestus | Childe | Cinema |
| Byssus | Callus | Carapa | Caudex | Cesura | Chiled | Cingle |
| By-time | Calmly | Carbon | Caudle | Cesure | Chilli | Cinque |
| By-view | Calory | Carboy | Caught | Cetate | Chilly | Cintre |
| By-walk | Calpac | Cardia | Cauker | Cetine | Chimer | Cipher |
| By-wipe | Caltha | Cardol | Caulis | Chabuk | Chinch | Cippus |
| Byword | Calver | Careen | Causal | Chacma | Chined | Circar |
| Bywork | Camail | Career | Causer | Chafer | Chinee | Circle |
| Byzant | Camass | Careme | Causey | Chaffy | Chinky | Circum |
| | Camata | Caress | Cautel | Chagan | Chinse | Circus |
| | Camber | Carfax | Cauter | Chaise | Chintz | Cirque |
| **C** | Camera | Carfox | Cavass | Chalet | Chippy | Cirrus |
| Cabala | Camese | Carica | Caveat | Chalky | Chirpy | Cissus |
| Cabana | Camion | Caries | Cavern | Chance | Chisel | Cisted |

### SIX-LETTER WORDS—*continued*

| | | | | | | |
|---|---|---|---|---|---|---|
| Cistic | Clotty | Coigne | Convey | Coryza | Cranky | Cruise |
| Cistus | Cloudy | Coiner | Convoy | Cosher | Cranny | Cruive |
| Citess | Clough | Cojoin | Conyza | Cosier | Crants | Crumby |
| Cither | Cloven | Coldly | Cooing | Cosily | Crasis | Crummy |
| Citing | Clover | Collar | Cooker | Cosine | Cratch | Crunch |
| Citole | Cloyed | Collet | Cookie | Cosmic | Crater | Crural |
| Citric | Clumps | Collie | Cooler | Cosmos | Cravat | Cruset |
| Citril | Clumpy | Collop | Coolie | Cossas | Craved | Crusie |
| Citron | Clumsy | Collum | Coolly | Cosset | Craven | Crusta |
| Citrul | Clunch | Colmar | Coombe | Costal | Craver | Crusty |
| Citrus | Clupea | Colmey | Coonty | Costly | Crayer | Crutch |
| Civics | Clutch | Colony | Cooper | Coteau | Crayon | Crying |
| Civies | Coachy | Colour | Cootie | Cotise | Crazed | Cubage |
| Civism | Coaita | Colter | Copang | Cottar | Creach | Cubica |
| Claggy | Coarse | Column | Copeck | Cotter | Creagh | Cubism |
| Clammy | Coatee | Colure | Copier | Cotton | Creaky | Cubist |
| Claque | Coaxer | Comarb | Coping | Cotyla | Creamy | Cuboid |
| Claret | Cobalt | Comart | Copped | Cotyle | Creant | Cubsha |
| Clarty | Cobble | Co-mate | Copper | Coucal | Crease | Cuckoo |
| Clatch | Cobcal | Combat | Coppin | Cougar | Creasy | Cuddie |
| Clatty | Cobnut | Comber | Copple | Coulee | Create | Cuddle |
| Clause | Cobres | Comedo | Copula | County | Crèche | Cudgel |
| Claver | Cobric | Comedy | Copyer | Couped | Credit | Cuerpo |
| Clavis | Coburg | Comely | Coquet | Coupee | Creeky | Cuffin |
| Clawed | Cobweb | Comfit | Corage | Couper | Creepy | Cuisse |
| Clayes | Coccus | Comfry | Corban | Couple | Creese | Cuiter |
| Clayey | Coccyx | Coming | Corbel | Coupon | Creesh | Culdee |
| Cleave | Cochin | Comity | Corbie | Courap | Cremor | Culler |
| Cleché | Cockal | Commit | Corcle | Course | Crenel | Cullet |
| Cledge | Cocked | Commix | Corded | Cousin | Creole | Cullis |
| Cledgy | Cocker | Common | Cordon | Couter | Crepon | Culmen |
| Clench | Cocket | Comose | Corium | Covent | Cressy | Cultch |
| Clergy | Cockle | Compel | Corked | Covert | Cretic | Culter |
| Cleric | Cocksy | Comply | Corker | Covess | Cretin | Cultus |
| Cleuch | Cocoon | Compot | Cormus | Coving | Crevet | Culver |
| Cleugh | Codber | Concha | Cornea | Cowage | Crewel | Cumber |
| Clever | Codded | Conchy | Corned | Coward | Crible | Cummer |
| Clevis | Codder | Concur | Cornel | Cowboy | Crinal | Cummin |
| Cliché | Codger | Conder | Corner | Cowish | Cringe | Cuneal |
| Client | Codify | Condor | Cornet | Cowled | Crises | Cupful |
| Cliffy | Codist | Confab | Cornua | Cowman | Crisis | Cupman |
| Clifty | Codlin | Confer | Corody | Cow-pox | Crispy | Cupola |
| Climax | Coelom | Confit | Corona | Cowrie | Crista | Cupped |
| Clinch | Coerce | Confix | Corozo | Coyish | Critic | Cupper |
| Clingy | Coeval | Congee | Corpse | Coyote | Croaky | Cupric |
| Clinic | Coffee | Conger | Corpus | Coypou | Croats | Cupula |
| Clione | Coffer | Congou | Corral | Cozier | Croche | Cupule |
| Clique | Coffin | Conics | Corrie | Crabby | Crocus | Curacy |
| Cloaca | Coffle | Coniin | Corsac | Craber | Cronet | Curara |
| Cloche | Cogent | Conima | Corsak | Crabro | Crooks | Curare |
| Cloddy | Coggie | Conine | Corset | Cradle | Croppy | Curari |
| Clodly | Coggle | Conium | Cortes | Crafty | Crosse | Curate |
| Cloggy | Cognac | Conjee | Cortex | Cragge | Crotch | Curcas |
| Clonic | Coheir | Conner | Corvée | Craggy | Croton | Curdle |
| Clonus | Cohere | Conoid | Corvet | Crambo | Crouch | Curfew |
| Closer | Cohorn | Consul | Corvus | Crampy | Croupy | Curiet |
| Closet | Cohort | Contra | Corymb | Cranch | Crouse | Curler |
| Clothe | | Convex | | Crania | Crowdy | Curlew |

## SIX-LETTER WORDS—*continued*

| | | | | | | |
|---|---|---|---|---|---|---|
| Currie | Daidle | Deaden | Degage | Desert | Diking | Dobbie |
| Cursed | Daiker | Deadly | Degree | Design | Dilate | Dobbin |
| Curser | Daimio | Deafen | Degust | Desine | Dilogy | Docent |
| Cursus | Dainty | Deafly | Dehors | Desire | Dilute | Docile |
| Curtal | Dakoit | Dealer | Dehort | Desist | Dimity | Docity |
| Curtly | Dalila | Dearie | Deific | Desman | Dimmer | Docked |
| Curtsy | Dallop | Dearly | Deject | Desmid | Dimple | Docker |
| Curule | Damage | Dearth | Delate | Despot | Dindle | Docket |
| Curvet | Damask | Deasil | Delete | Detach | Dinful | Doctor |
| Cuscus | Dammar | Debark | Deliac | Detail | Dinged | Dodded |
| Cushat | Dampen | Debase | Delian | Detain | Dingey | Dodder |
| Cuspid | Damper | Debate | Delice | Detect | Dinghy | Doddle |
| Cussed | Damply | Debile | Delict | Detent | Dingle | Dodger |
| Custom | Damsel | Deblai | Deluce | Detest | Dinner | Dodkin |
| Custos | Damson | Debosh | Delude | Detort | Dinnle | Dodman |
| Cutcha | Dancer | Debout | Deluge | Detour | Diodon | Doffer |
| Cutler | Dander | Débris | Delver | Devall | Diplex | Dogana |
| Cutlet | Dandie | Debtee | Demain | Devest | Diploe | Dogate |
| Cut-off | Dandle | Debtor | Demand | Device | Dipnoi | Dog-bee |
| Cut-out | Danger | Decade | Demean | Devise | Dipody | Dog-box |
| Cutter | Dangle | Decamp | Dement | Devoid | Dipper | Dogfly |
| Cuttle | Daniel | Decani | Demise | Devoir | Dipsas | Dog-fox |
| Cuttoe | Danish | Decant | Demiss | Devote | Dipyre | Doggar |
| Cyanic | Danite | Decare | Demure | Devour | Dirdum | Dogged |
| Cyclic | Danton | Deceit | Denary | Devout | Direct | Dogger |
| Cyclus | Daphne | Decent | Dengue | Dewani | Dirham | Dog-mad |
| Cygnet | Dapper | Decern | Denial | Dewitt | Dirhem | Doiled |
| Cygnus | Dapple | Decide | Denier | Dewlap | Dirtum | Doings |
| Cymbal | Darger | Decile | Dennet | Dexter | Dirzee | Doited |
| Cymoid | Daring | Decima | Denote | Dextro | Disarm | Dolent |
| Cymose | Darken | Decime | Dental | Dezink | Disbar | Dolium |
| Cymous | Darkey | Decker | Dentel | Dharma | Disbud | Dollar |
| Cymric | Darkle | Deckle | Dentex | Dhobie | Discal | Dollop |
| Cynara | Darkly | Decoct | Dentil | Dhooly | Discus | Dolman |
| Cynics | Darnel | Decode | Dentin | Dhurra | Dismal | Dolmen |
| Cyphel | Darner | Decree | Denude | Diadem | Disman | Dolose |
| Cypher | Darter | Decrew | Deodar | Diamyl | Dismay | Dolour |
| Cy-près | Dartle | Decury | Depart | Diaper | Disown | Domain |
| Cypris | Dartre | Dedans | Depend | Diatom | Dispel | Dom-boc |
| Cyprus | Dasher | Deduce | Depict | Dibber | Disple | Domett |
| Cystic | Datary | Deduct | Deploy | Dibble | Distal | Domify |
| Cystis | Dative | Deepen | Depone | Dicast | Distil | Domino |
| | Datura | Deeply | Deport | Dicker | Disuse | Domite |
| | Dauber | Deface | Depose | Dickey | Dither | Donary |
| **D** | Daubry | Defame | Depute | Dictum | Dition | Donjon |
| | Daucus | Defeat | Deputy | Didder | Ditone | Donkey |
| Dabber | Dauner | Defect | Derail | Diddle | Dittay | Donsie |
| Dabble | Dautie | Defend | Derain | Diesis | Dittos | Donzel |
| Dacker | Davina | Deffly | Derate | Dieted | Diurna | Doocot |
| Dacoit | Davine | Defier | Derbio | Dieter | Divali | Doodle |
| Dactyl | Davits | Defile | Deride | Differ | Divers | Doolie |
| Daddle | Dawdle | Define | Derive | Digamy | Divert | Dopper |
| Daedal | Dawish | Deflex | Dermal | Digest | Divest | Doquet |
| Daemon | Dawtie | Deflux | Dermic | Digger | Divide | Dorado |
| Daftly | Day-bed | Deform | Dermis | Diglot | Divine | Dorbie |
| Dagger | Day-fly | Defoul | Dernal | Digram | Divoto | Dorcas |
| Daggle | Dazzle | Defray | Desart | Dikast | Dizain | Dorian |
| Dagoba | Deacon | Deftly | Descry | Dik-dik | Doable | Dorism |

## SIX-LETTER WORDS—*continued*

| | | | | | | | |
|---|---|---|---|---|---|---|---|
| Dormer | Drolly | Dupery | Edible | Eltchi | Enfire | Entrée |
| Dormie | Dromic | Dupion | Editor | Elvish | Enfold | Entune |
| Dornic | Dromon | Duplex | Eel-oil | Elwand | Enform | Envied |
| Dorsal | Dromos | Dupper | Eel-pot | Embace | Enfree | Envier |
| Dorsel | Drongo | Durain | Eerily | Embale | Engage | Enwall |
| Dorsum | Dropax | Durant | Efface | Emball | Engaol | Enwind |
| Dosage | Dropsy | Durbar | Effect | Embalm | Engild | Enwomb |
| Dossal | Drosky | Durden | Effeir | Embank | Engine | Enwrap |
| Dossel | Drossy | Durdum | Effere | Embark | Engird | Enzone |
| Dosser | Drouge | Duress | Effete | Embase | Englut | Enzyme |
| Dossil | Droumy | Durgan | Effigy | Emblem | Engore | Eocene |
| Dotage | Drouth | Durham | Efflux | Embody | Engulf | Eolian |
| Dotant | Drover | Durian | Efform | Emboil | Enhalo | Eolith |
| Dotard | Drowse | During | Effort | Emboss | Enigma | Eostre |
| Dotish | Drowsy | Durion | Effray | Embrue | Enisle | Eothen |
| Dottle | Drudge | Durity | Effuse | Embryo | Enjail | Eozoic |
| Douane | Drumly | Duskey | Egence | Emerge | Enjoin | Eozoon |
| Double | Drupel | Duskin | Egeran | Emesis | Enlace | Eparch |
| Douche | Drused | Duster | Egesta | Emetic | Enlard | Epaule |
| Doughy | Druses | Duyker | Egg-cup | Emetin | Enlink | Epeira |
| Doukar | Drybob | Dyadic | Eggery | Emeute | Enlist | Ephebe |
| Dourly | Dryfly | Dyeing | Eggler | Emmesh | Enlock | Ephori |
| Doused | Dryish | Dynamo | Egg-nog | Emmove | Enmesh | Epigee |
| Douter | Dryite | Dynast | Egoism | Empair | Enmity | Epizoa |
| Dowery | Dry-rot | Dysury | Egoist | Empale | Enmove | Epodic |
| Dowlas | Dry-rub | Dyvour | Egoity | Empark | Enmure | Eponym |
| Downed | Dualin | Dzeren | Egress | Empasm | Ennead | Epopee |
| Dowser | Dubash | Dzeron | Egriot | Empawn | Ennuye | Epulis |
| Doyley | Dubber | | Eident | Empery | Enodal | Equant |
| Dozing | Dubbin | **E** | Eidola | Empire | Enough | Equate |
| Drabby | Ducker | | Eighth | Employ | Enrace | Equine |
| Drachm | Dudder | Eadish | Eighty | Empusa | Enrage | Equity |
| Draffy | Dudeen | Eaglet | Eirack | Empuse | Enrail | Eraser |
| Drafts | Dudish | Earbob | Either | Emrods | Enrank | Erbium |
| Dragon | Dudism | Ear-cap | Ekeing | Emucid | E nrapt | Erebus |
| Draper | Dueful | Earing | Elaeis | Emunge | Enrich | Erenow |
| Drapes | Duello | Earlap | Elance | Enable | Enring | Eriach |
| Drapet | Duenna | Earthy | Elanet | Enamel | Enrobe | Eringo |
| Drappy | Duetto | Ear-wax | Elapse | Encage | Enroll | Erinys |
| Drawee | Duffel | Earwig | Elater | Encamp | Enroot | Ermine |
| Drawer | Duffer | Easily | Elator | Encase | Ensate | Eroded |
| Drazel | Duffle | Eassel | Elchee | Encash | Enseal | Erotic |
| Dreamy | Dugong | Easter | Eldest | Encave | Enseam | Errand |
| Dreary | Dugout | Eatage | Elding | Encope | Ensear | Errant |
| Dredge | Duiker | Eathly | Elegit | Encore | Ensign | Errata |
| Dreggy | Dukery | Ecarte | Elemin | Encyst | Ensile | Eryngo |
| Dreich | Dulcet | Ecbole | Elench | End-all | Ensoul | Escape |
| Drench | Dumbly | Echoer | Eleven | Endear | Ensure | Escarp |
| Dressy | Dum-dum | Echoic | Elfish | Ending | Entail | Eschar |
| Dreuls | Dumose | Eclair | Elicit | Endite | Entame | Eschew |
| Drifts | Dumous | Eclegm | Elisor | Endive | Entent | Escort |
| Drifty | Dumple | Ectype | Elixir | Endoss | Entera | Escrol |
| Drivel | Dun-cow | Ecurie | Elk-nut | Endure | Entice | Escrow |
| Driven | Dunder | Eczema | Elleck | Enecia | Entire | Escudo |
| Driver | Dunker | Eddish | Ellops | Energy | Entity | Eskimo |
| Droger | Dunlin | Eddoes | Elodes | Enerve | Entoil | Esloin |
| Drogue | Dunlop | Edenic | Elohim | Enface | Entomb | Esnecy |
| Droich | Dunner | Edging | Eloign | Enfest | Entrap | Espial |

### SIX-LETTER WORDS—*continued*

| | | | | | | |
|---|---|---|---|---|---|---|
| Espier | Expect | Famble | Feller | Fillet | Flaxen | Foison |
| Esprit | Expend | Family | Fellic | Fillip | Flayer | Fokker |
| Essene | Expert | Famine | Felloe | Filose | Fleche | Folded |
| Essera | Expire | Famish | Fellow | Filter | Fledge | Folder |
| Essoin | Expiry | Famous | Felony | Filthy | Fledgy | Foliar |
| Estate | Export | Fanged | Felter | Fimble | Fleece | Folier |
| Esteem | Expose | Fangle | Feltre | Finale | Fleech | Foliot |
| Estray | Expugn | Fangot | Female | Finder | Fleecy | Follia |
| Etcher | Exsect | Fanion | Fencer | Findon | Flench | Follow |
| Eterne | Exsert | Fannel | Fender | Fineer | Flense | Foment |
| Ethics | Extant | Fanner | Fenian | Finely | Fleshy | Fondle |
| Ethiop | Extasy | Fantan | Fenman | Finery | Fletch | Fondly |
| Ethnic | Extend | Fantom | Fennec | Finger | Fleury | Fontal |
| Etnean | Extent | Faquir | Fennel | Finial | Flewed | Footed |
| Etymon | Extern | Farand | Feodal | Fining | Flexor | Footer |
| Etypic | Extine | Farcin | Feriae | Finish | Flight | Footle |
| Eucain | Extort | Fardel | Ferial | Finite | Flimsy | Foozle |
| Euchre | Eyalet | Farina | Ferine | Finlet | Flinch | Forage |
| Eulogy | Eyelet | Farmed | Ferity | Finnan | Flinty | Forbid |
| Eunomy | Eyelid | Farmer | Ferrel | Finned | Flisky | Forced |
| Eunuch | Eyepit | Farrow | Ferret | Finner | Flitch | Forcer |
| Euonym | Eyrant | Fasces | Ferric | Finnic | Flitty | Forded |
| Eupion | | Fascia | Ferula | Fiorin | Floaty | Fore-by |
| Eureka | | Fasten | Ferule | Firing | Flocci | Foredo |
| Eurite | | Fastly | Fervid | Firkin | Flocky | Forego |
| Eutaxy | **F** | Faster | Fescue | Firlot | Floppy | Forest |
| Evanid | | Fat-hen | Festal | Firman | Floral | Forfex |
| Evener | Fabian | Father | Fester | Firmed | Floran | Forgat |
| Evenly | Fabled | Fathom | Fetial | Firmly | Floret | Forger |
| Evilly | Fabler | Fatted | Fetich | Fiscal | Florid | Forget |
| Evince | Fabric | Fatten | Fetish | Fisgig | Florin | Forgot |
| Evolve | Façade | Faucal | Fetter | Fisher | Flossy | Forhow |
| Examen | Facete | Fauces | Fettle | Fissle | Floury | Forlay |
| Exarch | Facial | Faucet | Feudal | Fistic | Flouse | Formal |
| Exceed | Facies | Faulty | Fewter | Fitche | Floush | Format |
| Except | Facile | Faunal | Fiacre | Fitchy | Flower | Formed |
| Excern | Facing | Fautor | Fiancé | Fitful | Fluate | Former |
| Excess | Factor | Favose | Fiasco | Fitter | Flucan | Formic |
| Excide | Factum | Favour | Fibber | Fixing | Fluent | Fornix |
| Excise | Facula | Fawned | Fibred | Fixity | Fluffy | Forpet |
| Excite | Faddle | Fawner | Fibril | Fixive | Flurry | Forpit |
| Excuse | Fading | Faying | Fibrin | Fixure | Fluted | Forrel |
| Excuss | Faecal | Feague | Fibula | Fizgig | Fluter | Forrit |
| Exedra | Faeces | Fealty | Fickle | Fizzle | Flushy | Forsay |
| Exempt | Faerie | Featly | Fictor | Flabby | Flyman | Forted |
| Exequy | Faffle | Feazes | Fiddle | Flacon | Fly-net | Forthy |
| Exeunt | Fag-end | Fecial | Fidget | Flaggy | Fly-nut | Fossil |
| Exhale | Faggot | Feckly | Fierce | Flagon | Focile | Foster |
| Exhort | Faille | Fecula | Fifish | Flamen | Focoso | Fother |
| Exhume | Fainty | Fecund | Figaro | Flanch | Fodder | Fotmal |
| Exilic | Fairly | Fedary | Figure | Flange | Foeman | Fought |
| Exitus | Faitor | Feeble | Fikery | Flanks | Foetal | Foully |
| Exodic | Falcon | Feebly | Fikish | Flashe | Foetor | Fourbe |
| Exodus | Fallal | Feeder | Filago | Flashy | Foetus | Fourth |
| Exogen | Fallen | Feeler | Filfot | Flatly | Fog-bow | Foutre |
| Exomis | Fallow | Feline | Filial | Flatus | Fogram | Fowler |
| Exotic | Falter | Felled | Filing | Flaunt | Foible | Fox-bat |
| Expand | Faluns | Fellah | Filler | Flavin | Foiler | |

**SIX-LETTER WORDS**—*continued*

| | | | | | | |
|---|---|---|---|---|---|---|
| Foxish | Fugato | Gaffle | Garlic | German | Glaive | Gomuto |
| Foyble | Fugile | Gagger | Garner | Germen | Glance | Goodly |
| Fracas | Fulfil | Gaggle | Garnet | Germin | Glassy | Googly |
| Fracid | Fulgid | Gaiety | Garous | Gerund | Glazer | Gooroo |
| Fragor | Fulgor | Gainer | Garran | Gervao | Gleamy | Gopher |
| Fraise | Fulham | Gainly | Garret | Gervas | Gledge | Gopura |
| Framer | Fulica | Gainst | Garron | Gestic | Gleety | Goramy |
| Franzy | Fullam | Gaited | Garrot | Getter | Glibly | Gorged |
| Frappe | Fullan | Gaiter | Garrya | Gew-gaw | Glider | Gorget |
| Fratch | Fuller | Galage | Garter | Geyser | Globin | Gorgon |
| Frater | Fulmar | Galago | Garuda | Ghazal | Gloomy | Gor-hen |
| Fratry | Fulvid | Galaxy | Garvie | Ghazel | Gloria' | Goring |
| Frazil | Fumado | Galban | Gas-bag | Gheber | Glossy | Gospel |
| Freely | Fumage | Galeas | Gashly | Ghebre | Glover | Gossan |
| Freety | Fumble | Galega | Gasify | Ghetto | Glower | Gossip |
| Freeze | Family | Galena | Gas-jet | Ghurka | Glozer | Gothic |
| Freity | Fummel | Galiot | Gasket | Giaour | Glucic | Gotten |
| Fremit | Fumous | Galium | Gaskin | Gibber | Gluish | Gourdy |
| French | Funded | Galley | Gasman | Gibbet | Glumal | Gousty |
| Frenne | Fundus | Gallic | Gas-tar | Gibbon | Glumly | Govern |
| Frenum | Funest | Gallio | Gateau | Gib-cat | Glumps | Gowdie |
| Frenzy | Fungal | Gallon | Gather | Giblet | Gluten | Gowfer |
| Fresco | Fungia | Gallop | Gatten | Gifted | Glutin | Gowned |
| Frette | Fungic | Gallow | Gauche | Giggit | Glycin | Gowpen |
| Fretty | Fungin | Galoon | Gaucho | Giggle | Glycol | Gozzan |
| Friary | Fungus | Galoot | Gaucie | Giglet | Gnarly | Graces |
| Friday | Funkia | Galore | Gauger | Giglot | Gnarry | Gradin |
| Fridge | Funnel | Galosh | Gaupus | Gigman | Gnawer | Gradus |
| Friend | Furfur | Gamash | Gavial | Gigolo | Gneiss | Grafin |
| Frieze | Furore | Gambet | Gawpus | Gilded | Gnetum' | Grainy |
| Fright | Furrow | Gambit | Gazebo | Gilder | Gnomic | Graith |
| Frigid | Furzen | Gamble | Gazoon | Gillie | Gnomon | Grakle |
| Frigot | Fusain | Gambol | Geason | Gilpey | Gnosis | Gramme |
| Fringe | Fusion | Gamely | Gebbie | Gilpin | Goatee | Grange |
| Fringy | Fusted | Gamete | Geezer | Gimbal | Gobang | Granny |
| Frisky | Fustet | Gaming | Geisha | Gimlet | Gobbet | Grassy |
| Frivol | Fustic | Gammer | Gemara | Gimmal | Gobbin | Grater |
| Frizel | Fusure | Gammon | Gemini | Gimmer | Gobble | Gratin |
| Froggy | Futile | Gander | Gemmae | Ginete | Goblet | Gratis |
| Froise | Future | Ganesa | Gemman | Gingal | Goblin | Gravel |
| Frolic | Fuzzle | Ganger | Gemmho | Ginger | Go cart | Graven |
| Fronde | Fylfot | Gangue | Gemote | Gingko | Godown | Graver |
| Frosty | | Gannet | Gender | Gingle | Godson | Graves |
| Frothy | | Ganoid | Genera | Ginkgo | Godwit | Gravid |
| Frouzy | | Gantry | Geneva | Ginnet | Goetic | Grazer |
| Frower | **G** | Gaoler | Genial | Girder | Goffer | Grease |
| Frowst | Gabber | Gaping | Genius | Girdle | Goggle | Greats |
| Frowsy | Gabble | Garage | Gennet | Girkin | Goglet | Greasy |
| Frowzy | Gabbro | Garble | Gentle | Girnel | Goidel | Greave |
| Frozen | Gabion | Garçon | Gently | Gitana | Goitre | Greece |
| Frugal | Gablet | Garden | Gentoo | Gitano | Golden | Greedy |
| Fruict | Gadder | Gardon | Gentry | Giusto | Golfer | Greens |
| Fruity | Gadfly | Garget | Genual | Giving | Golias | Greeny |
| Frumpy | Gadget | Gargil | Geodic | Gizzen | Gollar | Greese |
| Frutex | Gadine | Gargle | Geomys | Glacis | Golore | Greeve |
| Fucate | Gadoid | Gargol | George | Gladly | Golosh | Gregal |
| Fucoid | Gaelic | Garial | Gerant | Glagol | Gommer | Gretna |
| Fuddle | Gaffer | Garish | Gerbil | Glairy | Gomuti | Griece |

## SIX-LETTER WORDS—*continued*

| | | | | | | |
|---|---|---|---|---|---|---|
| Grieve | Gun-wad | Halser | Hawser | Hermit | Hogget | Huddle |
| Grille | Gunyah | Halter | Haybox | Hernia | Hog-pen | Huddup |
| Grilse | Gurgle | Halved | Haymow | Heroic | Hogsty | Huffer |
| Grimly | Gurjon | Halves | Hazard | Heroin | Hoiden | Hugely |
| Gringo | Gurkha | Hamate | Hazily | Herpes | Holder | Huller |
| Griper | Gurnet | Hamble | Hazing | Herren | Holily | Humane |
| Grippe | Gurrah | Hamite | Headed | Hersal | Holloa | Humble |
| Grisly | Gusher | Hamlet | Header | Hersed | Hollow | Humbly |
| Grison | Gusset | Hammal | Healer | Hesper | Holpen | Humbug |
| Gritty | Guttae | Hammam | Health | Hesvan | Homage | Humect |
| Grocer | Guttee | Hammer | Hearer | Hetman | Homely | Humefy |
| Groggy | Gutter | Hamose | Hearse | Hexade | Homily | Humery |
| Gromel | Guttle | Hamous | Hearth | Heyday | Homing | Humete |
| Gromet | Guzzle | Hamper | Hearty | Hiatus | Hominy | Humhum |
| Groove | Gymnic | Handle | Heater | Hiccup | Honest | Humian |
| Groser | Gypsum | Hangar | Heathy | Hidage | Honour | Humine |
| Grotto | Gyrate | Hanger | Heaume | Hidden | Hooded | Humite |
| Ground | Gyrose | Hanjar | Heaven | Hiding | Hoofed | Hummel |
| Grouse | | Hanker | Heaver | Hiemal | Hookah | Hummer |
| Grovel | | Hansel | Heaves | Higgle | Hooker | Hummie |
| Grower | **H** | Hansom | Hebrew | Higher | Hookey | Hummum |
| Growth | Habble | Hantle | Hecate | Highly | Hooper | Humour |
| Groyne | Habile | Happen | Heckle | Hijrah | Hoopoe | Humous |
| Grubby | Hachel | Harass | Hectic | Hilary | Hoopoo | Humped |
| Grudge | Hackee | Harden | Hector | Hilled | Hooter | Hunger |
| Gru-gru | Hacket | Hardly | Heddle | Hilsah | Hooven | Hungry |
| Grumly | Hackle | Hareld | Hedera | Hilted | Hooves | Hunker |
| Grumph | Hackly | Harier | Hedger | Hindee | Hopdog | Hunnic |
| Grumpy | Haddie | Harish | Heehaw | Hinder | Hop-fly | Hunter |
| Grundy | Haddin | Harken | Heeler | Hindoo | Hopper | Hurden |
| Grutch | Hading | Harlot | Hegira | Hippic | Hoppet | Hurdle |
| Gryfon | Hadith | Harman | Heifer | Hippus | Hopple | Hurler |
| Grysie | Haemal | Harmel | Height | Hircin | Horary | Hurley |
| Guacho | Haemic | Harper | Hejira | Hircus | Horner | Hurrah |
| Guamin | Haffet | Harrow | Heliac | Hirmoi | Hornet | Hurter |
| Guddle | Haffle | Hartal | Helium | Hirmos | Hornie | Hurtle |
| Gueber | Hagbut | Haslet | Helmet | Hirple | Horrid | Hushed |
| Guebre | Hagden | Hasten | Helper | Hirsel | Horror | Husked |
| Guelph | Hagged | Hatbox | Helvin | Hirsle | Hosier | Husker |
| Guffaw | Haggis | Hathor | Hemina | Hispid | Hostel | Hussar |
| Guggle | Haggle | Hat-peg | Hemmer | Histie | Hot-bed | Hussif |
| Guider | Haglet | Hatpin | Hempen | Hitchy | Hotpot | Hustle |
| Guidon | Haiduk | Hatred | Henbit | Hither | Houdah | Hyades |
| Guiler | Haique | Hatted | Herald | Hitter | Houdan | Hyaena |
| Guills | Haired | Hatter | Herbal | Hoarse | Hounds | Hybrid |
| Guilty | Hairst | Haught | Herbar | Hoaxee | Hourly | Hydria |
| Guinea | Hakeem | Hauler | Herded | Hoaxer | Housel | Hydric |
| Guiser | Halfer | Haunch | Herdic | Hoazin | Housty | Hydrid |
| Guitar | Halion | Hautin | Hereat | Hobble | Howdah | Hydrus |
| Gulden | Hallan | Hauyne | Hereby | Hobjob | Howdie | Hyemal |
| Guller | Hallel | Havana | Herein | Hobnob | Howker | Hyetal |
| Gullet | Halloa | Havers | Hereof | Hockey | Howler | Hygeia |
| Gulley | Halloo | Having | Hereon | Hockle | Howlet | Hyksos |
| Gun-man | Hallow | Hawhaw | Heresy | Hodden | Hoyden | Hylism |
| Gunnel | Hallux | Hawked | Hereto | Hoddle | Hubble | Hymnal |
| Gunner | Haloed | Hawker | Heriot | Hodman | Hubbly | Hymnic |
| Gun-shy | Haloid | Hawkey | Hermae | Hogged | Hubbub | Hyphae |
| Gunter | Halsed | Hawkie | Hermes | Hogger | Huckle | Hyphen |

## SIX-LETTER WORDS—*continued*

| | | | | | | |
|---|---|---|---|---|---|---|
| Hypnum | Implex | Ingest | Invert | Jagged | Jocose | Kakapo |
| Hyssop | Impone | Ingulf | Invest | Jagger | Jocund | Kalium |
| | Import | Inhale | Invite | Jaghir | Jogger | Kalmia |
| | Impose | Inhaul | Invoke | Jaguar | Joggle | Kalong |
| | Impost | Inhere | Inwall | Jailer | Johnny | Kalpis |
| **I** | Impugn | Inhive | Inward | Jailor | Joiner | Kamees |
| | Impure | Inhoop | Inwick | Jambee | Jolter | Kamela |
| Iambic | Impute | Inhume | Inwith | Jambok | Jordan | Kamila |
| Iambus | Inbond | Inject | Inwork | Jambul | Joseph | Kamera |
| Iatric | Inborn | Injure | Inworn | Jampan | Joskin | Kamsin |
| Iberis | Inbred | Injury | Inwrap | Jangle | Josser | Kanaka |
| Ibidem | Incage | Inkbag | Inyala | Janker | Jostle | Kanten |
| Iblees | Incarn | Inknit | Iodate | Jargon | Jotter | Kanuck |
| Ice-age | Incase | Inknot | Iodide | Jarool | Jounce | Kaolin |
| Ice-axe | Incask | Inkpot | Iodine | Jarrah | Jovial | Karmic |
| Ice-cap | Incast | Inlace | Iodism | Jarvey | Jovian | Kaross |
| Iceman | Incavo | Inlaid | Iodist | Jasher | Jowler | Karroo |
| Ice-saw | Incept | Inland | Iodize | Jasper | Jowter | Kavass |
| Icicle | Incest | Inlier | Iolite | Jataka | Joyful | Kebbie |
| Isonic | Inched | Inlock | Ionian | Jaunce | Joyous | Keblah |
| Ideate | Incise | Inmate | Ionize | Jaunty | Jubate | Keckle |
| Idiasm | Incite | Inmost | Iranic | Jaw-box | Jubbah | Kecksy |
| Idiocy | Inclip | Innate | Ireful | Jeames | Judaic | Keddah |
| Idolon | Income | Inning | Irenic | Jeerer | Judean | Kedged |
| Idolum | Incony | Innuit | Iridal | Jejune | Judger | Kedger |
| Ignaro | Incult | Inrail | Iridin | Jennet | Judica | Keeker |
| Ignite | Incuse | Inroad | Irised | Jerboa | Jugate | Keeled |
| Ignore | Incuss | Inrush | Iritic | Jeered | Jugful | Keeler |
| Iguana | Indart | Insane | Iritis | Jereed | Juggle | Keelie |
| Ill-got | Indeed | Inseam | Ironer | Jerked | Jujube | Keener |
| Illude | Indent | Insect | Ironic | Jerker | Jug-jug | Keenly |
| Illume | Indian | Insert | Isabel | Jerkin | Julian | Keeper |
| Imband | Indict | Inship | Isagon | Jersey | Jumart | Kelkel |
| Imbank | Indign | Inside | Isatis | Jervin | Jumble | Kelpie |
| Imbark | Indigo | Insist | Isatic | Jessed | Jument | Kelson |
| Imbibe | Indite | Insole | Island | Jester | Jumper | Kelter |
| Imbody | Indium | Inspan | Isobar | Jesuit | Juncus | Keltic |
| Imboil | Indoor | Instal | Isodia | Jetsam | Jungle | Keltie |
| Imbrue | Induce | Instar | Isogon | Jetson | Jungly | Kennel |
| Imbued | Induct | Instep | Isohel | Jettee | Junior | Kentle |
| Immane | Induna | Instil | Isopod | Jetton | Junker | Kerion |
| Immask | Ineunt | Instop | Isonym | Jewess | Junket | Kerite |
| Immesh | Infall | Insult | Issuer | Jewish | Jurant | Kermes |
| Immune | Infame | Insure | Italic | Jibber | Jurist | Kernel |
| Immure | Infamy | Intact | Itself | Jiboya | Justle | Kerria |
| Impact | Infant | Intake | Ivigar | Jiffey | Justly | Kersey |
| Impair | Infect | Intend | Izzard | Jigger | Juzail | Keslop |
| Impale | Infeff | Intent | | Jiggle | Jymold | Ketone |
| Impalm | Infelt | Intern | **J** | Jigjog | | Kettle |
| Impark | Infest | Intine | | Jig-saw | **K** | Keuper |
| Imparl | Infirm | Intoed | Jabber | Jillet | | Keyage |
| Impart | Inflow | Intomb | Jabble | Jimson | Kabala | Keypin |
| Impave | Influx | Intone | Jabiru | Jingal | Kabook | Khalif |
| Impawn | Infold | Intort | Jacana | Jingle | Kabyle | Kiaugh |
| Impede | Inform | Intuse | Jacent | Jinnee | Kaffir | Kibble |
| Impend | Infula | Inulin | Jackal | Jobber | Kafila | Kiblah |
| Impens | Infuse | Invade | Jacket | Job-lot | Kaftan | Kibosh |
| Imping | Ingate | Invent | Jadery | Jockey | Kaiser | Kicker |
| Impish | | | Jadish | | | |

## SIX-LETTER WORDS—*continued*

| | | | | | | |
|---|---|---|---|---|---|---|
| Kidder | K'thibh | Lancer | Leaden | Libyan | Listen | Lorate |
| Kiddle | Kuklux | Lancet | Leader | Lichen | Lister | Lorcha |
| Kiddow | Kumbuk | Landau | Leafed | Licker | Litany | Lordly |
| Kid-fox | Kumbul | Landed | League | Lictor | Litchi | Lorica |
| Kidnap | Kumiss | Lander | Lealty | Liebig | Lither | Loring |
| Kidney | Kummel | Langet | Leamer | Lieder | Lithia | Loriot |
| Kiekie | Kunkur | Langur | Leanly | Lierne | Lithic | Losing |
| Kilerg | Kurkee | Lankly | Lean-to | Lifter | Litmus | Lotion |
| Killas | Kyloes | Lanner | Leaper | Ligate | Litter | Loudly |
| Killer | | Lapdog | Leaser | Ligger | Little | Lounge |
| Killow | **L** | Lapful | Leaved | Lights | Lituus | Louver |
| Killut | | Lappel | Leaven | Lignum | Lively | Louvre |
| Kilted | Laager | Lapper | Leaver | Lignin | Livery | Lovage |
| Kilter | Labefy | Lappet | Lecher | Ligula | Living | Lovely |
| Kiltie | Labial | Larder | Lector | Ligule | Lizard | Loving |
| Kimmer | Labile | Lardon | Ledger | Ligure | Lloyd's | Lowery |
| Kimono | Labium | Lariat | Leetle | Likely | Loaden | Lowest |
| Kinate | Labour | Larrup | Leeway | Liking | Loader | Lowing |
| Kincob | Labret | Larval | Legacy | Lilied | Loafer | Lubber |
| Kindle | Labrum | Larynx | Legate | Limbec | Loathe | Lubric |
| Kindly | Laccic | Lascar | Legato | Limbed | Loathy | Lucent |
| Kinema | Lac-dye | Lasher | Leg-bye | Limber | Lobate | Lucina |
| Kingly | Laches | Lasket | Legend | Limbus | Lobose | Luckie |
| Kinkle | Lacing | Lassie | Legged | Liming | Lobule | Lucumo |
| Kipper | Lacker | Laster | Legion | Limmer | Locale | Luffer |
| Kirbeh | Lackey | Lastly | Legist | Limner | Locate | Luetic |
| Kirkin | Lacrnus | Lateen | Legume | Limous | Lochan | Lugged |
| Kirtle | Lacoum | Lately | Leiger | Limpet | Locker | Lugger |
| Kismet | Lactic | Latent | Leipoa | Limpid | Locket | Luggie |
| Kisser | Lacuna | Latest | Lender | Linage | Lock-up | Lumbal |
| Kit-bag | Ladder | Lathen | Length | Linden | Locust | Lumbar |
| Kitcat | Laddie | Lather | Lenify | Lineal | Lodger | Lumber |
| Kitten | Lading | Latian | Lenity | Linear | Lofter | Lumper |
| Kittle | Ladino | Latish | Lenten | Lingam | Loggan | Lunacy |
| Kittly | Lagena | Latria | Lentil | Lingel | Loggat | Lunary |
| Klepht | Lag-end | Latten | Lentor | Linger | Logger | Lunate |
| Knacky | Laggen | Latter | Lenvoy | Linget | Loggia | Lunged |
| Knaggy | Lagger | Launce | Leonid | Lingot | Log-hut | Lunkah |
| Knarry | Lagoon | Launch | Lepton | Linhay | Log-log | Lunula |
| Knawel | Lagune | Laurel | Lesion | Lining | Logman | Lunule |
| Knight | Laical | Laurin | Lessee | Linnet | Lohock | Lupine |
| Knitch | Laidly | Lavabo | Lessen | Linsey | Loimic | Lurdan |
| Knobby | Laithe | Lavage | Lesser | Lintel | Loiter | Lurden |
| Knotty | Lakist | Lavish | Lesson | Lintie | Loligo | Lurker |
| Knower | Lallan | Lavolt | Lessor | Lionel | Lolium | Lusiad |
| Kobalt | Lambda | Lawful | Lethal | Lionet | Loller | Luster |
| Kobang | Lambie | Lawday | Letter | Liplet | Lollop | Lustic |
| Kobold | Lamely | Lawing | Lettic | Lipoma | Loment | Lustre |
| Koodoo | Lament | Lawyer | Leucin | Lipped | Lonely | Luting |
| Kopeck | Lamina | Laxist | Leucol | Lippen | Longan | Lutist |
| Kosher | Lamish | Laxity | Levant | Lipper | Longer | Lutose |
| Kosmos | Lammas | Lay-day | Levite | Lippie | Loofah | Luxate |
| Ko-tows | Lammer | Laying | Levity | Liquid | Looker | Luxury |
| Kousso | Lammie | Layman | Lewdly | Liquor | Looped | Luzula |
| Kowtow | Lampad | Lay-out | Liable | Lisbon | Looper | Lyceum |
| Kraken | Lampas | Lazily | Libant | Lisper | Loosen | Lydian |
| Krasis | Lampic | Lazuli | Libate | Lissom | Lopper | Lydite |
| Kreese | Lanary | Leaded | Libken | Listel | Loquat | Lymphy |
| | Lanate | | | | | |

## SIX-LETTER WORDS—*continued*

| | | | | | | |
|---|---|---|---|---|---|---|
| Lyrate | Manana | Masher | Medley | Mettle | Misfit | Monist |
| Lyrism | Manche | Mashie | Medusa | Mewler | Misget | Monkey |
| Lyrist | Manchu | Masjid | Meeken | Miasma | Mishap | Monody |
| **M** | Mandom | Masked | Meekly | Micher | Mishmi | Monoid |
| | Manege | Masker | Meetly | Mickle | Mishna | Monosy |
| Mabola | Manful | Maslin | Megass | Micmac | Misken | Montem |
| Macaco | Mangal | Masora | Megilp | Micron | Miskin | Monton |
| Macies | Manger | Masque | Megohm | Midage | Mislay | Montre |
| Mackle | Mangle | Masses | Megrim | Mid-air | Missee | Moolah |
| Macled | Maniac | Massif | Mellay | Midday | Missal | Mooned |
| Macron | Manila | Masted | Melley | Midden | Missay | Mooner |
| Macula | Manioc | Mastel | Mellit | Middle | Missel | Moonet |
| Macule | Manito | Master | Mellow | Midget | Misset | Mooruk |
| Madcap | Manned | Mastic | Melody | Mid-leg | Missis | Moorva |
| Madden | Manner | Mathes | Melter | Mid-off | Missus | Mooter |
| Madder | Manque | Matico | Melton | Midrib | Mister | Mopish |
| Madman | Mantel | Maties | Member | Mid-sea | Mistle | Mopoke |
| Madona | Mantic | Matrix | Memnon | Midway | Misuse | Moppet |
| Madras | Mantis | Matron | Memoir | Mighty | Mitral | Mopsey |
| Maenad | Mantle | Matted | Memory | Mignon | Mitten | Morale |
| Maggot | Manton | Matter | Menace | Mihrab | Miurus | Morass |
| Magian | Mantra | Mature | Ménage | Mikado | Mizzen | Morbid |
| Magilp | Mantua | Maugre | Mender | Milady | Mizzle | Moreen |
| Magism | Manual | Maumet | Menhir | Milden | Mizzly | Morgay |
| Magnes | Manure | Maundy | Menial | Mildew | Moated | Morgue |
| Magnet | Maraud | Mauser | Meninx | Mildly | Mobcap | Morian |
| Magnum | Marble | Mawkin | Mennad | Milieu | Mobile | Morion |
| Magpie | Marbly | Mawmet | Mensal | Milken | Mob law | Morish |
| Maguey | Marcid | May-bug | Mental | Milker | Mocker | Morkin |
| Magyar | Margay | May-day | Mentor | Milled | Modena | Morlop |
| Mahoun | Marged | May-dew | Menura | Miller | Modern | Mormon |
| Mahout | Margin | Mayfly | Mercer | Millet | Modest | Morned |
| Maidan | Margot | May-hap | Merely | Milord | Modify | Morone |
| Maiden | Marian | Mayhem | Merger | Milsey | Modish | Morose |
| Maigre | Mariet | Maying | Merino | Milter | Modist | Morris |
| Mailed | Marine | Mazard | Merkin | Mimbar | Modius | Morrow |
| Mainly | Marish | Mazily | Merlin | Mimosa | Modocs | Morsel |
| Mainor | Marist | Meadow | Merlon | Minbar | Module | Mortal |
| Make-up | Marked | Meager | Merman | Mincer | Moffle | Mortar |
| Malady | Marker | Meagre | Merops | Minded | Mohair | Morula |
| Malaga | Market | Meaker | Merula | Minder | Mohawk | Mosaic |
| Malate | Marmot | Mealer | Mesail | Mingle | Mohock | Moslem |
| Maleic | Marone | Mealie | Mescal | Minify | Moider | Mosque |
| Malgre | Maroon | Meanly | Mesial | Mining | Moiety | Mostic |
| Malice | Marque | Measly | Mesian | Minion | Moirae | Mostly |
| Malign | Marram | Meatal | Mesjid | Minish | Molech | Mother |
| Malism | Marrer | Meathe | Meslin | Minium | Molest | Motile |
| Malkin | Marron | Meatus | Mespot | Minnie | Moline | Motion |
| Mallee | Marrot | Meazel | Messin | Minnow | Mollah | Motive |
| Mallet | Marrow | Meddle | Mestee | Minoan | Moloch | Motley |
| Mallow | Marshy | Medial | Metage | Minter | Molten | Mot-mot |
| Maltha | Martel | Median | Meteor | Minuet | Moment | Motory |
| Mammal | Marten | Medick | Mether | Minute | Monday | Mottle |
| Mammee | Martin | Medico | Method | Miosis | Monera | Mought |
| Mammer | Martyr | Medism | Methyl | Mirage | Monger | Moujik |
| Mammet | Marvel | Medium | Métier | Mirror | Mongol | Mouldy |
| Mammon | Mascle | Medius | Metope | Miscue | Monied | Moulin |
| Manage | Mascot | Medlar | Metric | Misery | Monism | Mounty |

SIX-LETTER WORDS—*continued*

| | | | | | | |
|---|---|---|---|---|---|---|
| Mouser | Mussal | Nardus | Neuter | Norman | Obduce | Ollamh |
| Moutan | Mussel | Nargil | Newing | Norroy | Obelus | Omasal |
| Mouthy | Mustac | Narial | Newish | Nosean | Oberon | Omasum |
| Mouton | Mustee | Narine | New-sad | No-side | Obeyer | Ombros |
| Movies | Muster | Narrow | Nibbed | Nosing | Obiism | Omelet |
| Moving | Mutage | Narwal | Nibble | Nostoc | Obiter | Omened |
| Mowing | Mutate | Nasard | Nicely | Notary | Object | Omnify |
| Mozing | Mutely | Nasion | Nicene | Notice | Objure | Omnium |
| Mucate | Mutine | Nasute | Nicety | Notify | Oblate | Onager |
| Muchell | Muting | Natant | Niched | Notion | Oblige | Oncome |
| Muchly | Mutiny | Nation | Nicher | Notour | Oblong | Oncost |
| Mucite | Mutism | Native | Nickel | Nougat | Oboist | Ondine |
| Mucker | Mutter | Natrix | Nicker | Nought | Obolus | Onding |
| Muckle | Mutton | Natron | Nidder | Nounal | Obsess | Oneyer |
| Mucoid | Mutual | Natter | Nidget | Nousle | Obtain | Onfall |
| Mucous | Mutule | Nattes | Nidose | Novena | Obtend | Onflow |
| Muddle | Mutuum | Nature | Niello | Novene | Obtest | Oniony |
| Muffin | Muzhik | Naught | Niffer | Novice | Obtund | Onrush |
| Muffle | Muzzle | Nausea | Niffle | Noways | Obtuse | Onward |
| Mugger | Myaria | Nautch | Nigger | Nowise | Obvert | Onymal |
| Mugget | Myelon | Nautic | Niggle | Nowyed | Occamy | Oodles |
| Mulier | Mygale | Neaped | Nighly | Noyade | Occult | Oogeny |
| Mulish | Myitis | Near-by | Nigric | Noyous | Occupy | Ooidal |
| Mullah | Myopia | Nearly | Nilgai | Nozzle | Ocelot | Oolite |
| Mulled | Myopic | Neatly | Nilgau | Nuance | Octans | Oology |
| Muller | Myosin | Nebbuk | Nimble | Nubbin | Octant | Oolong |
| Mullen | Myosis | Neb-neb | Nimbly | Nubble | Octave | Oomiak |
| Mullet | Myotic | Nebris | Nimbus | Nubbly | Octavo | Opaque |
| Mulley | Myriad | Nebula | Nimrod | Nubile | Octile | Opener |
| Multum | Myrica | Nebule | Ninety | Nuchal | Octroi | Openly |
| Mumble | Myrtle | Nebuly | Nipper | Nuclei | Ocular | Ophite |
| Mummer | Myrtus | Necked | Nipter | Nucule | Oddity | Opiane |
| Mumper | Myself | Nectar | Nirles | Nudely | Odious | Opiate |
| Mundic | Mystic | Need-be | Nitric | Nudity | Oecium | Oppose |
| Mundil | Mythic | Needer | Nitter | Nuggar | Oedema | Oppugn |
| Munshi | Mythus | Needle | Nivose | Nugget | Oerlay | Optics |
| Murage | Myxine | Needly | No-ball | Nullah | Offend | Optime |
| Murder | Myxoma | Negate | Nobble | Number | Office | Option |
| Murine | | Nemean | Nobody | Numnah | Offing | Orache |
| Murmur | | Nephew | Nocake | Nuncio | Offish | Oracle |
| Murphy | **N** | Nereid | Nocent | Nuncle | Offset | Orally |
| Murren | Nacket | Nereis | Nochel | Nuphar | Ogamic | Orange |
| Murrey | Naevus | Nerine | Noctua | Nurser | Ogival | Orator |
| Musang | Nagana | Nerite | Nodder | Nutant | Ogling | Orbate |
| Muscal | Nagari | Nerium | Noddle | Nutmeg | Ogress | Orbita |
| Muscat | Nagger | Neroli | Nodose | Nut-oil | Oidium | Orchid |
| Muscle | Naiant | Nerval | Nodule | Nutria | Oil-bag | Orchil |
| Musena | Nailer | Nerved | Noetic | Nutter | Oilery | Orchis |
| Museum | Namely | Neshen | Noggin | Nuzzer | Oil-gas | Orcine |
| Mushed | Nandoo | Neshki | Nomade | Nuzzle | Oil-man | Ordain |
| Musing | Nanism | Nestle | Nomial | Nyanza | Oil-nut | Ordeal |
| Musive | Nankin | Nestor | Nonage | Nympha | Oldish | Ordure |
| Musket | Nanoid | Nether | Nonary | | Oleate | Oreide |
| Musk-ox | Napery | Netted | Non-con | **O** | Oleose | Orexis |
| Muslim | Napkin | Nettle | Non-ego | Oafish | Oleron | Orgasm |
| Muslin | Nappal | Neural | Non-est | Oarage | Oliver | Orgeat |
| Musmon | Napron | Neuric | Noodle | Oarium | Olivet | Orgies |
| Musnud | Nardoo | Neuron | Normal | Oarlap | Olivil | Orgues |

### SIX-LETTER WORDS—*continued*

| | | | | | | |
|---|---|---|---|---|---|---|
| Orient | Outwin | Palish | Parish | Peacod | Perdue | Piecer |
| Origan | Outwit | Palkee | Parity | Peahen | Period | Pieled |
| Origin | Ovally | Pallah | Parker | Peaked | Perish | Pieman |
| Oriole | Ovated | Pallas | Parkin | Peanut | Perkin | Pierce |
| Orison | Overby | Pallet | Parley | Pea-ore | Permit | Piffle |
| Ormolu | Overdo | Pallid | Parody | Pearly | Pernis | Pigeon |
| Ormuzd | Overgo | Pallor | Parole | Pebble | Perone | Piggin |
| Ornary | Ovibos | Palmar | Parral | Pebbly | Perron | Pignut |
| Ornate | Ovisac | Palmer | Parrel | Pecker | Persic | Pigsty |
| Oroide | Ovular | Palolo | Parrot | Pecten | Person | Pilaff |
| Orphan | Owelty | Pal-pal | Parsee | Pectic | Persue | Pilary |
| Orphic | Owlery | Palped | Parson | Pectin | Pertly | Pileum |
| Orpine | Owling | Palpus | Partan | Pedale | Peruke | Pileus |
| Orrery | Owlish | Palter | Parter | Pedant | Peruse | Pilfer |
| Orrice | Oxalic | Paltry | Partim | Pedate | Pesade | Piling |
| Ortive | Oxalis | Palwar | Partly | Peddle | Peseta | Pillar |
| Oscule | Oxbird | Pampas | Parure | Pedlar | Peshwa | Pillau |
| Osiery | Ox-eyed | Pamper | Parvis | Pedler | Pester | Pillow |
| Osiris | Oxford | Panada | Passée | Peeced | Pestle | Pilose |
| Osmium | Oxgall | Panama | Passer | Peeler | Petard | Pilous |
| Osmose | Oxgang | Panary | Passim | Peenge | Petary | Pilula |
| Osprey | Oxgate | Pander | Pastel | Peeper | Petite | Pilule |
| Ossein | Oxhead | Pandit | Pastil | Peepul | Petrel | Pimple |
| Ossify | Ox-heel | Pandur | Pastor | Peerie | Petrol | Pimply |
| Ostent | Oxland | Panful | Pastry | Peewit | Petted | Pinang |
| Ostium | Ox-like | Panisc | Patchy | Peg-leg | Pettle | Pin-cop |
| Ostler | Oxtail | Panmug | Patent | Peg-top | Peweep | Pinder |
| Ostmen | Oxygen | Pannel | Patera | Peinct | Pewter | Pineal |
| Ostrea | Oxygon | Panner | Pathan | Pelage | Pharos | Pinery |
| Otalgy | Oxymel | Pannus | Pathic | Pelike | Phasel | Pingle |
| Otaria | Oyster | Panser | Pathos | Pellet | Phasis | Pinion |
| Otiose | Ozoena | Panter | Patina | Pelota | Phasma | Pinite |
| Otitis | Ozonic | Panton | Patine | Pelter | Pheese | Pinked |
| Ottava | | Pantry | Patois | Peltry | Phenic | Pinner |
| Oulong | **P** | Papacy | Patrol | Pelvic | Phenix | Pinnet |
| Ouster | | Papain | Patron | Pelvis | Phenol | Pinnie |
| Outask | Pacify | Papery | Pattee | Pencil | Phenyl | Pintle |
| Outbar | Packer | Papish | Patten | Pengun | Phinoc | Pinxit |
| Outbid | Packet | Papism | Patter | Penman | Phlegm | Pioned |
| Outbud | Padder | Papist | Pattle | Penful | Phleme | Pioner |
| Outbye | Paddle | Pappus | Paunch | Pennal | Phleum | Pipage |
| Outcry | Padnag | Papuan | Pauper | Penned | Phloem | Piping |
| Outfit | Paduan | Papula | Pausal | Penner | Phobos | Pipkin |
| Outfly | Paeony | Parade | Pauser | Pennon | Phocal | Pippin |
| Outing | Paging | Parage | Pavage | Pensee | Pholas | Piquet |
| Outjet | Pagoda | Paramo | Pavane | Pensum | Phrase | Piracy |
| Outlaw | Pagode | Parang | Pavier | Pentad | Phylum | Pirate |
| Outlay | Paigle | Paraph | Paving | Penult | Physic | Pirnie |
| Outlet | Pained | Parcae | Pavior | Penury | Piaffe | Pisang |
| Outlie | Painim | Parcel | Pavise | People | Piazza | Pisces |
| Outman | Painty | Pardon | Pawnee | Pepita | Picard | Pistil |
| Output | Pajock | Pareil | Pawner | Peplis | Picked | Pistol |
| Outrun | Pakeha | Parent | Paw-paw | Peplum | Picker | Piston |
| Outset | Palace | Parfay | Pawwaw | Peplus | Picket | Pitaka |
| Outsit | Palama | Parget | Paxwax | Pepper | Pickle | Pitchy |
| Outsum | Palate | Pariah | Pay-day | Pepsin | Picnic | Pithos |
| Outtop | Palely | Parian | Paynim | Peptic | Picric | Pitier |
| Outvie | Paling | Paring | Peachy | Perdie | Pidgin | Pitman |

| | | | | | | |
|---|---|---|---|---|---|---|
| Pitsaw | Poetic | Porter | Preyer | Pulpit | Pygarg | Rabban |
| Pitted | Poetry | Portly | Priest | Pulque | Pyosis | Rabbet |
| Placer | Pogrom | Posada | Prieve | Pulvil | Pyrame | Rabbin |
| Placet | Poiser | Poseur | Primal | Pulwar | Pyrene | Rabbit |
| Placid | Poison | Posing | Primer | Pumice | Pyrite | Rabble |
| Plagal | Polack | Posnet | Primet | Pummel | Pyrola | Rabies |
| Plague | Polder | Posset | Primly | Pumped | Pyrope | Raceme |
| Plaguy | Police | Possum | Primus | Pumper | Python | Rachis |
| Plaice | Policy | Postal | Prince | Punchy | | Racial |
| Plaint | Poling | Postea | Priory | Puncto | **Q** | Racily |
| Plaise | Polish | Poster | Priser | Pundit | Quadra | Racing |
| Planch | Polite | Postil | Prismy | Punica | Quaere | Racker |
| Planer | Polity | Potage | Prison | Punier | Quagga | Racket |
| Planet | Pollan | Potale | Privet | Punish | Quaggy | Rackle |
| Plaque | Pollen | Potash | Prizer | Punkah | Quahog | Racoon |
| Plashy | Poller | Potass | Procès | Punner | Quaich | Raddle |
| Plasma | Pollex | Potato | Profit | Punnet | Quaigh | Radial |
| Platan | Pollux | Pot-boy | Projet | Punter | Quaint | Radian |
| Plated | Polony | Poteen | Proker | Pupate | Quaker | Radish |
| Platen | Polyad | Potent | Proleg | Pupoid | Quarry | Radium |
| Plater | Polype | Pother | Prolix | Puppet | Quarte | Radius |
| Platey | Pomace | Potion | Prompt | Purana | Quarto | Radoub |
| Player | Pomade | Pot-lid | Proped | Purdah | Quartz | Radula |
| Pleach | Pommel | Potman | Propel | Purely | Quatch | Raffee |
| Please | Pomona | Potted | Proper | Purest | Quaver | Raffia |
| Pledge | Pompom | Potter | Proser | Purfle | Queasy | Raffie |
| Pleiad | Pompon | Pottle | Prosit | Purfly | Queest | Raffle |
| Plenty | Poncho | Pouffe | Protea | Purger | Queint | Rafter |
| Plenum | Ponder | Poulpe | Proton | Purify | Quelch | Ragged |
| Pleugh | Ponent | Pounce | Proven | Purism | Quelea | Raggee |
| Pleura | Pongee | Pourer | Prover | Purist | Quench | Raggle |
| Plevin | Pontac | Pousse | Pruner | Purity | Querpo | Raging |
| Plexor | Pontee | Pouter | Prying | Purler | Querry | Raglan |
| Plexus | Pontic | Powder | Psoric | Purlin | Quesal | Ragman |
| Pliant | Pontil | Powter | Psyche | Purple | Quezal | Ragout |
| Pliers | Ponton | Pow-wow | Pteris | Purser | Quhilk | Rag-tag |
| Plight | Poodle | Praise | Pterna | Pursue | Quidam | Raguly |
| Plinth | Poogye | Prance | Pteron | Purvey | Quight | Raible |
| Plonge | Pooler | Prater | Ptisan | Pusher | Quihye | Raider |
| Plough | Poonac | Praxis | Ptosis | Pushto | Quijal | Railer |
| Plover | Poorly | Prayer | Public | Pushtu | Quince | Raiser |
| Plucky | Popery | Preace | Pucker | Putage | Quinch | Raisin |
| Pluffy | Popgun | Preach | Pudder | Puteal | Quinic | Rajput |
| Plumed | Popish | Prease | Puddle | Puteli | Quinoa | Rakery |
| Plumpy | Poplar | Preces | Puddly | Putlog | Quinsy | Rakish |
| Plunge | Poplin | Précis | Pueblo | Putois | Quinta | Rallus |
| Plural | Popper | Predal | Puffed | Putrid | Quinze | Ramble |
| Plushy | Poppet | Preeve | Puffer | Puttee | Quirky | Ramcat |
| Plyers | Popple | Prefer | Puffin | Putter | Quitch | Rameal |
| Pneuma | Porgie | Prefix | Pug-dog | Puttie | Quiver | Rament |
| Poachy | Porism | Prepay | Pugree | Puttoo | Quorum | Ramify |
| Pocked | Porite | Presee | Puisne | Puture | Quoteř | Ramism |
| Pocket | Porker | Preses | Puking | Puzzel | Quotha | Rammel |
| Podded | Porket | Presto | Puling | Puzzle | Quotum | Rammer |
| Podial | Porose | Preter | Pulkha | Pycnid | | Ramoon |
| Podite | Porous | Pretor | Puller | Pycnon | **R** | Ramose |
| Podium | Porret | Pretty | Pullet | Pyemia | Rabate | Ramous |
| Podura | Portal | Pre-war | Pulley | Pyemic | Rabato | Ramper |

## SIX-LETTER WORDS—*continued*

| | | | | | | |
|---|---|---|---|---|---|---|
| Ramrod | Ravage | Reddog | Rehash | Repass | Retund | Rideau |
| Ramson | Ravine | Redeem | Rehead | Repast | Return | Ridged |
| Ramule | Ravish | Red-eye | Re-heal | Repeal | Retuse | Ridgel |
| Ranche | Rawish | Red-gum | Rehear | Repeat | Retyre | Ridgil |
| Rancho | Ray-oil | Red-hot | Re-heat | Repeck | Reurge | Riding |
| Rancid | Razure | Redlac | Reigle | Repent | Revamp | Riever |
| Randan | Razzia | Red-mad | Reiter | Repine | Reveal | Rifely |
| Randle | Reader | Redoak | Reiver | Replum | Revere | Riffle |
| Random | Really | Redout | Reject | Repone | Reverb | Rifler |
| Randon | Realty | Redowa | Rejoin | Report | Revers | Rigger |
| Ranger | Reamer | Redraw | Rejolt | Repose | Revert | Riggle |
| Rangia | Reaper | Redtop | Relaid | Repour | Revery | Riggot |
| Ranine | Rearer | Reduce | Relais | Repped | Revest | Riglan |
| Ranker | Reason | Reduct | Reland | Repugn | Revict | Riglet |
| Rankle | Reasty | Reduit | Relate | Repute | Review | Rigour |
| Rankly | Reaver | Redwud | Relent | Requit | Revile | Rigout |
| Ransom | Reavow | Reebok | Relict | Re-rail | Revire | Rillet |
| Rantan | Rebate | Re-echo | Relief | Re-read | Revise | Rimist |
| Ranter | Rebato | Reechy | Relier | Resail | Revive | Rimlet |
| Ranula | Rebeck | Reeded | Relish | Resale | Revoke | Rimmer |
| Raphia | Rebind | Reeden | Relive | Rescue | Revolt | Rimmon |
| Raphis | Rebite | Reeder | Reload | Reseat | Reward | Rimose |
| Rapido | Reboil | Reefer | Relove | Reseau | Rewood | Rimous |
| Rapier | Reborn | Reeler | Reluct | Resect | Reword | Rimple |
| Rapine | Rebuff | Refait | Relume | Reseda | Rhagon | Rimsaw |
| Rappee | Rebuke | Refill | Remain | Resell | Rhapis | Rimula |
| Rappel | Rebury | Re-find | Remake | Resend | Rhebok | Rindle |
| Rapper | Recall | Refine | Remand | Resent | Rhesus | Ringer |
| Raptor | Recant | Reflet | Remark | Reship | Rheumy | Rinser |
| Rarefy | Recast | Reflex | Remast | Reside | Rhexia | Rioter |
| Rarely | Recede | Reflow | Remble | Resign | Rhinae | Ripeck |
| Rarity | Recent | Reflux | Remedy | Resile | Rhinal | Ripely |
| Rasant | Recept | Refold | Remind | Resiny | Rhizic | Ripper |
| Rascal | Recess | Refoot | Remise | Resist | Rhusma | Ripple |
| Rasher | Recipe | Reform | Remiss | Resorb | Rhymer | Ripply |
| Rashly | Recite | Refuge | Remora | Resort | Rhymic | Rippon |
| Rasing | Reckon | Refund | Remord | Restem | Rhyssa | Riprap |
| Rasion | Recoal | Refuse | Remote | Restio | Rhythm | Ripsaw |
| Rasper | Recoct | Refute | Remove | Result | Rhyton | Rising |
| Rasure | Recoil | Regain | Rempli | Resume | Rialto | Risala |
| Ratany | Recoin | Regale | Rename | Retail | Riancy | Risban |
| Rateen | Record | Regard | Renard | Retain | Ribald | Risker |
| Rather | Recoup | Regent | Renate | Retake | Riband | Risley |
| Ratify | Rectal | Regest | Render | Retama | Ribbed | Risqué |
| Rating | Rector | Regian | Renege | Retard | Ribbon | Ritely |
| Ration | Rectum | Regild | Rennet | Retent | Ribibe | Ritter |
| Ratite | Rectus | Régime | Renown | Retial | Riblet | Ritual |
| Ratlin | Recuil | Regina | Rental | Retina | Riccia | Rivage |
| Ratoon | Recule | Region | Renter | Retire | Richen | Rivery |
| Rat-pit | Recumb | Regius | Renule | Retold | Riches | Rivina |
| Rattan | Recure | Regive | Renvoy | Retort | Richly | Rivose |
| Rat-tat | Recuse | Reglet | Reopen | Retose | Rickle | Rizzer |
| Ratten | Redact | Reglow | Repace | Retoss | Rictal | Rizzle |
| Ratter | Redbud | Regnal | Repack | Retour | Rictus | Roamer |
| Rattle | Redcap | Regnum | Repaid | Retrad | Riddel | Roarer |
| Raucid | Redden | Regret | Repair | Retral | Ridden | Robalo |
| Raucle | Redder | Regula | Repand | Retree | Ridder | Robber |
| Raught | Reddle | Rehang | Repart | Retrim | Riddle | Robbin |

SIX-LETTER WORDS—*continued*

| | | | | | | |
|---|---|---|---|---|---|---|
| Roberd | Rotula | Rum-tum | Sajene | Santon | Scaler | Scramb |
| Rob-roy | Rotund | Rundle | Sakieh | Santur | Scales | Scramp |
| Robust | Roture | Runkle | Salaam | Sapful | Scalma | Scrape |
| Roccus | Rouble | Runlet | Salary | Sapium | Scamel | Scrawl |
| Rochea | Roucou | Runman | Salewe | Sapper | Scanty | Scrawm |
| Rochet | Rouget | Runnel | Salian | Sappho | Scapha | Screak |
| Rockel | Rought | Runner | Salify | Sap-rot | Scapus | Scream |
| Rocker | Rouman | Runnet | Salina | Sapyga | Scarab | Screed |
| Rocket | Rounce | Runrig | Saline | Sarcel | Scarce | Screen |
| Rockie | Rouncy | Ruppia | Salite | Sarcen | Scarph | Screes |
| Rococo | Rouser | Ruscus | Saliva | Sardel | Scarry | Screwy |
| Roddin | Router | Rushen | Sallal | Sargus | Scarus | Scribe |
| Rodent | Routle | Rusher | Sallet | Sarlac | Scatch | Scrike |
| Roggan | Rovery | Russel | Sallie | Sarlak | Scathe | Scrime |
| Roggle | Roving | Russet | Sallow | Sarlyk | Scathy | Scrimp |
| Roinek | Rowing | Rustic | Salmis | Sarong | Scatty | Scrine |
| Roland | Royena | Rustle | Salmon | Sarsen | Scaury | Script |
| Roller | Rubace | Rustre | Saloon | Sarsia | Scazon | Scrive |
| Romage | Rubato | Rusure | Saloop | Sartor | Scelio | Scrobe |
| Romaic | Rubber | Rutela | Salter | Sasine | Scenic | Scroll |
| Romant | Rubble | Rutile | Saltie | Sastra | Scerne | Scroop |
| Romany | Rubbly | Rutter | Saltly | Satara | Scheik | Scruff |
| Romero | Rubian | Ruttle | Saltus | Sateen | Schelm | Scrunt |
| Romish | Rubied | Rypeck | Salute | Satine | Schema | Scruto |
| Romper | Rubify | | Salver | Satiny | Scheme | Scruze |
| Rondel | Rubigo | **S** | Salvia | Satire | Schemy | Scuffy |
| Rondle | Rubine | | Salvor | Sative | Schene | Sculsh |
| Ronion | Rubric | Sabalo | Samara | Satrap | Schism | Scummy |
| Ronyon | Ruckle | Sabean | Samare | Saturn | Schist | Scurff |
| Roofer | Rudder | Sabian | Sambar | Saucer | School | Scurfy |
| Rooker | Ruddle | Samboo | Sauger | Schorl | Scurry |
| Rookie | Rudely | Sabine | Sambur | Saulge | Schout | Scurvy |
| Rookle | Ruddoc | Sacbut | Samely | Saulie | Sciara | Scutch |
| Roomed | Rueful | Saccos | Samian | Saumur | Sciath | Scutum |
| Roomer | Ruelle | Sachel | Samiel | Sauria | Scient | Scylla |
| Roopit | Ruffed | Sachem | Samiot | Saurus | Scilla | Scythe |
| Rooter | Ruffer | Sachet | Samite | Savage | Scious | 'Sdeath |
| Rootle | Ruffin | Sacker | Samlet | Savant | Sclate | Sdeign |
| Ropery | Ruffle | Sacque | Samoan | Savate | Sclave | Sea-ape |
| Roquet | Rufous | Sacral | Sampan | Savine | Sclera | Sea-bar |
| Rosary | Rugate | Sacred | Sample | Savory | Scobby | Sea-bat |
| Roscid | Rugged | Sacrum | Samshu | Savour | Scogie | Sea-boy |
| Roseal | Rugger | Sadden | Samyda | Savvey | Scolex | Sea-bun |
| Rosery | Rugine | Saddle | Sancho | Sawder | Scolia | Sea-cap |
| Rosied | Rugosa | Sadina | Sandal | Saw-fly | Sconce | Sea-cat |
| Rosier | Rugose | Sadism | Sanded | Sawneb | Scopus | Sea-cob |
| Rosily | Rugous | Safely | Sandix | Sawney | Scorch | Sea-cow |
| Rosing | Ruiner | Safety | Sandyx | Sawpit | Scorer | Sea-dog |
| Rosiny | Ruling | Sagely | Sanely | Sawset | Scoria | Sea-ear |
| Rostel | Rulley | Sagene | Sangar | Sawyer | Scorse | Sea-eel |
| Roster | Rumble | Saggar | Sangha | Saxony | Scorza | Sea-egg |
| Rosula | Rum-bud | Sagger | Sanies | Saying | Scotch | Sea-fan |
| Rotary | Rumkin | Sagina | Sanify | Saynay | Scoter | Sea-fir |
| Rotate | Rummer | Sagoin | Sanity | Sbirro | Scotia | Sea-fog |
| Rotche | Rumour | Saguin | Sanjak | Scabby | Scouth | Sea-fox |
| Rotgut | Rumper | Sailer | Sannop | Scaean | Scovan | Sea-god |
| Rother | Rumple | Sailor | Sanpan | Scaith | Scoved | Sea-hen |
| Rotten | Rumpus | Sairly | Santir | Scalar | Scovel | Sea-hog |

## SIX-LETTER WORDS—*continued*

| | | | | | | | |
|---|---|---|---|---|---|---|---|
| Sealer | Seizor | Seroon | Shekel | Sicker | Sinker | Sledge |
| Seaman | Sejant | Serous | Shelfy | Sickle | Sinner | Sleeky |
| Sea-mat | Sejoin | Serpet | Shelly | Sickly | Sinnet | Sleepy |
| Sea-maw | Seldom | Serula | Shelta | Sicsac | Sinter | Sleets |
| Seamer | Select | Serval | Shelty | Sicyos | Sintoc | Sleety |
| Seamew | Selene | Server | Shelve | Siddha | Siouan | Sleeve |
| Sea-mud | Selion | Sesame | Shelvy | Siddhi | Siphon | Sleezy |
| Seance | Seljuk | Sesban | She-oak | Siddow | Sipper | Sleigh |
| Sea-orb | Seller | Seseli | Sheppy | Siding | Sippet | Sleuth |
| Sea-owl | Semble | Sestet | Sherif | Sienna | Sipple | Slicer |
| Sea-pad | Semele | Set-off | Sherry | Sierra | Sircar | Slider |
| Sea-pea | Semese | Setose | Sheuch | Siesta | Sirdar | Slight |
| Sea-pen | Semita | Setous | Sheugh | Sifaka | Sirene | Slimsy |
| Sea-pie | Semite | Set-out | Shewel | Siffle | Sirius | Slinky |
| Sea-pig | Semmit | Settee | Shield | Sifter | Sirkar | Slippy |
| Sea-rat | Semola | Setter | Shifty | Sigher | Sirrah | Sliver |
| Searce | Semple | Settle | Shiism | Signal | Sirree | Slogan |
| Search | Sempre | Setule | Shiite | Signer | Sirupy | Sloken |
| Sea-rod | Senary | Severe | Shikar | Signet | Siskin | Sloomy |
| Season | Senate | Sevres | Shimmy | Signor | Sissoo | Sloppy |
| Sea-way | Sendal | Sewage | Shindy | Silage | Sister | Sloshy |
| Sebate | Sender | Sewing | Shiner | Silent | Sitter | Slouch |
| Secale | Senega | Sexfid | Shinny | Silica | Sizing | Slough |
| Secant | Senhor | Sextan | Shinto | Siline | Sizzle | Slovak |
| Secede | Senile | Sextet | Shinty | Silken | Skater | Sloven |
| Secern | Senior | Sextic | Shippo | Sillon | Skathe | Slowly |
| Secesh | Sennet | Sexton | Shippy | Silpha | Skeary | Sludge |
| Seckel | Sennit | Sexual | Shiraz | Silure | Skeely | Sludgy |
| Secohm | Senora | Shabby | Shirty | Silvan | Skelly | Slugga |
| Second | Sentry | Shadow | Shiver | Silver | Skerry | Sluice |
| Secret | Sepawn | Shaduf | Shoaly | Simbil | Sketch | Sluicy |
| Sector | Sephen | Shaggy | Shoddy | Simial | Skewer | Slumpy |
| Secund | Sepium | Shairl | Shofar | Simian | Skiing | Slurry |
| Secure | Sepose | Shairn | Shogun | Simile | Skilly | Slushy |
| Sedate | Sepsin | Shakal | Shoppy | Simkin | Skilts | Smalls |
| Sedent | Sepsis | Shaken | Shorer | Simmer | Skimpy | Smarty |
| Sedged | Septal | Shaker | Shorts | Simnel | Skinny | Smatch |
| Sedile | Septan | Shalli | Should | Simony | Skitty | Smeary |
| Seduce | Septet | Shalot | Shovel | Simoon | Skiver | Smeath |
| Seeded | Septic | Shaman | Shower | Simoom | Skivie | Smegma |
| Seeder | Septon | Shamer | Shrewd | Simorg | Sklent | Smelly |
| Seeing | Septum | Shammy | Shriek | Simous | Skruff | Smerky |
| Seeker | Sequel | Shamoy | Shrift | Simpai | Skryer | Smiddy |
| Seelde | Sequin | Shanny | Shrike | Simper | Skurry | Smight |
| Seemer | Serail | Shanty | Shrill | Simple | Skyish | Smilax |
| Seemly | Serang | Shaper | Shrimp | Simply | Slabby | Smiler |
| See-saw | Serape | Sharer | Shrine | Simson | Slaggy | Smilet |
| Seethe | Seraph | Sharpy | Shrink | Simurg | Slangy | Smirch |
| Seggan | Serdab | Shaver | Shrite | Sinaic | Slap-up | Smirky |
| Seggar | Serein | Shavie | Shrive | Sindoc | Slashy | Smitch |
| Seghol | Serena | Sheafy | Shroff | Sindon | Slatch | Smiter |
| Seiche | Serene | Shears | Shroud | Sinewy | Slater | Smithy |
| Seiner | Serial | Sheath | Shruff | Sinful | Slaver | Smoker |
| Seised | Serian | Sheave | Shucks | Singer | Slavey | Smooth |
| Seisin | Serica | Shebat | Siccan | Single | Slavic | Smouch |
| Seison | Series | Sheeny | Siccar | Singly | Slayer | Smudge |
| Seizer | Seriph | Sheers | Sicken | Sinian | Sleave | Smudgy |
| Seizin | Sermon | Sheikh | Sicker | Sinism | Sleazy | Smugly |

SIX-LETTER WORDS—*continued*

| | | | | | | |
|---|---|---|---|---|---|---|
| Smurry | Soller | Spadix | Sponge | Stapes | Stoory | Stuggy |
| Smutch | So-long | Spahee | Spongy | Staple | Storax | Stumps |
| Smutty | Solute | Spalax | Spooky | Starch | Storer | Stumpy |
| Snabby | Solver | Spandy | Spoony | Staree | Storey | Stupid |
| Snacot | Sombre | Sparer | Sposhy | Starer | Storge | Stupor |
| Snaggy | Somite | Spares | Spotty | Starry | Stormy | Sturdy |
| Snappy | Somnus | Sparge | Spouse | Starve | Stound | Stylar |
| Snarer | Sonant | Sparke | Sprack | Stasis | Stover | Stylet |
| Snatch | Sonata | Sparre | Spraid | Stater | Stower | Stylus |
| Snathe | Soncie | Sparry | Sprain | Stathe | Straik | Stymie |
| Sneeze | Sonned | Sparse | Sprawl | Static | Strain | Styrax |
| Sniffy | Sonnet | Sparth | Spread | Statua | Strait | Stythe |
| Snifty | Sonsie | Sparve | Sprent | Statue | Strake | Suable |
| Sniper | Sontag | Spathe | Spring | Status | Strand | Subdue |
| Snippy | Soodra | Spavin | Sprint | Stayer | Strass | Subfeu |
| Snivel | Soojee | Specie | Sprite | Stayne | Strata | Subito |
| Snobby | Soorma | Specky | Sprong | Stayre | Strath | Sublet |
| Snooze | Soosoo | Speech | Sprout | Steady | Strawy | Suburb |
| Snorer | Soothe | Speedy | Spruce | Steamy | Strayt | Suborn |
| Snorty | Sophic | Speiss | Spruit | Steare | Streak | Subtil |
| Snotty | Sopite | Spelin | Sprung | Steboy | Stream | Subtle |
| Snouty | Sopper | Spence | Sprunt | Steedy | Streek | Subtly |
| Snubby | Sorbet | Spense | Spuddy | Steely | Street | Suburb |
| Snudge | Sorbic | Sperre | Spulye | Steepy | Strene | Subway |
| Snuffy | Sorbin | Sperse | Spunge | Steeve | Stress | Succin |
| Snugly | Sordes | Spetch | Spunky | Stemma | Striae | Succus |
| Soaker | Sordet | Spewer | Spurge | Stench | Strich | Sucken |
| Sobeit | Sordid | Sphene | Spurne | Steppe | Strick | Sucker |
| Socage | Sordor | Sphere | Spurry | Stereo | Strict | Sucket |
| Soccer | Sorely | Sphery | Sputum | Sterve | Stride | Suckle |
| Social | Sorner | Sphinx | Spyism | Steven | Strife | Sudary |
| Socius | Sorose | Spical | Squail | Stewer | Striga | Sudden |
| Socket | Sorrel | Spicer | Squall | Stibic | Strike | Sudder |
| Socman | Sorrow | Spider | Squama | Sticky | String | Suffer |
| Sodaic | Sorter | Spiffy | Squame | Stiddy | Stripe | Suffix |
| Sodden | Sortes | Spight | Square | Stifle | Stripy | Sufism |
| Sodium | Sortie | Spigot | Squash | Stigma | Strive | Sugary |
| Soever | Sossle | Spilth | Squawk | Stigme | Stroam | Suggil |
| Sofett | Sothic | Spilus | Squeak | Stilar | Strode | Suidae |
| Soffit | Sotnia | Spinal | Squeal | Stilly | Stroke | Suitor |
| Sofism | Souari | Spined | Squill | Stilty | Stroll | Suivez |
| Soften | Sought | Spinel | Squint | Stinty | Stroma | Sulcus |
| Softly | Soujee | Spinet | Squire | Stingo | Stromb | Sullen |
| Sogged | Souper | Spinny | Squirm | Stingy | Strond | Sultan |
| Soirée | Souple | Spiral | Squirt | Stipel | Strong | Sultry |
| Solace | Source | Spired | Stable | Stines | Strook | Sumach |
| Soland | Sourly | Spiric | Stably | Stirps | Stroup | Summer |
| Solano | Soutar | Spirit | Stacte | Stitch | Strout | Summit |
| Soldan | Souter | Spital | Stadda | Stithy | Strove | Summon |
| Solder | Soviet | Splash | Stadia | Stiver | Struck | Sumpit |
| Solein | Sovran | Spleen | Stager | Stocky | Struma | Sunbow |
| Solely | Sowans | Splent | Stagey | Stodge | Strung | Sunday |
| Solemn | Sow-bug | Splice | Staith | Stodgy | Strunt | Sunder |
| Solert | Sowens | Spline | Stalky | Stoker | Stryde | Sundew |
| Soleus | Sowter | Splint | Stamen | Stolen | Stubby | Sundog |
| Solito | Sozzle | Splore | Stance | Stolid | Stucco | Sundry |
| Solive | Sozzly | Spoffy | Stanch | Stolon | Studio | Sun-god |
| Sollar | Spacer | Spoken | Stanza | Stoner | Stuffy | Sun-hat |

## SIX-LETTER WORDS—*continued*

| | | | | | | |
|---|---|---|---|---|---|---|
| Sunken | Syndaw | Tamanu | Tartly | Telugu | Themis | Tickly |
| Sunket | Syndic | Tamara | Tascal | Temper | Thenal | Tid-bit |
| Sunlit | Synema | Tambac | Tasker | Temple | Thenar | Tidder |
| Sunned | Synepy | Tamber | Taslet | Tenace | Thence | Tiddle |
| Sunset | Syntax | Tamboo | Tassel | Tenant | Theory | Tidily |
| Supawn | Sypher | Tamely | Tasset | Tender | Thesis | Tierce |
| Superb | Syphon | Tamine | Tassie | Tendon | Thetch | Tie-rod |
| Supine | Syrian | Taminy | Taster | Tenner | Thetic | Tie-wig |
| Supper | Syriac | Tamise | Tatler | Tennis | Thewed | Tiffin |
| Supple | Syrinx | Tamkin | Tatter | Tenrec | Thibet | Tights |
| Supply | Syrtic | Tammuz | Tattie | Tenson | Thible | Tilery |
| Surbet | Syrtis | Tampan | Tattle | Tensor | Thieve | Tiller |
| Surbed | Syrupy | Tamper | Tattoo | Tented | Thinly | Tilmus |
| Surcle | System | Tampoe | Taught | Tenter | Thirds | Tilter |
| Surely | Syzygy | Tampon | Taupie | Tenure | Thirst | Timbal |
| Surety | | Tam-tam | Taurus | Tenuto | Thirty | Timber |
| Surrey | **T** | Tan-bed | Tauted | Tenzon | Tholus | Timbre |
| Surtax | | Tandem | Tauten | Tepefy | Thorah | Timely |
| Survey | Tabard | Tanged | Tautie | Teraph | Thoral | Timist |
| Suslik | Tabefy | Tangie | Tautog | Terbic | Thorax | Tincal |
| Sutile | Taberd | Tangle | Tavern | Tercel | Thorny | Tindal |
| Sutler | Tabler | Tangly | Tavers | Tercet | Thorpe | Tinder |
| Suttee | Tables | Tanist | Tavert | Teredo | Though | Tineid |
| Suttle | Tablet | Tanite | Tawdry | Terete | Thowel | Tingis |
| Suture | Tabour | Tanjib | Tawery | Tergal | Thrall | Tingle |
| Svelte | Tabret | Tanker | Tawpie | Tergum | Thrash | Tinguy |
| Swaddy | Tacker | Tankia | Tawtie | Termer | Thrave | Tinkal |
| Swaggy | Tacket | Tanner | Tawtog | Termes | Thrawn | Tinker |
| Swampy | Tackle | Tannic | Tchick | Termly | Thread | Tinkle |
| Swanky | Tactic | Tannin | Teacup | Termor | Threap | Tinman |
| Swanny | Tactus | Tanpit | Teagle | Ternal | Threat | Tinned |
| Swardy | Taenia | Tanrec | Teague | Terrel | Threep | Tinner |
| Swarth | Tag-end | Tantra | Teapot | Terret | Threne | Tinpot |
| Swarve | Tagger | Tanzib | Teapoy | Territ | Thresh | Tinsel |
| Swashy | Taglia | Taoism | Tearer | Terror | Thrice | Tinter |
| Swatch | Taguan | Taoist | Teasel | Tester | Thrift | Tipcat |
| Swathe | Tahona | Tao-Tai | Teaser | Tetchy | Thrill | Tipper |
| Swathy | Taigle | Tapeti | Tea-set | Tether | Thrips | Tippet |
| Sweard | Tailed | Tapist | Teathe | Tetrad | Thrist | Tipple |
| Sweaty | Tailor | Tapper | Tea-urn | Tetrao | Thrive | Tiptoe |
| Sweeny | Tailye | Tappet | Teazel | Tetter | Throat | Tip-top |
| Sweepy | Taisch | Tappit | Teazle | Tettix | Throne | Tipula |
| Swerve | Tajaçu | Target | Tebeth | Teuton | Throng | Tirade |
| Sweven | Take-in | Targum | Tedder | Tewart | Throve | Tirret |
| Swinck | Taking | Tariff | Te Deum | Textus | Thrown | Tirrit |
| Swinge | Talbot | Tarnal | Tedium | Thairm | Thrush | Tirwit |
| Swiper | Talcky | Tarmac | Teemer | Thaler | Thrust | Tisane |
| Swipes | Talent | Tarpan | Teetee | Thalia | Thwack | Tissue |
| Swipey | Talian | Tarpon | Teeter | Thanks | Thwart | Tit-bit |
| Swirly | Talion | Tarpum | Teethe | Thatch | Thyite | Titely |
| Switch | Talker | Tarras | Tegmen | Theave | Thymol | Tither |
| Swivel | Tallat | Tarsal | Teinds | Theban | Thymus | Titled |
| Swound | Tallet | Tarsel | Telary | Thecal | Thyrse | Titler |
| Sycite | Tallot | Tarsia | Teledu | Thecla | Tibial | Ti-tree |
| Sycoma | Tallow | Tarsus | Telega | Theine | Ticken | Titter |
| Sylvan | Talmud | Tartan | Telesm | Theirs | Ticker | Tittle |
| Symbal | Tamale | Tartar | Teller | Theism | Ticket | Tittup |
| Symbol | | | Telson | Theist | Tickle | Tmesis |

SIX-LETTER WORDS—*continued*

| | | | | | | |
|---|---|---|---|---|---|---|
| Tobine | Torpid | Tricot | Tumbly | Tycoon | Uncape | Ungown |
| Tocher | Torpor | Trifid | Tumefy | Tylote | Uncart | Ungual |
| Tocsin | Torque | Trifle | Tumour | Tymbal | Uncase | Unguis |
| Toddle | Torrid | Trigla | Tum-tum | Tympan | Uncate | Ungula |
| Toecap | Torsel | Trigly | Tumult | Typhon | Uncial | Ungyve |
| Toffee | Torula | Trigon | Tundra | Typhus | Unclad | Unhair |
| Tofore | Tosser | Trilby | Tundun | Typify | Unclew | Unhand |
| Toggle | Toss-up | Trimly | Tungus | Typist | Unclog | Unhang |
| Toiler | Totter | Trinal | Tunker | Tyrant | Uncock | Unhasp |
| Toilet | Tottie | Tringa | Tunnel | Tyrian | Uncoif | Unhead |
| Toison | Toucan | Triode | Tupaia | Tyrite | Uncoil | Unheal |
| Toledo | Touchy | Triple | Tupelo | Tystie | Uncoin | Unhele |
| Toller | Toupee | Triply | Turaco | Tzetze | Uncolt | Unhelm |
| Tol-lol | Touser | Tripod | Turban | | Uncord | Unhewn |
| Tolsey | Tousle | Tripos | Turbid | | Uncork | Unhive |
| Toltec | Touter | Triste | Turbit | **U** | Uncowl | Unhold |
| Tolter | Toutie | Triton | Turbot | Uakari | Uncurl | Unholy |
| Toluic | Towage | Triune | Turdus | Uberty | Undate | Unhook |
| Toluol | Toward | Trivet | Tureen | Ubiety | Undeaf | Unhoop |
| Tomand | Towery | Trocar | Turfen | Uglify | Undean | Unhung |
| Tomato | Towhee | Troche | Turgid | Uglily | Undeck | Unhurt |
| Tomaun | Towser | Troggs | Turgor | Ugrian | Undern | Unhusk |
| Tombac | Toy-dog | Trogon | Turion | Ugsome | Undine | Uniate |
| Tombak | Toyful | Troika | Turkey | Uigite | Undock | Unible |
| Tombic | Toyish | Trojan | Turkis | Ulitis | Undoer | Unific |
| Tomboc | Toyman | Trolly | Turner | Ullage | Undone | Uniola |
| Tomboy | Trabal | Trompe | Turney | Ulling | Undose | Uniped |
| Tom-cat | Trabea | Trophi | Turnip | Ulmous | Undraw | Unique |
| Tomcod | Tracer | Trophy | Turnus | Ulnare | Unduke | Unison |
| Tomial | Trader | Tropic | Turrel | Ulosis | Undull | Unital |
| Tomium | Tragic | Troppo | Turret | Ulster | Unduly | United |
| Tompon | Tragus | Trough | Turtle | Ultimo | Uneasy | Uniter |
| Tompot | Trance | Troupe | Turves | Ultion | Uneath | Unjust |
| Tomtit | Tranka | Trover | Tuskar | Umbery | Unedge | Unkard |
| Tomtom | Trapan | Trowel | Tusked | Umbles | Uneven | Unkent |
| Toname | Trapes | Truant | Tusker | Umbral | Uneyed | Unkept |
| Tongue | Trappy | Trudge | Tusser | Umbrel | Unface | Unketh |
| Tonish | Trashy | Truism | Tussis | Umbril | Unfair | Unkind |
| Tonite | Trauma | Truite | Tussle | Umlaut | Unfast | Unking |
| Tonsil | Travel | Trusty | Tutrix | Umpire | Unfeed | Unkiss |
| Tooart | Travis | Trygon | Tutsan | Unable | Unfelt | Unknit |
| Tooter | Treaty | Trying | Tu-whit | Unawed | Unfile | Unknot |
| Toothy | Treble | Tsamba | Tu-whoo | Unbank | Unfine | Unlace |
| Tootle | Trebly | Tsetse | Tuyere | Unbear | Unfirm | Unlade |
| Too-too | Trefle | Tubage | Twaite | Unbelt | Unfist | Unlaid |
| Topaza | Tremex | Tubful | Tweeny | Unbend | Unfold | Unlash |
| Top-dog | Tremle | Tub-gig | Twelve | Unbent | Unfool | Unlast |
| Top-hat | Tremor | Tubing | Twenty | Unbias | Unform | Unlead |
| Topful | Trench | Tubule | Twicer | Unbind | Unfree | Unleal |
| Tophet | Trepan | Tucker | Twiggy | Unbitt | Unfurl | Unlent |
| Tophus | Trepid | Tucket | Twight | Unbolt | Ungain | Unless |
| Topman | Tressy | Tuffet | Twilly | Unbone | Ungear | Unlich |
| Topper | Trevet | Tufted | Twiner | Unboot | Ungild | Unlike |
| Topple | Triact | Tufter | Twinge | Unborn | Ungill | Unlime |
| To-rent | Triage | Tugger | Twitch | Unbred | Ungilt | Unline |
| Torero | Tribal | Tuille | Two-ply | Uncage | Ungird | Unlink |
| Torose | Tricar | Tulwar | Two-way | Uncalm | Ungirt | Unlive |
| Torous | Tricky | Tumble | Tyburn | Uncamp | Unglue | Unload |

## SIX-LETTER WORDS—*continued*

| | | | | | | |
|---|---|---|---|---|---|---|
| Unlock | Unspin | Uphroe | Usurer | Veddah | Viable | Volant |
| Unlord | Unstep | Upkeep | Usward | Vehmic | Viands | Volata |
| Unlove | Unstop | Upland | Utgard | Veined | Viatic | Volery |
| Unlute | Unsung | Uplean | Utmost | Velary | Viator | Volley |
| Unmade | Unsure | Uplift | Utopia | Velate | Vibrio | Volume |
| Unmake | Untack | Uplock | Uveous | Velite | Vicary | Volute |
| Unmask | Untame | Uplook | Uvular | Vellet | Victim | Volvox |
| Unmeet | Untell | Upmost | | Vellon | Victor | Vomica |
| Unmiry | Untent | Up-pile | **V** | Vellum | Vicuna | Vomito |
| Unmoor | Untidy | Upping | | Veloce | Vidame | Voodoo |
| Un-nail | Untied | Uppish | Vacant | Velour | Vidual | Vorant |
| Un-nest | Untile | Up-prop | Vacate | Velure | Vielle | Vorago |
| Un-neth | Untold | Uprear | Vacher | Velvet | Viewer | Vortex |
| Unowed | Untomb | Uprise | Vacuum | Vendee | Viewly | Votary |
| Unpack | Untorn | Uproar | Vadium | Vender | Vigour | Voting |
| Unpaid | Untrim | Uproll | Vagary | Vendor | Vihara | Voudou |
| Unpick | Untrod | Uproot | Vagina | Vendue | Viking | Voulge |
| Unpray | Untrue | Uprose | Vagous | Veneer | Vilely | Voyage |
| Unprop | Untuck | Uprush | Vagrom | Venery | Vilify | Vulcan |
| Unpure | Untune | Upsees | Vaidic | Veneur | Villus | Vulgar |
| Unquit | Unturf | Upseek | Vailer | Venger | Vinage | Vulvar |
| Unread | Unturn | Upsend | Vainly | Venial | Vinery | |
| Unreal | Unused | Upshot | Vaisya | Venite | Vinose | **W** |
| Unreel | Unveil | Upside | Vakass | Vennel | Vinous | Wabble |
| Unrein | Unvote | Upsoar | Vakeel | Venose | Vintry | Wabbly |
| Unrent | Unwarm | Upstay | Valgus | Venous | Violan | Wadded |
| Unrest | Unwarp | Upsway | Valise | Venter | Violet | Waddie |
| Unring | Unwary | Uptake | Valkyr | Ventil | Violin | Waddle |
| Unripe | Unwell | Uptear | Vallar | Verbal | Virago | Wading |
| Unrobe | Unwept | Uptilt | Valley | Verdoy | Virent | Wadmal |
| Unroll | Unwily | Uptoss | Vallum | Verdun | Virgin | Wadset |
| Unroof | Unwind | Uptown | Valour | Vergee | Virile | Waeful |
| Unroot | Unwire | Upturn | Valued | Verger | Virole | Wafery |
| Unrope | Unwise | Upward | Valuer | Verify | Virose | Waffle |
| Unrude | Unwish | Upways | Valved | Verily | Virous | Wafter |
| Unruly | Unwist | Upwell | Valval | Verity | Virtue | Waggle |
| Unsafe | Unwoof | Upwind | Vamose | Vermes | Visage | Waggon |
| Unsaid | Unwork | Urania | Vamper | Vermil | Viscid | Wag-wit |
| Unseal | Unworn | Uranic | Vandal | Vermin | Viscum | Wahabi |
| Unseam | Unwrap | Uranus | Vanish | Vernal | Viscus | Wailer |
| Unseat | Unyoke | Uraeum | Vanity | Verrel | Vishnu | Waiter |
| Unseel | Upbear | Uraeus | Vanner | Verrey | Vision | Waiver |
| Unseen | Upbind | Uratic | Vapour | Versal | Visite | Walker |
| Unself | Upblow | Urbane | Varech | Versed | Visier | Walkyr |
| Unsent | Upbray | Urchin | Varied | Verser | Visive | Wallah |
| Unsewn | Upcast | Uremia | Varier | Verset | Visual | Walled |
| Unshed | Upcoil | Uremic | Varlet | Versus | Vitric | Waller |
| Unship | Upcurl | Urgent | Varmin | Vertex | Vivace | Wallet |
| Unshod | Upfill | Urnful | Varsal | Vervet | Vivary | Wallop |
| Unshoe | Upflow | Uropod | Varuna | Vesica | Vivers | Wallow |
| Unshot | Upgaze | Ursine | Vassal | Vesper | Vivify | Walnut |
| Unshut | Upgrow | Urtica | Vastly | Vessel | Vivres | Walrus |
| Unsoft | Upgush | Urvant | Vastus | Vestal | Vizier | Wamble |
| Unsold | Uphand | Usable | Vaudoo | Vested | Vocule | Wammus |
| Unsoot | Upheap | Usager | Vaulty | Vestry | Voiced | Wampee |
| Unsoul | Upheld | Usance | Vaward | Vetchy | Voicer | Wampum |
| Unsown | Uphill | Useful | Veadar | Vetust | Voided | Wandle |
| Unspar | Uphold | Ustion | Vector | Vexing | Voider | Wandoo |

### SIX-LETTER WORDS—*continued*

| | | | | | | |
|---|---|---|---|---|---|---|
| Wander | Weapon | Whilst | Winnow | Worser | Yarpha | Zebeck |
| Wangle | Wearer | Whimsy | Winsey | Worthy | Yarrow | Zechin |
| Wanion | Weasel | Whiner | Winter | Woundy | Yaupon | Zenana |
| Wankle | Weaver | Whinge | Wintle | Wou-wou | Yclept | Zendik |
| Wanter | Weazen | Whinny | Wintry | Wow-wow | Yearly | Zenith |
| Wanton | Webbed | Whippy | Wirily | Wraith | Yeasty | Zephyr |
| Wapiti | Web-eye | Whirry | Wiring | Wrasse | Yellow | Zereba |
| Wapper | Wedded | Whisht | Wisard | Wrathy | Yelper | Zeriba |
| Wappet | Weeded | Whisky | Wisdom | Wreath | Yenite | Zeugma |
| Warble | Weeder | Whiten | Wisely | Wrench | Yeoman | Ziamet |
| War-cry | Weekly | Whites | Wisher | Wretch | Yer-nut | Zigzag |
| Warden | Weeper | Wholly | Wisket | Wrethe | Yester | Zillah |
| Warder | Weever | Whydah | Wistly | Wright | Yogism | Zincky |
| Warely | Weevil | Wicked | Withal | Writer | Yoicks | Zingel |
| Warily | Weight | Wicken | Withed | Writhe | Yojana | Zircon |
| Warman | Welder | Wicker | Wither | Wroken | Yoking | Zither |
| Warmer | Welkin | Wicket | Within | Wuther | Yolked | Zodiac |
| Warmly | Welted | Widely | Witted | Wuzzle | Yonder | Zoetic |
| Warmth | Welter | Wieldy | Wittol | Wyvern | Yonker | Zonary |
| Warner | Wendic | Wifely | Witwal | | Yorker | Zonate |
| Warped | Wesand | Wigeon | Wively | **X** | Youthy | Zonnar |
| Warper | Wester | Wigged | Wivern | Xangti | You-uns | Zonoid |
| Warray | Wet-bob | Wiggle | Wizard | Xenial | Yowley | Zonula |
| Warren | Wether | Wigwag | Wizier | Xenium | Y-track | Zonule |
| War-tax | Wezand | Wigwam | Wobble | Xenops | Yttria | Zonure |
| Warted | Whaler | Wilder | Wobbly | Xoanon | Yttric | Zooeal |
| Washer | Whally | Wildly | Woeful | Xylite | Yucker | Zoonal |
| Wash-up | Whaten | Wilful | Wolfer | Xyloid | | Zoonic |
| Wastel | Whatna | Wilily | Wombat | Xyster | | Zoozoo |
| Waster | Whatso | Willer | Womera | Xystos | **Z** | Zoster |
| Watery | Wheely | Willet | Wonder | Xystus | Zabian | Zouave |
| Wattle | Wheeze | Willow | Woning | | Zabism | Zounds |
| Waucht | Wheezy | Wimble | Wonted | | Zabrus | Zufolo |
| Waught | Whelky | Wimple | Wooded | **Y** | Zaccho | Zumate |
| Wavery | Whenas | Wincer | Wooden | Yaffle | Zaffer | Zunian |
| Wavure | Whence | Wincey | Woodie | Yagger | Zaffre | Zygite |
| Wax-end | Wherry | Winder | Wooing | Yahveh | Zaimet | Zygoma |
| Waxing | Wheugh | Windle | Woolly | Yaksha | Zamite | Zygose |
| Wax-red | Wheyey | Window | Worded | Yammer | Zander | Zymase |
| Waylay | Whewer | Wind-up | Worker | Yankee | Zapote | Zymate |
| Weaken | Whidah | Winged | Wormul | Yanker | Zareba | Zymite |
| Weakly | Whiles | Winker | Wornil | Yaourt | Zarape | Zymoid |
| Wealth | Whilly | Winkle | Worrit | Yapock | Zarnec | Zymome |
| Weanel | Whilom | Winner | Worsen | Yarely | Zealot | Zythum |

## Seven-Letter Words

| **A** | | | | | |
|---|---|---|---|---|---|
| | Abattis | Abietin | Abreast | Abstain | Acaleph |
| | Abature | Abigail | Abridge | Abusion | Acantha |
| Aaronic | Abb-wool | Abigeat | Abroach | Abusive | Acardia |
| Abacist | Abdomen | Ability | Abscess | Abuttal | Acarina |
| Abactor | Abduced | Abjudge | Abscind | Abutter | Accable |
| Abaddon | Abetter | Abjurer | Absciss | Abysmal | Acceder |
| Abaisse | Abettor | Ablepsy | Abscond | Abyssal | Acclaim |
| Abalone | Abeyant | Abluent | Absence | Academe | Accoast |
| Abandon | Abiding | Abolish | Absinth | Academy | Accollé |
| Abashed | Abietic | Abraxas | Absolve | Acadian | Accompt |

SEVEN-LETTER WORDS—*continued*

| | | | | | |
|---|---|---|---|---|---|
| Account | Address | Agelong | Alcaics | Already | Amusing |
| Accourt | Adducer | Agendum | Alcayde | Alsatia | Amusive |
| Accrete | Addulce | Ageusia | Alcazar | Alsirat | Amutter |
| Accurst | Adenoid | Aggrace | Alchemy | Altered | Amylene |
| Accusal | Adenose | Aggrate | Alchymy | Althaea | Amyline |
| Accuser | Adenous | Aggress | Alcohol | Althorn | Amyloid |
| Acerate | Adherer | Aggroup | Alcoran | Alumina | Anacard |
| Acerbic | Adhibit | Agilely | Alecost | Alumine | Anaemia |
| Acerose | Adipoma | Agility | Alegill | Alumish | Anaemic |
| Acerous | Adipose | Agister | Ale-hoof | Alumnus | Anagoge |
| Acetary | Adipous | Agistor | Alembic | Alunite | Anagogy |
| Acetate | Adipsia | Agitate | Alength | Alveary | Anagram |
| Acetify | Adjoint | Agitato | Alertly | Alveate | Analect |
| Acetone | Adjourn | Agnamed | Aletude | Alveole | Analogy |
| Acetose | Adjudge | Agnatic | Alewife | Amalgam | Analyse |
| Acetous | Adjunct | Agnomen | Alfalfa | Amandin | Analyst |
| Achaean | Adjutor | Agonism | Algarot | Amateur | Anapest |
| Achates | Admiral | Agonist | Algates | Amative | Anarchy |
| Acheron | Admired | Agonize | Algebra | Amatory | Anatase |
| Achieve | Admirer | Agraffe | Algific | Amazing | Anatomy |
| Acholia | Adolode | Aground | Alhenna | Ambages | Anatron |
| Acidify | Adonean | Agynous | Alicant | Ambarie | Anchovy |
| Acidity | Adonise | Aheight | Alidade | Ambient | Ancient |
| Aciform | Adossed | Ahriman | Alienee | Ambitus | Ancress |
| Acinose | Adrenal | Aiblins | Aliener | Ambling | Andante |
| Acinous | Adulate | Aidance | Aliform | Amboyna | Andarac |
| Acknown | Adusted | Aidless | Aliment | Ambrein | Andiron |
| Aclinic | Advance | Aigulet | Alimony | Ambroid | Android |
| Acology | Advened | Ailanto | Aliquot | Ambs-ace | Anelace |
| Acolyte | Advenes | Aileron | Alkanet | Amellus | Anemone |
| Acolyth | Adverse | Ailette | Alkenna | Amenage | Aneroid |
| Aconite | Adviser | Ailment | Alkoran | Amenity | Anethol |
| Acouchy | Advised | Aimless | Alledge | Amental | Angaria |
| Acquest | Advowee | Air-base | Alleged | Amentia | Angelic |
| Acquire | Aeolian | Air-bath | Allegro | Amentum | Angelot |
| Acquist | Aeolist | Air-bone | All-good | Ames-ace | Angelus |
| Acrisia | Aeonian | Air-cell | All-hail | Amiable | Angerly |
| Acreage | Aerator | Air-flue | All-heal | Amiably | Angevin |
| Acrobat | Aerobia | Air-hole | Allonge | Amidine | Anglice |
| Acrogen | Aerobic | Airless | Allowed | Amildar | Anglify |
| Acronic | Aetnean | Air-line | Alloxan | Ammeter | Angling |
| Acroter | Affable | Airling | Allseed | Ammiral | Angrily |
| Acrotic | Affably | Air-lock | All-wise | Ammonal | Anguine |
| Actinia | Affiche | Airport | Almadie | Ammonia | Anguish |
| Actinic | Affined | Airpump | Almagra | Amnesia | Angular |
| Actress | Afflict | Air-raid | Almaign | Amnesty | Aniline |
| Actuary | Afforce | Air-sacs | Almanac | Amongst | Anility |
| Actuate | Affront | Airshed | Almight | Amorist | Animate |
| Aculeus | Aflaunt | Airship | Almoign | Amorosa | Animism |
| Acutely | African | Airtrap | Almoner | Amorose | Animist |
| Adactyl | Aftward | Ajutage | Almonry | Amorous | Aniseed |
| Adagial | Against | Alameda | Almsbox | Amorpha | Ankress |
| Adamant | Agalaxy | Alamode | Alms-fee | Amotion | Annates |
| Adamite | Agamist | Alamort | Almsman | Ampassy | Annatto |
| Adapter | Agamous | Alantin | Alnager | Amphora | Annelid |
| Adaptor | Agatine | Alberia | Aloetic | Amplify | Annotto |
| Addable | Agatize | Albumen | Alongst | Ampoule | Annoyer |
| Addible | Ageless | Albumin | Alp-horn | Ampulla | Annuent |

SEVEN-LETTER WORDS—*continued*

| | | | | | |
|---|---|---|---|---|---|
| Annuity | Apitpat | Arduous | Askance | Atoning | Avocado |
| Annular | Apocope | Arenose | Asperse | Atropal | Avoider |
| Annulet | Apogean | Areolar | Asphalt | Atrophy | Avowant |
| Anodyne | Apology | Arghool | Asphyxy | Atropia | Awarder |
| Anomaly | Apoplex | Arguing | Aspirin | Atropin | Awe-band |
| Anorexy | Apostil | Argyria | Asprawl | Attaché | Aweless |
| Anormal | Apostle | Aricina | Aspread | Attaint | Awesome |
| Anosmia | Apotomy | Aricine | Asprout | Attempt | Awfully |
| Another | Apparel | Aridity | Asquint | Attical | Awkward |
| Ansated | Appeach | Arietta | Assagai | Attinge | Awlwort |
| Antacid | Appease | Arilled | Assapan | Attired | Awnless |
| Ant-bear | Apperil | Arillus | Assault | Attract | Axiform |
| Antefix | Applaud | Aripple | Assayer | Attrist | Axillar |
| Ant-eggs | Appoint | Armhole | Assegai | Attrite | Axle-box |
| Antenna | Apprise | Armiger | Assegay | Aubaine | Axle-pin |
| Anthill | Apprize | Armilla | Assever | Auberge | Axolotl |
| Anthoid | Approof | Armless | Ass-head | Auction | Azarole |
| Anthrax | Approve | Armoire | Assiege | Audible | Azimuth |
| Anticly | Appulse | Armoric | Assizer | Audibly | Azotise |
| Anticor | Apricot | Armoury | Assizes | Audient | Azotite |
| Anticum | Aproned | Arnotto | Assizor | Auditor | Azotize |
| Antient | Apropos | Arousal | Assuage | Augitic | Azotous |
| Antilog | Apsidal | Arraign | Assumed | Augment | Azurean |
| Antique | Apteral | Arrange | Assumer | Augural | Azurine |
| Antlike | Apteryx | Arrayed | Assurer | Aurally | Azurite |
| Ant-lion | Apthous | Arreach | Asswage | Aurated | Azygous |
| Antonym | Aptness | Arriere | Astatic | Aureate | Azymite |
| Anviled | Aptotic | Arrival | Asteism | Aureity | Azymous |
| Anxiety | Apyrexy | Arrived | Asteria | Aurelia | |
| Anxious | Apyrous | Arsenal | Asterid | Aureola | |
| Anybody | Aquatic | Arsenic | Astoned | Aureole | |
| Anyways | Aqueous | Article | Astound | Auricle | |
| Anywhen | Aquilon | Artisan | Astraea | Aurited | |
| Anywise | Arabian | Artiste | Astrand | Aurochs | **B** |
| Apagoge | Arabine | Artless | Astrict | Auroral | |
| Apagogy | Arabism | Aruspex | Astride | Ausonia | Baalism |
| Apanage | Arabist | Asarone | Astylar | Auspice | Baalite |
| Apatite | Arachis | Asbolin | Asudden | Austere | Babbler |
| Apaumee | Aramaic | Ascaris | Asunder | Austral | Babiism |
| Ape-hood | Aramean | Ascetic | Ataghan | Autarch | Babyish |
| Apellis | Aramite | Ascians | Ataraxy | Autocar | Babyism |
| Apepsia | Arbiter | Ascites | Atavism | Autonym | Babylon |
| Apertor | Arblast | Ascitic | Atelene | Autopsy | Baccara |
| Apeshly | Arbored | Ascribe | Atelier | Auxesis | Baccare |
| Aphasia | Arboret | Asepsis | Athalia | Auxetic | Baccate |
| Aphasic | Arbutus | Aseptic | Athanor | Avarice | Bacchic |
| Aphelia | Arcaded | Asexual | Atheism | Avenage | Bacchus |
| Aphemia | Arcadia | Ashamed | Atheist | Avenger | Bacilli |
| Aphesis | Arcanum | Ash-fire | Atheize | Aventre | Backare |
| Aphetic | Archaic | Ash-heap | Atheous | Average | Backend |
| Aphides | Archeal | Ash-hole | Athirst | Averted | Backing |
| Aphonia | Archery | Ashiver | Athleta | Averter | Backlog |
| Aphonic | Archeus | Ash-tray | Athlete | Aviates | Backset |
| Aphrite | Arching | Asiarch | Athrill | Aviator | Bactris |
| Aphthae | Archway | Asiatic | Athwart | Avidity | Baddish |
| Apician | Arc-lamp | Asinego | Atomism | Aviette | Badiaga |
| Apieces | Arcuate | Asinigo | Atomist | Aviform | Badjane |
| Apishly | Ardency | Asinine | Atomize | Avigato | Badness |
| | | | | | Baffler |

## SEVEN-LETTER WORDS—*continued*

| | | | | | |
|---|---|---|---|---|---|
| Bagasse | Bardish | Baudric | Bee-moth | Bepinch | Bettong |
| Baggage | Bardism | Bausond | Beeswax | Beplume | Betutor |
| Bagging | Bardlet | Bauxite | Beetfly | Beprose | Between |
| Bagman | Bargain | Bawcock | Beffana | Bequest | Betwixt |
| Bagpipe | Barilla | Bawdily | Beggary | Bequote | Bewitch |
| Bahadur | Bar-iron | Bawdkin | Begging | Bereave | Bezetta |
| Bailage | Bark-bed | Bawling | Beghard | Bergylt | Bezique |
| Bailing | Barkery | Bayonet | Begloom | Berhyme | Biasing |
| Bailiff | Bark-pit | Baysalt | Begonia | Berline | Biaxial |
| Baillie | Barmaid | Bay-tree | Begored | Berried | Bibasic |
| Baiting | Barmkin | Bay-wood | Begrime | Bertram | Biblist |
| Balance | Barnaby | Bay-yarn | Begroan | Besaint | Bichord |
| Balanus | Barnagh | Beached | Beguard | Besayle | Bickern |
| Balcony | Barning | Beading | Beguile | Beseech | Bicycle |
| Baldish | Barn-owl | Beadman | Beguine | Beseeke | Biddery |
| Baldric | Baronet | Bearded | Behight | Beshame | Bidding |
| Baleful | Baroque | Beardie | Behoney | Beshine | Biffings |
| Balista | Barrace | Bearing | Behoove | Beshmet | Bifidly |
| Balking | Barrack | Bearish | Beinked | Beshone | Bifilar |
| Ballade | Barrage | Bearpit | Bejewel | Beshrew | Bigener |
| Ballast | Barrico | Beastly | Beknave | Besides | Biggish |
| Ballium | Barrier | Beatify | Beknown | Besiege | Bighorn |
| Balloon | Barring | Beating | Belated | Beslave | Bigness |
| Balmily | Barruly | Beauish | Belcher | Beslime | Bigoted |
| Balming | Bar-shoe | Beavery | Beldame | Besmear | Bigotry |
| Balneum | Bar-shot | Bebeeru | Beleper | Besmoke | Bilboes |
| Balsamy | Bartram | Because | Belgard | Besnuff | Biliary |
| Bambino | Barwood | Becharm | Belgian | Besogno | Bilious |
| Bamming | Barytes | Becloud | Belgium | Besonio | Billing |
| Banbury | Barytic | Bedawin | Belibel | Bespate | Billion |
| Bandage | Basbleu | Bedelry | Believe | Bespeak | Billman |
| Bandana | Bascule | Bederal | Belittle | Bespeed | Billowy |
| Bandbox | Basenet | Bedevil | Bellies | Bespice | Bilobed |
| Bandeau | Bashful | Bedewer | Bellman | Bespirt | Biltong |
| Bandian | Bashlyk | Bedfast | Bellona | Bespoke | Bimanal |
| Banding | Basilar | Bedgown | Bellows | Bespout | Bindery |
| Bandlet | Basilic | Bedight | Beloved | Bestain | Binding |
| Bandore | Basinet | Bedizen | Beltane | Bestead | Bindweb |
| Bandrol | Basking | Bedmate | Belting | Bestial | Binocle |
| Bandsaw | Baslard | Bedouin | Bemazed | Bestick | Biogeny |
| Baneful | Bassock | Bedpost | Bemouth | Bestill | Biology |
| Banging | Bassoon | Bed-rest | Bemused | Bestorm | Biotaxy |
| Banking | Bastile | Bedrock | Bencher | Bestrew | Biotics |
| Banksia | Basting | Bedroom | Bendlet | Bestrid | Biotine |
| Banning | Bastion | Bedropt | Beneath | Bestuck | Biotite |
| Bannock | Batable | Bedside | Benefit | Betaine | Bipedal |
| Banquet | Bateful | Bedsore | Bengali | Bethank | Biplane |
| Banshee | Bathing | Bedtick | Benight | Bethink | Bipolar |
| Bantery | Bathman | Bedtime | Benison | Bethral | Birchen |
| Banting | Batiste | Bedward | Benzene | Bethrow | Bircher |
| Baptism | Batsman | Bedwarf | Benzine | Bethumb | Birdeye |
| Baptist | Battels | Bedwork | Benzoic | Bethump | Birding |
| Baptize | Battery | Bee-bird | Benzoin | Betimes | Birdman |
| Baracan | Battill | Beechen | Benzole | Betitle | Biretta |
| Barbate | Batting | Beef-tea | Benzoyl | Betoken | Birling |
| Barbell | Battish | Bee-glue | Bepaint | Betread | Birlinn |
| Barbing | Battled | Beehive | Bepatch | Betroth | Biscuit |
| Barbule | Battler | Beeline | Bepearl | Betting | Bismite |

## SEVEN-LETTER WORDS—*continued*

Bismuth
Bistort
Bitless
Bittern
Bitters
Bittock
Bittour
Bitumed
Bitumen
Bivalve
Bivious
Bivouac
Bizarre
Blabber
Blacken
Blackey
Blackly
Bladder
Blandly
Blanket
Blankly
Blarney
Blasted
Blaster
Blatant
Blatter
Blawort
Bleakly
Blemish
Blender
Blesbok
Blessed
Blether
Bletted
Blewart
Blewits
Blighty
Blinder
Blister
Bloated
Bloater
Blobber
Blomary
Blooded
Bloomer
Blossom
Blotchy
Bloting
Blotter
Blow-fly
Blow-gun
Blowzed
Blubber
Blucher
Blue-cap
Blue-eye
Blue-gum
Blue-jay

Blueing
Bluffly
Blunder
Blunger
Bluntly
Blurred
Blushet
Bluster
Boarder
Boarish
Boaster
Boat-car
Boat-fly
Boatful
Boating
Boatman
Bobadil
Bobbery
Bobbing
Bobbish
Bob-sled
Bob-stay
Bobtail
Bocking
Bocland
Bodeful
Bodikin
Bog-bean
Boggard
Boggart
Boggler
Bog-land
Bog-moss
Bog-rush
Boiling
Boletic
Boletus
Bollard
Bolling
Bologna
Bolster
Bolting
Bombard
Bombast
Bonanza
Bonasus
Bondage
Bonding
Bondman
Bone-ace
Bone-ash
Bone-bed
Bonetta
Bonfire
Bonnily
Bookful
Booking
Bookish

Booklet
Bookman
Booming
Boomkin
Boonder
Boorish
Booster
Bootied
Boot-leg
Boracic
Bordage
Bordman
Bordure
Boredom
Bornite
Borough
Borstal
Boscage
Boshbok
Bossage
Botanic
Botargo
Botcher
Bottine
Bottler
Bottony
Bouchet
Boudoir
Bouilli
Boulder
Boulimy
Boulter
Boultin
Bouncer
Bounden
Bounder
Bouquet
Bourder
Bourdon
Bourlaw
Boutade
Bowback
Bow-bent
Bow-hand
Bowlder
Bowless
Bowline
Bowling
Bow-shot
Box-coat
Boxhaul
Box-iron
Box-kite
Box-tree
Box-wood
Boycott
Boyhood
Brabble

Braccia
Braccio
Bracing
Bracken
Bracket
Bracted
Bradawl
Brahman
Brahmin
Braille
Brained
Bramble
Brambly
Branchy
Brander
Brandle
Brangle
Branlin
Bran-new
Bransle
Brantle
Brasier
Brasero
Brasset
Brassie
Brattle
Bravado
Bravely
Bravery
Bravura
Brawner
Braying
Brazier
Brazing
Breachy
Breaded
Breadth
Breaker
Breathe
Breccia
Breeder
Brevier
Brevity
Brewage
Brewery
Brewing
Briabot
Bribery
Brickle
Bricole
Bridler
Bridoon
Briefly
Briered
Brigade
Brigand
Brimful
Brimmed

Brimmer
Brinded
Brindle
Brinish
Brinjal
Brioche
Brisket
Briskly
Bristle
Bristly
Brisure
British
Brittle
Britzka
Broaden
Broadly
Brocade
Brocage
Brocard
Brocked
Brocket
Brodkin
Broider
Broiler
Brokage
Brokery
Broking
Bromate
Bromide
Bromine
Bromize
Broncho
Brothel
Brother
Brought
Brownie
Bruchus
Brucine
Brucite
Bruckle
Bruiser
Brulyie
Brulzie
Brumous
Brunion
Brusque
Brustle
Brutify
Brutish
Brutism
Bryozoa
Bubalis
Bubbler
Bubonic
Bubukle
Buceros
Buckeen
Buckeye

Bucking
Buckish
Buckism
Buckler
Buckram
Bucksaw
Bucolic
Budding
Budgero
Budgers
Budging
Budless
Buffalo
Buffing
Buffoon
Bugaboo
Bugbear
Bugloss
Bugwort
Builder
Buirdly
Buisson
Bukshee
Bulbose
Bulbous
Bulbule
Bulchin
Bulging
Bulimea
Bullace
Bullary
Bullate
Bullbat
Bull-bee
Bulldog
Bull-fly
Bullion
Bullish
Bullock
Bulrush
Bulwark
Bumbage
Bumbaze
Bumboat
Bummalo
Bummock
Bumping
Bumpkin
Bunched
Bungler
Bunkage
Bunking
Bunting
Buoyage
Buoyant
Buphaga
Burdash
Burdock

SEVEN-LETTER WORDS—*continud*

| | | | | | |
|---|---|---|---|---|---|
| Burette | Cabiric | Caloric | Cap-a-pie | Carosse | Cattish |
| Burgeon | Caboose | Calorie | Capcase | Carotid | Catwhin |
| Burgage | Cab-rank | Calotte | Capelin | Carouse | Caudate |
| Burgess | Cachexy | Caloyer | Caperer | Carping | Caudron |
| Burghal | Cacique | Calpack | Capital | Carrack | Cauline |
| Burgher | Cackler | Caltrap | Capitan | Carrier | Caulker |
| Burglar | Cacodyl | Caltrop | Capitol | Carrion | Caustic |
| Burlace | Cacoepy | Calumba | Caporal | Carroty | Cautery |
| Burmise | Cacolet | Calumet | Capouch | Cartage | Caution |
| Burning | Cadaver | Calumny | Caprate | Cartoon | Cavalry |
| Burnish | Caddice | Calvary | Caprice | Carving | Cavetto |
| Burnous | Caddish | Calycle | Caprine | Carvist | Caviare |
| Bur-reed | Cadenas | Camaieu | Caproic | Caryota | Cayenne |
| Burrhel | Cadence | Camayeu | Caprone | Cascade | Cazique |
| Burrock | Cadency | Camboge | Capsize | Cascara | Ceasing |
| Bursary | Cadenza | Cambism | Capstan | Caseate | Cebidae |
| Bursten | Cadmean | Cambist | Capsula | Caseine | Cedared |
| Burthen | Cadmium | Cambium | Capsule | Caselaw | Cedilla |
| Bur-weed | Cadrans | Camblet | Captain | Caseman | Cedrate |
| Burying | Caesium | Cambrel | Caption | Caseous | Cedrela |
| Bushcat | Caesura | Cambric | Captive | Cashier | Cedrine |
| Bushman | Cafenet | Cambuca | Capture | Cassada | Ceiling |
| Busking | Caffeic | Camelot | Capuche | Cassava | Celadon |
| Bustard | Cainite | Camelry | Capulet | Cassino | Cellist |
| Bustler | Caisson | Camorra | Capulin | Cassius | Cellule |
| Butcher | Caitiff | Campana | Caracal | Cassock | Celsius |
| Butlery | Caitive | Camphor | Caramel | Casting | Cenacle |
| Butment | Cajeput | Campion | Caranna | Castlet | Cension |
| Butt-end | Cajoler | Camwood | Carauna | Cast-off | Censual |
| Buttery | Cajuput | Canakin | Caravan | Castral | Censure |
| Buttock | Calaber | Can-buoy | Caravel | Casuist | Centage |
| Buttons | Calamus | Candent | Caraway | Catalan | Centaur |
| Buttony | Calando | Candied | Carbide | Catalpa | Centavo |
| Butyric | Calcify | Candify | Carbine | Catapan | Centime |
| Buxeous | Calcine | Candock | Carcake | Catarrh | Centner |
| Buxomly | Calcite | Candour | Carcase | Catasta | Central |
| Buyable | Calcium | Canella | Carcass | Catawba | Centric |
| Buzzard | Calculi | Canhook | Cardecu | Cat-bird | Century |
| Buzzing | Caldron | Cankery | Cardiac | Catboat | Ceramic |
| By-and-by | Calèche | Cannery | Cardoon | Catcall | Cerasin |
| Bygoing | Calends | Cannula | Carduus | Catcher | Cerated |
| Bynempt | Caliban | Canonic | Careful | Catchup | Cereals |
| Byously | Caliber | Canonry | Cariboo | Catechu | Cereous |
| Byplace | Calibre | Canopic | Caribou | Cateran | Cerotic |
| Byrlady | Caliche | Canopus | Cariole | Caterer | Certain |
| Byronic | Calicle | Cantata | Carious | Cat-eyed | Certify |
| Byssine | Calipee | Canteen | Carking | Cat-fall | Cerulin |
| Byssoid | Caliver | Canthus | Carline | Catfish | Cerumen |
| Bything | Calking | Canting | Carlism | Cathead | Cerused |
| | Callant | Cantion | Carlist | Cathode | Cervine |
| | Call-boy | Cantlet | Carlock | Cathole | Cesious |
| **C** | Calling | Cantoon | Carmine | Cathood | Cession |
| | Callous | Cantred | Carnage | Catlike | Cesspit |
| Cabaret | Calluna | Cantrip | Carnify | Catling | Cestoid |
| Cabbage | Calmant | Canvass | Carnose | Catmint | Cetacea |
| Cabbala | Calming | Canzone | Caroche | Cat-salt | Chablis |
| Cabeiri | Calmuck | Capable | Carolus | Cat's-paw | Chabouk |
| Cabesse | Calomel | Capably | Caromel | Cattalo | Chacone |

SEVEN-LETTER WORDS—*continued*

| | | | | | |
|---|---|---|---|---|---|
| Chafery | Checker | Chisleu | Cirrous | Clitter | Cobiron |
| Chaffer | Cheddar | Chisley | Cissoid . | Clivers | Cobloaf |
| Chafing | Cheeper | Chitter | Cistern | Clivity | Cob-wall |
| Chagrin | Cheerer | Chitwah | Citable | Cloacal | Cocagne |
| Chalaza | Cheetah | Chlamys | Citadel | Clobber | Cocaine |
| Chaldee | Chelate | Chloral | Citator | Clocker | Cocalon |
| Chalder | Chelone | Chloric | Cithara | Clogger | Cochlea |
| Chalice | Chemise | Chlorid | Cithern | Cloison | Cocinic |
| Challis | Chemism | Chobdar | Citizen | Clootie | Cockade |
| Chalone | Chemist | Choctaw | Citrate | Closely | Cockeye |
| Chamade | Chemosh | Choleic | Citrene | Close-up | Cocking |
| Chamber | Chequer | Cholera | Citrine | Closing | Cockled |
| Chamfer | Cherish | Choltry | Cittern | Closure | Cockler |
| Chamlet | Chermes | Chooser | Civilly | Clot-bur | Cockney |
| Chamo's | Cheroot | Chopine | Clabber | Clothed | Cockpit |
| Champac | Chervil | Chopper | Clachan | Clothes | Cock-shy |
| Champak | Chessel | Chorale | Clacker | Clotted | Coco-nut |
| Chancel | Chested | Choreus | Cladode | Clotter | Cocotte |
| Chancre | Cheston | Chorion | Clamant | Cloture | Coctile |
| Changer | Chevied | Chorist | Clamber | Clouded | Coction |
| Channel | Cheviot | Choroid | Clammed | Clouted | Codeine |
| Chanson | Chevron | Chortle | Clamour | Clovate | Codfish |
| Chanter | Chianti | Chowder | Clamped | Clovery | Codicil |
| Chantor | Chiasma | Chowter | Clamper | Cloying | Codilla |
| Chantry | Chibouk | Chrisom | Clapnet | Clubbed | Codille |
| Chaotic | Chicane | Chromic | Clapper | Clubber | Codling |
| Chapeau | Chicken | Chronic | Clarain | Club-law | Coehorn |
| Chaplet | Chicory | Chuckie | Clarify | Club-man | Coelebs |
| Chapman | Chiding | Chuckle | Clarion | Clumber | Coeliac |
| Chapped | Chiefly | Chukkur | Clarity | Clumped | Coenure |
| Chappie | Chiefry | Churchy | Clasper | Clumper | Coequal |
| Chapter | Chiffon | Churrus | Classic | Cluniac | Coexist |
| Charact | Chiffre | Chutney | Classis | Cluster | Cogence |
| Charade | Chigger | Chyazic | Clastic | Clutter | Cogency |
| Charger | Chignon | Chylify | Clatter | Clypeal | Coggery |
| Charily | Chikara | Chylous | Claught | Clypeus | Cogging |
| Chariot | Childly | Chymify | Clavate | Clysmic . | Cognate |
| Charism | Chilean | Chymist | Clavier | Clyster | Cognize |
| Charity | Chiliad | Chymous | Claying | Coachee | Cogwood |
| Charley | Chilian | Ciboria | Clayish | Coagent | Cohabit |
| Charlie | Chiller | Cichlid | Clay-pit | Coalbed | Coherer |
| Charmer | Chillum | Ciconia | Cleaner | Coalbox | Cohibit |
| Charnel | Chiloma | Cidaris | Cleanly | Coal-gas | Coinage |
| Charpie | Chimera | Ciliary | Cleanse | Coaling | Coining |
| Charpoy | Chimere | Ciliate | Clearer | Coalise | Coition |
| Charqui | Chimney | Cimbric | Clearly | Coalite | Cojuror |
| Charter | Chincha | Cimeter | Cleaver | Coalman | Cola-nut |
| Chasing | Chinese | Cimicic | Cleddyo | Coalpit | Coldish |
| Chassis | Chingle | Cindery | Clement | Coaltar | Coldpig |
| Chasten | Chinned | Cinerea | Clerisy | Coal-tit | Colibri |
| Chateau | Chinook | Cipolin | Clerkly | Coaming | Colicky |
| Chattah | Chipaxe | Circean | Clicker | Co-annex | Colitis |
| Chattel | Chip-hat | Circled | Clicket | Coarsen | Collate |
| Chatter | Chipped | Circler | Climate | Coastal | Collaud |
| Chauvin | Chipper | Circlet | Climber | Coaster | Collect |
| Cheapen | Chirped | Circuit | Clinker | Coating | Colleen |
| Cheaply | Chirper | Cirrate | Clinoid | Co-axial | College |
| Cheater | Chirrup | Cirrose | Clipper | Cobbler | Collide |

### SEVEN-LETTER WORDS—*continued*

| | | | | | |
|---|---|---|---|---|---|
| Collier | Concept | Conteck | Cornist | Council | Craving |
| Colloid | Concern | Contemn | Cornlaw | Counsel | Crawler |
| Collude | Concert | Contend | Corn-rig | Counter | Crazily |
| Colobus | Concise | Content | Cornual | Country | Creance |
| Colonel | Concoct | Contest | Cornute | Coupler | Creatin |
| Coloury | Concord | Context | Cornuto | Couplet | Creator |
| Coltish | Concrew | Contort | Cornvan | Coupure | Credent |
| Coluber | Concupy | Contour | Corolla | Courage | Creeing |
| Columba | Concuss | Control | Coronal | Courant | Creeper |
| Columel | Condemn | Contund | Coroner | Courier | Creepie |
| Combine | Condign | Contuse | Coronet | Courlan | Cremate |
| Combing | Condite | Convene | Corouis | Courser | Cremona |
| Combust | Condole | Convent | Correct | Courter | Crenate |
| Cometic | Condone | Convert | Corrode | Couthie | Crenaux |
| Comfort | Conduce | Convict | Corrody | Courtly | Creosol |
| Comfrey | Conduct | Convive | Corrupt | Couteau | Crepane |
| Comical | Conduit | Convoke | Corsage | Couvade | Cresset |
| Comique | Condyle | Cookery | Corsair | Covelet | Crested |
| Comitia | Coneine | Cooking | Corsite | Coverts | Cretify |
| Command | Confect | Cooling | Corslet | Coveted | Cretism |
| Commark | Confess | Coolish | Corsned | Cow-bane | Cretose |
| Commend | Confest | Coon-can | Cortege | Cowbird | Crevice |
| Comment | Confide | Coontie | Cortile | Cowcalf | Crewels |
| Commere | Confine | Coopery | Corvine | Cowered | Cribble |
| Commode | Confirm | Copaiba | Corydon | Cowhage | Cricket |
| Commons | Conflux | Copaiva | Corylus | Cowheel | Cricoid |
| Commove | Conform | Copious | Corypha | Cowherd | Crim-con |
| Commune | Confuse | Copland | Cosaque | Cowhide | Crimine |
| Commute | Confute | Coppery | Coshery | Cow-itch | Crimini |
| Compact | Congeal | Coppice | Cosmism | Cowlick | Crimper |
| Company | Congest | Copping | Cosmist | Cowlike | Crimple |
| Compare | Congree | Copular | Cossack | Cowslip | Crimson |
| Compart | Congrue | Copyism | Costard | Cow-tree | Crinate |
| Compass | Conical | Copyist | Costate | Cowweed | Crincum |
| Compear | Conifer | Coquito | Costean | Coxcomb | Cringer |
| Compeer | Coniine | Coracle | Costive | Coyness | Cringle |
| Compend | Conject | Coranto | Costrel | Cozener | Crinite |
| Compete | Conjoin | Corbean | Costume | Crabbed | Crinkle |
| Compile | Conjure | Corbeil | Coterie | Crabite | Crinoid |
| Complex | Conjury | Corcass | Cotfolk | Craboil | Crinose |
| Complin | Connate | Corcule | Cothurn | Cracked | Cripple |
| Complot | Connect | Cordage | Cotidal | Cracker | Crisped |
| Comport | Conning | Cordate | Cotinga | Crackle | Crisper |
| Compose | Connive | Cordial | Cotland | Cracowe | Crispin |
| Compost | Connote | Cording | Cottage | Cragged | Crisply |
| Compote | Conquer | Cordite | Cottice | Craigie | Crizzel |
| Compter | Consent | Corinth | Cottier | Crambus | Crizzle |
| Compute | Consign | Co-rival | Cottoid | Cramesy | Croaker |
| Comrade | Consist | Corkage | Cottony | Crammer | Crochet |
| Comtism | Console | Corking | Cottown | Crampon | Crocket |
| Comtist | Consort | Corkleg | Couchee | Cranage | Croesus |
| Conacre | Conspue | Cornage | Coucher | Cranial | Crofter |
| Conatus | Constat | Corn-cob | Cougher | Cranium | Croisés |
| Concave | Consult | Corneal | Couldst | Crankle | Croodle |
| Conceal | Consume | Cornfly | Couleur | Crannog | Crooked |
| Concede | Consute | Cornice | Couloir | Craping | Crooned |
| Conceit | Contact | Cornine | Coulomb | Crapnel | Crooner |
| Concent | Contain | Cornish | Coulter | Craunch | Cropear |

SEVEN-LETTER WORDS—*continued*

Cropful
Cropped
Cropper
Croquet
Crosier
Croslet
Crossed
Crossly
Crotalo
Crottle
Crouper
Croupon
Crowbar
Crowded
Crowder
Crowdie
Crowger
Crowner
Crownet
Crowtoe
Crozier
Crucial
Crucian
Crucify
Crucite
Crudely
Crudity
Cruelly
Cruelty
Cruiser
Cruisie
Cruller
Crumble
Crumbly
Crumpet
Crumple
Crunkle
Cruorin
Crupper
Crusade
Crusado
Crusher
Crusian
Cryogen
Cryptic
Crystal
Ctenoid
Cubbing
Cubbish
Cubebin
Cubical
Cubicle
Cubital
Cubited
Cubitus
Cuckold
Cuculus
Cudbear

Cuddled
Cudweed
Cuinage
Cuirass
Cuisine
Cuittle
Culette
Culling
Cullion
Culprit
Cultism
Cultist
Culture
Culvert
Cumarin
Cumbent
Cumshaw
Cumulus
Cuneate
Cunette
Cunning
Cup-gall
Cupmoss
Cupping
Cuprite
Cup-rose
Curable
Curacao
Curacoa
Curator
Curcuma
Cure-all
Curette
Curioso
Curious
Curling
Currach
Curragh
Currant
Current
Currier
Currish
Cursing
Cursive
Cursory
Curtail
Curtain
Curtana
Curtate
Curt-axe
Curtsey
Curvate
Curvity
Cushion
Custard
Custode
Custody
Custrel

Cut-away
Cuticle
Cutlass
Cutlery
Cut-worm
Cuvette
Cyanate
Cyanide
Cyanine
Cyanite
Cycling
Cyclist
Cycloid
Cyclone
Cyclops
Cyclorn
Cymbalo
Cynical
Cyperus
Cypress
Cyprian
Cyprine
Cypriot
Cystine
Cystoid
Cystoma
Cystose
Cytisus
Cytitis
Czardas
Czarina
Czarism
Czechic

**D**

Dabbler
Dabster
Dacoity
Daddock
Dag-lock
Dagwood
Dahline
Daisied
Dakoity
Dallier
Dalriad
Dambrod
Damnify
Damosel
Damozel
Dampish
Danakil
Dandify
Dangled

Dangler
Dankish
Dansker
Dantean
Dantist
Daphnal
Daphnia
Daphnin
Dapifer
Darbies
Darcall
Darcock
Dariole
Darkish
Darling
Darrain
Darrein
Dartars
Dashpot
Dastard
Dasypus
Dasyure
Datable
Dataria
Datisca
Datival
Daubery
Daubing
Daunder
Daunton
Dauphin
Dawdler
Day-book
Day-coal
Day-lily
Daylon
Day-maid
Day-peep
Day's-man
Day-star
Daytime
Dayvite
Day-work
Dazzler
Deadeye
Deadish
Deadmen
Dead pay
Deadset
Dead-top
Deaf-nut
Deanery
Dearnly
Deasiul
Deasoil
Deathly
Deatzia
Debacle

Debaser
Debater
Debauch
Debitor
Debouch
Decadal
Decagon
Decanal
Decapod
Decayed
Decayer
Decease
Deceive
Decency
Decharm
Deciare
Decided
Decider
Decidua
Decimal
Decking
Deckled
Declaim
Declare
Decline
Decorum
Decreet
Decrial
Decrier
Decrown
Decuman
Decuple
Dedimus
Deedful
Deedily
Deep-fit
Deep-sea
Defacer
Defamer
Default
Defence
Defiant
Deficit
Defiler
Definer
Deflate
Deflect
Deflour
Deforce
Defraud
Defunct
Degrade
Dehisce
Deicide
Deictic
Deiform
Deiseal
Deistic

Delaine
Delapse
Delator
Delayer
Deleble
Delenda
Delible
Delight
Delilah
Delimit
Deliver
Delphic
Delphin
Deltaic
Deltoid
Deluder
Demayne
Dementi
Demerit
Demerse
Demesne
Demigod
Demirep
Demonic
Demonry
Demotic
Denizen
Densely
Density
Dentary
Dentate
Dentels
Dentine
Dentise
Dentist
Dentize
Dentoid
Denture
Deodand
Deodate
Depaint
Deplete
Deplore
Deplume
Deponed
Deposal
Deposed
Deposit
Deprave
Depress
Deprive
Deraign
Derange
Derbend
Derider
Dermoid
Dernful
Dernier

SEVEN-LETTER WORDS—*continued*

| | | | | | |
|---|---|---|---|---|---|
| Derrick | Diamond | Diocese | Dismals | Djereed | Doorway |
| Dervish | Diander | Dioecia | Dismask | Djerrid | Dor-hawk |
| Descant | Diapase | Dionaea | Dismast | Dobhash | Dorking |
| Descend | Diapasm | Diopsis | Dismayd | Docetae | Dorlach |
| Descent | Diarchy | Diopter | Dismayl | Docetic | Dormant |
| Deserve | Diarial | Diorama | Dismiss | Docible | Dornick |
| Desired | Diarian | Diorism | Disnest | Docious | Dornock |
| Desirer | Diarise | Diorite | Disobey | Dockage | Dor-tour |
| Desmine | Diarist | Dioxide | Dispair | Dockize | Dossier |
| Desmoid | Diatoms | Diploma | Dispark | Docquet | Dottard |
| Despair | Dibasic | Dipolar | Dispart | Doddart | Dottrel |
| Despise | Dibbled | Diptera | Dispend | Dodgery | Doublet |
| Despite | Dibbler | Diptych | Displace | Doeskin | Doubted |
| Despoil | Diceing | Direful | Display | Dogbane | Doubter |
| Despond | Dice-box | Dirt-bed | Dispone | Dog-belt | Doucely |
| Dessert | Diceras | Dirtily | Disport | Dog-bolt | Douceur |
| Destine | Dichord | Dirt-pie | Dispose | Dogcart | Doucine |
| Destiny | Dickens | Disable | Dispost | Dog-days | Doughty |
| Destroy | Dictate | Disally | Dispute | Dogeate | Doupion |
| Details | Diction | Disavow | Disrank | Dogfish | Dovecot |
| Deterge | Didache | Disband | Disrate | Doggish | Dovekie |
| Determa | Diddled | Disbark | Disrobe | Doggrel | Dovelet |
| Detinue | Diddler | Disbend | Disroot | Doghead | Dowable |
| Detract | Dididae | Discage | Disrupt | Dog-hole | Dowager |
| Detrain | Die-away | Discant | Disseat | Doghood | Dowcets |
| Detrude | Diedral | Discard | Dissect | Dog-like | Dowdily |
| Develop | Diehard | Discase | Dissent | Dog-rose | Dowered |
| Deviate | Dietary | Discept | Dissert | Dog's-ear | Down-bed |
| Devilet | Dietine | Discern | Distaff | Dogship | Dozenth |
| Devilry | Dietist | Discerp | Distain | Dog-sick | Drabber |
| Devious | Die-work | Discoid | Distant | Dogskin | Drabbet |
| Devisee | Difform | Discord | Distend | Dog's-rue | Drabble |
| Deviser | Diffuse | Discous | Distent | Dog-star | Drabler |
| Devisor | Digamma | Discide | Distich | Dog-tick | Drachma |
| Devolve | Digging | Discure | Distoma | Dog-trot | Dracina |
| Devotee | Dightly | Discuss | Distort | Dog-vane | Dracine |
| Devoter | Digital | Disdain | Distune | Dogwood | Draft-ox |
| Dewanny | Diglyph | Disease | Disturb | Dolabra | Drag-bar |
| Dewclaw | Dignify | Disedge | Distyle | Doleful | Draggle |
| Dewdrop | Dignity | Disfame | Disused | Dollied | Dragman |
| Dew-fall | Digraph | Disform | Diswarn | Dollier | Drag-net |
| Dewlapt | Digress | Disgown | Diswont | Dolldom | Dragoon |
| Dewless | Digynia | Disgust | Disyoke | Dollman | Drainer |
| Dew-pond | Dilater | Dishelm | Ditcher | Dolphin | Drapery |
| Dew-worm | Dilator | Dishful | Dittany | Doltish | Drappie |
| Dextral | Dilemma | Dishing | Dittied | Domable | Drastic |
| Dextrin | Dile-oil | Dishmat | Diurnal | Domical | Draught |
| Dhagoba | Dilling | Dishome | Diverge | Dominie | Drawbar |
| Dhoolie | Diluent | Dishorn | Diverse | Dominus | Draw-boy |
| Dhurrie | Diluter | Disjoin | Divided | Donator | Drawing |
| Diabase | Dimeter | Disjune | Divider | Donnerd | Drawler |
| Diabolo | Dim-eyed | Disleaf | Diviner | Donnert | Draw-net |
| Diacope | Dimgary | Disleal | Divisor | Donnish | Drayage |
| Diadrom | Dimmish | Dislike | Divorce | Donnism | Drayman |
| Diagram | Dimness | Dislimb | Divulge | Donship | Dreadly |
| Dialect | Dimpled | Dislimn | Dizened | Doomful | Dreamer |
| Dialist | Dinette | Dislink | Dizzard | Dooring | Dredger |
| Dialyze | Dinmont | Disload | Dizzily | Doormat | Dreeing |

SEVEN-LETTER WORDS—*continued*

| | | | | | |
|---|---|---|---|---|---|
| Dresden | Duchess | Dyslogy | Ecorché | Elf-bolt | Empanel |
| Dresser | Duck-ant | Dysnomy | Ecoutes | Elfland | Emperil |
| Drevill | Ducking | Dysopsy | Ecstasy | Elf-lock | Emperor |
| Dribble | Ductile | Dysuria | Ectasis | Elfshot | Emphyma |
| Driblet | Duddery | Dysuric | Ecthyma | Elfwort | Empight |
| Drifter | Dudgeon | Dyticus | Ectopia | Elimate | Empiric |
| Driller | Due-bill | Dyvoury | Ectopic | Elision | Emplead |
| Drinker | Dueller | | Ectozoa | Elk-wood | Employe |
| Drip-tip | Dueness | | Ectypal | Ellagic | Emplume |
| Driving | Duffing | **E** | Edacity | Ellipse | Empower |
| Drizzle | Dukedom | Eagerly | Edelite | Ellwand | Empress |
| Drizzly | Dulcify | Eanling | Edental | Elogist | Emprise |
| Drogher | Dulcine | Ear-ache | Edictal | Elogium | Emptier |
| Drogman | Dulcite | Ear-drop | Edifice | Elohist | Emption |
| Drognet | Dulcose | Ear-drum | Edifier | Elusion | Empyema |
| Droichy | Dullard | Ear-hole | Edition | Elusive | Emulate |
| Drolled | Dullish | Earldom | Educate | Elusory | Emulous |
| Droller | Dulness | Earless | Eductor | Elution | Emulsic |
| Dromond | Dumpish | Earlock | Eelbuck | Elysian | Emulsin |
| Dronish | Dun-bird | Earmark | Eel-fare | Elysium | Emu-wren |
| Drookit | Duncery | Earnest | Eel-pout | Elytral | Enactor |
| Droplet | Dunciad | Earning | Eel-punt | Elytron | Enamour |
| Drop-net | Duncish | Earpick | Effable | Elytrum | Enarmed |
| Drosera | Dun-fish | Earring | Effects | Elzevir | Encauma |
| Droshky | Dungeon | Earshot | Effendi | Emanant | Encenia |
| Drought | Dunging | Earthed | Efforce | Emanate | Enchafe |
| Droukit | Dunkers | Earthen | Effulge | Embargo | Enchain |
| Drouthy | Dunnage | Earthly | Egality | Embassy | Enchant |
| Drowner | Dunning | Easeful | Eggbird | Embathe | Enchase |
| Drubber | Dunnish | East-end | Egg-cosy | Emblaze | Encheer |
| Drudger | Dunnock | Eastern | Egg-flip | Emblema | Enchyma |
| Drugger | Duodena | Easting | Egilops | Emblica | Enclasp |
| Drugget | Dupable | Eatable | Egotise | Embloom | Enclave |
| Druidic | Durable | Ebb-tide | Egotism | Embogue | Enclose |
| Drumble | Durably | Ebonise | Egotist | Embolus | Encloud |
| Drummer | Duramen | Ebonist | Egotize | Embosom | Encrust |
| Drunken | Durance | Ebonite | Egrette | Embound | Endemic |
| Drusian | Durante | Ebonize | Eidolon | Embowel | Enderon |
| Dryades | Dureful | Ebriety | Eirenic | Embower | Endiron |
| Drybeat | Durmast | Ebrious | Ejector | Emboxed | Endless |
| Drybone | Dursley | Ecbasis | Elaidic | Embrace | Endlong |
| Dry-dock | Duskily | Ecbatic | Elaidin | Embraid | Endmost |
| Dry-eyed | Duskish | Ecbolic | Elastic | Embrail | Endogen |
| Dryfoot | Dustbin | Ecdemic | Elastin | Embrave | Endorse |
| Dryness | Dustman | Ecdysis | Elatery | Embread | Endosis |
| Dry-rent | Dustpan | Echappé | Elatine | Embroil | Endower |
| Dry-salt | Duteous | Echelle | Elation | Embrown | Endship |
| Dryshod | Dutiful | Echelon | Elderly | Embrute | Endurer |
| Dualism | Duumvir | Echidna | Eleatic | Embryon | Endways |
| Dualist | Dweller | Echimyd | Elector | Emerald | Endwise |
| Duality | Dwindle | Echinus | Electro | Emerite | Energic |
| Dualize | Dyalyse | Echoing | Elegant | Emerods | Enfelon |
| Duarchy | Dyarchy | Echoism | Elegiac | Emicant | Enfeoff |
| Dubbing | Dye-wood | Echoist | Elegise | Eminent | Enfiled |
| Dubiate | Dye-work | Eclipse | Elegist | Emirate | Enflesh |
| Dubiety | Dyingly | Eclogue | Elegize | Emongst | Enforce |
| Dubious | Dynamic | Ecology | Element | Emotion | Enframe |
| Ducally | Dynasty | Economy | Elevate | Emotive | Engaged |

SEVEN-LETTER WORDS—*continued*

| | | | | | |
|---|---|---|---|---|---|
| Engager | Entreat | Eremite | Euchymy | Exility | Facture |
| English | Entropy | Ergoted | Euclase | Exitial | Faculae |
| Englobe | Entrust | Erineum | Eucrasy | Exodist | Facular |
| Engloom | Entwine | Erinite | Eugenia | Exogamy | Faculty |
| Engorge | Entwist | Erinnys | Eugenic | Exomion | Fadaise |
| Engrace | Envault | Eristic | Eugenin | Exotism | Faddish |
| Engraff | Envelop | Erl-king | Eulogic | Expanse | Faddism |
| Engraft | Envenom | Ermelin | Eupepsy | Exparte | Faddist |
| Engrail | Envious | Ermined | Euphony | Expense | Faddled |
| Engrain | Environ | Ermines | Euphroe | Expiate | Fadedly |
| Engrasp | Enwheel | Erodent | Eupnaea | Explain | Faecula |
| Engrave | Enwoman | Erosion | Euripus | Explode | Faggery |
| Engross | Enwoven | Erosive | Euritic | Exploit | Fagging |
| Enguard | Epacrid | Eroteme | Euryale | Explore | Fagotto |
| Enhance | Epagoge | Errable | Eustyle | Exposal | Fahlerz |
| Enjoyer | Eparchy | Erratic | Euterpe | Exposed | Faience |
| Enlarge | Epaulet | Erratum | Eutonia | Exposer | Failing |
| Enlight | Epergne | Errhine | Evangel | Expound | Failure |
| Enliven | Ephebus | Erudite | Evanish | Express | Faintly |
| Enniche | Ephelis | Erugate | Evasion | Expulse | Fairily |
| Ennoble | Epicarp | Erupted | Evasive | Expunge | Fairing |
| Enomoty | Epicede | Escaper | Evening | Expurge | Fairish |
| Enounce | Epicene | Eschara | Evictor | Exscind | Fairway |
| Enquire | Epicism | Escheat | Evident | Extatic | Faithed |
| Enquiry | Epicist | Escroll | Evil-eye | Extense | Faitour |
| Enrange | Epicure | Escuage | Evinces | Extinct | Falbala |
| Enrheum | Epidemy | Esculin | Evitate | Extract | Falcade |
| Enridge | Epidote | Eserine | Evocate | Extreat | Falcula |
| Enripen | Epigeal | Esopian | Evolute | Extreme | Faldage |
| Enrough | Epigene | Esotery | Ewe-lamb | Extrude | Faldfee |
| Enround | Epigone | Espadon | Ewe-neck | Exuviae | Falerne |
| Enslave | Epigram | Esparto | Exacter | Exuvial | Fallacy |
| Ensnare | Episode | Espinel | Exactly | Eyeball | Fallals |
| Ensnarl | Epistle | Espouse | Exactor | Eyebeam | Falling |
| Ensober | Epitaph | Esquire | Exalgin | Eye-bolt | Falsely |
| Enstamp | Epithem | Essayer | Exalter | Eyebrow | Falsify |
| Ensteep | Epithet | Essence | Examine | Eyedrop | Falsish |
| Enstyle | Epitome | Essenes | Example | Eyeflap | Falsism |
| Ensuing | Epizoan | Essoign | Exangia | Eyehole | Falsity |
| Ensweep | Epizoon | Estival | Exarchy | Eyelash | Famulus |
| Entasia | Epochal | Estoile | Excerpt | Eyeless | Fanatic |
| Entasis | Epulary | Estrade | Excheat | Eyeliad | Fancied |
| Entente | Equable | Estreat | Exciter | Eyeshot | Fancier |
| Enterer | Equably | Estrich | Exclaim | Eyesore | Fanfare |
| Enteric | Equally | Estuary | Exclave | Eyespot | Fangled |
| Enteron | Equator | Esurine | Exclude | Eyewash | Fan-palm |
| Entheal | Equerry | Etaerio | Excreta | Eye-wink | Fantail |
| Enthral | Equinal | Etagere | Excrete | | Fantasm |
| Enthuse | Equinia | Etching | Excurse | | Fantast |
| Enticer | Equinox | Eternal | Execute | **F** | Fantasy |
| Entitle | Equites | Etesian | Exedrae | | Faradic |
| Entomic | Erasion | Etheria | Exegete | Fabliau | Faraway |
| Entonic | Erasure | Ethical | Exergue | Fabrile | Farceur |
| Entotic | Erected | Ethiops | Exhaust | Fabular | Farcied |
| Entozoa | Erecter | Ethmoid | Exhibit | Faceted | Farcify |
| Entrail | Erectly | Etiolin | Exhumer | Faction | Farcing |
| Entrain | Erector | Etonian | Exigent | Factive | Fardage |
| Entrant | Erelong | Euaemia | Exilian | Factual | Farmery |

SEVEN-LETTER WORDS—*continued*

| | | | | | |
|---|---|---|---|---|---|
| Farming | Fen-fire | Figment | Fiskery | Flinder | Foggage |
| Farmost | Fengite | Figtoll | Fissile | Flinger | Foggdom |
| Farness | Fennish | Figural | Fission | Flip-dog | Foggily |
| Farrago | Feodary | Figwort | Fissive | Flipper | Foghorn |
| Farrand | Feoffee | Filacer | Fissure | Flitter | Fogless |
| Farrier | Feoffer | Filager | Fistlaw | Floater | Fogring |
| Farthel | Feoffor | Filaria | Fistula | Floccus | Fogyish |
| Farther | Ferdwit | Filberd | Fitched | Flockly | Fogyism |
| Fascets | Fermata | Filbert | Fitcher | Flookan | Foiling |
| Fasciae | Ferment | Filcher | Fitchet | Floorer | Foister |
| Fascial | Fernery | Filemot | Fitchew | Floreal | Foldage |
| Fascine | Fern-owl | Filiate | Fitment | Florist | Folding |
| Fascism | Ferrara | Filibeg | Fitness | Floroon | Foliage |
| Fashery | Ferrate | Filical | Fitting | Floruit | Foliate |
| Fashion | Ferrous | Filices | Fitweed | Flotage | Folioed |
| Fast-day | Ferrugo | Filling | Fixable | Flotant | Foliole |
| Fastens | Ferrule | Filming | Fixedly | Flotsam | Foliose |
| Fasting | Fertile | Fimbria | Fixings | Flounce | Folious |
| Fastish | Feruled | Fimetic | Fixture | Flouter | Fomites |
| Fatally | Fervent | Finable | Flaccid | Flowage | Fondant |
| Fateful | Fervour | Finally | Flacker | Flowery | Fondler |
| Fat-head | Festive | Finance | Flacket | Flowing | Fontlet |
| Fatigue | Festoon | Finback | Flackie | Fluence | Foodful |
| Fatling | Festuca | Finched | Flaffer | Fluency | Foogler |
| Fatlute | Fetcher | Finding | Flagman | Fluidal | Foolery |
| Fatness | Fetlock | Finecut | Flaming | Fluidic | Fooling |
| Fattish | Feudary | Finesse | Flaneur | Fluidly | Foolish |
| Fatuity | Feudist | Fin-fish | Flanged | Flukily | Footboy |
| Fatuous | Feu-duty | Fin-foot | Flanker | Flummox | Foothot |
| Faulted | Fevered | Finical | Flannel | Flumped | Footing |
| Faulter | Fewness | Finicin | Flapped | Flunkey | Footman |
| Faunist | Fiancee | Finicky | Flapper | Fluoric | Footpad |
| Favours | Fibbery | Finless | Flaring | Flusher | Foot-rot |
| Fawning | Fibroid | Finlike | Flashed | Fluster | Footway |
| Fayence | Fibroin | Finnish | Flasher | Flustra | Fopling |
| Fearful | Fibroma | Fin-toed | Flasket | Flutina | Foppery |
| Feaster | Fibrose | Fiorite | Flatten | Fluting | Foppish |
| Feather | Fibrous | Fire-arm | Flatter | Flutist | Forager |
| Feature | Fibster | Firebox | Flaught | Flutter | Foramen |
| Febrile | Fibular | Firedog | Flaunty | Fluvial | Forayer |
| Feculum | Ficaria | Firefly | Flavian | Fluxide | Forbade |
| Federal | Fictile | Fireman | Flavine | Fluxion | Forbear |
| Feeding | Fiction | Fire-new | Flavour | Fluxive | Forceps |
| Fee-farm | Fictive | Fire-pan | Flecked | Flyaway | Forcing |
| Feeling | Fidalgo | Fire-pot | Flecker | Fly-blow | Forcque |
| Fee-tail | Fiddler | Firmary | Fleecer | Flyboat | Forearm |
| Felidae | Fiddley | Firstly | Fleerer | Fly-book | Fore-bow |
| Felinae | Fidgety | Fishday | Fleetly | Fly-flap | Foreday |
| Felonry | Fielded | Fishery | Fleming | Fly-leaf | Fore-end |
| Felsite | Fielder | Fish-fag | Flemish | Fly-line | Foreign |
| Felspar | Fierily | Fish-fly | Flesher | Fly-rail | Forelay |
| Felting | Fifteen | Fishgig | Fleshly | Flyting | Foreleg |
| Felucca | Fifthly | Fishgod | Fleuret | Fly-trap | Foreman |
| Felwort | Fig-cake | Fishify | Flexile | Foaling | Foreran |
| Feminal | Figgery | Fishing | Flexion | Fodient | Forerun |
| Femoral | Fig-gnat | Fish-maw | Flexure | Foe-like | Foresay |
| Fencing | Fighter | Fish-oil | Flicker | Fog-bank | Foresee |
| Fen-duck | Fig-leaf | Fishway | Flighty | Fog-bell | Foretie |

## SEVEN-LETTER WORDS—*continued*

| | | | | | |
|---|---|---|---|---|---|
| Foretop | Frailty | Froward | Fuscous | Gamebag | Gavotte |
| Forever | Fraised | Fructed | Fusible | Game-egg | Gayness |
| Forfang | Framing | Fruggin | Fussily | Gameful | Gaysome |
| Forfeit | Frampel | Fruiter | Fustian | Gametal | Gazeebo |
| Forfend | Francic | Frumper | Futchel | Gametic | Gazeful |
| Forgery | Franion | Frustum | Futhorc | Gammock | Gazelle |
| Forging | Frankly | Frutify | Futtock | Gampish | Gazette |
| Forgive | Frantic | Fubbery | Fuzzily | Ganglia | Gearing |
| Forgone | Fratchy | Fucated | | Gangrel | Gehenna |
| Forhail | Fratery | Fuchsia | **G** | Gang-saw | Gelable |
| Forhent | Fraught | Fuchsin | | Gangway | Gelatin |
| Forlaid | Fraying | Fucused | Gabbard | Ganoids | Gelding |
| Forlore | Frazzle | Fuddler | Gabbart | Gantlet | Gelidly |
| Forlorn | Freaked | Fuelled | Gabbler | Gapping | Gellock |
| Formate | Freckle | Fueller | Gabeler | Garbage | Gemmate |
| Formful | Freckly | Fuguist | Gabelle | Garbler | Gemmery |
| Formula | Freedom | Fulcrum | Gaddish | Garboil | Gemmule |
| Fornent | Freeman | Fulgent | Gadelle | Gardant | Gemsbok |
| Forpine | Freezer | Fulgora | Gadling | Garfish | Genappe |
| Forsake | Freiged | Fulgour | Gadroon | Garland | General |
| Forslow | Freight | Fullage | Gadsman | Garment | Generic |
| Forswat | Frenate | Fullery | Gadwall | Garnish | Genesis |
| Fortify | Freshen | Full-hot | Gaekwar | Garotte | Genetic |
| Fortlet | Fresher | Fullpay | Gapping | Garpike | Genette |
| Fortune | Freshes | Fulmine | Gaikwar | Garvock | Genevan |
| Forward | Freshet | Fulness | Gainful | Gas-buoy | Genipap |
| Forwent | Freshly | Fulsome | Gaining | Gas-coal | Genista |
| Forworn | Fretful | Fulvous | Gainsay | Gas-coke | Genital |
| Fossick | Fret-saw | Fumaria | Gairish | Gaseity | Genitor |
| Fossway | Fretted | Fumaric | Galatea | Gaseous | Genoese |
| Foudrie | Fretten | Fumbler | Galeate | Gas-fire | Genteel |
| Fougade | Fretter | Fumette | Galeeny | Gashful | Gentian |
| Foughty | Friable | Fumiter | Galenic | Gaskins | Gentile |
| Foulard | Friarly | Funaria | Galette | Gas-lamp | Genuine |
| Foulder | Fribble | Funeral | Galilee | Gasmain | Geodesy |
| Foumart | Friesic | Fungate | Galipot | Gas-mask | Geogony |
| Founder | Frigate | Fungite | Gallant | Gaspipe | Geology |
| Foundry | Frijole | Fungold | Galla-ox | Gasping | Geonomy |
| Fourgon | Fringed | Fungous | Gallate | Gas-ring | Georama |
| Foveate | Fripper | Funicle | Galleon | Gassing | Geordie |
| Foveola | Friseur | Funnily | Gallery | Gassoul | Georgic |
| Foveole | Frisian | Furbish | Gall-fly | Gas-tank | Gerenda |
| Fovilla | Frisker | Furcate | Gallice | Gastral | Germane |
| Fowling | Frisket | Furcula | Galling | Gastric | Gesture |
| Fox-case | Frislet | Furfair | Galliot | Gateman | Getable |
| Fox-evil | Frisure | Furioso | Gallium | Gateway | Getting |
| Foxhunt | Fritter | Furious | Gallize | Gatling | Ghastly |
| Foxlike | Frizzle | Furlong | Gall-nut | Gaudery | Gherkin |
| Foxship | Frizzly | Furmety | Galloon | Gaudily | Ghostly |
| Foxtail | Frogbit | Furnace | Gallows | Gauffer | Giantly |
| Fox-trap | Frogery | Furnish | Galoche | Gauffre | Giantry |
| Fox-trot | Frogged | Furrier | Galopin | Gauging | Gibbose |
| Frabbit | Fronded | Furring | Galumph | Gaulish | Gibbous |
| Fraches | Frontal | Further | Gambado | Gaulter | Giblets |
| Fracted | Fronted | Furtive | Gambier | Gauntly | Giddily |
| Fraenum | Fronton | Fusarol | Gambist | Gauntry | Giggler |
| Fragile | Frosted | Fuscine | Gambler | Gavelet | Gig-mill |
| Frailly | Frounce | Fuscite | Gambrel | Gavilan | Gilding |

SEVEN-LETTER WORDS—*continued*

| | | | | | |
|---|---|---|---|---|---|
| Gillian | Glottis | Goodnow | Grapple | Grommet | Gushing |
| Gill-lid | Glowing | Goorkha | Grasper | Groomed | Guttate |
| Gimbals | Glozing | Goosery | Grassed | Grooved | Gutwort |
| Gimblet | Glucide | Gorcock | Grasser | Grossly | Guzzler |
| Gin-fizz | Glucina | Gor-crow | Grassum | Grotian | Gwiniad |
| Gingham | Glucose | Gordian | Gratify | Grouper | Gwyniad |
| Gingili | Gluepot | Gordius | Grating | Grouser | Gymnast |
| Ginging | Glumose | Gorilla | Gravely | Growler | Gynecic |
| Ginning | Glumous | Gormand | Gravied | Grown-up | Gyronny |
| Ginseng | Gluteal | Goshawk | Graving | Grub-axe | Gytrash |
| Gin-shop | Glutean | Gosling | Gravita | Grubber | |
| Giraffe | Gluteus | Gosnick | Gravity | Grubble | |
| Girasol | Glutton | Gossipy | Gravure | Grudged | **H** |
| Girding | Glyphic | Gossoon | Gray-fly | Grudger | Habitat |
| Girdler | Glyptic | Gouache | Graylay | Gruffly | Habited |
| Girlish | Gmelina | Goulard | Grayowl | Grumble | Habitué |
| Girlond | Gnarled | Goulash | Grazier | Grummet | Hachure |
| Girrock | Gnathal | Gourami | Grazing | Grumose | Hackbut |
| Gittern | Gnathic | Gourmet | Greased | Grumous | Hackery |
| Gizzard | Gnawing | Gournet | Greaser | Grundel | Hacking |
| Glacial | Gnostic | Goutily | Greaten | Grunter | Hackler |
| Glacier | Go-ahead | Gowman | Greatly | Gruyere | Hacklet |
| Gladden | Goatish | Grab-bag | Greaves | Gryphon | Hacklog |
| Gladful | Gobbing | Grabber | Grecian | Guanaco | Hackney |
| Gladius | Gobbler | Grabble | Grecise | Guanine | Hacksaw |
| Gladwyn | Gobelin | Gracile | Grecism | Guarana | Hadding |
| Glaikit | Goddess | Grackle | Grecize | Guarish | Haddock |
| Glamour | Godetia | Gradate | Grecque | Gubbins | Haemony |
| Glanced | Godhead | Gradely | Greenly | Gudgeon | Haffets |
| Glasses | Godhood | Gradine | Greenth | Guenons | Hafnium |
| Glaucus | Godless | Gradino | Gremial | Guerdon | Hagdown |
| Glazier | Godlike | Gradual | Grenade | Guereza | Hagfish |
| Glazing | Godlily | Graffer | Grey-hen | Guerite | Haggada |
| Gleaner | Godling | Grafter | Greyish | Guesser | Haggard |
| Glebous | Godroon | Grained | Greylag | Guester | Haggish |
| Gleeful | Godsend | Grainer | Griddle | Guiacum | Haggler |
| Gleeman | Godship | Grallae | Griding | Guidage | Hagseed |
| Glenoid | Godward | Grallic | Griffin | Guilder | Hagship |
| Gliadin | Goggled | Gramary | Griffon | Guildry | Hagweed |
| Glimmer | Goggles | Grammar | Grimace | Guipure | Haining |
| Glimpse | Goitred | Grampus | Grimily | Guisard | Hair-oil |
| Glisten | Golding | Granary | Griming | Gullery | Hairpin |
| Glister | Goldney | Grandad | Grinder | Gullied | Halacha |
| Glitter | Goliard | Grandam | Gr'pper | Gum-boil | Halakah |
| Gloamed | Goliath | Grandee | Gripple | Gummous | Halberd |
| Gloated | Golping | Grandly | Gr'quas | Gum-rash | Halcyon |
| Globard | Gombeen | Grandma | Griskin | Gum-tree | Half-cup |
| Globate | Gomelin | Grandpa | Grisled | Gunboat | Half-one |
| Globoid | Gomeril | Granger | Gristle | Gun-deck | Half-pay |
| Globose | Gonagra | Granite | Gristly | Gun-fire | Half-way |
| Globous | Gondola | Grannom | Grizzle | Gunnage | Half-wit |
| Globule | Gonidia | Grantee | Grizzly | Gunnery | Halibut |
| Gloried | Good bye | Granter | Grobian | Gunning | Halidom |
| Glorify | Good day | Grantor | Grocery | Gun-port | Halitus |
| Glosser | Goodden | Granule | Grogram | Gun-room | Hallage |
| Glossic | Goodeen | Grapery | Grogran | Gunshot | Hallian |
| Glottal | Goodish | Graphic | Groined | Gunwale | Hallier |
| Glottic | Goodman | Grapnel | Grolier | Gurnard | Hallion |

SEVEN-LETTER WORDS—*continued*

| | | | | | |
|---|---|---|---|---|---|
| Hallyon | Hastler | Hedeoma | Hessian | Hoghood | Hosiery |
| Halogen | Hatable | Hederal | Hetaira | Hogmane | Hospice |
| Halting | Hatband | Hederic | Hexagon | Hog-plum | Hostage |
| Halyard | Hatcase | Hedonic | Hexapla | Hogskin | Hostess |
| Hamburg | Hatchel | Heedful | Hexapod | Hogwash | Hostile |
| Hamites | Hatcher | Heel-tap | Heyduck | Hogweed | Hostler |
| Hamitic | Hatchet | Heftily | Heypass | Holdall | Hotflue |
| Hammock | Hateful | Hegumen | Hicatee | Holding | Hot-foot |
| Hamster | Hatrack | Heigh-ho | Hiccupy | Holibut | Hotness |
| Hamular | Hatrail | Heinous | Hickory | Holiday | Hotspur |
| Hamulus | Hauberk | Heirdom | Hickway | Holland | Hottrod |
| Hanaper | Haughty | Heiress | Hidalgo | Holmium | Hot-wall |
| Handbag | Haulage | Helcoid | Hideous | Holster | Houghed |
| Handful | Haulier | Helical | Hiemate | Holy-day | Housage |
| Handily | Haunchy | Hell-cat | Higgled | Homager | Housing |
| Handjar | Haunted | Hellene | Higgler | Homelot | Howbeit |
| Handler | Haunter | Hell-hag | Highday | Homelyn | Howdy-do |
| Handsaw | Hautboy | Hellish | High-fed | Homeric | However |
| Handsel | Hauteur | Helmage | Highlow | Hommock | Howling |
| Hangdog | Haut-pas | Helosis | Hightop | Homonym | Huddler |
| Hanging | Havanna | Helotry | Highway | Honesty | Hueless |
| Hangman | Haverel | Helpful | Hilding | Honeyed | Huffily |
| Hang-net | Haviour | Helping | Hillmen | Honiton | Huffish |
| Hansard | Hawbuck | Helving | Hillock | Hoôdlum | Hugeous |
| Hanster | Hawk-bit | Hemione | Hilltop | Hoodman | Hulking |
| Hanuman | Hawk-owl | Hemlock | Himself | Hoodock | Hulsean |
| Hapless | Hayband | Hemming | Hindbow | Hookpin | Humanly |
| Happify | Haycock | Hemopsy | Hipbelt | Hoopooh | Humbler |
| Happily | Hayfork | Henbane | Hip-gout | Hop-back | Humbuzz |
| Harbour | Hayloft | Hencoop | Hipknot | Hopbind | Humdrum |
| Hardily | Hayrick | Hennery | Hiplock | Hopbine | Humeral |
| Hardish | Haytier | Henotic | Hip-roof | Hopflea | Humerus |
| Hardock | Hayward | Henpeck | Hipshot | Hopeful | Humette |
| Hard-pan | Hazelly | Henting | Hirable | Hopkiln | Humidly |
| Hardrun | Headbag | Henwife | Hircine | Hoplite | Humming |
| Hardset | Headily | Hepatic | Hirsute | Hopoast | Hummock |
| Hardwon | Headman | Heptade | Hissing | Hop-pole | Humoral |
| Harelip | Head-sea | Herbage | Histrio | Hoptree | Humulin |
| Haricot | Headway | Herbary | History | Hop-vine | Humulus |
| Harlock | Healing | Herbist | Hitcher | Hop-yard | Hunches |
| Harmala | Healthy | Herblet | Hittite | Hordein | Hundred |
| Harmful | Hearing | Herbose | Hive-bee | Hordeum | Hungred |
| Harmine | Hearken | Herbous | Hoarder | Hording | Hunting |
| Harmony | Hearsal | Herdman | Hoatzin | Horizon | Hurdies |
| Harmost | Hearsay | Hereout | Hobbish | Hormone | Hurdler |
| Harness | Hearted | Heretic | Hobbism | Hornbar | Hurkaru |
| Harpist | Hearten | Herisse | Hobbist | Horn-bug | Hurling |
| Harpoon | Heathen | Heritor | Hobbler | Horning | Hurrier |
| Harrier | Heather | Herling | Hoblike | Hornish | Hurtful |
| Harshen | Heating | Hernial | Hobnail | Hornito | Hurtoir |
| Harshly | Heavers | Heroine | Hockday | Horn-mad | Husband |
| Hartall | Heavily | Heroism | Hoe-cake | Horn-nut | Hushaby |
| Harvest | Heaving | Heroize | Hogback | Horn-owl | Hushion |
| Hashish | Hebenon | Heronry | Hogcote | Horrent | Huskily |
| Hassock | Hebraic | Herring | Hoggers | Horrify | Hussite |
| Hastate | Heckler | Herself | Hoggery | Horsely | Hustler |
| Hastily | Hectare | Hership | Hoggish | Hoseman | Huswife |
| Hasting | Hectoid | Heshvan | Hog-herd | Hosanna | Hutment |

### SEVEN-LETTER WORDS—*continued*

| | | | | | |
|---|---|---|---|---|---|
| Hyaline | Ignobly | Improve | Ingenue | Inthral | Itacist |
| Hyalite | Illapse | Impulse | Ingesta | Intrant | Italian |
| Hyaloid | Ill-bred | Imputer | Inglobe | Intreat | Italics |
| Hydatid | Illegal | In-and-in | Ingoing | Introit | Itemise |
| Hydrant | Illeism | Inanity | Ingraft | Intrude | Iteracy |
| Hydrate | Ill-fame | Inaptly | Ingrain | Intrust | Iterant |
| Hydriad | Illicit | Inbeing | Ingrate | Intwine | Iterate |
| Hydride | Illness | Inboard | Ingress | Intwist | Ivoried |
| Hydroid | Ill-time | Inbreak | Ingross | Inutile | Ivy-bush |
| Hydrous | Ill-turn | Inbreed | Inhabit | Invader | Ixolite |
| Hygeian | Ill-used | Inburst | Inhaler | Invalid | |
| Hygiene | Ill-will | Incense | Inhaust | Inveigh | **J** |
| Hyloist | Imagery | Inchase | Inherit | Inverse | |
| Hymnary | Imagine | Inchest | Inherse | Invexed | Jacamar |
| Hymnist | Imamate | Inchpin | Inhibit | Invious | Jacchus |
| Hymnody | Imbathe | Incised | Inhuman | Invised | Jacinth |
| Hyodont | Imbiber | Incisor | Initial | Inviter | Jackass |
| Hypogea | Imblaze | Inciter | Injelly | Invoice | Jackdaw |
| Hyppish | Imbosom | Incivil | Injoint | Involve | Jackpot |
| Hypural | Imbound | Inclasp | Injurer | Inwards | Jacksaw |
| Hystrix | Imbowed | Inclave | Inkhorn | Inweave | Jack-tar |
| | Imbower | Incline | Inkling | Inwheel | Jacobin |
| **I** | Imbreke | Inclose | Inkneed | Inwoven | Jacobus |
| | Imbrown | Incloud | Inkwell | Ioduret | Jaconet |
| Iambics | Imbrute | Include | Inlayer | Ipomaea | Jadedly |
| Iambise | Imburse | Incomer | Inmeats | Iracund | Jadeite |
| Iberian | Imitant | Incrust | Innerve | Iranian | Jaggery |
| Icarian | Imitate | Incubus | Innuent | Irenics | Jaghire |
| Icebelt | Immense | Incudes | Inquest | Iricism | Jahvist |
| Iceberg | Immerge | Incurve | Inquire | Irideae | Jainism |
| Icebird | Immerse | Indexer | Inquiry | Iridine | Jalapic |
| Iceboat | Immoral | Indices | Insanie | Iridise | Jalapin |
| Ice-fall | Impaint | Inditer | Insculp | Iridium | Jalouse |
| Ice-fern | Impalsy | Indoors | Inshell | Irishry | Jambone |
| Ice-floe | Impanel | Indorse | Inshore | Irksome | Jamdain |
| Ice-foot | Impasse | Indrawn | Insider | Ironing | Jamdari |
| Icepack | Impaste | Inducer | Insight | Ironist | Jamewar |
| Icepail | Impasto | Indulge | Insinew | Isatine | Jamrach |
| Ice-spar | Impavid | Indwell | Insipid | Ischial | Jangada |
| Ice-wall | Impeach | Inearth | Insnare | Ischium | Jangler |
| Ichabod | Impearl | Ineptly | Insooth | Ischury | Janitor |
| Ichnite | Imperil | Inertia | Inspect | Iserine | Jannock |
| Ichthys | Impetus | Inertly | Inspire | Isidium | Janting |
| Iciness | Impeyan | Inexact | Install | Islamic | January |
| Icteric | Impiety | Infancy | Instant | Isleman | Jargoon |
| Idalian | Impinge | Infanta | Instate | Ismatic | Jarkman |
| Ideally | Impious | Infante | Instead | Isodoma | Jarring |
| Idiotcy | Implant | Infaust | Insteep | Isodont | Jashawk |
| Idiotic | Implate | Inferno | Instill | Isoëtes | Jasmine |
| Idlesse | Implead | Infidel | Instyle | Isogamy | Jaspery |
| Idolise | Implied | Infield | Insular | Isogeny | Jaspoid |
| Idolism | Implore | Inflamè | Insulin | Isohyet | Jaunder |
| Idolist | Imposer | Inflate | Insulse | Isolate | Javelin |
| Idolize | Impound | Inflect | Insurer | Isonomy | Jawbone |
| Idylist | Imprese | Inflict | Intense | Isopoda | Jawfall |
| Idyllic | Impress | Infulae | Integer | Issuant | Jawfoot |
| Igneous | Imprest | Infuser | Interim | Isthmus | Jaw-hole |
| Ignoble | Imprint | Ingener | Interne | Itacism | Jawrope |

SEVEN-LETTER WORDS—*continued*

| | | | | | |
|---|---|---|---|---|---|
| Jealous | Judcock | Kenosis | Kneeler | Ladrane | Lappish |
| Jedcock | Juffers | Kenotic | Kneepan | Ladybug | Laputan |
| Jeddart | Jugated | Kentish | Knitter | Ladycow | Lapwing |
| Jeering | Juggins | Keramic | Knittle | Lady-day | Lapwork |
| Jehovah | Juggler | Keratin | Knobbed | Ladyfly | Larceny |
| Jejunum | Juglans | Kermess | Knobble | Ladyish | Lard-oil |
| Jellied | Jugular | Kernish | Knobbly | Ladyism | Lardoon |
| Jellify | Jujitsu | Kestrel | Knocked | Laetare | Largely |
| Jellyby | Jujutsa | Ketchup | Knocker | Laggard | Largess |
| Jemadar | Jumbler | Keybolt | Knock-on | Lagging | Largish |
| Jenkins | Jumping | Keycold | Knoller | Lagomys | Larking |
| Jeofail | Juncate | Keyhole | Knopped | Lagopus | Larmier |
| Jeopard | Juncous | Keynote | Knopper | Laicize | Larrups |
| Jerking | Juniper | Keyring | Knotted | Lairage | Larvate |
| Jerquer | Junkman | Keyseat | Knowall | Lakelet | Lashing |
| Jessamy | Jupette | Khamsin | Knowing | Lakshmi | Laskets |
| Jessant | Jupiter | Khanate | Knuckle | Lamaism | Lassock |
| Jestful | Jurally | Kheddah | Koftgar | Lamaist | Lastage |
| Jesting | Jury-box | Khediva | Koranic | Lamb-ale | Lastery |
| Jewelry | Juryman | Khedive | Koumiss | Lambags | Lasting |
| Jew's-ear | Jussive | Khotbah | Kreatin | Lambent | Latakia |
| Jezebel | Justice | Kibitka | Kremlin | Lambkin | Latebra |
| Jezhail | Justify | Kickoff | Krishna | Lamella | Latches |
| Jib-boom | Juvenal | Kidling | Krooboy | Lametta | Latchet |
| Jib-door | Juwanza | Kikumon | Kruller | Lamiger | Latence |
| Jigajog | | Killdee | Krupsis | Laminal | Latency |
| Jigging | | Killick | Krypton | Laminar | Lateral |
| Jiggish | **K** | Killjoy | Kuh-horn | Lamiter | Lateran |
| Jim-crow | Kabbala | Killock | Kumquat | Lampass | Latiner |
| Jinglet | Kaddish | Kiln-dry | Kursaal | Lampate | Lathing |
| Jobbery | Kainite | Kilting | Kyanise | Lampern | Latrine |
| Jobbing | Kakodyl | Kinchin | Kyanite | Lampfly | Latrobe |
| Jocular | Kalends | Kindler | Kyanize | Lampion | Lattice |
| Joggles | Kalmuck | Kindred | | Lampoon | Latvian |
| Jog-trot | Kamerad | Kinetic | | Lamprey | Laugher |
| Johnian | Kamichi | Kingcup | **L** | Lanated | Launder |
| Joinder | Kampong | Kingdom | | Landing | Laundry |
| Joinery | Kantian | Kinglet | Labarum | Landman | Laurite |
| Jointed | Kantism | Kinless | Labiate | Landtag | Lauwine |
| Jointer | Kantist | Kinship | Labrose | Land-tax | Lavalla |
| Jointly | Kapitia | Kinsman | Laccine | Langaha | Lavotta |
| Jollify | Karagan | Kippage | Laceman | Langate | Lawbook |
| Jollily | Karaite | Kipshop | Lacerta | Langite | Lawcalf |
| Jollity | Karatas | Kipskin | Lacinia | Langued | Lawless |
| Jongler | Katydid | Kirimon | Lack-all | Languet | Law-list |
| Jonquil | Kebbock | Kirkton | Lacking | Languid | Law-lord |
| Jookery | Kebbuck | Kirtled | Lac-lake | Languor | Law-lore |
| Jotting | Kecking | Kitchen | Laconic | Langure | Lawsuit |
| Joukery | Kedging | Kitling | Lacquer | Laniard | Laxator |
| Journal | Kedlack | Klipdas | Lactate | Laniary | Laxness |
| Journey | Keelage | Knacker | Lacteal | Laniate | Lay-days |
| Joyance | Keeling | Knapper | Lactean | Lanolin | Layette |
| Joyless | Keelman | Knapple | Lactine | Lantern | Layland |
| Jubilee | Keelson | Knarled | Lactose | Lanyard | Laylord |
| Judaise | Keeping | Knavery | Lactuca | Laocoon | Lazaret |
| Judaism | Keitloa | Knavish | Lacunal | Lapelle | Lazarly |
| Judaist | Kennick | Kneader | Lacunar | Lapilli | Lazybed |
| Judaize | Kenning | Kneecap | Ladanum | Lappior | Leading |

## SEVEN-LETTER WORDS—*continued*

| | | | | | |
|---|---|---|---|---|---|
| Leafage | Leprose | Lingism | Locular | Lowland | Macaque |
| Leaf-bud | Leprosy | Lingual | Loculus | Low-life | Mace-ale |
| Leaf-fat | Leprous | Linkage | Locusta | Lowlily | Machete |
| Leafing | Lesbian | Linkboy | Lodging | Lowness | Machine |
| Leaflet | Lethean | Linkman | Loftily | Lowtide | Mackite |
| Leaguer | Letheon | Linnean | Logbook | Loyally | Macrame |
| Leakage | Lettern | Linsang | Logchip | Loyalty | Maculae |
| Leaking | Lettish | Linseed | Loggats | Lozenge | Madbred |
| Leaning | Lettuce | Lioncel | Loghead | Lozengy | Maddest |
| Learned | Leucine | Lioness | Log-heap | Lubbard | Madding |
| Learner | Leucism | Lionise | Logical | Lucanus | Madeira |
| Leasing | Leucite | Lionism | Logline | Lucarne | Madling |
| Leasowe | Leucoma | Lionize | Log-reel | Lucency | Madness |
| Leather | Leucous | Lipborn | Log-roll | Lucerne | Madonna |
| Leaving | Levator | Lip-good | Log-ship | Lucidly | Madoqua |
| Lechery | Levelly | Liquate | Logwood | Lucifer | Madrier |
| Lectern | Leveret | Liquefy | Loiters | Lucigen | Madrone |
| Lection | Levitic | Liqueur | Lollard | Luckily | Madwort |
| Lectual | Levying | Lissome | Lomaria | Luggage | Maestro |
| Lecture | Lexical | Listful | Lombard | Lugmark | Maffick |
| Lecturn | Lexicon | Listing | Long-ago | Lugsail | Mappled |
| Leechee | Liaison | Literal | Longbow | Lugworm | Magenta |
| Leefang | Liassic | Lithate | Longest | Lullaby | Maggoty |
| Leegage | Libbard | Lithely | Long-hop | Lumbago | Magical |
| Leemost | Liberal | Lithium | Longing | Lumping | Magnate |
| Lee-side | Liberty | Lithoid | Longish | Lumpish | Magneto |
| Lee-tide | Library | Litotes | Long-leg | Lunated | Magnify |
| Leeward | Librate | Littery | Long-run | Lunatic | Mahaleb |
| Legally | Licence | Lituate | Loobily | Lunette | Mahatma |
| Legatee | License | Liturge | Looking | Lunular | Mahdism |
| Leg-bail | Lich-owl | Liturgy | Lookout | Lunulet | Mahdist |
| Leggers | Licitly | Livable | Looming | Lupulin | Mahjong |
| Legging | Lidless | Livened | Looning | Lupulus | Mahound |
| Leggism | Lie-abed | Live-oak | Loopers | Lurcher | Mahseer |
| Leghorn | Lighten | Livered | Looping | Lurdane | Mailbag |
| Legible | Lighter | Llanero | Loosely | Luskish | Mailcar |
| Legibly | Lightly | Loading | Lopping | Lustful | Mailing |
| Legiron | Lignage | Loaming | Lording | Lustily | Mainour |
| Legitim | Lignify | Loaning | Lordkin | Lustral | Maintop |
| Legless | Lignine | Loather | Lorette | Lustrum | Maister |
| Legumin | Lignite | Loathly | Lorgnon | Luteous | Maizena |
| Leidger | Lignose | Lobcock | Lorimer | Luthern | Majesty |
| Leister | Ligular | Lobelet | Loriner | Lutrine | Majorat |
| Leisure | Lily-pad | Lobelia | Losable | Lychnic | Malacca |
| Lemmata | Limbate | Lobiped | Lottery | Lychnis | Malaise |
| Lemming | Limbing | Lobster | Loukoum | Lycopod | Malaria |
| Lemnian | Lime-pit | Lobular | Lounder | Lyddite | Malayan |
| Lemures | Liminal | Lobulus | Lounger | Lyingly | Malefic |
| Lending | Limited | Lobworm | Loutish | Lymphad | Malicho |
| Lengthy | Limiter | Locally | Lovable | Lyncean | Malison |
| Lenient | Limning | Lochial | Loveday | Lynchet | Mallard |
| Lentigo | Limnite | Lockage | Loveman | Lyrated | Malleus |
| Lentisk | Limosis | Lockian | Lovered | Lyrical | Malmsey |
| Lentoid | Limping | Lockist | Loverly | | Maltese |
| Lentous | Limpkin | Lock-jaw | Low-bell | | Malting |
| Leonero | Linctus | Lockman | Low-born | **M** | Maltman |
| Leonine | Lineage | Lock-out | Lowdown | Macabre | Maltose |
| Leopard | Lineate | Lockram | Lowered | Macadam | Mamelon |

## SEVEN-LETTER WORDS—*continued*

| | | | | | |
|---|---|---|---|---|---|
| Mammary | Margosa | Matting | Melaena | Mid-lent | Mirador |
| Mammate | Marikin | Mattins | Melange | Mid-life | Mirbane |
| Mammock | Mariner | Mattock | Melanic | Midmost | Misborn |
| Mammoth | Mariput | Maudlin | Melanin | Midnoon | Miscall |
| Mammula | Marital | Maunder | Melasma | Midrash | Miscast |
| Manacle | Markhor | Maurist | Melilot | Midriff | Miscite |
| Manager | Marking | Mauther | Mellite | Midship | Miscopy |
| Manakin | Marline | Mawkish | Mellowy | Midwife | Misdate |
| Manatee | Marling | Mawseed | Melodic | Miemite | Misdeal |
| Manchet | Marlite | Mawworm | Melrose | Mightst | Misdeed |
| Manchoo | Marlpit | Maxilla | Melting | Migrant | Misdeem |
| Mandate | Markman | Maximal | Membral | Migrate | Misdiet |
| Mandioc | Marmite | Maximum | Memento | Mildewy | Misdoer |
| Mandola | Marmose | Maybird | Menacer | Mileage | Misdone |
| Mandora | Marplot | Mayduke | Mending | Milfoil | Misdraw |
| Mandrel | Marquee | May-game | Mengate | Miliary | Miserly |
| Mandril | Marquis | Maylady | Mengite | Miliola | Misfall |
| Mangler | Married | Maylily | Meniver | Militar | Misfare |
| Mangold | Marrowy | May-morn | Mensual | Militia | Misfire |
| Manhole | Marsala | Mayoral | Menthol | Milkily | Misform |
| Manhood | Marshal | Maypole | Mention | Milking | Misgive |
| Manihoc | Martext | Maytime | Mercery | Milkman | Mishear |
| Manihot | Martial | Mayweed | Mercify | Milksop | Mishmee |
| Manikin | Martini | Mazagan | Mercury | Mill-cog | Mishnah |
| Manilio | Martlet | Mazarin | Merited | Mill-dam | Mishnic |
| Manilla | Marxian | Mazdean | Merling | Millier | Misjoin |
| Manille | Marybud | Mazeful | Mermaid | Milling | Misknow |
| Maniple | Mascled | Mazurka | Merrily | Million | Mislays |
| Manitou | Mascule | Mazzard | Mersion | Milreis | Mislead |
| Mankind | Meacock | Mesally | Milvine | Mislike |
| Manless | Mashing | Meadowy | Meseems | Mimesis | Mislive |
| Manlike | Mashlim | Mealark | Mesodic | Mimetic | Misluck |
| Man-made | Mashlum | Mealman | Mesquit | Mimical | Mismark |
| Manning | Mashtub | Meander | Message | Mimicry | Misname |
| Mannish | Masonic | Meaning | Messiah | Mimulus | Misplay |
| Mannite | Masonry | Measled | Messing | Minaret | Misrate |
| Mansard | Massage | Measles | Mestino | Mincing | Misread |
| Mansion | Masseur | Measure | Mestizo | Mindful | Misrule |
| Mantlet | Massive | Meat-pie | Metayer | Minding | Missaid |
| Man-trap | Massora | Meat tea | Metazao | Mineral | Misseem |
| Mantuan | Mastaba | Meat-tub | Metazoa | Minerva | Missend |
| Manuard | Mastery | Mechlin | Methane | Minever | Missent |
| Manumit | Mastful | Meconic | Metoche | Mingler | Missile |
| Manurer | Mastick | Medalet | Metonic | Miniate | Missing |
| Maormor | Mastiff | Meddler | Metopic | Minibus | Mission |
| Mappery | Masting | Mediacy | Metrics | Minikin | Missish |
| Mappist | Mastoid | Mediant | Metrify | Minimal | Missive |
| Marabou | Matador | Mediate | Metrist | Minimum | Misstep |
| Maracan | Matchet | Medical | Mettled | Minimus | Missuit |
| Marathi | Materia | Medulla | Mexican | Minious | Mistake |
| Marbled | Matinal | Medusae | Mezquit | Miniver | Mistell |
| Marbler | Matinée | Medusan | Miasmal | Minster | Misterm |
| Marcato | Matrass | Meerkat | Microbe | Mintage | Mistery |
| Märchen | Matress | Meeting | Microhm | Mintman | Mistful |
| Marcher | Mat-reed | Megaera | Middest | Minuend | Mistico |
| Maremma | Matrice | Mega-erg | Midgard | Miocene | Mistily |
| Margent | Matross | Mega-fog | Midhour | Mirable | Mistime |
| Margode | Mattery | Meiosis | Midland | Miracle | Mistral |

## SEVEN-LETTER WORDS—*continued*

| | | | | | |
|---|---|---|---|---|---|
| Mistune | Monodic | Mottled | Mumping | Mystery | Needily |
| Misturn | Monodon | Mottoed | Mumpish | Mystics | Neesing |
| Misween | Monsoon | Moucher | Muncher | Mystify | Negated |
| Miswend | Monster | Mouflon | Mundane | Mythist | Negatur |
| Misyoke | Montant | Mouille | Mundify | Mytilus | Neglect |
| Mithras | Montero | Moulder | Mungeet | Myxopod | Neglige |
| Mitosis | Monthly | Mouldie | Munjeet | | Negress |
| Mixable | Montoir | Mounted | Munnion | | Negrito |
| Mixedly | Monture | Mounter | Munting | | Negroid |
| Mixible | Moodily | Mourner | Muntjak | **N** | Negundo |
| Mixtion | Mooktar | Mousery | Muraena | | Neither |
| Mixture | Mooneye | Mousing | Murexan | Nacarat | Nelumbo |
| Mizmaze | Moonish | Mousmee | Murgeon | Nacelle | Nemesic |
| Mjolnir | Moonlit | Mouther | Muriate | Nacodah | Nemesis |
| Moabite | Moonset | Movable | Murkily | Nacrite | Nemoral |
| Moanful | Moorage | Movably | Murrain | Nacrous | Neogene |
| Mobbish | Moorery | Mowburn | Murrine | Naevoid | Neolite |
| Mobsman | Moorhen | Mozarab | Murrion | Naevose | Neology |
| Mockery | Moorill | Mozetta | Murther | Nailery | Neozoic |
| Mocking | Mooring | Mucific | Muscite | Nailrod | Nepotic |
| Mock-sun | Moorish | Mucigen | Muscled | Naively | Neptune |
| Modally | Mootmen | Mudbath | Muscoid | Naivety | Nereite |
| Modesty | Moraine | Mudboat | Museful | Nakedly | Nervate |
| Modicum | Moraler | Mud-cart | Musette | Namable | Nervine |
| Modiste | Morally | Mudcone | Mushing | Nandine | Nervose |
| Modular | Morassy | Muddied | Musical | Nankeen | Nervous |
| Modulus | Morbose | Muddily | Musimon | Naphtha | Nervule |
| Modwall | Morceau | Mudding | Muskbag | Napless | Nervure |
| Moellon | Mordant | Mud-fish | Muskcat | Nardine | Nesiote |
| Mofette | Mordent | Mudflat | Muskily | Nargile | Nest-egg |
| Mohican | Morella | Mud-hole | Musk-rat | Narrate | Nestled |
| Mohsite | Morrello | Mudlark | Musrole | Narthex | Nestler |
| Moidert | Morglay | Mud-scow | Mustang | Narwhal | Netball |
| Moidore | Moriche | Mud-wall | Mustard | Nasalis | Netfish |
| Moineau | Moringa | Mudwort | Mustela | Nasally | Netsuke |
| Moisten | Morisco | Mueddin | Mustily | Nasarde | Netting |
| Molasse | Morling | Muezzin | Musting | Nascent | Nettler |
| Mole-rat | Mormops | Muffler | Mutable | Nastily | Nettles |
| Molimen | Morning | Mufflon | Mutably | Nathmoe | Network |
| Mollify | Morocco | Muggard | Mutanda | Nattery | Neurine |
| Molline | Morphew | Muggent | Muttony | Nattily | Neuroma |
| Mollusc | Morphia | Muggins | Muzarab | Natural | Neurose |
| Mollusk | Morphic | Muggish | Muzzily | Natured | Neutral |
| Molossi | Morrhua | Mugwort | Myalgia | Naughty | Newborn |
| Momenta | Morrice | Mugwump | Myalgic | Nautile | Newcome |
| Monacid | Morrion | Mulatto | Myarian | Navarch | Newmade |
| Monadic | Morsure | Mulette | Mycelia | Navette | Newness |
| Monarch | Mortice | Mullein | Mycetes | Nayward | Newsboy |
| Moneral | Mortier | Mullion | Mycosis | Nayword | Newsman |
| Moneran | Mortify | Mullock | Mycotic | Nead-end | Nibbler |
| Moneron | Mortise | Multoca | Myeloid | Nealogy | Niblick |
| Moneyed | Mosaism | Multure | Mylodon | Nearest | Nictate |
| Moneyer | Moschus | Mumbler | Mynheer | Nebulae | Nidging |
| Mongrel | Moselle | Mummery | Myogram | Nebular | Nigella |
| Monitor | Mosshag | Mummied | Myology | Necking | Niggard |
| Monkery | Motacil | Mummify | Myotomy | Necklet | Niggery |
| Monkish | Moth-eat | Mumming | Myrrhic | Necktie | Niggler |
| Monocle | Mothery | Mummock | Myrrhol | Nectary | Nightly |

## SEVEN-LETTER WORDS—*continued*

Nigrine
Nigrite
Nilotic
Nimiety
Ninthly
Niobean
Niobium
Nippers
Nipping
Nirvana
Nitency
Nithing
Nitrate
Nitrify
Nitrite
Nitrose
Nitrous
Niveous
Noachic
Nobbler
Nobless
Noctuid
Noctule
Nocturn
Nocuous
Nodated
Nodding
Nodical
Nodular
Noduled
Nodulus
Noemics
Noetian
Nogging
Noiance
Noisily
Noisome
Nomadic
Nomancy
Nomarch
Nombles
Nombril
Nominal
Nominee
Non-acid
Nonaged
Nonagon
Nonplus
Non-stop
Nonsuch
Nonsuit
Nonterm
Nonuser
Noology
Noonday
Nooning
Norimon
Norland

Norther
Nosebag
Nosegay
Noseled
Nostril
Nostrum
Notable
Notably
Notaeum
Notanda
Notchel
Notedly
Notitia
Noumena
Nourice
Notelet
Nothing
Nourish
Noursle
Novalia
Novelty
Nowhere
Noxious
Noyance
Noysome
Nuclear
Nuclein
Nuclear
Nucleus
Nullify
Nullity
Numbers
Numbles
Numeral
Numeric
Nummary
Nunatak
Nun-buoy
Nunhood
Nunnery
Nunnish
Nuptial
Nurling
Nursery
Nurture
Nutbush
Nutgall
Nut-hook
Nutmeal
Nut-pine
Nutting
Nut-tree
Nylghau
Nymphal
Nymphic
Nymphly

## O

Oak-bark
Oak-fern
Oak-gall
Oakling
Oarfish
Oarlock
Oarsman
Oatcake
Oatmalt
Oatmeal
Obconic
Obelion
Obelise
Obelisk
Obelize
Obesity
Obitual
Obligee
Obliger
Obligor
Oblique
Obloquy
Obolary
Obovate
Obovoid
Obscene
Obscure
Obsequy
Observe
Obtrude
Obverse
Obviate
Obvious
Ocarina
Occiput
Occlude
Oceania
Oceanic
Oceanid
Oceanus
Ocellar
Ocellus
Oceloid
Ochroid
Octagon
Octapla
October
Octofid
Octopod
Octopus
Octuple
Octylic
Oculate
Oculist
Odalisk

Odaller
Oddment
Oddness
Odforce
Odorine
Odorous
Odyssey
Oedemia
Oedipus
Oellade
Oenomel
O'ercome
Oestrum
Oestrus
Offcome
Offence
Offense
Offerer
Offhand
Officer
Offscum
Offside
Offward
Oghamic
Ogreish
Ogygian
Oilbird
Oilcake
Oil-gold
Oil-meal
Oil-palm
Oilshop
Oilskin
Oil-well
Oldness
Oldster
Oldtime
Olefine
Olifant
Oligist
Olitory
Olivary
Olivine
Olympic
Olympus
Omental
Omentum
Omicron
Ominous
Omnibus
Omnific
Onanism
Onanist
One-eyed
Onefold
Oneness
Onerary
Onerous

Oneself
Ongoing
Onicolo
Onoclea
Onology
Onshore
Onstead
Onwards
Onychia
Onymise
Oodlins
Oögraph
Oolitic
Oologic
Oometry
Oozings
Opacity
Opacous
Opaline
Opalise
Opaque
Opalize
Opening
Operant
Operate
Operose
Opetide
Ophidia
Ophiura
Opiated
Opinant
Opining
Opinion
Oporice
Opossum
Oppidan
Opposed
Opposer
Opposit
Oppress
Opsonic
Opsonin
Optical
Optimum
Options
Opulent
Opuntia
Opuscle
Oraison
Orarium
Orarian
Orarion
Oration
Oratory
Oratrix
Orbital
Orb-like
Orchard

Orderer
Orderly
Ordinal
Ordinee
Oreades
Organic
Organon
Organry
Organum
Orgiast
Oriency
Orifice
Orleans
Orogeny
Orology
Orotund
Orphean
Orphism
Orphrey
Orsedew
Orthite
Orthros
Orvieto
Ortolan
Osborne
Oscheal
Oscines
Oscular
Osiered
Osmanli
Osmious
Osmosis
Osmotic
Osmunda
Osselet
Osseous
Ossicle
Ossipic
Ossuary
Osteoid
Ostiary
Ostiole
Ostitis
Ostrich
Otalgia
Otarine
Otocyst
Otolith
Otology
Ottoman
Ourself
Outbrag
Outburn
Outcast
Outcome
Outcrop
Outdare
Outdoor

## SEVEN-LETTER WORDS—*continued*

| | | | | | |
|---|---|---|---|---|---|
| Outedge | Outward | Ox-stall | Pallium | Parbake | Patrist |
| Outface | Outwear | Oxyopia | Pallone | Parboil | Patroon |
| Outfall | Outweed | Oxysalt | Palmary | Pardale | Pattern |
| Outflow | Outwell | Oxytone | Palmate | Pardieu | Pattras |
| Out-foot | Outwind | Ozonize | Palmery | Pareira | Paucity |
| Outgage | Outwing | Ozonous | Palming | Parella | Pauline |
| Outgate | Outwith | | Palmist | Parelle | Paunchy |
| Outgive | Outwork | | Palm-oil | Parergy | Paviage |
| Outgoer | Ouvrage | **P** | Palmyra | Paresis | Paviour |
| Outgrow | Ovarial | | Palpate | Paretic | Pawning |
| Outgush | Ovarian | Pabular | Palsied | Paritor | Paxiuba |
| Outhaul | Ovation | Pabulum | Paludal | Parking | Payable |
| Outhire | Oventit | Pacable | Pampero | Parlour | Pay-bill |
| Outjest | Overact | Pacated | Panacea | Parlous | Pay-dirt |
| Outland | Overall | Pachisi | Panache | Parodic | Pay-list |
| Outlash | Overawe | Pachyma | Panagia | Parotic | Payment |
| Outlast | Overbid | Pacific | Pancake | Parotid | Paynise |
| Outleap | Overbuy | Package | Pandean | Parotis | Pay-roll |
| Outlier | Overdue | Pack-ice | Pandect | Parquet | Paysage |
| Outline | Overdye | Packing | Pandion | Parsley | Peacher |
| Outlive | Overeat | Packman | Pandora | Parsnep | Peacoat |
| Outlook | Overeye | Pack-wax | Pandore | Parsnip | Peacrub |
| Outmate | Overfar | Packway | Pandour | Partake | Peacock |
| Outmost | Overfly | Paction | Pandura | Partial | Peacrab |
| Outmove | Overget | Padding | Paneity | Parting | Peafowl |
| Outname | Overjoy | Paddled | Panicky | Partite | Peaking |
| Outness | Overlap | Paddler | Panicle | Partlet | Peakish |
| Outpace | Overlay | Paddock | Panicum | Partner | Peanism |
| Outpart | Overlie | Padella | Panikin | Parture | Pearled |
| Outpeer | Overman | Padisha | Pannade | Parvenu | Pearlin |
| Outplay | Overnet | Padlock | Pannage | Parvise | Peasant |
| Outport | Overpay | Padrone | Pannier | Paschal | Peascod |
| Outpost | Overply | Pad-tree | Pannose | Pascual | Peasoup |
| Outpour | Overred | Paenula | Panocha | Pasquil | Peat-bed |
| Outpray | Overrun | Paeonin | Panoply | Pasquin | Peat-bog |
| Outrage | Oversea | Pageant | Pan-pike | Passade | Peat-hag |
| Outraze | Oversee | Paginal | Pansied | Passado | Pebbled |
| Outride | Overset | Pahlavi | Panther | Passage | Pebrine |
| Outroad | Oversew | Pailful | Pantile | Passant | Peccant |
| Outroar | Overtax | Paillon | Pantler | Passing | Peccary |
| Outroot | Overtly | Painful | Panurgy | Passion | Peccavi |
| Outrush | Overtop | Paining | Papally | Passive | Peckish |
| Outsail | Ovidian | Painter | Paphian | Pass-key | Pectate |
| Outsell | Oviduct | Pajamas | Papilio | Passman | Pectine |
| Outshot | Oviform | Pakfong | Papilla | Pastern | Pectose |
| Outside | Ovoidal | Paktong | Papmeat | Pastime | Peddler |
| Outsize | Ovology | Palabra | Papoose | Pasture | Pedesis |
| Outsoar | Ovulary | Paladin | Pappose | Patamar | Pedicel |
| Outsold | Ovulite | Palamae | Pappous | Patcher | Pedicle |
| Outsole | Owenite | Palatal | Papular | Patella | Pedlary |
| Outspan | Owleyed | Palaver | Papyrus | Paterae | Pedrail |
| Outstay | Owl-like | Pale-ale | Parable | Pathway | Peeling |
| Outstep | Oxalate | Paleous | Paracme | Patient | Peelite |
| Outtalk | Oxalite | Paletot | Parados | Patness | Peerage |
| Outturn | Oxidate | Palette | Paradox | Patonce | Peeress |
| Outvote | Oxidise | Palfrey | Paragon | Patrial | Peevers |
| Outwalk | Oxidize | Palilia | Parapet | Patrico | Peevish |
| Outwall | Oxonian | Palinal | Parasol | Patriot | Peeweep |

## SEVEN-LETTER WORDS—*continued*

| | | | | | |
|---|---|---|---|---|---|
| Pegasus | Percuss | Pewrent | Pierage | Pinkish | Planner |
| Pehlevi | Perdure | Pewtery | Pierced | Pinnace | Plantar |
| Peishwa | Peregal | Pfennig | Piercer | Pinnate | Planter |
| Pelagic | Pereion | Phacoid | Pierian | Pinnock | Planula |
| Pelasgi | Perelle | Phaeton | Pierrot | Pinnoed | Planury |
| Pelican | Perfect | Phalanx | Pietism | Pinnula | Planxty |
| Pelisse | Perfidy | Phallic | Pietist | Pinnule | Plasmic |
| Pellage | Perform | Phallus | Piewife | Pintado | Plaster |
| Pelopid | Perfume | Phantom | Piffero | Pintail | Plastic |
| Peloria | Perfuse | Pharaoh | Piffled | Pintpot | Plastid |
| Peloric | Pergola | Pharynx | Piggery | Pinwork | Platane |
| Peltase | Perhaps | Pheesar | Pigeyed | Pioneer | Plateau |
| Peltate | Periapt | Phenate | Pigging | Pioning | Platina |
| Pelting | Peridot | Phenoic | Piggish | Piously | Plating |
| Penally | Perigee | Philter | Pightle | Piperic | Platoon |
| Penalty | Perique | Philtree | Pig-iron | Pipette | Platter |
| Penance | Periwig | Phlegmy | Piglead | Pipless | Plaudit |
| Penates | Perjure | Phloeum | Pigmean | Pipping | Play-day |
| Pencase | Perjury | Phocine | Pigment | Piquing | Playful |
| Pendant | Perking | Phoebus | Pigskin | Piragua | Playing |
| Pendent | Perlite | Phoenix | Pigtail | Piratic | Pleader |
| Pending | Perlous | Phonate | Pikelet | Pirogue | Pleased |
| Peneian | Permagy | Phonics | Pikelin | Piscary | Pleaser |
| Penfish | Permian | Phoresy | Pikeman | Piscina | Plectre |
| Penfold | Permute | Photism | Pikrite | Piscine | Pledgee |
| Penguin | Peropod | Phraser | Pilcher | Pismire | Pledger |
| Penicil | Perpend | Phratry | Pilealy | Pistole | Pledget |
| Pen-name | Perplex | Phrenic | Pileate | Pitapat | Pleiads |
| Pennant | Perrier | Phrensy | Pilfery | Pitcher | Plenary |
| Pennate | Persant | Physics | Pilgrim | Pit-coal | Plenish |
| Pennied | Perseus | Phytoid | Pilkins | Piteous | Plenist |
| Pennill | Persian | Piacere | Pillage | Pitfall | Pleroma |
| Penning | Persist | Piaffer | Pillbox | Pithead | Pleural |
| Pensile | Persona | Pianino | Pillion | Pithily | Pleuron |
| Pension | Pertain | Pianism | Pillory | Pitiful | Plexure |
| Pensive | Perturb | Pianist | Pillows | Pitmirk | Pliable |
| Pentact | Pertuse | Pianola | Pillowy | Pitting | Pliably |
| Pentane | Perusal | Piarist | Piltock | Pittite | Pliancy |
| Pentice | Perused | Piaster | Pilular | Pituita | Plicate |
| Pentile | Peruser | Piastre | Pimelic | Pituite | Pliform |
| Pentzia | Pervade | Pibroch | Pimenta | Pitying | Pliskie |
| Pentone | Pervert | Picador | Pimento | Pivotal | Plodder |
| Peonage | Peshito | Picamar | Pimping | Pivoted | Plotful |
| Peonism | Peskily | Piccage | Pimpled | Pixy-led | Plotter |
| Peotomy | Pesters | Piccolo | Pin-case | Placard | Plottie |
| Peperin | Pestled | Piceous | Pincers | Placate | Plouter |
| Peppery | Petasus | Pickaxe | Pincher | Placebo | Plucker |
| Pepsine | Petered | Pickeer | Pinches | Placket | Plugger |
| Peptics | Peterel | Picotee | Pindari | Placoid | Plumage |
| Peptone | Petiole | Picotte | Pineoil | Placula | Plumber |
| Perbend | Petrary | Picquet | Pinetum | Plafond | Plumbic |
| Percale | Petrean | Picrate | Pinfish | Plagium | Plumbum |
| Percase | Petrify | Picrine | Pinfold | Plaided | Plumcot |
| Percept | Petrine | Picrite | Pingaid | Plainly | Plumery |
| Percher | Petrous | Pictish | Pinguin | Plaiter | Plumist |
| Percine | Pettily | Pict·ure | Pinhold | Planary | Plummer |
| Percoct | Pettish | Piddock | Pinhole | Planish | Plummet |
| Percoid | Petunia | Piebald | Pinkeye | Planked | Plumose |

SEVEN LETTER WORDS—*continued*

| | | | | | |
|---|---|---|---|---|---|
| Plumous | Pompelo | Potargo | Prejink | Privily | Protend |
| Plumped | Pompion | Potassa | Prelacy | Privity | Protest |
| Plumper | Pompire | Potator | Prelate | Prizage | Proteus |
| Plumply | Pomposo | Potelot | Prelect | Probang | Protyle |
| Plumula | Pompous | Potence | Prelude | Probate | Prouder |
| Plumule | Ponceau | Potency | Premial | Probity | Proudly |
| Plunder | Pondage | Potheen | Premier | Problem | Provand |
| Plunger | Poniard | Pot-herb | Premise | Proceed | Provant |
| Plunket | Pontage | Pothead | Premiss | Process | Provend |
| Plurisy | Pontiff | Pot-hole | Premium | Proctor | **Proving** |
| Pluvial | Pontile | Pothook | Prender | Procure | Proverb |
| Plywood | Pontine | Potiche | Preoral | Procyon | Provide |
| Poaceae | Pontoòn | Pot-luck | Prepaid | Prodigy | Provine |
| Poacher | Popcorn | Potoroo | Prepare | Produce | Proviso |
| Pochard | Popedom | Potshop | Presage | Product | Provoke |
| Pockpit | Popeyes | Pot-shot | Present | Proface | Provost |
| Podagra | Poppied | Pottage | Preside | Profane | Prowess |
| Podesta | Popping | Pottery | Presser | Profess | Prowest |
| Poditic | Poppled | Potting | Prester | Proffer | Prowler |
| Podrida | Popshot | Pouched | Presume | Profile | Proxime |
| Poe-bird | Popular | Poulard | Pretend | Profuse | Proximo |
| Poetess | Popweed | Poulter | Pretext | Progeny | Prudent |
| Poetics | Porcate | Poultry | Pretone | Program | Prudery |
| Poetise | Porcine | Pounced | Pretzel | Project | Prudish |
| Poetize | Porifer | Poundal | Prevail | Prolate | Pruning |
| Pointed | Porkpie | Pounder | Prevene | Prolegs | Prurigo |
| Pointel | Porosis | Poverty | Prevent | Prolong | Prussic |
| Pointer | Porotic | Powdery | Previse | Promise | Prythee |
| Poising | Porpess | Powered | Prewarn | Promote | Psalter |
| Poitrel | Porrect | Poynant | Preyful | Pronaos | Pschent |
| Polacca | Porrigo | Practic | Preying | Pronate | Psoatic |
| Pole-axe | Portage | Praetor | Priapic | Pronely | Psychal |
| Polecat | Port-bar | Prairie | Priapus | Pronged | Psychic |
| Polemic | Portend | Praiser | Pricker | Pronota | Ptarmic |
| Polenta | Portent | Praisine | Pricket | Pronoun | Pterion |
| Policed | Portico | Prakrit | Prickle | Prootic | Pteroma |
| Politic | Portify | Praline | Prickly | Propale | Pterope |
| Pollard | Portion | Pranker | Pridian | Propend | Ptomain |
| Poll-axe | Portman | Prating | Prigger | Prophet | Ptyalin |
| Pollack | Portray | Prattle | Primacy | Propine | Puberal |
| Pollent | Porzana | Pravity | Primage | Propose | Puberty |
| Poll-man | Posaune | Praying | Primary | Propugn | Publish |
| Pollock | Posited | Preachy | Primate | Prorate | Pucelle |
| Poll-tax | Possess | Prebend | Primely | Prorsad | Puceron |
| Pollute | Postage | Precede | Primero | Prorsal | Puckery |
| Poloist | Post-bag | Precept | Primine | Prosaic | Puckish |
| Polyact | Postboy | Precipe | Priming | Prosect | Pudding |
| Polygon | Post-day | Precise | Primmed | Prosify | Puddler |
| Polygyn | Posteen | Predate | Primsie | Prosily | Puddock |
| Polyopy | Postern | Predial | Primula | Prosing | Pudency |
| Polypus | Postfix | Predict | Princox | Prosody | Pudenda |
| Polyzoa | Posting | Predone | Prinker | Prosoma | Pudical |
| Pomatum | Postman | Predoom | Printer | Prosper | Pueblan |
| Pomeloe | Posture | Pre-empt | Prisage | Protean | Puerile |
| Pomeroy | Post-war | Preface | Pristis | Protect | Puff-box |
| Pomfret | Potable | Prefect | Prithee | Protégé | Puffery |
| Pommage | Potager | Prefine | Privacy | Proteid | Puffily |
| Pommard | Potance | Preform | Private | Protein | Puffing |

## SEVEN LETTER WORDS—*continued*

| | | | | | |
|---|---|---|---|---|---|
| Pugaree | Pygopus | Quetzal | Radicel | Rancour | Reality |
| Puggery | Pyjamas | Quibble | Radicle | Rangers | Realize |
| Pugging | Pyloric | Quicken | Radious | Ranidae | Reannex |
| Puggree | Pylorus | Quickly | Radular | Ransack | Reapman |
| Pug-mill | Pynkado | Quiddit | Raffish | Rantock | Reapply |
| Pug-nose | Pyramid | Quiddle | Raffler | Ranular | Reargue |
| Pullman | Pyretic | Quiesce | Raffled | Rapeful | Rearise |
| Pulpify | Pyrexia | Quieten | Raftdog | Rapeoil | Réaumur |
| Pulpous | Pyrexic | Quieter | Rafting | Rapidly | Reawake |
| Pulsate | Pyrites | Quietly | Rag-bolt | Raploch | Rebelly |
| Pulsion | Pyritic | Quietus | Rag-bush | Rapping | Rebirth |
| Pulture | Pyrogen | Quilled | Rag-dust | Rapport | Rebloom |
| Pummace | Pyrosis | Quillet | Rageful | Rapture | Reboant |
| Pumpage | Pyrotic | Quillon | Rag-fair | Rarebit | Rebound |
| Pumpion | Pyrrhic | Quilted | Raggery | Rasores | Rebrace |
| Pumpkin | Pythiad | Quilter | Ragshop | Rastrum | Rebuild |
| Pumprod | Pythian | Quinary | Ragtime | Ratable | Rebuker |
| Puncher | Pyxidia | Quinate | Raguled | Ratably | Reburse |
| Punctum | | Quinine | Ragweed | Ratafia | Recarry |
| Pungent | | Quinnat | Ragwool | Rat-a-tat | Receipt |
| Punjabi | **Q** | Quinone | Ragwork | Ratchel | Receive |
| Punnage | Qua-bird | Quintad | Ragwort | Ratchet | Recency |
| Punster | Quackle | Quintal | Rail-car | Ratchil | Recheat |
| Puntgun | Quadrat | Quintan | Railing | Rathole | Recital |
| Puranic | Quadrel | Quintet | Railsaw | Ratitae | Reciter |
| Purflew | Quadric | Quintic | Railway | Ratline | Reclaim |
| Purging | Quaffer | Quintin | Raiment | Ratling | Réclame |
| Puritan | Quahaug | Quittal | Rainbow | Rat-tail | Reclasp |
| Purlieu | Quakery | Quitter | Rain-map | Ratteen | Recline |
| Purline | Qualify | Quizzer | Raising | Rattery | Reclose |
| Purling | Quality | Quodlin | Rajpoot | Ratting | Recluse |
| Purloin | Quamash | Quondam | Rakshas | Rattler | Recoast |
| Purples | Quannet | Quoniam | Rallier | Rat-trap | Recount |
| Purport | Quantic | Quotity | Ralline | Raucity | Recoupé |
| Purpose | Quantum | | Ramadan | Raucous | Recoure |
| Purpura | Quarrel | | Ramazan | Ravager | Recover |
| Purpure | Quartan | **R** | Rambade | Ravelin | Recross |
| Purrock | Quarter | Rabanna | Rambler | Ravener | Recruit |
| Pursuer | Quartet | Rabbler | Ramekin | Ravined | Rectify |
| Pursuit | Quartic | Rabboni | Ramenta | Rawbone | Rection |
| Purveys | Quartzy | Rabidly | Rameous | Rawcold | Rectory |
| Purview | Quashee | Rabific | Ram-head | Rawhead | Rectrix |
| Pushful | Quashey | Rabinet | Ramilie | Rawhide | Recurve |
| Pushing | Quassia | Rabious | Ramline | Rawness | Red-bird |
| Pushpin | Quatern | Raccoon | Rammish | Rawport | Red-book |
| Pushtoo | Quavery | Racecup | Rampage | Rayless | Redcent |
| Pustule | Quayage | Racemed | Rampant | Rayonée | Redclay |
| Putamen | Queachy | Racemic | Rampart | Reacher | Red-coat |
| Putrefy | Queenly | Raceway | Rampick | Readily | Redcock |
| Puttier | Queerly | Rackety | Rampier | Reading | Redcrag |
| Putting | Queller | Racking | Rampike | Readmit | Red-deer |
| Puttock | Quercus | Racquet | Rampion | Readopt | Redding |
| Puzzler | Querela | Raddock | Rampler | Readorn | Reddish |
| Pyaemia | Querent | Radiale | Ramskin | Reagent | Red-drum |
| Pyaemic | Querist | Radiant | Ramsons | Realgar | Red-fish |
| Pycnite | Quernal | Radiata | Ramstam | Realise | Red-hand |
| Pyebald | Quester | Radiate | Ramulus | Realism | Red-head |
| Pygmean | Questor | Radical | Rancher | Realist | Red-lead |

SEVEN LETTER WORDS—*continued*

| | | | | | |
|---|---|---|---|---|---|
| Red-legs | Regrade | Replant | Restore | Rhamnus | Ringman |
| Redness | Regraft | Replead | Resurge | Rhatany | Ringnet |
| Red-nose | Regrant | Replete | Retable | Rhemish | Ringsaw |
| Redoubt | Regrate | Replevy | Retaker | Rhenish | Riolite |
| Redound | Regrede | Replica | Retiary | Rhesian | Rioting |
| Redpoll | Regreet | Replier | Reticle | Rhizina | Riotise |
| Redorse | Regress | Replume | Retinal | Rhizine | Riotous |
| Redraft | Regular | Repoint | Retinol | Rhizoid | Ripieno |
| Redress | Regulus | Reposal | Retinue | Rhizoma | Riposte |
| Redrive | Rehouse | Reposer | Retiped | Rhizome | Ripping |
| Red-root | Reinter | Reposit | Retiral | Rhizota | Rippler |
| Redsear | Reissue | Repress | Retired | Rhizote | Ripplet |
| Red-seed | Rejoice | Reprief | Retouch | Rhodeus | Rippock |
| Redskin | Rejoint | Reprint | Retourn | Rhodian | Ripsack |
| Red-tail | Rejourn | Reprise | Retrace | Rhodium | Risberm |
| Red-tape | Rejudge | Reprive | Retract | Rhodope | Risible |
| Reducer | Relabel | Reproof | Retrait | Rhodora | Risibly |
| Redweed | Relapse | Reprove | Retrate | Rhombic | Risotto |
| Redwing | Related | Reprune | Retread | Rhombus | Rissole |
| Redwood | Relater | Reptant | Retreat | Rhubarb | Ristori |
| Re-edify | Relator | Reptile | Retrial | Rhymist | Rittock |
| Reeding | Release | Repulse | Retrude | Rhyncho | Rivalry |
| Reefing | Reliant | Repurge | Retruse | Rhyphus | Riveret |
| Re-elect | Relieve | Requere | Rettery | Rhytina | Riveter |
| Reeming | Relievo | Request | Retting | Rib-band | Rivière |
| Re-enact | Relight | Requiem | Reunify | Ribbing | Rivulet |
| Re-endow | Relique | Require | Reunion | Ribless | Rizomed |
| Re-enjoy | Remanet | Requite | Reunite | Riblike | Roadbed |
| Re-enter | Remarry | Reredos | Reutter | Ricasso | Roadcar |
| Re-entry | Remblai | Rescind | Revalue | Ricehen | Road-hog |
| Re-erect | Remeant | Re-score | Revelry | Richest | Roading |
| Re-expel | Remercy | Rescuer | Revenge | Ricinus | Roadman |
| Refeoff | Remerge | Reseize | Revenue | Rickers | Road-map |
| Referee | Remiges | Reserve | Reverer | Rickets | Roadway |
| Refined | Remigia | Reshape | Reverie | Rickety | Roaring |
| Refiner | Remiped | Resiant | Reverse | Ricksha | Roaster |
| Reflame | Remnant | Resider | Reversi | Ridable | Robbery |
| Reflect | Remodel | Residue | Reverso | Riddler | Robinet |
| Refloat | Remorse | Resolve | Revestu | Ridered | Robinia |
| Reforge | Remould | Resound | Reviler | Ridotto | Rockcam |
| Re-found | Remount | Respeak | Revince | Riffler | Rock-doe |
| Refract | Removal | Respect | Revisal | Rigging | Rock-eel |
| Refrain | Removed | Respell | Reviser | Riggish | Rock-elm |
| Reframe | Remover | Respire | Revisit | Riggite | Rockery |
| Refresh | Remphan | Respite | Revisor | Righten | Rockily |
| Refugee | Reneger | Resplit | Revival | Righter | Rock-oil |
| Refusal | Renerve | Respond | Reviver | Rightly | Rock-tar |
| Refuser | Renewal | Ressaut | Revivor | Rigidly | Rodlike |
| Refuter | Renewer | Restamp | Revolve | Rigsdag | Rodline |
| Regalia | Rent-day | Restant | Revomit | Rig-veda | Rodomel |
| Regally | Rentier | Restate | Rewaken | Riksdag | Rodring |
| Regatta | Renuent | Restaur | Reweigh | Rilievo | Rodster |
| Regence | Reorder | Rest-day | Rewrite | Rimbase | Roebuck |
| Regency | Repaint | Restful | Reynard | Rimfire | Roedeer |
| Regible | Repiner | Restiff | Rhabdom | Rimless | Roguery |
| Regimen | Repique | Restily | Rhabdus | Ringdog | Roguish |
| Regnant | Replace | Restive | Rhaetic | Ringent | Roinish |
| Regorge | Replait | Restock | Rhagose | Ringlet | Roinous |

SEVEN-LETTER WORDS—*continued*

| | | | | |
|---|---|---|---|---|
| Roister | Rotator | Ruddily | Saccade | Saltire | Sarasin |
| Rokeage | Rotchie | Ruddock | Saccata | Saltish | Sarcasm |
| Rokelay | Rotchet | Ruderal | Saccate | Salt-pan | Sarcelé |
| Rollick | Rotella | Rudesby | Saccule | Salt-pit | Sarcina |
| Rollock | Rotifer | Ruewort | Sackage | Saluter | Sarcine |
| Rollway | Rotonde | Ruellia | Sackbut | Salvage | Sarcode |
| Romaika | Rottolo | Ruffian | Sackful | Salving | Sarcoid |
| Romalea | Rotular | Ruffler | Sacking | Sambhar | Sarcoma |
| Romance | Rotunda | Rugging | Sacodes | Sambhur | Sarcous |
| Romanic | Rotundo | Ruinate | Sacrary | Sambuca | Sardine |
| Romaunt | Rouched | Ruinous | Sacrate | Sambuke | Sardius |
| Romeine | Rouerie | Rulable | Sacring | Samiote | Sargina |
| Rommany | Rouelle | Rullion | Sacrist | Samisen | Sarigue |
| Rompers | Roughen | Rumbler | Saddler | Samnite | Sarking |
| Rompish | Rougher | Ruminal | Sad-eyed | Samolus | Sarment |
| Ronchil | Roughie | Rummage | Sadiron | Samovar | Sarplar |
| Rondeau | Roughly | Rummily | Sadness | Samoyed | Sarpler |
| Rondure | Roulade | Rumness | Sadtree | Sampler | Sarsnet |
| Rongeur | Rouleau | Rump-fed | Saffian | Samshoo | Sartage |
| Ronquil | Roundel | Rumpost | Saffron | Samurai | Sashery |
| Roofing | Rounder | Rumshop | Sagaman | Sanable | Sassaby |
| Rooflet | Roundly | Runaway | Sagathy | Sanctum | Satanic |
| Rookery | Round-up | Rundale | Sagesse | Sanctus | Satchel |
| Rook-pie | Rousant | Rundled | Saggard | Sandbag | Satiate |
| Roomage | Rousing | Rundlet | Sagitta | Sand-bed | Satiety |
| Roomful | Rouster | Running | Sagouin | Sand-box | Satinet |
| Roomily | Routhie | Ruptile | Saguaro | Sand-boy | Satiric |
| Rooster | Routier | Ruption | Sahlite | Sand-bug | Satisfy |
| Rootage | Routine | Ruptive | Sailing | Sand-bur | Satrapy |
| Rootcap | Routish | Rupture | Saimiri | Sand-dab | Satsuma |
| Rootery | Routous | Rurally | Sainted | Sand-eel | Sattara |
| Rootlet | Rowable | Rusalka | Saintly | Sanders | Satteen |
| Ropalic | Rowboat | Rush-mat | Sairing | Sand-fly | Satyral |
| Ropeway | Rowdily | Rush-nut | Saivism | Sanding | Satyric |
| Rorqual | Rowlock | Russety | Salable | Sandish | Satyrus |
| Rosalia | Rowport | Russian | Salably | Sand-jet | Saucily |
| Rosated | Royalet | Russify | Salamba | Sand-lob | Saunter |
| Roseate | Royally | Russula | Salamis | Sand-pit | Saurian |
| Rosebay | Royalty | Rustful | Saliant | Sand-rat | Sauroid |
| Rosebit | Roynish | Rustily | Salicin | Sangsue | Sausage |
| Rosebox | Roytish | Rustred | Salient | Sanhita | Sautoir |
| Rosebud | Rozelle | Rustler | Saliere | Sanicle | Savable |
| Rose-bug | Rub-a-dub | Ruthful | Saligot | Sanious | Savanna |
| Rosecut | Rubasse | Ruttish | Salique | Sankhya | Save all |
| Rosehaw | Rubbing | Rye-moth | Salival | Sapajou | Saveloy |
| Rosehip | Rubbish | Rye-wolf | Sallowy | Saperda | Savings |
| Roselet | Rubella | Rye-worm | Salmiac | Sap-head | Saviour |
| Rosella | Rubeola | Ryotwar | Salpian | Sapient | Savoury |
| Roselle | Rubiate | | Salpinx | Sapless | Saw-back |
| Roseola | Rubican | | Salsafy | Sapling | Sawbill |
| Rosered | Rubicel | | Salsify | Saponin | Sawdust |
| Rosette | Rubicon | **S** | Salsola | Sapphic | Sawfile |
| Rosland | Rubific | | Saltant | Sapples | Sawfish |
| Rosolio | Rubiron | Sabaism | Saltate | Sapsago | Sawhorn |
| Rostral | Rubious | Sabaoth | Salt-box | Sap-tube | Sawmill |
| Rostrum | Ruching | Sabbath | Salt-cat | Sapwood | Saw-whet |
| Rosular | Ruction | Sabeism | Saltern | Saracen | Saw-wort |
| Rotalia | Ruddied | Sabella | Saltier | Sarafan | Saxhorn |
| | | Saburra | | | |

SEVEN-LETTER WORDS—*continued*

| | | | | | |
|---|---|---|---|---|---|
| Saxonic | Science | Scrubby | Sea-gown | Sea-wing | Semi-ape |
| Sayette | Sciolto | Scrudge | Seagull | Sea-wold | Semi-god |
| Scabbed | Scirpus | Scruffy | Sea-haar | Sea-wolf | Semilor |
| Scabble | Scissel | Scrunch | Sea-hall | Sea-worm | Seminal |
| Scabies | Scissil | Scruple | Sea-hare | Sebacic | Seminar |
| Scabrid | Scissor | Scudder | Sea-hawk | Sebilla | Semiped |
| Scaddle | Sciurus | Scuddle | Sea-holm | Sebundy | Semital |
| Scaglia | Scleral | Scudler | Seakale | Secancy | Semitic |
| Scalade | Scleria | Scuffle | Sea-king | Seceder | Semoted |
| Scalado | Scobina | Sculler | Sea-lace | Sechium | Senator |
| Scalary | Scoffer | Sculpin | Sea-lark | Seclude | Sencion |
| Scalder | Scolder | Scumber | Sea-legs | Secondo | Send-off |
| Scaldic | Scolite | Scumble | Sealery | Secrecy | Senecio |
| Scalene | Scollop | Scummer | Sea-like | Secrete | Senegal |
| Scaling | Scomber | Scunner | Sea-lily | Sectant | Seniory |
| Scalled | Scooner | Scupper | Sea-line | Sectary | Sensate |
| Scallop | Scooper | Scuppet | Sea-lion | Sectile | Sensile |
| Scalops | Scooter | Scurril | Sea-luce | Section | Sension |
| Scalpel | Scoppet | Scurrit | Sea-maid | Sectist | Sensism |
| Scalper | Scoptic | Scutage | Sea-mall | Sective | Sensist |
| Scamble | Scoriae | Scutate | Seamark | Secular | Sensory |
| Scammel | Scorify | Scutter | Sea-mile | Securer | Sensual |
| Scammum | Scorner | Scuttle | Sea-mink | Sedilia | Sentine |
| Scamper | Scorper | Scymnus | Sea-monk | Seducer | Sepiary |
| Scandal | Scorpio | Scyphus | Seamset | Seeable | Sepioid |
| Scandix | Scotice | Scytale | Sea-moss | See-cawk | Sepiost |
| Scantle | Scotism | Scythed | Sea-ooze | Seed-bag | Seppuku |
| Scantly | Scotist | Scythic | Sea-pass | Seedbed | Septate |
| Scapnet | Scotoma | Sea-bank | Sea-pear | Seedbud | Septime |
| Scapple | Scotomy | Sea-bass | Sea-peck | Seed-cod | Septole |
| Scapula | Scourer | Sea-beam | Sea-pert | Seedful | Sequela |
| Scarify | Scourge | Sea-bear | Sea-pike | Seedily | Sequent |
| Scarlet | Scourse | Sea-beat | Sea-pink | Seed-lac | Sequoia |
| Scathed | Scouter | Sea-beet | Sea-pork | Seed-lop | Serapis |
| Scatter | Scraggy | Sea-belt | Seaport | Seed-oil | Serbian |
| Scauper | Scraich | Seabird | Sea-reed | Seeming | Serenoa |
| Scavage | Scraigh | Sea-boat | Sea-risk | Seepage | Serfage |
| Scenery | Scranch | Sea-born | Sea-roll | Seether | Serfdom |
| Scepsis | Scranky | Sea-calf | Sea-room | Segment | Seriate |
| Sceptic | Scranny | Sea-card | Sea-rose | Seggrom | Sericin |
| Sceptre | Scraper | Sea-clam | Sea-ruff | Seismal | Sericon |
| Sceptry | Scrappy | Sea-coal | Sea-salt | Seismic | Seriema |
| Schappe | Scratch | Sea-cock | Sea-sick | Seisura | Seringa |
| Schelly | Scrawly | Sea-cook | Seaside | Seiurus | Serinus |
| Schemer | Scrawny | Sea-coot | Sea-slug | Seizing | Seriola |
| Schepen | Screech | Sea-corn | Sea-tang | Seizure | Serious |
| Scherif | Screeve | Sea-crab | Seating | Sejeant | Serpent |
| Scherzo | Screwer | Sea-crow | Sea-toad | Selache | Serpigo |
| Schesis | Scribal | Sea-dace | Sea-tost | Selenic | Serpula |
| Schetic | Scrieve | Sea-dove | Sea-turn | Self-fed | Serrate |
| Schinus | Scrimer | Sea-duck | Sea-view | Selfish | Serried |
| Schisma | Scrimpy | Sea-fire | Sea-wall | Selfism | Serrous |
| Schlich | Scringe | Sea-fish | Sea-wane | Selfist | Servage |
| Schnaps | Scritch | Sea-foam | Sea-ware | Selinium | Servant |
| Scholar | Scroggy | Sea-folk | Seaward | Seltzer | Servian |
| Schorly | Scrooge | Sea-fowl | Sea-weed | Selvage | Service |
| Sciatic | Scrouge | Sea-gage | Sea-whip | Sematic | Servile |
| Scibile | Scroyle | Sea-girt | Sea-wife | Semeion | Servite |

### SEVEN-LETTER WORDS—*continued*

| | | | | | |
|---|---|---|---|---|---|
| Sesamum | Shearer | Showily | Silkman | Sjambok | Skeekly |
| Sessile | Sheathe | Showman | Sillago | Skaddle | Sleeper |
| Session | Sheathy | Shreddy | Sillery | Skating | Sleight |
| Sestina | Sheaved | Shrieve | Sillily | Skeeter | Slender |
| Sestine | She-bang | Shright | Silurus | Skelder | Slicker |
| Sestole | Shebeen | Shrilly | Silvern | Skellum | Slidder |
| Setaria | Shedder | Shrinal | Silvery | Skelter | Sliding |
| Set-back | Shellac | Shrivel | Simarre | Skepful | Slighty |
| Set-down | Sheller | Shriver | Similar | Skeptic | Slimily |
| Settima | Shelter | Shrouds | Similia | Skepsis | Sliness |
| Settimo | Sheltie | Shroudy | Similor | Sketchy | Slinger |
| Setting | Sheppey | Shrubby | Simious | Skewgee | Slipper |
| Settler | Sherbet | Shucker | Simitar | Skidder | Slipway |
| Set-wall | Shereef | Shudder | Simpkin | Skilful | Slither |
| Set-work | Sheriff | Shuffle | Simpler | Skilled | Slitter |
| Seventh | Sherris | Shunner | Simpson | Skillet | Slobber |
| Seventy | Shifter | Shunter | Simular | Skimmer | Slocken |
| Several | Shiitic | Shutter | Simurgh | Skinful | Slogger |
| Sex-foil | Shikari | Shuttle | Sinapin | Skinker | Slombry |
| Sexless | Shilpit | Shyness | Sinapis | Skinner | Slotter |
| Sextain | Shimmer | Shyster | Sin-born | Skipper | Slouchy |
| Sextans | Shingle | Sialoid | Sin-bred | Skippet | Sloughy |
| Sextant | Shingly | Siamang | Sincere | Skirret | Slovaks |
| Sextile | Shipboy | Siamese | Sinewed | Skirter | Slubber |
| Shackle | Shipful | Siccate | Singing | Skitter | Sludger |
| Shadfly | Shipman | Siccity | Singles | Skittle | Slumber |
| Shadily | Shippen | Sick-bay | Singlet | Skiving | Slummer |
| Shadine | Shipper | Sick-bed | Sin-gult | Skolion | Slunken |
| Shading | Shipway | Sickish | Sinical | Skulker | Slurred |
| Shadoof | Shippon | Sickled | Sinless | Skulpin | Slyness |
| Shadowy | Shipton | Sic-like | Sinoper | Sky-blue | Smacker |
| Shafted | Shirker | Side-arm | Sinopia | Sky-born | Smaragd |
| Shagged | Shiness | Sidebox | Sinopis | Sky-high | Smarten |
| Shaheen | Shirley | Sidecar | Sinople | Skylark | Smartly |
| Shaitan | Shirred | Sidecut | Sin-sick | Skyline | Smasher |
| Shakily | Shittah | Sideral | Sinsyne | Skysail | Smash-up |
| Shallon | Shittim | Side-rod | Sinuate | Skyward | Smatter |
| Shallop | Shivery | Sienese | Sinuose | Slabber | Smeddum |
| Shallot | Shizoku | Sienite | Sinuous | Slacken | Smeller |
| Shallow | Shoaler | Sifflet | Sin-worn | Slacker | Smelter |
| Shamble | Shocker | Sighful | Siredon | Slackly | Smerlin |
| Shammer | Shoeboy | Sightly | Sirenian | Slainte | Smicker |
| Shampoo | Shoepeg | Sigmate | Sirgang | Slamkin | Smickly |
| Shandry | Shoe-tie | Sigmoid | Sirloin | Slander | Smicket |
| Shangie | Shooter | Signate | Sirname | Slanket | Smidgen |
| Shangti | Shopboy | Signify | Sirocco | Slantly | Smiling |
| Shanked | Shopman | Signior | Sistine | Slapper | Smittle |
| Shanker | Shorage | Signora | Sistrum | Slasher | Smokily |
| Shapely | Shoring | Signory | Sitfast | Slather | Smoking |
| Sharded | Shorten | Sikhism | Sithens | Slating | Smolder |
| Sharker | Shortly | Silence | Sittine | Slatter | Smoothe |
| Sharpen | Shotgun | Silenus | Situate | Slavdom | Smother |
| Sharper | Shotted | Silesia | Sivaite | Slavery | Smudger |
| Sharpie | Shotten | Silicic | Sixfold | Slavish | Smuggle |
| Sharply | Shouter | Silicle | Sixteen | Sledded | Smytrie |
| Shaster | Show-box | Silicon | Sixthly | Sleeken | Snabble |
| Shastra | Showend | Siliqua | Sixtine | Sleeker | Snaffle |
| Shatter | Showery | Silique | Sizable | Sleekit | Snagged |

SEVEN-LETTER WORDS—*continued*

| | | | | | |
|---|---|---|---|---|---|
| Snagger | Soldado | Souffle | Sperket | Sponson | Stachys |
| Snakish | Soldier | Soulful | Spermic | Sponsor | Staddle |
| Snapper | Solicit | Sounder | Sphenic | Spooney | Stadium |
| Snarler | Solidly | Soundly | Spheral | Spoorer | Stagery |
| Snatchy | Solidum | Soupçon | Spheric | Sporoid | Stagger |
| Sneaker | Solidus | Souring | Sphyrna | Sporous | Staidly |
| Sneck-up | Soliped | Sourish | Spicate | Sporran | Stainer |
| Snedden | Soloist | Sourock | Spicery | Sporter | Staithe |
| Sneerer | Solomon | Soursop | Spicily | Sporule | Stalder |
| Snicker | Solonic | Soutane | Spicous | Spotted | Stalely |
| Sniffle | Solpuga | Souther | Spicose | Spotter | Stalker |
| Snifter | Soluble | Southly | Spicula | Spousal | Stalled |
| Snigger | Solvend | Sowback | Spicule | Spouter | Stamina |
| Sniggle | Solvent | Spacial | Spidery | Spraich | Stammel |
| Sniping | Somatic | Spaddle | Spignel | Spraint | Stammer |
| Snipper | Somehow | Spadone | Spiller | Sprayey | Stamnos |
| Snippet | Someone | Spaeman | Spiling | Spreagh | Stamper |
| Snirtle | Somital | Spairge | Spiloma | Spriggy | Standel |
| Snooded | Somitic | Spaling | Spinach | Spright | Stander |
| Snooker | Somnial | Spancel | Spinage | Springe | Stand-up |
| Snoozer | Sonance | Spangle | Spinate | Springy | Staniel |
| Snoring | Sonancy | Spangly | Spindle | Sprunny | Stannel |
| Snorter | Sonchus | Spaniel | Spindly | Spulzie | Stannic |
| Snotter | Sondeli | Spanish | Spinner | Spulyie | Stannum |
| Snouted | Songful | Spanker | Spinney | Spumous | Stanyel |
| Snow-box | Songman | Spanner | Spinode | Spun-hay | Stapler |
| Snow-fed | Sonless | Span-new | Spinose | Spun-out | Starchy |
| Snow-fly | Sonnite | Sparely | Spinous | Spur-dog | Starken |
| Snow-ice | Sonship | Sparing | Spinula | Spuriae | Starkly |
| Snowing | Soother | Sparger | Spinule | Spurner | Starlit |
| Snowily | Soothly | Sparkle | Spiraea | Spurrer | Starter |
| Snowish | Sootish | Sparrer | Spirant | Spurrey | Startle |
| Snow-man | Sophism | Sparrow | Spirity | Spurtle | Start-up |
| Snow-owl | Sophist | Spartan | Spirket | Spur-way | Statant |
| Snuffer | Sophora | Spastic | Spirtle | Sputter | Stately |
| Snuffle | Sopient | Spathed | Spirula | Spy-boat | Statice |
| Snuggle | Soprano | Spathic | Spitbox | Spyhole | Statics |
| Snugify | Sorbate | Spatial | Spitted | Squabby | Station |
| Snuzzle | Sorbent | Spatter | Spitter | Squacco | Statism |
| Soakage | Sorbian | Spattle | Spittle | Squaddy | Statist |
| Soaking | Sorbine | Spatula | Spizine | Squails | Stative |
| Soap-pan | Sorbite | Spatule | Splashy | Squalid | Statued |
| Soarant | Sorbish | Spawner | Spleeny | Squally | Stature |
| Soaring | Sorcery | Speaker | Spleget | Squalor | Statute |
| Sobbing | Sordine | Special | Splenic | Squalus | Staunch |
| Soberly | Sordono | Species | Splodge | Squarer | Stealer |
| Soboles | Sorehon | Specify | Splodgy | Squashy | Stealth |
| Socager | Sorghum | Speckle | Splotch | Squatty | Steamer |
| Soccage | Sorites | Spectra | Splurge | Squeasy | Stearic |
| Society | Sororal | Spectre | Splurgy | Squeeze | Stearin |
| Sockeye | Sorosis | Speeder | Spodium | Squelch | Steepen |
| Sofa-bed | Sorrily | Spelean | Spoffle | Squiffy | Steeper |
| Softish | Sospiro | Spelder | Spoiler | Squinch | Steeple |
| Soilcap | Sostrum | Speller | Spolium | Squinny | Steeply |
| Soilure | Sotadic | Spelter | Spondee | Squitch | Steerer |
| Sojourn | Sottish | Spencer | Spondyl | Sraddha | Stelene |
| Sokeman | Soubise | Spender | Sponger | Stabber | Stellar |
| Solanum | Souchet | Sperate | Sponsal | Stabler | Stelled |

## SEVEN-LETTER WORDS—*continued*

| | | | | | |
|---|---|---|---|---|---|
| Stelths | Stormer | Suasion | Sugared | Sursize | Synacmy |
| Stemlet | Stotter | Suasive | Suggest | Surtout | Synapte |
| Stempel | Stouten | Suasory | Suicide | Surview | Synaxis |
| Stemple | Stoutly | Suavely | Suicism | Survive | Syncope |
| Stemson | Stowage | Suavity | Suiform | Suspect | Synergy |
| Stenchy | Straiks | Subacid | Suiting | Suspend | Synesis |
| Stencil | Straint | Subadar | Sulcate | Suspire | Synocil |
| Stentor | Strange | Subbing | Sulkily | Sustain | Synodal |
| Stepney | Stratum | Sub-bass | Sullage | Sutlery | Synodic |
| Stepper | Stratus | Subdean | Sullens | Sutling | Synonym |
| Stepson | Strayer | Subdual | Sulphur | Sutural | Synotus |
| Sterile | Strayne | Subduce | Sultana | Sutured | Synovia |
| Sterlet | Streaky | Subduct | Sumless | Swabber | Syntony |
| Sternal | Streamy | Subdued | Summary | Swaddle | Syringa |
| Sternly | Stretch | Subduer | Summist | Swagger | Syringe |
| Sternum | Stretto | Subedar | Summons | Swagman | Systole |
| Sterven | Striate | Subedit | Sumpter | Swahili | Systyle |
| Steward | Stridor | Suberic | Sun-bath | Swallet | **T** |
| Stewish | Striges | Subfusc | Sunbeam | Swallow | Tabanus |
| Stew-pan | Strigil | Subfusk | Sunbeat | Swankie | Tabaret |
| Stewpot | Striker | Subgens | Sunbird | Swanpan | Tabella |
| Sthenia | Stringy | Subject | Sunburn | Swarded | Tabetic |
| Sthenic | Striped | Subjoin | Sunclad | Swarthy | Tabidly |
| Stibial | Striver | Sublate | Sundari | Swasher | Tabific |
| Stibium | Strobic | Sublime | Sundawn | Swatter | Tabinet |
| Stichic | Strocal | Submiss | Sundial | Swearer | Tableau |
| Stichos | Stroker | Subnude | Sundown | Sweater | Tabling |
| Sticker | Stroken | Suboval | Sunfish | Swedish | Tabloid |
| Stickle | Strophe | Subpena | Sunless | Sweeper | Taborer |
| Stiffen | Stubbed | Subrent | Sunlike | Sweeten | Taboret |
| Stiffly | Stubble | Subsalt | Sunmyth | Sweetly | Tabrere |
| Stiller | Stubbly | Subside | Sunnite | Swellet | Tabular |
| Stilted | Stuckle | Subsidy | Sunrise | Swelter | Tacitly |
| Stilton | Stuck-up | Subsign | Sunrose | Sweltry | Tackety |
| Stinger | Studdle | Subsist | Sunspot | Swerver | Tactful |
| Stinker | Student | Subsoil | Sunward | Swifter | Tactics |
| Stinter | Studied | Subsume | Sunwise | Swiftly | Tactile |
| Stipend | Studier | Subtack | Suppawn | Swiller | Taction |
| Stipple | Stuffer | Subtend | Support | Swimmer | Tactual |
| Stiptic | Stumble | Subtile | Suppose | Swindge | Tadorna |
| Stipula | Stumbly | Subtype | Supreme | Swindle | Tadpole |
| Stipule | Stummel | Suburbs | Surance | Swinery | Taedium |
| Stirrer | Stumper | Subvene | Surbase | Swingel | Taffeta |
| Stirrup | Stunner | Subvert | Surbate | Swinger | Taffety |
| Stoical | Stunted | Succade | Surcoat | Swingle | Taggers |
| Stomach | Stupefy | Succeed | Surdity | Swinish | Tag-sore |
| Stomata | Stupent | Success | Surface | Swisher | Tag-tail |
| Stonied | Stupose | Succour | Surfeit | Swither | Tailage |
| Stonily | Stuprum | Succula | Surfman | Switzer | Tail-end |
| Stooker | Sturnus | Succumb | Surgent | Swizzle | Tailing |
| Stooper | Stutter | Succuss | Surgeon | Swollen | Tailzie |
| Stooter | Stygian | Suckler | Surgery | Sybotic | Tai-ping |
| Stop-gap | Stylate | Sucrose | Surlily | Sycosis | Take-off |
| Stoping | Stylish | Suction | Surloin | Syenite | Talaria |
| Stopper | Stylist | Sudoral | Surmise | Sylphid | Talaric |
| Stopple | Stylite | Suffete | Surname | Sylvite | Talaunt |
| Storage | Styloid | Suffice | Surpass | Symbion | Talcite |
| Storied | Styptic | Suffuse | Surplus | Symptom | Talcose |

## SEVEN-LETTER WORDS—*continued*

| | | | | | |
|---|---|---|---|---|---|
| Talcous | Tardily | Tensity | Thecate | Tideway | Toddler |
| Taleful | Tarheel | Tensive | Theorbo | Tidings | Toenail |
| Talipat | Tarhood | Tent-fly | Thereat | Tie-beam | Toftman |
| Taliped | Tarnish | Tenthly | Thereby | Tiercel | Togated |
| Talipes | Tarrace | Tentigo | Therein | Tiercet | Toggery |
| Talipot | Tarrier | Tentory | Thereof | Tiffany | Toilful |
| Taliput | Tarrock | Tentpeg | Thereon | Tighten | Tollbar |
| Talkies | Tarsier | Tent-pin | Thereto | Tightly | Toluene |
| Talking | Tartish | Tenuate | Theriac | Tigline | Tomally |
| Tallage | Tartlet | Tenuity | Thermal | Tigress | Tombola |
| Tallboy | Tascall | Tenuous | Thermic | Tigrine | Tomfool |
| Tallier | Tastily | Terbium | Thermit | Tigrish | Tompion |
| Tallish | Tataric | Tercine | Thermos | Tilbury | Tongued |
| Tallith | Tatouay | Terebra | Theroid | Tile-ore | To-night |
| Tallowy | Tatting | Terekia | Thether | Tile-red | Tonnage |
| Tally-ho | Tattled | Tergant | Theurgy | Tillage | Tonneau |
| Taloned | Tattler | Tergite | Thicken | Tilling | Tonsile |
| Tamable | Taunter | Term-fee | Thicket | Tilseed | Tonsure |
| Tamanoa | Taurian | Termite | Thickly | Tilting | Tontine |
| Tamarin | Taurine | Ternary | Thigger | Timbale | Tooling |
| Tamasha | Taxable | Ternery | Thiller | Timbrel | Toothed |
| Tambour | Taxably | Terrace | Thimble | Timeful | Toparch |
| Tamilic | Taxcart | Terrain | Thinker | Time-gun | Top-coat |
| Tammany | Taxicab | Terrene | Thirdly | Timeous | Topfull |
| Tamping | Tea-cake | Terrier | Thirsty | Timidly | Top-hole |
| Tampion | Teacher | Terrify | Thistle | Timothy | Topiary |
| Tamulic | Tearbag | Terrine | Thistly | Timpani | Topical |
| Tanadar | Tearful | Tersely | Thomism | Timpano | Topknot |
| Tanager | Tearing | Tersion | Thomist | Tinamou | Topless |
| Tanagra | Tearose | Tertial | Thorite | Tinchel | Topmast |
| Tangent | Tearpit | Tertian | Thorium | Tindery | Topmost |
| Tanghin | Tea-tree | Tessera | Thought | Tinfoil | Toponym |
| Tangram | Techily | Testacy | Thready | Tinkler | Topping |
| Tankage | Technic | Testate | Threave | Tinning | Topsail |
| Tankard | Tectrix | Testify | Thretty | Tinnock | Topside |
| Tanling | Tedious | Testily | Thristy | Tintage | Topsman |
| Tannage | Teemful | Testing | Thriver | Tinware | Topsoil |
| Tannate | Teeming | Testoon | Throaty | Tip-cart | Torbite |
| Tannery | Tegular | Testril | Through | Tipping | Torchon |
| Tanning | Telamon | Testudo | Thrower | Tippled | Torgoch |
| Tanride | Telesia | Tetanic | Thuggee | Tippler | Torment |
| Tanspud | Telling | Tetanus | Thulite | Tipsily | Tormina |
| Tantara | Telpher | Tetract | Thulium | Tipster | Tornado |
| Tantity | Temenos | Textile | Thumbed | Tirasse | Torpedo |
| Tantivy | Tempean | Textual | Thummim | Titania | Torpent |
| Tantony | Tempera | Texture | Thumper | Titanic | Torpify |
| Tantrum | Tempest | Thalian | Thunder | Tithely | Torqued |
| Tanyard | Templar | Thallic | Thurify | Tithing | Torrefy |
| Tapbolt | Templet | Thallus | Thwaite | Titlark | Torrent |
| Tapered | Tempter | Thalweg | Thyroid | Titling | Torsade |
| Tapetum | Tenable | Thammuz | Thyrsus | Titrate | Torsion |
| Tapioca | Tenancy | Thanage | Thyself | Titular | Torsive |
| Taplash | Tendril | Thannah | Tiaraed | Tituppy | Torsten |
| Tappish | Tenfold | Thapsia | Tibetan | Toaster | Torteau |
| Tap-room | Tenioid | Theatin | Tibicen | Tobacco | Tortile |
| Tap-root | Tenpins | Theatre | Tickler | To-brake | Tortive |
| Tapsman | Tensile | Thebaia | Tiddler | Tobyman | Tortrix |
| Tapster | Tension | Thebain | Tiderip | Toccata | Torture |

SEVEN-LETTER WORDS—*continued*

| | | | | | |
|---|---|---|---|---|---|
| Torulus | Trapeze | Tripsis | Tullian | Twofold | Unbrace |
| Torvous | Trapper | Trireme | Tumbler | Two-line | Unbraid |
| Toryism | Travail | Trisect | Tumbrel | Twoness | Unbrute |
| Tossily | Trawler | Triseme | Tumbril | Twosome | Unbuilt |
| Tosspot | Treacle | Trismus | Tumidly | Two-step | Unburnt |
| Totemic | Treader | Trisular | Tumular | Tylarus | Uncanny |
| Totient | Treadle | Tritely | Tumulus | Tylosis | Uncared |
| Tottery | Treason | Tritoma | Tunable | Tylotic | Unceded |
| Toucher | Treater | Tritone | Tunably | Tympano | Unchain |
| Toughen | Treddle : | Triumph | Tun-dish | Tympany | Uncharm |
| Toughly | Trefoil | Trivial | Tuneful | Typebar | Unchary |
| Touraco | Trehala | Trivium | Tunicle | Typhoon | Unchild |
| Tourist | Trellis | Trochee | Tunnage | Typhord | Uncinal |
| Tourney | Tremble | Trochus | Tunnery | Typhous | Uncinus |
| Tousled | Tremolo | Trodden | Turacin | Typical | Uncivil |
| Towards | Trental | Troggin | Turband | Typonym | Unclasp |
| Towboat | Trepang | Troller | Turbary | Tyranny | Unclean |
| Towered | Trepans | Trolley | Turbine | Tzarina | Unclear |
| Towline | Tressed | Trollop | Turcism | Tzigane | Uncling |
| Townish | Trestle | Trommel | Turfing | Tzigany | Uncloak |
| To-worne | Triable | Trompil | Turfite | **U** | Unclose |
| Towpath | Triatic | Trooper | Turgent | Ukelele | Uncloud |
| Towrope | Tribble | Trophic | Turgite | Ulcered | Uncouth |
| Toxical | Triblet | Tropics | Turkish | Ullaloo | Uncover |
| Toxodon | Tribune | Tropist | Turkois | Ulnaria | Uncrass |
| Toyshop | Tribute | Trotter | Turmoil | Ululant | Uncrown |
| Toysome | Triceps | Trouble | Turncap | Ululate | Unction |
| Toywort | Tricker | Trounce | Turnery | Umbered | Undated |
| Tracery | Trickle | Trousse | Turning | Umbilic | Undeify |
| Trachea | Trickly | Trowing | Turnkey | Umbonal | Undight |
| Trachle | Tricksy | Truancy | Turn-out | Umbrage | Underdo |
| Tracing | Tricorn | Trucker | Turpeth | Umbrian | Undergo |
| Tracker | Trident | Truckle | Turquet | Umbrine | Undoing |
| Tractor | Triduan | Trudgen | Tussock | Umbrose | Undrape |
| Trading | Triduum | Truffle | Tussore | Umpired | Undrawn |
| Traduce | Trifler | Trullan | Tutamen | Umpteen | Undress |
| Traffic | Triform | Trumpet | Tutelar | Umwhile | Undried |
| Tragedy | Trigamy | Truncal | Tutenag | Unacted | Undying |
| Trailer | Trigger | Trundle | Tutored | Unaided | Uneared |
| Trained | Triglot | Trustee | Tutulus | Unaired | Unearth |
| Trainer | Trigram | Truster | Tutwork | Unalist | Uneaten |
| Traipse | Trilabe | Tryable | Twaddle | Unaptly | Unequal |
| Traitor | Trilith | Trypsin | Twangle | Unarmed | Unexact |
| Traject | Trilogy | Tryptic | Twankay | Unasked | Unfaded |
| Tramcar | Trimera | Trysail | Twattle | Unaware | Unfaith |
| Trammel | Trimmer | T-square | Tweedle | Unbaked | Unfence |
| Tramper | Trinary | Tubbing | Twelfth | Unbated | Unfiled |
| Trample | Trindle | Tubfast | Twibill | Unbeget | Unfitly |
| Trampot | Tringle | Tub-fish | Twiddle | Unbegun | Unfixed |
| Tramway | Trinity | Tubicen | Twiggen | Unbess | Unflame |
| Tranced | Trinket | Tubular | Twining | Unblest | Unflesh |
| Tranect | Trinkle | Tuckout | Twinkle | Unblind | Unflush |
| Trangle | Triolet | Tuefall | Twinned | Unblock | Unfound |
| Trankum | Tripery | Tuesday | Twinter | Unblown | Unfrock |
| Trannel | Triplet | Tuesite | Twirler | Unborne | Unfumed |
| Transit | Tripoli | Tugging | Twister | Unbosom | Unfused |
| Transom | Tripoly | Tuition | Twitten | Unbound | Ungiven |
| Tranter | Tripper | Tulchan | Twitter | Unbowed | Unglaze |

### SEVEN-LETTER WORDS—*continued*

| | | | | | |
|---|---|---|---|---|---|
| Unglove | Unorder | Unswear | Uptrain | Vandyke | Ventrad |
| Ungodly | Unowned | Unsweet | Uptrill | Vanessa | Ventral |
| Ungored | Unpaint | Unswept | Upwards | Van-foss | Ventric |
| Ungrate | Unpanel | Unsworn | Upwhirl | Vanilla | Venture |
| Unguent | Unpaved | Untaken | Uraemia | Vanning | Veranda |
| Unhable | Unpenal | Untamed | Uralite | Vansire | Verbena |
| Unhandy | Unperch | Untaxed | Uranite | Vantage | Verbose |
| Unhappy | Unplace | Unthink | Uranium | Vanward | Verdant |
| Unhardy | Unplait | Untiled | Urgency | Vapidly | Verdict |
| Unhasty | Unplant | Untired | Urocyon | Vapoury | Verdure |
| Unheard | Umplumb | Untombs | Urohyal | Vaquero | Vergent |
| Unheart | Unplume | Untooth | Ursinal | Varanus | Veriest |
| Unheedy | Unqueen | Untried | Urtical | Varcuse | Veritas |
| Unhinge | Unquiet | Untruce | Useless | Variant | Vermeil |
| Unhired | Unraked | Untruly | Usitate | Variate | Vermian |
| Unhitch | Unravel | Untruss | Usually | Varices | Vermily |
| Unhoard | Unready | Untruth | Usurper | Variety | Vermuth |
| Unhoped | Unreeve | Untwine | Utensil | Variola | Vernant |
| Unhorse | Unrivet | Untwist | Utilise | Variole | Vernate |
| Unhouse | Unrough | Unurged | Utility | Various | Vernier |
| Uniaxal | Unroyal | Unusage | Utilize | Varmint | Veronal |
| Unicorn | Unruled | Unusual | Utopian | Varnish | Verruca |
| Unideal | Unsaint | Unvexed | Utricle | Varsity | Versant |
| Unifoil | Unsated | Unvowed | Utterer | Varvels | Versify |
| Uniform | Unscale | Unwaged | Utterly | Vatican | Version |
| Unitary | Unscaly | Unweary | Uxorial | Vaudois | Versual |
| Unitate | Unscrew | Unweave | | Vaulter | Versute |
| Unition | Unsense | Unwhipt | **V** | Vaunter | Vertigo |
| Unitive | Unsexed | Unwitch | Vacancy | Vavasor | Veruled |
| Unitize | Unshale | Unwitty | Vaccine | Vayvode | Verules |
| Unjoint | Unshape | Unwoman | Vachery | Vection | Vervain |
| Unkempt | Unshell | Unwooed | Vacuist | Vedanga | Vervels |
| Unknown | Unshorn | Unwound | Vacuity | Vedanta | Vesicae |
| Unladen | Unshown | Unwoven | Vacuole | Vedette | Vesical |
| Unlatch | Unsized | Unwrung | Vacuous | Veering | Vesicle |
| Unlearn | Unsling | Unyoked | Vafrous | Vegetal | Vespine |
| Unleash | Unslung | Unzoned | Vaginal | Vehicle | Vestige |
| Unleave | Unsmote | Upblaze | Vagrant | Veiling | Vesting |
| Unlevel | Unsolid | Upborne | Vaguely | Veinage | Vestlet |
| Unlimed | Unsound | Upbound | Vaivode | Veining | Vestral |
| Unlived | Unspell | Upbraid | Valance | Veinlet | Vesture |
| Unloose | Unspent | Upbrast | Valence | Veinous | Veteran |
| Unlucky | Unspied | Upbreak | Valency | Veinule | Vetiver |
| Unlusty | Unspike | Upburst | Valeric | Velamen | Vettura |
| Unmanly | Unspilt | Upclimb | Valiant | Velaria | Vexilla |
| Unmarry | Unsplit | Upheave | Validly | Velours | Viaduct |
| Unmeant | Unspoil | Upraise | Valinch | Vellumy | Vialful |
| Unmeted | Unstack | Upright | Vallary | Velvety | Viarian |
| Unmixed | Unstaid | Uprisen | Vallate | Venally | Vibices |
| Unmoist | Unstate | Uprouse | Valonia | Venatic | Vibrant |
| Unmoral | Unsteel | Upshort | Valvate | Vendace | Vibrate |
| Unmould | Unsteps | Upspear | Valvlet | Venerer | Vibrato |
| Unmoved | Unstick | Upstand | Valvula | Venison | Vibrion |
| Unnamed | Unsting | Upstart | Valvule | Venomed | Viceroy |
| Unnerve | Unstock | Upsurge | Vamoose | Ventage | Vicinal |
| Unnoble | Unstuck | Upsweep | Vampire | Ventail | Vicious |
| Unnoted | Unstung | Upswell | Vamplet | Ventose | Victory |
| Unoften | Unsunny | Uptrace | Vanadic | Vent-peg | Victrix |

SEVEN-LETTER WORDS—*continued*

| | | | | | |
|---|---|---|---|---|---|
| Victual | Vocable | Waivode | Wastrel | Welding | Whipsaw |
| Vicugna | Vocalic | Waiwode | Watcher | Welfare | Whip-top |
| Videnda | Vocally | Wakeful | Watchet | Well-met | Whirler |
| Vidette | Vocular | Wakener | Watered | Well-set | Whirret |
| Vidimus | Voglite | Walking | Waterer | Welsher | Whisker |
| Viduity | Voicing | Wallaba | Wattled | Welting | Whisket |
| Viduage | Voiding | Wallaby | Wavelet | Wencher | Whiskey |
| Viduate | Voivode | Wallach | Waverer | Wendish | Whisper |
| Viewing | Volable | Wallack | Waveson | Wenlock | Whistle |
| Vigonia | Volante | Wall-eye | Waxbill | Wennish | Whistly |
| Vilayet | Volapuk | Walling | Waxdoll | Wergild | Whitely |
| Village | Volcano | Walloon | Wax-moth | Werwolf | Whither |
| Villain | Volsung | Wall-rue | Wax-palm | Western | Whiting |
| Villein | Voltage | Waltzer | Wax-tree | Westing | Whitish |
| Villose | Voltaic | Wametow | Waxwing | Wet-dock | Whitlow |
| Villous | Voluble | Wampish | Waxwork | Wetness | Whitsul |
| Viminal | Volubly | Wanghee | Way-bill | Wet-shod | Whitsun |
| Vinasse | Volumed | Wanhope | Wayfare | Wetting | Whittaw |
| Vinalia | Voluspa | Wanhorn | Waygone | Wettish | Whittle |
| Vinegar | Voluted | Wanness | Wayless | Whacker | Whoever |
| Vinewed | Vouchee | Wannish | Waymark | Whalery | Whomble |
| Vintage | Voucher | Wantage | Wayment | Whaling | Whommel |
| Vintner | Vowelly | Wanting | Waypost | Whangam | Whoobub |
| Violate | Voyager | Wantwit | Wayside | Whatnot | Whooper |
| Violent | Vulgate | Wapacut | Wayward | Whatten | Whopper |
| Violine | Vulpine | Waratah | Wayside | Wheaten | Whorled |
| Violist | Vulture | Warbler | Waywode | Wheedle | Whummle |
| Violone | Vulturn | Wardage | Wayworn | Wheeled | Widener |
| Virelay | Vulvate | Wardian | Wealden | Wheeler | Widgeon |
| Virgate | | Ward-wit | Wealthy | Wheezle | Widower |
| Virgule | **W** | Wareful | Weaning | Whelked | Wielder |
| Virtual | Wabbler | Warfare | Wearied | Whemmle | Wiggery |
| Visaged | Wabster | Warhoop | Wearily | Whereas | Wigging |
| Vis-a-vis | Wadable | Warison | Wearing | Whereat | Wiggler |
| Viscera | Wadding | Warlike | Wearish | Whereby | Wild-ass |
| Viscous | Waddled | Warlock | Weasand | Wherein | Wild-cat |
| Visible | Waddler | Warming | Weather | Whereof | Wilding |
| Visibly | Wad-hook | Warning | Weaving | Whereon | Wildish |
| Visiter | Wadmoll | Warpath | Webbing | Whereso | Wild-oat |
| Visitor | Wadsett | Warping | Web-eyed | Whereto | Willock |
| Visnomy | Waeness | Warrant | Web-foot | Wherret | Willowy |
| Visored | Waesome | Warrior | Web-toed | Whether | Wilsome |
| Vitally | Waftage | War-scot | Webster | Whetile | Wimbery |
| Vitamin | Wafting | Warship | Wedding | Whetter | Wimbrel |
| Vitiate | Wafture | Warsong | Wedging | Wheyish | Windage |
| Vitrain | Wagerer | Wart-hog | Wedlock | Whey-tub | Windbag |
| Vitreum | Waggery | Warwolf | Weedery | Whidder | Wind-egg |
| Vitrics | Waggish | Warworn | Weeding | Whiffle | Wind-gun |
| Vitrify | Wagoner | Washing | Weekday | Whilere | Windowy |
| Vitrina | Wagsome | Wash-off | Week-end | Whiling | Windrow |
| Vitrine | Wagtail | Washout | Weening | Whimper | Winebag |
| Vitriol | Wagwant | Washpot | Weeping | Whimple | Winefat |
| Vitular | Wahabee | Washtub | Weevily | Whimsey | Winglet |
| Vivency | Wailful | Wasp-fly | Weftage | Whinger | Winking |
| Viverra | Wailing | Waspish | Weigher | Whining | Winning |
| Vividly | Wainage | Wassail | Weighty | Whipper | Winnock |
| Vivific | Waister | Wastage | Welcher | Whippet | Winsome |
| Vixenly | Waiting | Wasting | Welcome | Whip-ray | Wireman |

### SEVEN-LETTER WORDS—*continued*

| | | | | | |
|---|---|---|---|---|---|
| Wireway | Woollen | Wrinkle | Yardarm | Zamouse | Zoccolo |
| Wishful | Woolman | Wrinkly | Yardman | Zanella | Zoilean |
| Wistful | Woolsey | Writing | Yarring | Zanjero | Zoilism |
| Wistiti | Woomera | Writhle | Yarrish | Zanyism | Zoilist |
| Withers | Woorali | Written | Yashmak | Zaphara | Zoisite |
| Without | Woorara | Wronger | Yawling | Zaptieh | Zolaism |
| Witless | Wording | Wrongly | Yawning | Zareeba | Zonular |
| Witling | Wordily | Wrought | Ycleped | Zarnich | Zonulet |
| Witloof | Wordish | Wrybill | Yeldrin | Zealant | Zonuras |
| Witness | Workbag | Wryneck | Yelling | Zealful | Zonurus |
| Wittily | Workbox | Wryness | Yelloch | Zealous | Zooecia |
| Witwall | Workday | Wuzzent | Yellows | Zebrine | Zoogamy |
| Wizened | Workman | Wych-elm | Yellowy | Zedoary | Zoogeny |
| Wobbler | Workshy | | Yestern | Zemstvo | Zoogony |
| Woesome | Worldly | | Yezidis | Zeolite | Zoolite |
| Wolf-cub | Worming | **X** | Yiddish | Zestful | Zoolith |
| Wolf-dog | Worried | Xanthic | Yielder | Zesting | Zoology |
| Wolfian | Worrier | Xanthin | Yodeler | Zetetic | Zoonite |
| Wolf-kin | Worship | Xenurus | Yolding | Zeuxite | Zoonomy |
| Wolf-net | Worsted | Xerasia | Yorkish | Zigzags | Zootaxy |
| Wolsung | Would-be | Xerodes | Yorkist | Zimocca | Zootomy |
| Womaned | Wouldst | Xerosis | Youngly | Zincali | Zopissa |
| Womanly | Wounded | Xerotes | Youngth | Zincite | Zorgite |
| Wommera | Wounder | Xerotic | Younker | Zincode | Zorilla |
| Wongshy | Wourali | Xiphias | Youthly | Zincoid | Zorille |
| Wood-ant | Wrangler | Xiphoid | Yorling | Zincous | Zorrino |
| Woodcut | Wrapped | Xylopia | Yravish | Zingane | Zotheca |
| Wood-god | Wrapper | | Yslaked | Zingano | Zuffolo |
| Woodman | Wreaked | | Yttrium | Zingari | Zurlite |
| Woodnut | Wreathe | **Y** | Yule-log | Zingaro | Zygaena |
| Wood-oil | Wreathy | | | Zionism | Zygoite |
| Wood-tar | Wrecker | Yachter | | Zionist | Zygosis |
| Wood-tin | Wrester | Yamadou | **Z** | Ziphius | Zymogen |
| Woolded | Wrestle | Yanking | Zabaism | Zithern | Zymosis |
| Woolder | Wriggle | Yapster | Zadkiel | Zizania | Zymotic |
| Woolfat | Wringer | Yardage | Zalacca | Zoarium | Zymurgy |

## Eight-Letter Words

| | | | | | |
|---|---|---|---|---|---|
| **A** | Abductor | Abluvion | Absolver | Acaulose | Accustom |
| | Abelians | Abnegate | Absonant | Acaulous | Aceldama |
| Aard-vark | Abelites | Abnodate | Absonous | Accensor | Acentric |
| Aard-wolf | Abelmosk | Abnormal | Absterge | Accentor | Acerbate |
| Aaronite | Aberrant | Abococke | Abstract | Accepter | Acerbent |
| Abaction | Aberring | Abomasum | Abstruse | Acceptor | Acerbity |
| Abatable | Abetment | Abomasus | Absurdly | Accident | Acervate |
| Abat-jour | Abeyance | Abradant | Abundant | Acclinal | Acescent |
| Abbattoir | Abeyancy | Abrasion | Abusable | Accolade | Acetated |
| Abat-voix | Abhorrer | Abrasive | Abutilon | Accolent | Achenium |
| Abbatial | Abiogeny | Abrastol | Abutment | Accorage | Acherset |
| Abdalavi | Abjectly | Abrogate | Abutting | Accouple | Acheweed |
| Abderian | Ablation | Abruptly | Academic | Accoutre | Achiever |
| Abderite | Ablative | Abscissa | Acalepha | Accredit | Achilous |
| Abdicant | Ablegate | Absentee | Acanthus | Accuracy | Achirite |
| Abdicate | Ableness | Absently | Acardiac | Accurate | Acicular |
| Abditory | Ablocate | Absinthe | Acarpous | Accursed | Acidific |
| Abducent | Ablution | Absolute | Acauline | Accusant | Acidness |

EIGHT-LETTER WORDS—*continued*

| | | | | | |
|---|---|---|---|---|---|
| Acidosis | Adularia | Ague-cake | Alitrunk | Amadavat | Analepsy |
| Acierage | Adulator | Ague-tree | Alizarin | Amandine | Analogic |
| Acnestis | Adultery | Aigrette | Alkahest | Amandola | Analogon |
| Acoemeti | Aduncous | Aiguille | Alkalify | Amanitin | Analogue |
| Aconitic | Adustion | Ailantus | Alkaline | Amaracus | Analyser |
| Acosmism | Advancer | Aillette | Alkalize | Amaranth | Analysis |
| Acoustic | Advisory | Air-brake | Alkaloid | Amazedly | Analytic |
| Acquaint | Advocacy | Air-brick | Alkermes | Amberite | Anapaest |
| Acreable | Advocate | Air-built | Allanite | Ambition | Anaphora |
| Acridian | Advoutry | Aircells | Allegory | Amblosis | Anarchal |
| Acridity | Advowson | Aircraft | Alleluia | Amblotic | Anarchic |
| Acrimony | Adynamia | Air-drain | Allerion | Amblygon | Anasarca |
| Acritude | Adynamic | Air-drawn | All-fired | Ambreada | Anathema |
| Acroatic | Aegrotat | Airedale | All-fours | Ambreate | Anatomic |
| Acrolith | Aerarian | Airiness | Alliance | Ambrosia | Ancestor |
| Acrostic | Aeration | Airplane | Alligate | Ambrosin | Ancestry |
| Acrotism | Aerially | Airpoise | Allision | Ambulant | Anchoret |
| Actinism | Aeriform | Airscrew | Allocate | Ambulate | Anconeal |
| Activate | Aerocyst | Airshaft | Allodial | Amenable | Andesine |
| Actively | Aerolite | Airspace | Allodium | Amenably | Andesite |
| Activism | Aerolith | Air-stove | Allogamy | Amenance | Anecdote |
| Activity | Aerology | Airtight | Allottee | American | Aneurism |
| Actually | Aeronaut | Airtrunk | Alloyage | Amethyst | Aneurysm |
| Acuition | Aerostat | Alacrity | Allspice | Amiantus | Angel-bed |
| Aculeate | Aesthete | Alarm-gun | Allusion | Amicable | Angelica |
| Adamitic | Aestival | Alarming | Allusive | Amicably | Anglican |
| Adaptive | Affamish | Alarmist | Allusory | Amissing | Angloman |
| Addendum | Affected | Albacore | Alluvial | Ammodyte | Angstrom |
| Adder-fly | Afferent | Albicore | Alluvion | Ammoniac | Angulate |
| Addicted | Affiance | Albiness | Alluvium | Ammonite | Animally |
| Addition | Affinage | Albinism | Almagest | Ammonium | Animated |
| Additive | Affinity | Albumess | Almighty | Amniotic | Animator |
| Addorsed | Affirmer | Alburnum | Almsdeed | Amoebean | Animetta |
| Adducent | Afflatus | Alcahest | Almsgate | Amoebeum | Anisette |
| Adductor | Affluent | Alcatras | Alomancy | Amoeboid | Annalise |
| Adenitis | Afforest | Alchemic | Alopecia | Amoebous | Annalist |
| Adenoids | Affright | Aldehyde | Alphabet | Amoretto | Annelida |
| Adeption | Affronté | Alderman | Alphenic | Amortize | Annexion |
| Adequacy | Affusion | Aleatory | Alpinist | Ampelite | Annotate |
| Adequate | Aftereye | Alebench | Alquifou | Amphibia | Announce |
| Adfected | Afterwit | Aleberry | Alsatian | Amphigen | Annually |
| Adherent | Agastric | Alehouse | Altarage | Amphoral | Annulary |
| Adhesion | Agenesis | Alembdar | Alterant | Amphoric | Annulate |
| Adhesive | Agential | Ale-stake | Alterego | Ampullar | Annuller |
| Adiantum | Ageustia | Aleurone | Alterity | Amputate | Annulose |
| Adjacent | Aggrieve | Alfresco | Alternat | Amuletic | Anorexia |
| Adjutage | Agiotage | Algerine | Altheine | Amurcous | Anorthic |
| Adjutant | Agistage | Algidity | Although | Amusable | Anourous |
| Adjutrix | Agitable | Algology | Altincar | Amusette | Anserine |
| Adjuvant | Agitator | Algorism | Altitude | Anabasis | Antacrid |
| Admiring | Aglimmer | Alguazil | Alto-clef | Anableps | Antalgic |
| Admonish | Agnation | Alhambra | Altruism | Anaconda | Anteater |
| Adoption | Agnostic | Alicante | Altruist | Anaglyph | Antecede |
| Adoptive | Agraphia | Alienage | Aluminic | Anagogic | Antedate |
| Adorable | Agrarian | Alienate | Aluminum | Anagraph | Antelope |
| Adorably | Agrestic | Alienism | Alunogen | Analecta | Antennae |
| Adroitly | Agrimony | Alienist | Alveolar | Analects | Antennal |
| Adscript | Agronomy | Aliquant | Alveolus | Analemma | Antepast |

## EIGHT-LETTER WORDS—*continued*

| | | | | | |
|---|---|---|---|---|---|
| Anteport | Apostacy | Archaean | Arterial | Astringe | Auto-da-fe |
| Anterior | Apostasy | Archaism | Artesian | Astunned | Autogamy |
| Anteroom | Apostate | Archaise | Artfully | Astutely | Auto-gyro |
| Anthelix | Aposteme | Archaize | Artifact | Asystole | Autology |
| Anthemis | Apostume | Archduke | Artifice | Ataraxia | Automata |
| Antheral | Apothegm | Archical | Artistic | Atheling | Automath |
| Anthesis | Appanage | Archival | Artistry | Athenian | Autonomy |
| Anthozoa | Apparent | Arehives | Aruspice | Atherine | Autopsia |
| Antiacid | Appeaser | Archlike | Aruspicy | Atheroma | Autoptic |
| Antiades | Appellee | Archlute | Arvicola | Athletic | Autotype |
| Antibody | Appellor | Archness | Aryanise | Atlantes | Autumnal |
| Anticize | Appendix | Archwise | Asbestic | Atlantic | Auxilear |
| Anticous | Appetent | Arcturus | Asbestos | Atlantis | Aventail |
| Antidote | Appetise | Ardently | Ascidium | Atmology | Aventine |
| Antilogy | Appetite | Arenaria | Ashleach | Atomical | Aventure |
| Antilope | Appetize | Areolate | Ashplant | Atomizer | Averment |
| Antimask | Applause | Argemone | Ashy-gray | Atonable | Avernian |
| Antimony | Apple-pie | Argental | Aspartic | Atremble | Aversant |
| Antinomy | Apple-pip | Argentan | Asperate | Atrocity | Aversely |
| Antinous | Appliqué | Argentic | Asperges | Atrophic | Aversion |
| Antiphon | Apposite | Argentum | Asperity | Atropine | Aviarist |
| Antipode | Appraise | Argonaut | Asphodel | Atropism | Aviation |
| Antipole | Apprizer | Arguable | Asphyxia | Atropous | Avifauna |
| Antipope | Approach | Argument | Aspirant | Attached | Aviseful |
| Antiport | Approval | Argutely | Aspirate | Attaghan | Avowable |
| Antistes | Approved | Arianise | Assailer | Attemper | Avowably |
| Antitype | Approven | Arianism | Assassin | Attender | Avowance |
| Antlered | Approver | Aridness | Assemble | Attester | Avowedly |
| Antrorse | Apricate | Arillary | Assembly | Attestor | Avulsion |
| Anything | Apricock | Aristate | Assenter | Atticism | Awakable |
| Anywhere | Apron-man | Armament | Assentor | Atticize | Awakener |
| Aoristic | Apterous | Armature | Asserter | Attitude | Awanting |
| Aortitis | Aptitude | Arm-chair | Assertor | Attorney | Awearied |
| Apagogic | Apyrefic | Armenian | Assessor | Attrited | Aweather |
| Apellous | Apyrexia | Armigero | Assident | Attritus | Axillary |
| Aperient | Aquarium | Armillet | Assiento | Audacity | Axletree |
| Apéritif | Aquarius | Arminian | Assiette | Audience | Axoidean |
| Aperture | Aquatint | Armorial | Assignat | Audition | Ayenbite |
| Aphanite | Aqueduct | Armorist | Assignee | Auditive | |
| Aphelion | Aquiform | Armourer | Assignor | Auditory | |
| Aphidian | Aquiline | Armozeen | Assinego | Augurate | **B** |
| Aphonous | Aquosity | Armozine | Assonant | Augurial | Babakoto |
| Aphorise | Arachnid | Aromatic | Assonate | Augustan | Babbling |
| Aphorism | Araignee | Arpeggio | Assorted | Augustly | Babeldom |
| Aphorist | Araneose | Arquebus | Assotted | Aularian | Babirusa |
| Aphorize | Araneous | Arrantly | Assuager | Aurelian | Babishly |
| Aphthous | Arapunga | Arrasene | Assurant | Aureoled | Baboodom |
| Apiarian | Arbalist | Arraught | Assyrian | Auricled | Babooism |
| Apiarist | Arbitral | Arrected | Asterias | Auricula | Babyhood |
| Aplastic | Arboreal | Arrester | Asterisk | Auriform | Baccarat |
| Aplustre | Arborist | Arrogant | Asterism | Aurilave | Bacchant |
| Apodosis | Arborous | Arrogate | Asteroid | Aurorean | Bachelor |
| Apogaeic | Arboured | Arrondée | Asthenia | Aurulent | Bacillar |
| Apograph | Arbuscle | Arrosion | Asthenic | Ausonian | Bacillus |
| Apollyon | Arbustum | Arsenate | Astomous | Auspices | Backband |
| Apologue | Arbutean | Arsenite | Astonied | Austrian | Backbite |
| Apophyge | Arcadian | Arsonite | Astonish | Autarchy | Backbond |
| Apoplexy | Arcature | Arsonist | Astragal | Autocrat | Backbone |

| | | | | | |
|---|---|---|---|---|---|
| Backdoor | Banality | Baronial | Beadwork | Befogged | Beri-beri |
| Backfall | Bandanna | Barouche | Beakiron | Befriend | Bernacle |
| Back-fire | Bandeaux | Bar-posts | Beam-bird | Befringe | Bernicle |
| Backhair | Bandelet | Barracan | Beamking | Begetter | Bernouse |
| Backhand | Banderol | Barracks | Beamless | Beggable | Berthage |
| Backlash | Bandfish | Barrator | Beam-tree | Beggarly | Bescrawl |
| Backmost | Banditti | Barratry | Bearable | Beginner | Bescream |
| Back-rent | Bandsman | Barrenly | Bearably | Begirdle | Bescreen |
| Backside | Bandying | Barrulet | Bearbind | Begrease | Beseemly |
| Backward | Banewort | Bar-shear | Bearbine | Begrudge | Besetter |
| Backwash | Bangster | Barterer | Bear-herd | Beguiler | Beshadow |
| Backworm | Bangtail | Bartisan | Bear-like | Behappen | Besidery |
| Baconian | Banister | Bartizan | Bear's-ear | .Beheadal | Besieger |
| Bacteria | Banjoist | Barytone | Bearskin | Behemoth | Besilver |
| Baculine | Bankable | Basaltic | Bearward | Beholden | Beslaver |
| Baculite | Bank-bill | Basanite | Beasties | Beholder | Besmirch |
| Badgerly | Bank-book | Bascinet | Beastish | Beinness | Besmutch |
| Badigeon | Bank-note | Baseball | Beatific | Bejesuit | Besnowed |
| Badinage | Bankrate | Base-born | Beaufrey | Belabour | Besotted |
| Baffetas | Bankrupt | Base-bred | Beaupere | Belamoor | Besought |
| Baffling | Banksman | Baseless | Beautify | Believer | Besouled |
| Bagpiper | Banlieue | Baseline | Beauxite | Belittle | Bespoken |
| Baguette | Bannered | Basement | Beavered | Bellbind | Bespread |
| Bailable | Banneret | Baseness | Bebeerin | Bell-bird | Besprent |
| Bailball | Bannerol | Base-viol | Becalmed | Bell-buoy | Bessemer |
| Bailbond | Banterer | Bashless | Bechamel | Bellcote | Bestiary |
| Baildock | Bantling | Basicity | Bechance | Bellpull | Bestowal |
| Bailment | Banxring | Basifier | Becoming | Bellrope | Bestower |
| Bailsman | Baphomet | Basilian | Bedabble | Bell-tent | Bestreak |
| Bajadere | Barbacan | Basilica | Bedaggle | Bellwort | Bestride |
| Bakemeat | Barbacon | Basilisk | Bedarken | Belly-god | Beteared |
| Bakshish | Barbaric | Basketry | Bedazzle | Bellying | Bethrall |
| Balancer | Barbated | Basquine | Bed-chair | Beloving | Bethwack |
| Balanite | Barbecue | Bassette | Bedeafen | Belzebub | Betongue |
| Balconet | Barberry | Bass-horn | Bedeguar | Bemuddle | Betrayal |
| Baldcoot | Barbette | Bassinet | Bedesman | Bemuffle | Betrayer |
| Baldhead | Barbican | Bass-viol | Bedeween | Bendable | Bettered |
| Baldness | Barbiton | Basterna | Bedlinen | Beneaped | Betuline |
| Baldpate | Bardling | Bastille | Bedmaker | Benedick | Bevelled |
| Baldrick | Bareback | Batavian | Bedplate | Benedict | Beverage |
| Baledock | Barebone | Bateless | Bed-quilt | Benefice | Bevilled |
| Bale-fire | Barefoot | Bathable | Bedrench | Benignly | Bewigged |
| Balister | Bareness | Bathorse | Bedright | Bénitier | Bewilder |
| Balistic | Baresark | Bath-room | Bedstaff | Benjamin | Bewinter |
| Balk-line | Bargeman | Batswing | Bedstead | Benzoate | Bewrayer |
| Ballader | Barghest | Battalia | Bedstraw | Bepepper | Bezonian |
| Balladry | Barillet | Battleax | Bed-table | Bepester | Bheestie |
| Ballcock | Baritone | Baudekin | Bee-bread | Bepommel | Bibation |
| Balliage | Barkmill | Baudrons | Beech-oil | Bepowder | Biblical |
| Ballista | Barnabas | Bawdrick | Bee-eater | Bepraise | Bibulous |
| Ballonet | Barnacle | Bayadere | Beefwood | Bequeath | Bicaudal |
| Ballroom | Barn-door | Bayardly | Beer-pump | Berberin | Bicrural |
| Ballyrag | Barnekin | Bayberry | Beer-shop | Berberry | Bicuspid |
| Balmoral | Barnyard | Bdellium | Beeswing | Bereaved | Biddable |
| Balneary | Barology | Beadlery | Beetling | Bergamot | Bidental |
| Balotade | Barometz | Beadroll | Beet-rave | Bergfall | Biennial |
| Balsamic | Baronage | Beadsman | Beetroot | Bergmehl | Bier-balk |
| Baluster | Baroness | Bead-tree | Beflower | Bergmote | Bifacial |

## EIGHT-LETTER WORDS—*continued*

| | | | | | |
|---|---|---|---|---|---|
| Biferous | Bisetous | Blooming | Bombiate | Botryoid | Brazenry |
| Bifidate | Bisexual | Blossomy | Bona-fide | Bottomry | Brazilin |
| Biforate | Bistoury | Blotting | Bona-roba | Botulism | Bread-nut |
| Bigamist | Bitingly | Blow-ball | Bondager | Bouffant | Breakage |
| Bigamous | Bitmaker | Blow-hole | Bond-debt | Boughten | Breakman |
| Bigaroon | Bitmouth | Blow-milk | Bondmaid | Bouillon | Breakvow |
| Big-boned | Bitnoben | Blowpipe | Bondsman | Bouncing | Breathed |
| Biggonet | Bittacle | Bludgeon | Bone-ache | Boundary | Breather |
| Bignonia | Bitterly | Blue-back | Bone-cave | Bountree | Bredsore |
| Big-swoln | Bivalent | Blue-bell | Bone-dust | Bourgeon | Breeches |
| Bijoutry | Bizcacha | Blue-bird | Bonelace | Bour-tree | Breeched |
| Bijugate | Blackart | Blue-book | Boneless | Boviform | Breeding |
| Bijugous | Blackcap | Bluecoat | Bongrace | Bow-brace | Breloque |
| Bilander | Blackfly | Blue-fish | Bonhomie | Bow-drill | Brennage |
| Bilberry | Black-gum | Bluefunk | Boniface | Bow-grace | Brethren |
| Bileduct | Blacking | Bluegown | Bonneted | Bowingly | Brettice |
| Bill-book | Blackish | Blueness | Bonspiel | Bow-piece | Brevetcy |
| Billfish | Blackleg | Bluenose | Bontebok | Bowsprit | Breviary |
| Billhead | Blackneb | Blue-pill | Booby-hut | Box-drain | Breviate |
| Billhook | Blackrod | Bluepoll | Boobyish | Box-elder | Breviped |
| Billiard | Blackwad | Bluewing | Boobyism | Boxlobby | Brevipen |
| Billowed | Bladdery | Bluntish | Boodhism | Box-pleat | Brewster |
| Billy-boy | Blamable | Blushful | Bookcase | Box-thorn | Briarean |
| Bilobate | Blamably | Blushing | Bookclub | Boyishly | Bribable |
| Bimanous | Blameful | Blustery | Book-debt | Braccate | Brickbat |
| Bimarine | Blancard | Boarding | Bookland | Bracelet | Brick-red |
| Bimensal | Blancher | Boarfish | Bookless | Brachial | Brick-tea |
| Binaural | Blandish | Boastful | Bookmark | Brackish | Bride-ale |
| Bindweed | Blastide | Boasting | Bookmate | Bracteal | Bride-bed |
| Binnacle | Blasting | Boatable | Book-name | Bradshaw | Briefman |
| Binomial | Blatancy | Boatbill | Book-oath | Bradypod | Brighten |
| Binoxide | Blazoner | Boathook | Book-post | Braggart | Brightly |
| Bioblast | Blazonry | Boat race | Bookshop | Bragging | Briguing |
| Biograph | Bleacher | Boat-rope | Bookworm | Brain-fag | Brimless |
| Biolytic | Bleakish | Bobbinet | Boothook | Brainish | Brindled |
| Biometry | Bleating | Bobolink | Boothose | Brain-pan | Brinepan |
| Bioplasm | Bleeding | Bob-white | Bootikin | Brake-man | Brinepit |
| Bioscope | Blenheim | Bock-beer | Bootjack | Brake-van | Briskish |
| Biparous | Blessing | Bockelet | Bootlace | Brambled | Britzska |
| Bipennis | Blimbing | Bockland | Bootlast | Brancard | Broacher |
| Biramous | Blindage | Bodement | Bootless | Brancher | Broad-axe |
| Bird-bolt | Blinding | Bodiless | Bootlick | Brandied | Broadish |
| Bird-cage | Blindman | Bodleian | Boot-tree | Brandish | Brocaded |
| Bird-call | Blinkard | Bodrages | Borachio | Brandise | Brocatel |
| Bird-eyed | Blinkers | Boeotian | Boracite | Brand-new | Broccoli |
| Birdlice | Blissful | Bog-berry | Bordeaux | Brantail | Brochure |
| Birdlike | Blistery | Bog-earth | Borderer | Brant-fox | Brodekin |
| Birdlime | Blithely | Bogeyism | Bordland | Brassage | Broidery |
| Birdseed | Blizzard | Bogey-man | Bord-lode | Brassard | Broiling |
| Bird's-eye | Blockade | Bog-house | Borecole | Brassart | Brokenly |
| Birthday | Blockish | Bog-latin | Boreworm | Brassica | Brokerly |
| Birthdom | Bloncket | Bog-whort | Borrower | Brassock | Bromelia |
| Birthing | Blood-hot | Bohemian | Borstall | Bratchel | Bronchic |
| Biscayan | Bloodily | Bold-face | Bosporus | Bratling | Bronzify |
| Biscotin | Bloodred | Boldness | Bostangi | Brattice | Bronzite |
| Bisector | Blood-tax | Bolt-boat | Botanist | Braunite | Brooding |
| Biserial | Blood-won | Bolt-head | Botanize | Brawling | Brooklet |
| Bisetose | Bloomery | Bolt-rope | Botchery | Brazenly | Brougham |

## EIGHT-LETTER WORDS—*continued*

| | | | | | |
|---|---|---|---|---|---|
| Browbeat | Buoyancy | Cabriole | Call-note | Canticle | Carnival |
| Browning | Burgamot | Cab-stand | Calmness | Canticum | Caroline |
| Brownish | Burganet | Cachalot | Calorist | Cantonal | Caroteel |
| Brownist | Burgeois | Cachemia | Calotype | Cantoris | Carousal |
| Brow-post | Burglary | Cachemic | Caltrops | Canvaser | Carousel |
| Browsick | Burgonet | Cachepot | Calvered | Canzonet | Carouser |
| Browsing | Burgrave | Cacholot | Calville | Capacity | Carraway |
| Bruilzie | Burgundy | Cachucha | Calycine | Capeline | Carriage |
| Brumaire | Burinist | Cachunde | Calycoid | Capellet | Carriole |
| Brunette | Burletta | Cackerel | Calymene | Caper-tea | Carritch |
| Brushing | Burnoose | Cacodoxy | Calyptra | Capibara | Cart-jade |
| Brussels | Burnt-ear | Cacology | Camassia | Capitano | Cart-load |
| Brutally | Burrower | Cadastre | Camatina | Capitate | Cartouch |
| Bryology | Burr-pump | Cadillac | Cambrian | Capnomor | Carucage |
| Bryonine | Bursalis | Caducean | Cameleer | Caponier | Carucate |
| Bubbling | Burschen | Caducity | Cameleon | Caponise | Caruncle |
| Bucanier | Bushbuck | Caducous | Cameline | Cap-paper | Caryatic |
| Buccinal | Busheler | Caesious | Camellia | Capriole | Caryatid |
| Buccinum | Business | Caesural | Camerate | Capriped | Caryokar |
| Buckbean | Buskined | Caffeine | Camisade | Caproate | Cascabel |
| Buckhorn | Busybody | Cageling | Camisado | Capsicum | Cascalho |
| Buck-jump | Busyless | Caillach | Camisole | Capstone | Casemate |
| Buckmast | Busyness | Caimacam | Camomile | Capsular | Casement |
| Buckshee | Butchery | Cajolery | Campaign | Captious | Case-shot |
| Buckshot | Butching | Calabash | Camphene | Capuccio | Case-worm |
| Buckskin | Butteris | Caladium | Camphine | Capuchin | Cashbook |
| Bucrania | Buttress | Calamary | Camstone | Capucine | Cashmere |
| Buddhism | Buttrice | Calambac | Canadian | Capybara | Cass-weed |
| Buddhist | Butyrate | Calamine | Canaigre | Carabine | Castanea |
| Buffcoat | Butyrine | Calamint | Canaille | Caracara | Castanet |
| Bufonite | Butyrous | Calamite | Canalize | Caracole | Castaway |
| Building | By-bidder | Calamity | Canarese | Caracoly | Cast-iron |
| Bulgaric | Bycocket | Calander | Canaster | Carapace | Castlery |
| Bulkhead | By-corner | Calandra | Cancrine | Carap-oil | Castrate |
| Bull-beef | By-design | Calangay | Cancroid | Carbolic | Castrato |
| Bull-calf | Bylander | Calathus | Candidly | Carbonic | Casually |
| Bulldose | By-matter | Calceate | Cane-hole | Carburet | Casualty |
| Bulletin | Bymotive | Calcedon | Cane-mill | Carcajou | Catacomb |
| Bull-frog | Byronism | Calc-spar | Canephor | Carcanet | Cataline |
| Bullhead | By-speech | Calc-tuff | Canicula | Cardamom | Catamite |
| Bullirag | By-street | Calculus | Canister | Card-case | Catapult |
| Bullring | By-stroke | Calendar | Canities | Cardiace | Cataract |
| Bull's-eye | | Calender | Cannabic | Cardigan | Cat-block |
| Bullweed | | Calf-less | Cannabin | Cardinal | Catching |
| Bullwort | | Calf-love | Cannabis | Cardioid | Catchfly |
| Bullyism | | Calfskin | Cannelon | Carditis | Category |
| Bullyrag | | Calibred | Cannibal | Careless | Catenary |
| Bulrushy | **C** | Calidity | Cannikin | Careworn | Cateress |
| Bummaloe | Cabalism | Caliduct | Cannular | Cargoose | Catering |
| Bummaree | Cabalist | Califate | Canoeist | Cariacou | Catharma |
| Buncombe | Caballer | Calipash | Canon-law | Caribbee | Cathedra |
| Bungalow | Cabinboy | Calipers | Canoness | Caricous | Catheter |
| Bunghole | Cabirian | Calippic | Canonist | Carillon | Cathetus |
| Bungling | Caboched | Calisaya | Canonize | Carinate | Cathisma |
| Bungvent | Cabochon | Calixtin | Canoodle | Carnally | Cathodal |
| Bunkered | Caboodle | Call-bird | Canorous | Carnauba | Catholic |
| Bunodont | Caboshed | Call-loan | Canstick | Carneous | Catiline |
| Buntline | Cabotage | Calliope | Canthook | Carnifex | Catodont |

EIGHT-LETTER WORDS—*continued*

| | | | | | |
|---|---|---|---|---|---|
| Catonian | Cerulean | Cheatery | Chondral | Circæan | Clay-marl |
| Catopsis | Cerulein | Cheating | Chondrin | Circuity | Claymill |
| Catstick | Cerusite | Cheerful | Chopness | Circular | Claymore |
| Caudated | Cervical | Cheerily | Chopping | Cirrhose | Clayweed |
| Caudicle | Cesarean | Cheering | Choragic | Cirrhous | Cleaning |
| Cauldron | Cesspool | Chelifer | Choragus | Cirriped | Cleanish |
| Caulicle | Cetacean | Chelonia | Chorally | Ciseleur | Cleansed |
| Causally | Cetology | Chemical | Chordata | Ciselure | Cleanser |
| Causerie | Cetraria | Chenille | Chording | Cistella | Clearage |
| Causeuse | Chaconne | Cherubic | Choregus | Cistvaen | Clear-cut |
| Causeway | Chafewax | Cherubim | Choriamb | Citation | Clearing |
| Cautious | Chaffery | Cheshire | Chorisis | Citatory | Cleavage |
| Cavalier | Chaffing | Chesible | Choultry | Citreous | Cleavers |
| Cavatina | Chaffron | Chessman | Chow-chow | Civeting | Clecking |
| Cavation | Chagrins | Chestnut | Choy-root | Civet-cat | Clematis |
| Caveator | Chainlet | Cheverel | Chrismal | Civilian | Clemence |
| Cavebear | Chairbed | Cheveril | Christen | Civilist | Clemency |
| Cavesson | Chairman | Cheville | Christom | Civility | Clemming |
| Cavicorn | Chaldaic | Chiasmus | Chromate | Civilize | Clerkage |
| Caviller | Chaldean | Chiastic | Chromite | Clackbox | Clerical |
| Celeriac | Chaldron | Chicaner | Chromium | Clacking | Clerkdom |
| Celerity | Chaliced | Chiccory | Chromule | Cladonia | Clerkery |
| Celibacy | Chalkpit | Chick-pea | Chthonic | Claimant | Clerkish |
| Celibate | Chambrel | Chiefage | Chuckies | Claiming | Cleverly |
| Cellarer | Chamelot | Chiefery | Chuffily | Clamancy | Cliental |
| Cellaret | Chamfron | Chiefess | Chummage | Clamming | Cliented |
| Cellular | Champion | Chiefrie | Chumming | Clamping | Climatic |
| Cemetery | Chancery | Childing | Chummery | Clanging | Climbing |
| Cenation | Chandler | Childish | Chump-end | Clangour | Clinamen |
| Cenobite | Chanfrin | Children | Chupatty | Clangous | Clincher |
| Cenotaph | Changing | Chiliasm | Churinga | Clanking | Clinical |
| Cenozoic | Chapbook | Chiliast | Churlish | Clannish | Clinique |
| Centaury | Chapelet | Chilling | Chylific | Clanship | Clinkant |
| Centiare | Chapelry | Chiltern | Chyluria | Clansman | Clippers |
| Centinel | Chaperon | Chimaera | Chymical | Clap-dish | Clipping |
| Centoist | Chapiter | Chimeric | Ciborium | Clapping | Cliquish |
| Centoism | Chaplain | Chinaman | Cicatrix | Clap-sill | Cliquism |
| Centroid | Chaptrel | Chinampa | Cicerone | Clap-trap | Clitella |
| Centuple | Charcoal | Chin-chin | Cicisbei | Claqueur | Clithral |
| Cephalgy | Chardoon | Chinscab | Cicisbeo | Clarence | Cloakage |
| Cephalic | Charfron | Chipmuck | Cicurate | Clarinet | Cloak-bag |
| Ceramics | Charlock | Chipmunk | Cider-cup | Clashing | Cloaking |
| Cerasine | Charming | Chipping | Ciderist | Clasping | Cloddish |
| Cerastes | Charneco | Chiragra | Ciderkin | Classify | Clodpate |
| Ceratite | Chartism | Chirping | Ci-devant | Classing | Clodpoll |
| Ceratode | Chartist | Chit-chat | Ciliated | Classman | Clogging |
| Ceratoid | Chasseur | Chivalry | Ciliform | Clatters | Cloister |
| Ceratose | Chastely | Chloasma | Cimbrian | Claudian | Clothier |
| Cereberus | Chastise | Chlorate | Cimolite | Clausure | Clothing |
| Cerealia | Chastity | Chloride | Cinchona | Clavated | Clotpoll |
| Cerealin | Chasuble | Chlorine | Cincture | Clavecin | Clotting |
| Cerebral | Chatelet | Chlorite | Cindrous | Claviary | Cloudage |
| Cerebric | Chatwood | Chloroid | Cinerary | Clavicle | Cloudery |
| Cerebrin | Chauffer | Chlorous | Cinereal | Claviger | Cloudily |
| Cerebrum | Chaunter | Choanite | Cingulum | Clawback | Cloudlet |
| Cerement | Chausses | Choicely | Cinnabar | Clawless | Clovered |
| Ceremony | Chawdron | Choleric | Cinnamic | Clawsick | Clownery |
| Cernuous | Chay-root | Choliamb | Cinnamon | Clay-cold | Clowning |

## EIGHT-LETTER WORDS—*continued*

| | | | | | |
|---|---|---|---|---|---|
| Clownish | Cockayne | Colonist | Concerto | Contrive | Corocore |
| Cloyless | Cock-bill | Colonize | Concetto | Conusant | Corollet |
| Cloyment | Cockboat | Colophon | Conchite | Convener | Coronach |
| Cloysome | Cock-crow | Colorate | Conchoid | Converge | Coronary |
| Clubable | Cockerel | Colorine | Conclave | Converse | Coronate |
| Clubbish | Cockeyed | Colossal | Conclude | Convexed | Coronium |
| Clubbism | Cockloft | Colossus | Concours | Convexly | Coronoid |
| Clubbist | Cock-shot | Colotomy | Concrete | Conveyer | Coronule |
| Club-fist | Cockshut | Coloured | Condense | Conveyor | Corporal |
| Clubfoot | Cockspur | Colstaff | Confalon | Convince | Corporas |
| Clubhaul | Cocksure | Columbic | Conferva | Convoked | Corragio |
| Club-land | Cocktail | Columnar | Confetti | Convolve | Corridor |
| Club-moss | Cocoa-nut | Columned | Confider | Convulse | Corrival |
| Club-room | Coctible | Comatose | Confined | Cony-skin | Corselet |
| Club-root | Codifier | Comatous | Confiner | Cony-wool | Corsican |
| Club-rush | Codpiece | Combiner | Conflate | Cook-room | Cortical |
| Clueless | Coercion | Combless | Conflict | Cook-shop | Corundum |
| Clumsily | Coercive | Comedian | Confound | Coolness | Corvette |
| Clupeoid | Coestate | Comedist | Confrere | Co-option | Corybant |
| Clustery | Coexpand | Comelily | Confront | Copatain | Corymbus |
| Clyfaker | Coextend | Cometary | Congener | Copepoda | Coryphée |
| Clypeate | Cofferer | Comitial | Congiary | Cophosis | Corystes |
| Coachbox | Cogently | Commando | Conglobe | Cophouse | Cosecant |
| Coach-dog | Cogitate | Commatic | Congreet | Copopsia | Cosherer |
| Coachful | Cognizor | Commence | Congress | Copperas | Cosenage |
| Coaching | Cognomen | Commerce | Congreve | Copy-book | Cosinage |
| Coachman | Cognosce | Commerge | Conicine | Copyhold | Cosiness |
| Coaction | Cognovit | Commoner | Conicity | Coquetry | Cosmetic |
| Coactive | Cogwheel | Commoney | Coniform | Coquette | Cosmical |
| Coagency | Coherent | Commonly | Conjoint | Coquilla | Cost-book |
| Coagulum | Cohesion | Commonty | Conjugal | Coracite | Cost-free |
| Coalesce | Cohesive | Communal | Conjunct | Coracoid | Costless |
| Coalfish | Cohobate | Compages | Conjurer | Coranach | Costmary |
| Coal-hole | Coiffeur | Compesce | Conjuror | Cordiner | Costumer |
| Coal-mine | Coincide | Compiler | Conjusto | Cordovan | Co-surety |
| Coal-ship | Co-inhere | Complain | Conniver | Corduroy | Coteline |
| Coalwork | Coistril | Complect | Conoidal | Cordwain | Co-tenant |
| Coamings | Cokernut | Complete | Conoidic | Cord-wood | Cothouse |
| Coarsely | Colander | Complice | Conquest | Co-regent | Cotillon |
| Coarsish | Colation | Complier | Conserve | Cork-tree | Cotquean |
| Co-assume | Colature | Compline | Consider | Corkwing | Cotswold |
| Coasting | Coldness | Componed | Consoler | Corkwood | Cottabus |
| Coat-card | Cole rape | Composer | Consomme | Cormogen | Cottager |
| Coat-link | Coleseed | Composto | Conspire | Cornacre | Cotyloid |
| Cobaltic | Colewort | Compound | Constant | Cornball | Couchant |
| Cobcoals | Coliseum | Compress | Construe | Corncake | Couching |
| Co-bishop | Collagen | Comprint | Consular | Corneous | Coulisse |
| Cobstone | Collapse | Comprise | Consulta | Cornetcy | Coumaric |
| Cobwebby | Collared | Comptoir | Consumer | Cornflag | Coumarin |
| Cocaigne | Collaret | Compulse | Consumpt | Cornicle | Countess |
| Coccagee | Collator | Computer | Contango | Cornific | Counting |
| Coccidia | Colleger | Conarial | Contempt | Cornland | Coupling |
| Cocculus | Colletic | Conarium | Contents | Cornloft | Courante |
| Cochlean | Colliery | Conation | Continue | Corn-mill | Couranto |
| Cochlear | Collogue | Conative | Contline | Corn-moth | Coursing |
| Cocinate | Colloquy | Concause | Contract | Cornpipe | Courting |
| Cockaded | Colluder | Conceder | Contrary | Corn-rent | Court-day |
| Cockatoo | Colonial | Conceive | Contrast | Corn-wain | Courtesy |

### EIGHT-LETTER WORDS—*continued*

| | | | | | |
|---|---|---|---|---|---|
| Courtier | Creatrix | Crotchet | Curlicue | Daintily | Deadness |
| Courtlet | Creature | Crotonic | Currency | Dairyman | Dead-pull |
| Couscous | Credence | Crottles | Curricle | Dalesman | Dead-rope |
| Cousinly | Credenda | Croupade | Curricle | Dallying | Dead-shot |
| Cousinry | Credible | Croupier | Cursitor | Dalmahoy | Dead-wall |
| Coutille | Credibly | Croupous | Cursores | Dalmatic | Dead-wind |
| Covenant | Creditor | Crowbill | Curtleax | Damaskin | Deadwood |
| Coventry | Creeping | Crowfoot | Curtness | Damassin | Deadwort |
| Covercle | Crematon | Crowmill | Curvital | Damboard | Deaf-mute |
| Coverlet | Cremosin | Crowning | Cuspidal | Dame-wort | Deafness |
| Coverlid | Crenelet | Crownlet | Cuspidor | Damnable | Deal-fish |
| Covertly | Crenelle | Crownsaw | Customed | Dampness | Deanship |
| Covetise | Creolian | Crow-silk | Customer | Dancette | Dearling |
| Covetous | Creosote | Cruciate | Cutchery | Dandriff | Dearness |
| Covinous | Crepance | Crucible | Cut-glass | Dandruff | Dearnful |
| Cowardly | Crepitus | Crucifer | Cuthbert | Dandyise | Deathbed |
| Cowberry | Crescent | Crucifix | Cutikins | Dandyish | Deathful |
| Cowgrass | Crescive | Crumenal | Cutpurse | Dandyism | Debility |
| Cowhouse | Cretonne | Cruorine | Cutwater | Danegelt | Debonair |
| Cow-leech | Creutzer | Crusader | Cyanogen | Danelagh | Debouche |
| Co-worker | Crevasse | Crustily | Cyanosis | Dane-weed | Debtless |
| Cowpilot | Cribbage | Crutchet | Cyanotic | Dane-wort | Debutant |
| Cowplant | Cribrate | Cryolite | Cyanuret | Danseuse | Decadent |
| Cow-wheat | Cribrose | Cubation | Cyanuric | Danubian | Decagram |
| Coxalgia | Cricetus | Cubature | Cyclamen | Dapedius | Decanter |
| Coxiness | Crimeful | Cubebine | Cycle-car | Daring-do | Deceased |
| Coxswain | Criminal | Cubiform | Cyclical | Darkness | Deceiver |
| Coystrel | Crimpage | Cuboidal | Cyclonic | Darksome | December |
| Coystril | Crinated | Cucumber | Cyclopic | Darraign | Decemfid |
| Cozenage | Cringing | Cucurbit | Cyclosis | Dartrow | Decemvir |
| Crabtree | Crispate | Cul-de-sac | Cylinder | Darrayne | Decently |
| Crabwood | Crisping | Culinary | Cymatium | Dastardy | Decerned |
| Crab-yaws | Cristate | Cullyism | Cynanche | Dasyures | Decigram |
| Crackjaw | Criteria | Culottic | Cynicism | Dateless | Decimate |
| Cracklin | Crithmum | Culpable | Cynogale | Date-line | Decipher |
| Cracknel | Critical | Culpably | Cynosure | Date-palm | Decision |
| Cracowes | Critique | Cultrate | Cyrenaic | Date-plum | Decisive |
| Cradling | Croaking | Culverin | Cyrillic | Date-tree | Decisory |
| Craftily | Croceous | Cumbrian | Cysticle | Datolite | Deck-hand |
| Cragsman | Crockery | Cumbrous | Cystitis | Daturine | Deck-load |
| Cramfull | Crocoite | Cumulate | Cytisine | Daubster | Declared |
| Cramoisy | Cromlech | Cumulose | Cytology | Daughter | Declinal |
| Crampons | Cromorna | Cunabula | Czarevna | Dauphine | Decliner |
| Crane-fly | Crop-comb | Cunarder | Czaritza | Davy-lamp | Decolour |
| Crankles | Cropping | Cuneated | Czechish | Daybreak | Decorate |
| Cratches | Crop-sick | Cuniform | | Day-dream | Decorous |
| Craw-craw | Crossbar | Cupboard | | Daylight | Decrease |
| Craw-fish | Crossbit | Cupidity | | Daysight | Decrepit |
| Crawling | Crossbow | Cupreous | | Day-woman | Decretal |
| Crayfish | Cross-bun | Curarine | | Dead-beat | Decurion |
| Creamery | Crosscut | Curarise | **D** | Deadborn | Dedation |
| Cream-nut | Crossing | Curassow | Dacryoma | Deadfull | Dedicant |
| Cream-pot | Crosslet | Curative | Dactylar | Deadhead | Dedicate |
| Creasote | Cross-row | Curatory | Dactylic | Dead-heat | Dedition |
| Creating | Cross-sea | Curbless | Daemonic | Dead-lift | Deedless |
| Creatine | Cross-tie | Curbroof | Daffodil | Deadlock | Deemster |
| Creation | Crossway | Curculio | Dagswain | Dead-loss | Deep-dyed |
| Creative | Crotched | Cureless | Dahabieh | Dead-meat | Deep-laid |

## EIGHT-LETTER WORDS—*continued*

| | | | | | |
|---|---|---|---|---|---|
| Deepmost | Demented | Derbyite | Devoutly | Dichroic | Dioritic |
| Deepness | Dementia | Der-doing | Dewberry | Diclinic | Dioscure |
| Deep-read | Demersal | Derelict | Dewiness | Dicrotic | Dipchick |
| Deer-hair | Demersed | Derision | Dewpoint | Dictated | Diplegia |
| Deer-herd | Demibain | Derisive | Dewstone | Dictator | Diplomat |
| Deer-lick | Demijohn | Derisory | Dextrine | Didactic | Diplopia |
| Deer-neck | Demilune | Derivate | Dextrose | Didactyl | D'pnoous |
| Deerskin | Demissly | Dermatic | Dextrous | Didapper | Dipsacus |
| Defaming | Demi-tint | Derogate | Diabasic | Didymium | Dipsosis |
| Defecate | Demitone | Derring-do | Diabetes | Didymous | Dipteral |
| Defenced | Demiurge | Describe | Diabetic | Diegesis | Dipteran |
| Defender | Demi-volt | Descried | Diablery | Dielytra | Dipteros |
| Defendee | Demi-wolf | Descrive | Diabolic | Die-stock | Directly |
| Deferent | Democrat | Deserter | Diachyma | Dietetic | Director |
| Deferred | Demolish | Deserver | Diaconal | Diffract | Direness |
| Deferrer | Demology | Designer | Diactrine | Diffused | Dirigent |
| Defiance | Demoness | Desilver | Diadelph | Diffuser | Diriment |
| Defilade | Demoniac | Desirous | Diademed | Digamous | Disabled |
| Definite | Demonian | Desk-work | Diadexis | Digamist | Disabuse |
| Deflower | Demonism | Desolate | Diadochi | Digester | Disadorn |
| Defluent | Demonist | Despatch | Diaglyph | Diggable | Disagree |
| Deforced | Demonize | Despight | Diagnose | Diggings | Disallow |
| Deforest | Demonomy | Despitch | Diagonal | Digitate | Disannex |
| Deformed | Dempster | Despisal | Diagrams | Digonous | Disannul |
| Deformer | Demurely | Despiser | Diagraph | Digynian | Disarmed |
| Defrauds | Demurred | Despotat | Diallage | Digynous | Disarray |
| Defrayal | Demurrer | Despotic | Dialling | Dihedral | Disaster |
| Defrayer | Demyship | Destrier | Dialogic | Dihedron | Disbench |
| Deftness | Denarius | Detached | Dialogue | Dikamali | Disbloom |
| Degender | Denature | Detailed | Dialuric | Dilatant | Disbosom |
| Deifical | Dendrite | Detailer | Dialyses | Dilation | Disbowel |
| Deisheal | Dendroid | Detainer | Dialysis | Dilative | Disburse |
| Dejected | Dendroit | Detecter | Dialytic | Dilatory | Discandy |
| Dejectly | Denegate | Detector | Dialyzer | Diligent | Discharm |
| Dejeuner | Denehole | Detested | Diameter | Dillybag | Discinct |
| Delation | Deniable | Detester | Diandria | Dilution | Disciple |
| Delectus | Denotate | Dethrone | Dianodal | Diluvial | Disclaim |
| Delegacy | Denounce | Detonate | Dianthus | Diluvian | Disclose |
| Delegate | Dentagra | Detonize | Diapason | Diluvion | Discount |
| Deleting | Dentated | Detrital | Diapente | Diluvium | Discover |
| Deletion | Denticle | Detrited | Diaphane | Dimerism | Discrase |
| Deletive | Dentized | Detritus | Diapnoic | Dimerous | Discreet |
| Deletory | Denudate | Detrusor | Diarized | Dimetric | Discrete |
| Delibate | Departed | Deuce-ace | Diaspora | Diminish | Discrown |
| Delicacy | Departer | Deucedly | Diaspore | Dimyaria | Diseased |
| Delicate | Depeinct | Develope | Diastase | Dinarchy | Disedify |
| Delirium | Depictor | Deviator | Diastema | Diner-out | Disembay |
| Delivery | Depilate | Devildom | Diastole | Ding-dong | Disendow |
| Delphian | Deponent | Deviless | Diastyle | Dinornis | Disenrol |
| Delphine | Deportee | Devilish | Diatomic | Dinosaur | Disflesh |
| Delubrum | Depraved | Devilism | Diatonic | Diocesan | Disfrock |
| Delusion | Depraver | Devilkin | Diatribe | Diœcian | Disgavel |
| Delusive | Depriver | Deviltry | Dibstone | Diogenic | Disgorge |
| Delusory | Depurate | Devolute | Dicacity | Diopside | Disgrace |
| Demagogy | Deputize | Devonian | Dice-coal | Dioptase | Disgrade |
| Demarche | Derailer | Devotion | Dicentra | Dioptric | Disguise |
| Demeaned | Derby-dog | Devourer | Dice-play | Dioramic | Dishabit |

## EIGHT-LETTER WORDS—*continued*

| | | | | | |
|---|---|---|---|---|---|
| Disherit | Distitle | Document | Donatory | Downweed | Droghing |
| Dishevel | Distomum | Doddered | Donnered | Doxology | Drollery |
| Dishorse | Distract | Dodecane | Donzella | Doziness | Drolling |
| Disinter | Distrain | Dodipoll | Dool-tree | Drabbett | Drollish |
| Disippus | Distrait | Dodipolt | Doom-palm | Drabette | Dromical |
| Disjoint | Distream | Dodonian | Doomsday | Drabbish | Drone-fly |
| Disjunct | Distress | Dogberry | Doomsman | Drabbled | Drooping |
| Disleave | District | Dog-brier | Door-bell | Drabbler | Dropping |
| Disliked | Distrust | Dog-cheap | Door-case | Dracaena | Drop-ripe |
| Disliken | Disunion | Dog-eared | Door-hawk | Dracanth | Dropsied |
| Dislodge | Disunite | Dog-faced | Doorless | Draconic | Drop-wise |
| Disloign | Disunity | Doge-ship | Door-nail | Draconin | Drop wort |
| Disloyal | Disusage | Doggedly | Door-post | Draffish | Drotchel |
| Dismally | Disvalue | Doggerel | Door-sill | Draft-bar | Droughty |
| Dismayed | Disvouch | Doggoned | Door-step | Dragbolt | Drowsily |
| Dismount | Disyoked | Dog-grass | Door-yard | Draggled | Drowsing |
| Disorbed | Ditch-dog | Dog-house | Doricism | Drag-hook | Drubbing |
| Disorder | Dithecal | Dog-latin | Dormancy | Drag-hunt | Drudgery |
| Disowned | Ditheism | Dogleech | Dormouse | Dragoman | Drudgism |
| Dispatch | Ditheist | Dog-louse | Dorsally | Dragonet | Druggist |
| Dispathy | Ditokous | Dogmatic | Dosology | Dragonne | Druidess |
| Dispeace | Ditty-bag | Dog's-bane | Dotardly | Dragsman | Druidish |
| Dispence | Ditty-box | Dog-sleep | Dotation | Drainage | Druidism |
| Dispense | Diuresis | Dogs-meat | Dotingly | Dramatic | Drumfire |
| Disperse | Diuretic | Dog's-nose | Dotterel | Drammock | Drumfish |
| Dispirit | Divagate | Dog-tired | Douanier | Dram-shop | Drumhead |
| Displace | Divalent | Dog-tooth | Doublets | Draughts | Drumming |
| Displait | Diverged | Dog-trick | Doubling | Draughty | Drummock |
| Displant | Diverter | Dog-watch | Doubloon | Drawable | Drunkard |
| Displode | Dividend | Dog-weary | Doubtful | Drawback | Dry-goods |
| Displume | Divident | Dog-wheat | Doubting | Drawbolt | Dry-nurse |
| Disponee | Dividing | Dog-whelk | Doubtive | Drawgate | Dry-plate |
| Disponer | Divi-divi | Doldrums | Doughboy | Draw-gear | Dry-point |
| Disponge | Dividual | Dolerite | Doughnut | Drawling | Dry-steam |
| Disposal | Divinely | Dolesome | Dourness | Draw-link | Dry-stone |
| Disposed | Divinify | Dolichos | Dovecote | Draw-well | Dry-stove |
| Disposer | Divinity | Dollared | Dove-eyed | Dreadful | Dualized |
| Dispread | Divinize | Dollhood | Dovelike | Dreamery | Dubitate |
| Disprize | Division | Dollship | Doveship | Dreamful | Ducatoon |
| Disproof | Divisive | Dolomite | Dovetail | Dreamily | Duckbill |
| Disprove | Divorced | Doloroso | Dowdyish | Drearily | Duck-hawk |
| Dispunge | Divorcee | Dolorous | Dowdyism | Dreggish | Duckling |
| Dispurse | Divorcer | Domainal | Dowelled | Drencher | Duck-mole |
| Disputed | Divulger | Domanial | Dowel-pin | Dressing | Duck-shot |
| Disputer | Dizzying | Domelike | Dowf-ness | Dribbler | Duck-weed |
| Disquiet | Dob-chick | Domesday | Downbear | Dribblet | Duelling |
| Disrober | Docetism | Domesman | Downbore | Driftage | Duellist |
| Disseize | Docetist | Domestic | Downcast | Driftice | Duelsome |
| Disserve | Dochmiac | Domicile | Downcome | Drift-net | Duettino |
| Dissever | Docility | Dominant | Downfall | Drift-way | Duettist |
| Dissight | Docimacy | Dominate | Downhaul | Drill-bow | Dukeling |
| Dissolve | Dockized | Domineer | Downhill | Drill-box | Duke-ship |
| Dissuade | Dockyard | Dominion | Downland | Drilling | Dulcimer |
| Distally | Doctoral | Dominium | Down-line | Drinking | Dulcitol |
| Distance | Doctored | Dominoes | Downpour | Dripping | Dull-eyed |
| Distaste | Doctorly | Donation | Downrush | Drivable | Dull-head |
| Disthene | Doctress | Donatism | Downtrod | Drizzled | Dullness |
| Distinct | Doctrine | Donative | Downward | Drofland | Dumb-cake |

EIGHT-LETTER WORDS—*continued*

| | | | | | |
|---|---|---|---|---|---|
| Dumb-cane | Earth-pea | Eel-grass | Elf-arrow | Emphatic | Endermic |
| Dumbness | Easeless | Eel-spear | Elf-child | Empierce | Endocarp |
| Dumb-show | Easement | Eeriness | Elidable | Employee | Endocyst |
| Dumosity | Easiness | Effecter | Eligible | Employer | Ebdoderm |
| Dumpling | Easterly | Effector | Eligibly | Emplunge | Endogamy |
| Duncedom | Eastland | Efferent | Elinguid | Empoison | Endorsee |
| Dun-diver | Eastmost | Efficacy | Ellipsis | Emporium | Endorser |
| Dungaree | Eastward | Effierce | Elliptic | Emptysis | Endosarc |
| Dungeree | Eau-de-vie | Effigial | Elocular | Empurple | Endrudge |
| Duodenal | Ebenezer | Effluent | Elongate | Empuzzle | Endymion |
| Duodenum | Ebionise | Effluvia | Eloquent | Empyesis | Energico |
| Duologue | Ebionism | Effusion | Elsewise | Empyreal | Energise |
| Duration | Ebionite | Effusive | Eludible | Empyrean | Energize |
| Duskness | Eblanine | Eftsoons | Elvanite | Emulator | Enervate |
| Dustball | Ebriated | Egestion | Elve-lock | Emulgent | Enfamish |
| Dust-cart | Eburnean | Egestive | Elvishly | Emulsify | Enfeeble |
| Dust-coat | Eburnine | Eggapple | Elydoric | Emulsine | Enfetter |
| Dust-hole | Ecaudate | Egg-glass | Elytrine | Emulsion | Enfierce |
| Dutchman | Ecclesia | Egg-plant | Emaciate | Emulsive | Enfilade |
| Dutiable | Eccrisis | Egg-shell | Embalmer | Enacting | Enflower |
| Duty-free | Eccritic | Egg-slice | Embattle | Enactive | Enforcer |
| Dwarfish | Echeance | Egg-spoon | Embezzle | Enacture | Enforest |
| Dwelling | Echinate | Egg-tooth | Embitter | Enallage | Enfreeze |
| Dye-house | Echinite | Egg-whisk | Emblazon | Enaluron | Engaging |
| Dye-stuff | Echinoid | Eglatere | Embolden | Enarched | Engender |
| Dynamics | Echinops | Egoistic | Embolism | Enascent | Engineer |
| Dynamism | Echiodon | Egophony | Embolite | Enaunter | Enginery |
| Dynamist | Echoless | Egyptian | Emborder | Encaenia | Engirdle |
| Dynamite | Eclampsy | Eighteen | Embosser | Encarpus | Englante |
| Dynastic | Eclectic | Eighthly | Embottle | Enceinte | Engoulee |
| Dyschroa | Ecliptic | Ejection | Embracer | Encharge | Engouled |
| Dysluite | Eclogite | Ejective | Embrasor | Enchisel | Engraver |
| Dysmenia | Economic | Elaidate | Embronze | Enchoric | Engrieve |
| Dysodile | Ecostate | Elaiodic | Embryous | Encircle | Engroove |
| Dysopsia | Ecphasis | Elaphine | Emendals | Enclisis | Enguiche |
| Dysorexy | Ecraseur | Elapsion | Emendate | Enclitic | Enhancer |
| Dyspathy | Ecstatic | Elatedly | Emergent | Encloser | Enharden |
| Dyspepsy | Ectoderm | Elaterin | Emerited | Enclothe | Enhearse |
| Dysphony | Ectozoan | Elder-gun | Emeritus | Encoffin | Enhunger |
| Dyspnoea | Ectropic | Eldorado | Emersion | Encollar | Enhydric |
| Dyspnoic | Ectrotic | Eldritch | Emetical | Encolour | Enjoiner |
| Dytiscid | Ecumenic | Election | Emiction | Encolure | Enkernel |
| Dystomic | Edacious | Elective | Emictory | Encomium | Enkindle |
| Dytiscus | Eddy-wind | Electric | Emigrant | Encradle | Enlarged |
| | Edentata | Electron | Emigrate | Encrease | Enlarger |
| | Edentate | Electrum | Eminence | Encrinal | Enlumine |
| | Edge-bone | Elegance | Eminency | Encrinic | Enmanché |
| | Edgeless | Elegancy | Emissary | Encroach | Enmarble |
| **E** | Edge-rail | Elegante | Emission | Encumber | Enmossed |
| | Edge-tool | Elegiast | Emissive | Encurled | Enneadic |
| Eagle-owl | Edgeways | Elenchic | Emissory | Encyclic | Enneagon |
| Eagle-ray | Edgewise | Elenchus | Emmanuel | Encysted | Enneatic |
| Ear-bored | Edginess | Elenctic | Emmarble | Encystis | Enormity |
| Earphone | Editress | Elephant | Empacket | Endamage | Enormous |
| Ear-shell | Educable | Eleusine | Empatron | Endanger | Enquirer |
| Earth-bag | Educator | Elevated | Empeople | Endeixis | Enravish |
| Earthfed | Educible | Elevator | Emperish | Endemial | Enricher |
| Earth-hog | Eduction | Eleventh | Emphasis | Endenize | Enroller |
| Earth-nut | | | | | |

### EIGHT-LETTER WORDS—*continued*

| | | | | | |
|---|---|---|---|---|---|
| Ensample | Epenetic | Eremitic | Estivate | Eurythmy | Exequies |
| Ensconce | Ephemera | Ereption | Estonian | Eusebian | Exercise |
| Ensemble | Ephesian | Erethism | Estoppel | Eutheria | Exergual |
| Enshield | Epiblast | Erewhile | Estovers | Eutrophy | Exertion |
| Enshrine | Epicalyx | Ergotine | Estrange | Evacuant | Exertive |
| Enshroud | Epicerie | Ergotise | Estridge | Evacuate | Exhalant |
| Ensiform | Epicolic | Ergotism | Esurient | Evadible | Exhalent |
| Ensigncy | Epicycle | Erigeron | Etcetera | Evaluate | Exhorter |
| Ensigned | Epidemic | Erminois | Eteostic | Evanesce | Exhumate |
| Ensilage | Epidotic | Erotesis | Eternise | Evangely | Exigeant |
| Enslaver | Epigeous | Erotetic | Eternity | Evasible | Exigence |
| Ensphere | Epigraph | Erotical | Eternize | Evection | Exigency |
| Enstyled | Epilepsy | Errantly | Ethereal | Even-down | Exigible |
| Ensuring | Epilogic | Errantry | Etherine | Evenfall | Exiguity |
| Enswathe | Epilogue | Errorist | Etherise | Evenness | Exiguous |
| Entackle | Epimeral | Eructate | Etherism | Evensong | Eximious |
| E ntailer | Epinasty | Erumpent | Etherize | Eventful | Exintine |
| Entangle | Epiornis | Eruption | Etherole | Eventide | Existent |
| Entastic | Epiphany | Eruptive | Ethicist | Eventual | Exitious |
| Entellus | Epiphora | Erycinia | Ethiopic | Evermore | Ex-libris |
| Entender | Epiphyte | Erysimum | Ethnarch | Eversion | Exophagy |
| Entering | Epiploce | Erythema | Ethnical | Everyday | Exorable |
| Enthrill | Epiploic | Escalade | Ethology | Everyone | Exorcise |
| Enthrone | Epiploon | Escalado | Ethylene | Everyway | Exorcism |
| Enticing | Epipolic | Escallop | Etiolate | Eviction | Exorcist |
| Entirely | Epipoeia | Escambio | Etiology | Evidence | Exorcize |
| Entirety | Episcopy | Escapade | Etrurian | Evildoer | Exordial |
| Entocele | Episemon | Escapado | Etruscan | Evilness | Exordium |
| Entomoid | Episodal | Escarped | Etypical | Evincive | Exosmose |
| Entoptic | Episodic | Eschalot | Eucalypt | Evitable | Exostome |
| Entozoal | Episperm | Eschewer | Eucharis | Evocator | Exoteric |
| Entozoic | Epistler | Escouade | Euchylia | Evolatic | Expecter |
| Entozoon | Epistyle | Esculent | Euctical | Evolvent | Expedite |
| Entr'acte | Epitasis | Escurial | Eugenics | Evulgate | Expertly |
| Entrails | Epitonic | Esoteric | Eugenism | Evulsion | Expiable |
| Entrance | Epitrite | Espalier | Eugenist | Ewigkeit | Expiator |
| Entreaty | Epitrope | Esparcet | Eugubine | Exacting | Expirant |
| Entremes | Epizooty | Especial | Eulogist | Exaction | Expiring |
| Entrench | Eplicate | Espibawn | Eulogium | Examinee | Explicit |
| Entrepas | Eponymic | Espiègle | Eulogize | Examiner | Exploder |
| Entrepot | Epopoeia | Espiotte | Euniceae | Examplar | Explorer |
| Entresol | Epsomite | Espousal | Euonymin | Excavate | Exponent |
| Enuresis | Epulotic | Espoused | Euonymus | Exceeder | Exported |
| Envapour | Equalise | Espouser | Eupatory | Exceptor | Exporter |
| Envassal | Equality | Esquisse | Eupatrid | Exchange | Exposure |
| Enveigle | Equalize | Essayish | Eupepsia | Excision | Exscinds |
| Envelope | Equalled | Essayist | Eupeptic | Excitant | Exserted |
| Enviable | Equation | Essaykin | Euphonia | Exciting | Extender |
| Enviably | Equiform | Essenism | Euphonic | Excitive | Extensor |
| Envisage | Equipage | Essoiner | Euphonon | Excretes | Exterior |
| Envolume | Equitant | Essonite | Euphrasy | Excursus | External |
| Enwallow | Equivoke | Essorant | Euphuise | Execrate | Externat |
| Enzootic | Eradiate | Estacade | Euphuism | Executer | Extoller |
| Eolipile | Erasable | Estancia | Euphuist | Executor | Extrados |
| Eolithic | Erastian | Esteemer | Euphuize | Exegesis | Extrorse |
| Epagogic | Erectile | Esthetic | Eupyrion | Exegetic | Exultant |
| Epalpate | Erection | Estimate | Eurasion | Exemplar | Exuviate |
| Epanodos | Erective | Estivage | European | Exequial | Eyeglass |

EIGHT-LETTER WORDS—*continued*

| | | | | | |
|---|---|---|---|---|---|
| Eyepiece | Falsette | Feaberry | Fen-goose | Fig-shell | Firehose |
| Eyesalve | Falsetto | Fearless | Fenugrec | Figulate | Fire-kiln |
| Eyesight | Fameless | Fearsome | Feoffing | Figuline | Firelock |
| Eyestone | Familiar | Feasible | Feracity | Figurant | Fire-plug |
| Eyetooth | Familism | Feasibly | Ferd-fare | Figurate | Fireship |
| Eyewater | Familist | Feast-day | Feretory | Figurial | Fireside |
| | Famished | Feastful | Ferinely | Figurine | Fire-step |
| | Famously | Feasting | Ferments | Figuring | Firetail |
| | Famulist | Feast-won | Fernally | Figurist | Firetrap |
| | Fan-blast | Feateous | Fernseed | Filagree | Fire-ward |
| **F** | Fanciful | Feathers | Fernshaw | Filament | Fire-weed |
| | Fandango | Feathery | Ferocity | Filarial | Firewood |
| Fabulise | Fanfaron | Featness | Ferreous | Filarius | Firmless |
| Fabulist | Fangless | Featured | Ferreted | Filatory | Firmness |
| Fabulize | Fanlight | Feblesse | Ferreter | Filature | First-aid |
| Fabulous | Fantasia | Febrific | Ferretto | File-fish | First-day |
| Face-ache | Fanwheel | February | Ferriage | Filially | Fishable |
| Face-card | Faradaic | Feckless | Ferruled | Filicoid | Fishball |
| Faceless | Faradise | Feculent | Ferrying | Filiform | Fishbeam |
| Facetiae | Faradism | Fedelini | Ferryman | Filigree | Fish-cake |
| Facially | Farcical | Federacy | Feruling | Filioque | Fishcoop |
| Facilely | Farcy-bud | Federary | Fervency | Filipina | Fish-glue |
| Facility | Fardeled | Federate | Fervidly | Filipino | Fish-hawk |
| Facingly | Farewell | Feeblish | Festally | Fillibeg | Fish-hook |
| Factious | Far-forth | Feed-head | Festival | Filliped | Fish-meal |
| Factotum | Faringee | Feed-pipe | Fetation | Filthily | Fish-pond |
| Faculous | Farinose | Feed-pump | Fetching | Filtrate | Fish-room |
| Fadeless | Farmable | Fee-grief | Feticide | Finalism | Fish-skin |
| Fadingly | Farmyard | Feetless | Fetishes | Finalist | Fish-tail |
| Fae-berry | Farriery | Feigning | Fettered | Finality | Fish-weir |
| Fagoting | Farrowed | Feinting | Feudally | Financed | Fish-wife |
| Faildike | Far-spent | Feldspar | Feverfew | Findable | Fissiped |
| Fainéant | Farthest | Felicide | Feverish | Finedraw | Fissured |
| Fainness | Farthing | Felicity | Feverous | Fineless | Fistiana |
| Fainting | Fascicle | Felinity | Fewtrils | Fineness | Fistinut |
| Faintish | Fascists | Fellable | Fibrilla | Fine-spun | Fistular |
| Fair-copy | Fashious | Fellah'n | Fibrosis | Finesser | Fitfully |
| Fairhand | Fastened | Fellinic | Fibulate | Fingered | Fitliest |
| Fairlead | Fastness | Fellness | Fibulous | Fingroms | Fivefold |
| Fairness | Fatalism | Fellowed | Fiddling | Finished | Fiveleaf |
| Fair-play | Fatalist | Fellowly | Fidelity | Finisher | Fixation |
| Fairydom | Fatality | Felo-de-se | Fidgeted | Finitely | Fixative |
| Fairyism | Fatherly | Felonous | Fidicula | Finitude | Fixature |
| Faithful | Fathomed | Felsitic | Fiducial | Finnikin | Fixidity |
| Fakement | Fatigate | Felstone | Field-bed | Finochio | Flabbily |
| Fakirism | Fatigued | Feltered | Field-day | Finscale | Flag-day |
| Falcated | Fattened | Feltwort | Field-gun | Fin-whale | Flagging |
| Falchion | Fattener | Femality | Fielding | Firearms | Flagrant |
| Falconer | Fattrels | Femerell | Fiendful | Fireback | Flag-ship |
| Falconet | Faubourg | Femicide | Fiendish | Fire-ball | Flag-worm |
| Falconry | Faultful | Feminine | Fiercely | Fire-bars | Flambeau |
| Falderal | Faultily | Feminist | Fiery-hot | Fireboat | Flamelet |
| Faldetta | Faulting | Feminize | Fiery-new | Fireclay | Flamingo |
| Fallable | Fauteuil | Fenberry | Fife-rail | Firecock | Flammule |
| Fallible | Fauvette | Fenceful | Fiftieth | Firedamp | Flanched |
| Fallibly | Favonian | Fencible | Fig-apple | Fire-eyed | Flanerie |
| Fallowed | Favourer | Fenester | Fig-eater | Fireflag | Flap-jack |
| Fall-trap | Fayalite | Fenestra | Fighting | Fire-hook | Flashing |

EIGHT-LETTER WORDS—*continued*

| | | | | | |
|---|---|---|---|---|---|
| Flashily | Floccule | Folksong | Foregone | Formiate | Fragrant |
| Flat-boat | Flockbed | Folktale | Forehand | Formless | Frailish |
| Flatfish | Flocking | Follicle | Forehead | Formulae | Framable |
| Flathead | Flogging | Follower | Fore-hook | Formular | Frame-saw |
| Flat-iron | Flooding | Fomenter | Foreknow | Formulas | Frampold |
| Flat-long | Flooking | Fondling | Forelaid | Forrader | Francatu |
| Flatness | Floorage | Fondness | Foreland | Forsaken | Frank-fee |
| Flat-race | Flooring | Fontanel | Forelays | Forslack | Franking |
| Flattery | Floppily | Fontange | Forelend | Forsooth | Frankish |
| Flatting | Florally | Foodless | Forelent | Forspeak | Franklin |
| Flattish | Florence | Fool-born | Forelift | Forspend | Frasling |
| Flatwise | Floriage | Foolscap | Forelock | Forstall | Fraudful |
| Flatworm | Florican | Fool-trap | Foremast | Forswear | Fräulein |
| Flaunter | Floridly | Football | Foremean | Forswink | Fraxinin |
| Flautist | Floscule | Foot-bath | Foremost | Forswonk | Fraxinus |
| Flawless | Flotilla | Footfall | Forename | Forthink | Freakful |
| Flax-comb | Flounder | Footgear | Forenoon | Fortieth | Freakish |
| Flax-lily | Flourish | Foot-halt | Forensal | Fortress | Freckled |
| Flax-mill | Floweret | Foothill | Forensic | Fortuist | Freeborn |
| Flax-seed | Fluently | Foothold | Forepart | Fortuity | Free-city |
| Flaxtail | Fluidify | Foot-iron | Forepast | Fortuned | Free-cost |
| Flax-weed | Fluidise | Footless | Forepeak | Forwards | Freedman |
| Flea-bane | Fluidism | Footling | Foreplan | Forwaste | Freehand |
| Flea-bite | Fluidity | Footmark | Fore-rank | Forweary | Freehold |
| Fleaking | Flummery | Footmuff | Fore-read | Forzando | Free-love |
| Flea-wort | Fluorene | Footnote | Forerent | Fossdyke | Freeness |
| Flecking | Fluoride | Footpace | Foresaid | Fossette | Free-port |
| Flection | Fluorine | Footpath | Foresail | Fossores | Free-reed |
| Fleering | Fluorite | Foot-post | Foreseen | Fosterer | Free-shot |
| Fleeting | Fluorous | Footrace | Foreseer | Fostress | Free-soil |
| Flenched | Flurried | Foot-rope | Foreship | Fougasse | Free-will |
| Fleshfly | Flush-box | Footrule | Foreshow | Foul-fish | Freezing |
| Flesh-pot | Flushing | Footsore | Foreside | Foulness | Fremitus |
| Fletcher | Flustery | Footstep | Foreslow | Foul-play | Frenetic |
| Flexible | Fluxible | Footwear | Forestal | Foundery | Frenulum |
| Flexibly | Fly-blown | Footworn | Forestay | Fountain | Frenzied |
| Flexuose | Flymaker | Foozling | Forester | Fountful | Frequent |
| Flexuous | Flypaper | Foraging | Forestry | Fourfold | Frescade |
| Flichter | Fly-speck | Foramina | Foretell | Fourling | Frescoed |
| Flighted | Fly-water | Forcedly | Foretime | Fourneau | Frescoer |
| Flimflam | Fly-wheel | Forceful | Foreward | Fourrier | Freshish |
| Flimsily | Foal-foot | Forcible | Forewarn | Foursome | Freshman |
| Flincher | Foamless | Forcibly | Forewent | Fourteen | Freshnew |
| Flinders | Focalise | Fordable | Forewind | Fourthly | Fretting |
| Flintify | Focalize | Forebear | Forewish | Fox-brush | Fretwork |
| Flipflap | Fodderer | Forebode | Foreword | Fox-chase | Friation |
| Flipflop | Fog-bound | Forebody | Foreyard | Fox-earth | Fribbler |
| Flippant | Fogeydom | Forecast | Forfairn | Foxglove | Friction |
| Flirting | Fog-smoke | Foredate | Forfends | Foxgrape | Friended |
| Flirtish | Foilable | Foredeck | Forgeman | Foxhound | Friendly |
| Flittern | Folderol | Foredone | Forgiver | Foxiness | Friesian |
| Flitters | Foldless | Foredoom | Forkedly | Fox-shark | Friesish |
| Flitting | Fold-yard | Foredoor | Forkhead | Fox-sleep | Frighten |
| Flixweed | Foliaged | Fore-edge | Forkless | Foziness | Frigidly |
| Floatage | Foliated | Forefeel | Forktail | Fraction | Frilling |
| Floating | Folkland | Forefelt | Formalin | Fracture | Frimaire |
| Floatsam | Folk-lore | Forefoot | Formally | Fragaria | Fringent |
| Floccose | Folkmote | Foregoer | Formerly | Fragment | Fringing |

EIGHT-LETTER WORDS—*continued*

| | | | | | |
|---|---|---|---|---|---|
| Frippery | Fullness | Gagtooth | Gapingly | Generale | Girondin |
| Frisette | Full-stop | Gaiement | Garbaged | Generant | Girthing |
| Friskful | Fulmined | Gainable | Garboard | Generate | Girt-line |
| Friskily | Fulminic | Gainless | Garcinia | Generous | Giveable |
| Fritting | Fumarole | Gainsaid | Gardener | Genesiac | Glabrate |
| Frizette | Fumatory | Gair-fowl | Gardenia | Genetics | Glabrous |
| Frizzler | Fumbling | Galactia | Gardyloo | Genetrix | Glaciate |
| Frocking | Fumeless | Galactic | Gare-fowl | Genevese | Gladiate |
| Frog-fish | Fumewort | Galactin | Garganey | Genially | Gladiole |
| Froggery | Fumigant | Galangal | Gargling | Genitive | Gladioli |
| Frogling | Fumigate | Galatian | Gargoyle | Genitrix | Gladness |
| Frog-spit | Fumingly | Galbanum | Garishly | Geniture | Gladsome |
| Fromward | Fumitory | Galeated | Garlicky | Genovese | Glairous |
| Frondage | Fumosity | Galenism | Garotter | Gentilic | Glandage |
| Frondent | Function | Galenist | Garreted | Geodesic | Glanders |
| Frondeur | Fundable | Galenite | Garrison | Geodetic | Glandule |
| Frondose | Fundless | Galenoid | Garrotte | Geognost | Glareous |
| Frondous | Funebral | Galerite | Garrulus | Geognosy | Glassful |
| Frontage | Funereal | Galilean | Gasalier | Geogonic | Glassily |
| Frontate | Furbelow | Gall-dust | Gaselier | Geolatry | Glassing |
| Frontier | Furcated | Galleass | Gas-gauge | Geomancy | Glassite |
| Fronting | Furcifer | Galliard | Gasiform | Geometer | Glass-pot |
| Frontlet | Furcular | Galliass | Gaslight | Geometry | Glaucium |
| Frontoon | Furfurol | Gallican | Gas-mains | Geonomic | Glaucoma |
| Frostily | Furibund | Gallipot | Gas-meter | Geophagy | Glaucous |
| Frosting | Furlough | Gallivat | Gasmotor | Geoponic | Gleaming |
| Frothery | Furmenty | Gallized | Gasogene | Georgian | Gleaning |
| Froth-fly | Furriery | Galloped | Gasolene | Geoscopy | Gleesome |
| Frothily | Furthest | Galloper | Gasoline | Geranium | Gleeting |
| Frothing | Furuncle | Galloway | Gas-stove | Germanic | Gliadine |
| Frou-frou | Fury-like | Galumphs | Gastight | Germinal | Glibness |
| Frounced | Fusarole | Galvanic | Gastraea | Gerocomy | Gliddery |
| Frowning | Fusel-oil | Gambeson | Gastrula | Gestural | Glissade |
| Fructify | Fusiform | Gambison | Gas-water | Ghastful | Glissaun |
| Fructose | Fusileer | Gambling | Gas-works | Ghoulish | Gloaming |
| Frugally | Fusilier | Gambogic | Gate-bill | Giantess | Globated |
| Fruitage | Fusteric | Gambroon | Gatefine | Giantism | Globular |
| Fruitbud | Futilely | Gamecock | Gateless | Giantize | Globulet |
| Fruitery | Futility | Gamelaws | Gate-vein | Gibingly | Globulin |
| Fruit-fly | Futurise | Gameness | Gatherer | Gib-staff | Glooming |
| Fruitful | Futurist | Gamesome | Gaudy day | Giftling | Gloomily |
| Fruiting | Futurity | Gamester | Gauntlet | Gigantic | Gloriole |
| Fruition | Fuzz-ball | Gammarus | Gavelman | Gig-lamps | Gloriosa |
| Fruitive | | Gammoned | Gavelock | Gillaroo | Glorious |
| Fruitlet | | Gammoner | Gawntree | Gill-flap | Glorying |
| Frumenty | | Gang-days | Gazement | Gilt-head | Glory-pea |
| Frumpish | | Gangetic | Gazogene | Gilt-tail | Glossary |
| Frustule | | Gangliac | Gelastic | Gimcrack | Glossily |
| Fugacity | **G** | Ganglion | Gelatine | Gingerly | Glow-lamp |
| Fugitive | | Ganglial | Gelation | Gingival | Glowworm |
| Fugleman | Gabarage | Gangrene | Geldable | Gin-horse | Gloxinia |
| Fulcrate | Gabbatha | Gangsman | Gelidity | Gin-house | Glucinum |
| Fulgency | Gabioned | Gangster | Gematria | Gin-sling | Glucosid |
| Fulgural | Gable-end | Gangweek | Geminate | Gipsydom | Glumness |
| Full-aged | Gadabout | Ganister | Geminous | Gipsyism | Glumpish |
| Fullback | Gadhelic | Gantlope | Gemmeous | Girasole | Glutaeus |
| Full-butt | Gadlings | Ganymede | Gemshorn | Girdling | Gluttony |
| Full-eyed | Gadzooks | Gaolbird | Gendarme | Girlhood | Glycerol |
| | Gaggling | | | | |

## EIGHT-LETTER WORDS—*continued*

| | | | | | |
|---|---|---|---|---|---|
| Glycogen | Goosecap | Greening | Guelphic | Hairless | Handsome |
| Glyconic | Goose-egg | Greenish | Guerilla | Hairline | Hand-work |
| Glyptics | Gorgeous | Green-fly | Guernsey | Hair-salt | Handyman |
| Gnarling | Gorgonia | Green-tea | Guicowar | Hairtail | Hangable |
| Gnarring | Gossamer | Greeting | Guidable | Hairwork | Hanger-on |
| Gnathism | Gossipry | Greffier | Guidance | Hairworm | Hangnail |
| Gnatling | Goujeers | Gressing | Guileful | Halation | Hangnest |
| Gnat-worm | Gourmand | Greyness | Guiltily | Haleness | Haquebut |
| Gnomical | Goutweed | Gridelin | Guimauve | Half-back | Haqueton |
| Gnomonic | Goutwort | Gridiron | Gulf-weed | Half-boot | Hara-kiri |
| Goa-cedar | Governor | Griefful | Gullible | Half-bred | Harangue |
| Goal-line | Gownsman | Grievous | Gulosity | Half-cock | Harasser |
| Goatherd | Graafian | Grillade | Gumption | Half-dead | Hardbake |
| Goatling | Grace-cup | Grillage | Gum-resin | Half-done | Hardbeam |
| Goat-moth | Graceful | Grimness | Gunmetal | Half-face | Hardener |
| Goatskin | Gracioso | Grindery | Gun-reach | Halfling | Hardhack |
| Goat's-rue | Gracious | Gripeful | Gunsmith | Half-mark | Hardness |
| Gobbling | Gradatim | Gripping | Gunstick | Halfmast | Hardship |
| Godchild | Gradient | Griselda | Gunstock | Half-moon | Hardtack |
| God's-acre | Graduand | Griseous | Gunstone | Half-note | Hardware |
| Godsmith | Graduate | Grisette | Gurgoyle | Half-past | Hardwood |
| God-speed | Graecism | Grizzled | Guttural | Half-pike | Harebell |
| Goethian | Graecize | Groanful | Gymkhana | Half-seas | Harefoot |
| Going-out | Graffiti | Groggery | Gymnasic | Half-suit | Harepipe |
| Goitered | Graffito | Grogging | Gymnical | Half-tide | Hari-kari |
| Goitrous | Grafting | Grog-shop | Gymnotus | Half-time | Harleian |
| Golconda | Grainage | Groining | Gynaecic | Half-tint | Harmless |
| Gold-dust | Graining | Gromwell | Gynander | Half-tone | Harmonic |
| Goldenly | Grain-tin | Grooming | Gynarchy | Halicore | Harmosty |
| Gold-fern | Graithly | Grooving | Gynecian | Haliotis | Harpings |
| Goldfish | Gralline | Grosbeak | Gynecium | Hall-door | Harridan |
| Gold-foil | Gralloch | Groschen | Gynerium | Halliard | Harrower |
| Gold-lace | Gramarye | Grossart | Gypseous | Hall-mark | Hartwort |
| Gold-leaf | Gramercy | Grounder | Gypsyism | Hallooed | Hastener |
| Gold-less | Grandeur | Grousing | Gyration | Hallowed | Hastings |
| Gold-lily | Granddad | Grouting | Gyratory | Halteres | Hatbrush |
| Gold-mine | Grandson | Growable | Gyroidal | Hamiform | Hatchery |
| Gold-size | Granitic | Growlery | Gyropter | Hamulate | Hatchety |
| Gold-wire | Granular | Grubbing | Gyrostat | Handball | Hatching |
| Golf-club | Graphics | Grubbled | | Handbell | Hatchway |
| Golgotha | Graphite | Gruesome | **H** | Handbill | Hatstand |
| Golliwog | Graphium | Grumbler | Habendum | Handbook | Hateable |
| Gomarist | Grasping | Grumness | Hability | Handcart | Hatteria |
| Gombroon | Grassing | Grumphie | Habitant | Handcuff | Hat-trick |
| Gonalgia | Grass-oil | Grundsel | Habitual | Handfast | Haunched |
| Gondelay | Grateful | Gryposis | Habitude | Handgear | Hauriant |
| Goneness | Gratiola | Grysbock | Hacienda | Handgrip | Haut-gout |
| Gonfalon | Gratuity | Guacharo | Hackbolt | Handicap | Havannah |
| Gonfanon | Gravamen | Guaicaol | Hacking | Handless | Havelock |
| Gongylus | Gravelly | Guaiacum | Haematic | Handline | Havildar |
| Gonidium | Gray-eyed | Guanchos | Haematin | Handling | Havocked |
| Goodeven | Grayling | Guaracha | Hagberry | Hand-list | Hawfinch |
| Good-lack | Grazioso | Guaranty | Haggadah | Handloom | Hawk-bell |
| Goodlier | Greasing | Guardage | Haggadic | Hand-made | Hawk-eyed |
| Good-folk | Greasily | Guardant | Hagtaper | Handmaid | Hawkmoth |
| Goodness | Grecized | Guardful | Hailshot | Handmill | Hawkweed |
| Goodwife | Greedily | Guardian | Hairbell | Hand-post | Hawthorn |
| Goodwill | Greenery | Guarding | Hair-lace | Handrail | Hay-fever |

EIGHT-LETTER WORDS—*continued*

| | | | | | |
|---|---|---|---|---|---|
| Hayfield | Hectorer | Hepatise | Highroad | Homefelt | Horseman |
| Hay-knife | Hectorly | Hepatite | High-tide | Homeland | Horse-way |
| Haymaker | Hedgehog | Hepatize | High-time | Homeless | Hosepipe |
| Haystack | Hedgepig | Heptagon | Higtaper | Homelike | Hose-reel |
| Hazarder | Hedgerow | Heptarch | Hilarity | Homelily | Hospital |
| Hazardry | Hedonics | Heraldic | Hillfolk | Homemade | Hospodar |
| Hazelnut | Hedonism | Heraldry | Hill-fort | Home-rule | Hostelry |
| Haziness | Hedonist | Herbaria | Hillocky | Homesick | Hostlers |
| Headache | Heedless | Herbelet | Hillside | Homespun | Hot-blast |
| Headachy | Heelball | Herbless | Hinderer | Homeward | Hotchpot |
| Headband | Hegelian | Hercules | Hinduism | Homicide | Hotelier |
| Headboom | Hegemony | Herd-book | Hipjoint | Homilist | Hothouse |
| Headfast | Hegumene | Herdsman | Hippuric | Homodont | Hot-press |
| Headgear | Heighten | Hereaway | Hippurid | Homogamy | Hot-short |
| Headland | Heirless | Heredity | Hireable | Homogeny | Hottonia |
| Headless | Heirloom | Hereinto | Hireless | Homology | Hot-water |
| Headline | Heirship | Hereunto | Hireling | Homonymy | Hour-hand |
| Headlong | Helcotic | Hereupon | Hirrient | Homotype | House-dog |
| Head-main | Heliacal | Herewith | Hirudine | Homotypy | House-fly |
| Head-mark | Helicoid | Herisson | Hispanic | Honestly | House-tax |
| Headmold | Heliosis | Heritage | Histioid | Honey-bag | Housling |
| Headmost | Heliozoa | Hermetic | Historic | Honey-bee | Hout-tout |
| Headnote | Hellborn | Hernioid | Histrion | Honeydew | Hovelled |
| Headpump | Hellbred | Hernshaw | Hitching | Honorary | Hoveller |
| Headrest | Hellenic | Heroical | Hitherto | Honourer | Hovering |
| Headring | Hellfire | Heroicly | Hiveless | Hoodwink | Howitzer |
| Headship | Hellgate | Heroized | Hivenest | Hoofless | Huckster |
| Headsman | Hellkite | Heroship | Hoactzin | Hoofmark | Huddling |
| Headtire | Hellical | Herpetic | Hoarding | Hook-worm | Hugeness |
| Head-wind | Hellward | Hertzian | Hoarsely | Hooligan | Huguenot |
| Headword | Helminth | Heruclid | Hoastman | Hoop-iron | Huia-bird |
| Headwork | Helmless | Hesitant | Hobbyism | Hopeless | Humanely |
| Healable | Helmsman | Hesitate | Hobbyist | Hopingly | Humanise |
| Healsome | Helotage | Hexagram | Hockherb | Hoppling | Humanism |
| Hearable | Helotism | Hexaplar | Hockling | Horatian | Humanist |
| Heartcam | Helpless | Hey-go-mad | Hock-tide | Hornbeak | Humanity |
| Heartily | Helpmate | Hibernal | Hoggerel | Hornbeam | Humanize |
| Heartlet | Helpmeet | Hibiscus | Hogmanay | Hornbill | Humation |
| Heartrot | Helvetic | Hiccatee | Hog-reeve | Hornbook | Humbless |
| Heathery | Hematine | Hiccough | Hogsbean | Hornfish | Humidify |
| Heath-hen | Hematite | Hiccuped | Hogscart | Hornfoot | Humidity |
| Heathpea | Hemiolie | Hickwall | Hog-score | Horngate | Humility |
| Heat-spot | Hemionus | Hiddenly | Hogshead | Horn-lead | Hummocky |
| Heat-unit | Hemiopia | Hiderope | Hogsteer | Hornless | Humorism |
| Heatwave | Hemipode | Hidrosis | Hoistway | Hornpipe | Humorist |
| Heavenly | Hemipter | Hidrotic | Holdback | Hornwork | Humorous |
| Hebdomad | Hemp-palm | Hielaman | Holdfast | Hornwort | Humoured |
| Hebetant | Hempseed | Hierarch | Holewort | Horologe | Humpback |
| Hebetate | Henchman | H´eratic | Holiness | Horology | Humpless |
| Hebetude | Henequen | Highborn | Hollands | Horrible | Humstrum |
| Hebraise | Henequin | Highbred | Holloaed | Horribly | Hung-beef |
| Hebraism | Henhouse | Highbrow | Hollowed | Horridly | Hungered |
| Hebraist | Henhussy | High-hung | Hollowly | Horrific | Hungrily |
| Hebraize | Heniquin | Highland | Holyrood | Horsebox | Huntress |
| Hecatomb | Henmould | High-life | Holyweek | Horse-boy | Huntsman |
| Heckymal | Henroost | Highmass | Homeborn | Horsecar | Hurdling |
| Hectical | Henwoman | Highmost | Homebred | Horsefly | Hurlbone |
| Hectored | Hepatica | Highness | Home-farm | Horse-hoe | Hurlwind |

**EIGHT-LETTER WORDS—*continued***

| | | | | | |
|---|---|---|---|---|---|
| Hurrying | Ice-plant | Imbument | Inactive | Indulger | Inhersed |
| Hurtless | Ice-sheet | Imitable | Inaquate | Induline | Inherses |
| Hush-mush | Ice-water | Imitator | Inarable | Indurate | Inhesion |
| Hustling | Ice-yacht | Immanent | Inasmuch | Indusial | Inholder |
| Huzzaing | Ichorous | Immanily | Inaurate | Indusium | Inhooped |
| Hyacinth | Ichthine | Immanity | Incanton | Industry | Inhuming |
| Hyalitis | Ichthyic | Immantle | Incasked | Induviae | Inimical |
| Hybodont | Icterine | Immasked | Incavate | Induvial | Iniquity |
| Hydatism | Idealess | Immature | Incensed | Indwells | Initiate |
| Hydatoid | Idealise | Imminent | Incensor | Inedible | Injected |
| Hydrated | Idealism | Immingle | Inceptor | Inedited | Injector |
| Hydrogen | Idealist | Immobile | Inchmeal | Inequity | Injuring |
| Hydromel | Ideality | Immodest | Inchoate | Inermous | Inkiness |
| Hydromys | Idealize | Immolate | Incident | Inertion | Inkmaker |
| Hydropic | Ideation | Immoment | Incircle | Inexpert | Inkstand |
| Hydropsy | Ideative | Immortal | Incisely | Infamise | Inkstone |
| Hydrotic | Identify | Immunise | Incision | Infamize | Inlacing |
| Hydruret | Identity | Immunity | Incisive | Infamous | Inlander |
| Hygienic | Ideogram | Impairer | Incisory | Infantly | Inlawing |
| Hylicism | Ideology | Impanate | Incisure | Infantry | Inlaying |
| Hylicist | Idiotish | Imparity | Incitant | Infecter | Innately |
| Hylobate | Idiotism | Imparter | Incivism | Infecund | Innative |
| Hylozoic | Idiotize | Impeller | Inclasps | Inferiae | Innerved |
| Hymeneal | Idlehood | Imperial | Incliner | Inferior | Innocent |
| Hymenean | Idleness | Imperium | Incloser | Infernal | Innovate |
| Hymenium | Idocrase | Impetigo | Incoming | Inferred | Innuendo |
| Hymn-book | Idolater | Impierce | Incomity | Infilter | Inornate |
| Hyoscine | Idolatry | Impleach | Incorpse | Infinite | Inquired |
| Hypalgia | Idoliser | Impledge | Increase | Infinito | Inquirer |
| Hyperion | Idolizer | Implicit | Increate | Infinity | Inrigged |
| Hyphened | Ignation | Implorer | Incubate | Infirmly | Insanely |
| Hyphenic | Ignition | Implunge | Incubous | Inflamed | Insanity |
| Hypnosis | Ignominy | Implying | Incumber | Inflamer | Inscient |
| Hypnotic | Ignorant | Impocket | Incurred | Inflator | Insconce |
| Hypobole | Illation | Impoison | Incurved | Inflatus | Inscribe |
| Hypocist | Illative | Impolicy | Incurves | Inflects | Inscroll |
| Hypogeal | Ill-blood | Impolite | Indagate | Inflexed | Inseamed |
| Hypogean | Illfated | Imponent | Indebted | Influent | Insected |
| Hypogene | Ill-faurd | Imporous | Indecent | Informal | Insecure |
| Hypogeum | Illinium | Imported | Invented | Informed | Inserted |
| Hypothec | Illision | Importer | Indevote | Informer | Inshrine |
| Hypozoan | Ill-timed | Imposing | Indevout | Infringe | Insignia |
| Hypozoic | Ill-times | Impostor | Indiaman | Infrugal | Insition |
| Hysteria | Ill-treat | Impotent | Indicant | Infumate | Insnarer |
| Hysteric | Illuding | Imprests | Indicate | Infusion | Insolate |
| | Illumine | Imprimis | Indictee | Infusive | Insolent |
| | Illuming | Imprints | Indicter | Infusory | Insomnia |
| | Illusion | Imprison | Indigene | Ingenium | Insomuch |
| **I** | Illusive | Improper | Indigent | Ingroove | Inspects |
| Ianthina | Illusory | Improver | Indigest | Ingrowth | Insphere |
| Iatrical | Illyrian | Impudent | Indirect | Inguilty | Inspired |
| Iceblink | Ilmenite | Impugner | Indocile | Inguinal | Inspirer |
| Icebound | Imaginal | Impunity | Indolent | Inhalant | Inspirit |
| Ice-brook | Imaginer | Impurely | Indorsee | Inhalent | Instable |
| Ice-cream | Imbecile | Impurity | Indorser | Inhaling | Instance |
| Ice-field | Imbellic | Impurple | Indrench | Inhearse | Instancy |
| Ice-float | Imbitter | Imputing | Inducing | Inherent | Instated |
| Icehouse | Imborder | Inaction | Inductor | Inhering | Instinct |
| Ice-ledge | | | | | |

## EIGHT-LETTER WORDS—*continued*

| | | | | | |
|---|---|---|---|---|---|
| Instruct | Inworked | Italiote | Jettison | Kalamdan | Kinkajou |
| Insucken | Iodizing | Itchmite | Jeweller | Kalevala | Kinsfolk |
| Insulate | Iodoform | Iterance | Jewishly | Kaleyard | Kirkyard |
| Insulter | Iodyrite | Iterated | Jew's-harp | Kalinite | Kiroumbo |
| Insurant | Ionicize | Ivory-nut | Jibbings | Kaliyuga | Kiss-curl |
| Intaglio | Iotacism | | Jickajog | Kalology | Kistvaen |
| Integral | Irefully | **J** | Jiggered | Kalotype | Kitefoot |
| Intended | Irenical | | Jigmaker | Kamadeva | Kittened |
| Intender | Irenicon | Jabberer | Jimcrack | Kanarese | Kittlish |
| Intently | Iriditis | Jackaroo | Jingling | Kanedar | Knabbing |
| Interact | Irisated | Jacketed | Jingoish | Kangaroo | Knackish |
| Interest | Iriscope | Jack-flag | Jingoism | Kanticoy | Knappish |
| Interior | Irishism | Jackfool | Jobation | Katakana | Knappled |
| Interlay | Ironbark | Jackwood | Jockeyed | Kauri-gum | Knapsack |
| Intermit | Ironclad | Jackyard | Jocosely | Keckling | Knapweed |
| Intermix | Iron-clay | Jacobean | Jocosity | Kedgeree | Knee-deep |
| Internal | Irongrey | Jacobite | Jocundly | Keel-boat | Kneeding |
| Interrex | Ironical | Jacquard | Johannes | Keel-haul | Kneeholm |
| Intertie | Iron-sand | Jaculate | Join-hand | Keenness | Knee-stop |
| Interval | Ironsick | Jaggedly | Jointing | Keepsake | Knickers |
| Intexine | Ironside | Jailbird | Joint-oil | Kenspeck | Knife-boy |
| Intimacy | Ironware | Jalousie | Jointure | Kephalic | Knightly |
| Intimate | Ironwood | Jambeaus | Jokingly | Kerasine | Knitting |
| Intimity | Ironwork | Jamboree | Jolthead | Keratose | Knocking |
| Intitule | Irrigate | Jampanee | Jonathan | Kerchief | Knock-out |
| Intombed | Irrision | Jangling | Jongleur | Kern-baby | Knotless |
| Intonate | Irritant | Janitrix | Jovially | Kernelly | Knotting |
| Intradcs | Irritate | Janizary | Jovialty | Kerosene | Knot-work |
| Intrench | Irrupted | Januform | Joyfully | Keyboard | Knowable |
| Intrepid | Isabelle | Japanese | Joyously | Key-bugle | Knuckled |
| Intrigue | Isagogic | Japanner | Joystick | Key-money | Koftgari |
| Intrinse | Ischuria | Japhetic | Jozerant | Keyplate | Koftwork |
| Intromit | Isengrim | Japonica | Jubilant | Keystone | Koheleth |
| Introrse | Islamism | Jararaka | Jubilate | Kickable | Kohlrabi |
| Intruded | Islamite | Jasponyx | Judaical | Kickshaw | Kolinsky |
| Intruder | Islamize | Jaundice | Judaiser | Kiefekil | Konistra |
| Intubate | Islanded | Jauntily | Judaized | Killadar | Koorbash |
| Inundant | Islander | Javanese | Judaizer | Kill-crop | Kourbash |
| Inundate | Islesman | Jaw-lever | Judgment | Killdeer | Kotowing |
| Inurbane | Isobaric | Jaw-tooth | Judicial | Killogie | Kreasote |
| Inustion | Isobront | Jazerant | Jugglery | Kiln-hole | Kreutzer |
| Invaried | Isocheim | Jealousy | Juggling | Kilodyne | Kurveyor |
| Invasion | Isocryme | Jeanette | Jugo-Slav. | Kilogram | Kyanized |
| Invasive | Isodicon | Jebusite | Julienne | Kilowatt | Kyllosis |
| Inveagle | Isodomon | Jehovist | Jumpseat | Kindless | |
| Invecked | Isodomum | Jejunely | Junction | Kindling | |
| Invected | Isogonic | Jellybag | Juncture | Kindness | **L** |
| Inveighs | Isolable | Jentling | Junk-ring | Kinetics | |
| Inveigle | Isomeric | Jeopardy | Jurassic | Kingbird | Labdanum |
| Inventer | Isonymic | Jeremiad | Juratory | King-crab | Labellum |
| Inventor | Isopathy | Jerkinet | Juristic | Kingfish | Labially |
| Investor | Isostacy | Jeroboam | Jurymast | Kinghood | Labiatæ |
| Invocate | Isothere | Jerquing | Justness | Kingless | Labiated |
| Invoiced | Isotherm | Jestbook | Juvenile | Kinglike | Laboured |
| Involute | Isotonic | Jesuited | | Kingling | Labourer |
| Inwardly | Issuable | Jesuitic | **K** | Kingpost | Laburnic |
| Inweaves | Issuance | Jesuitry | | Kingship | Laburnum |
| Inwheels | Isthmian | Jet-black | Kafflyeh | Kingwood | Lace-bark |
| | | | Kaimakam | | Laceboot |

**EIGHT-LETTER WORDS—*continued***

Lace-leaf
Lacerate
Lacewing
Lachesis
Lack-a-day
Laconism
Lacrosse
Lacrymal
Lacteous
Lactific
Lactucic
Lacunose
Lacunous
Ladleful
Ladybird
Lady-fern
Lady-help
Ladyhood
Ladylike
Ladylove
Ladyship
Lagthing
Lake-like
Lamantin
Lamasery
Lambdoid
Lambency
Lamblike
Lambling
Lambskin
Lame-duck
Lamellar
Lameness
Lamented
Lamenter
Laminary
Laminate
Lampless
Lamp-post
Lancegay
Lancelet
Land-crab
Land-damn
Landfall
Land-herd
Landlady
Landless
Landlock
Landlord
Landmark
Landnama
Landrail
Land-roll
Land-skip
Landslip
Landsman
Land-turn
Landward

Landwehr
Land-wind
Langrage
Langshan
Langsyne
Language
Languish
Lankness
Lanneret
Lanthorn
Lap-board
Lapelled
Lapidary
Lapidate
Lapidify
Lapidist
Lapillus
Lap-joint
Lappeted
Lapsable
Lapsided
Lapstone
Larboard
Larcener
Larderer
Largesse
Larkspur
Larrikin
Larruped
Larvated
Larynges
Lasslorn
Latch-key
Lateness
Latently
Laterite
Lathwork
Latibula
Latinise
Latinism
Latinist
Latinity
Latinize
Latitude
Latterly
Laudable
Laudably
Laudanum
Laughing
Laughter
Laureate
Lava-like
Lavation
Lavender
Laverock
Lavishly
Lawfully
Lawgiver

Lawmaker
Lawyerly
Laxation
Laxative
Lay-clerk
Lay-elder
Layering
Laystall
Lazarist
Lazarone
Laziness
Lazulite
Lead-mill
Leadsman
Leaf-lard
Leafless
Leafscar
Leanness
Leapfrog
Leap-year
Learning
Leasable
Leashing
Leathern
Leathery
Lecanora
Lecithin
Lecturer
Leeboard
Leefange
Leeshore
Left-hand
Leftward
Legalise
Legalism
Legalist
Legality
Legalize
Legatary
Legatine
Legation
Legerity
Legumine
Lemonade
Lemurine
Lemuroid
Lendable
Lengthen
Lenience
Leniency
Lenitive
Lentando
Lenticel
Lent-lily
Leperous
Lepidoid
Leporine
Lethargy

Leucitic
Leucosis
Levanter
Leveller
Leverage
Leviable
Levigate
Levirate
Levitate
Levulose
Lewdness
Lewdster
Libation
Libatory
Libeller
Liberate
Libretto
Licensed
Licensee
Licenser
Lichenic
Lichenin
Lichgate
Lichwake
Licorice
Lientery
Lifebelt
Lifeboat
Lifebuoy
Lifehold
Lifeless
Lifelike
Lifeline
Lifelong
Life-peer
Life-raft
Life-rate
Life-rent
Life-size
Life-time
Life-work
Liftable
Ligament
Ligation
Ligature
Lightbob
Lightful
Lighting
Lightish
Ligneous
Lignitic
Ligulate
Ligurite
Likeable
Likeness
Likewake
Likewise
Lilacine

Lily-star
Limacoid
Limation
Limature
Lima-wood
Lime-free
Limekiln
Limerick
Lime-sink
Lime-twig
Lime-wash
Limewort
Limitary
Limonite
Linament
Linarite
Linchpin
Lineally
Linearly
Line-fish
Linesman
Ling-bird
Lingerer
Lingerie
Linguist
Liniment
Linnæan
Linoleum
Linotype
Linstock
Lipæmia
Lipo-gram
Lipstick
Liquable
Liquidly
Liquored
Liripoop
Lirocone
Listener
Listless
Literacy
Literary
Literate
Literati
Literose
Litharge
Lithemia
Lithemic
Litherly
Litigant
Litigate
Littoral
Liturate
Liturgic
Liveable
Liveaxle
Livebait
Livelily

Livelong
Liveried
Liverish
Livewell
Lividity
Livingly
Lixivial
Lixivium
Loadline
Loadstar
Loanable
Loanword
Loathful
Loathing
Lobbying
Lobbyist
Loblolly
Localism
Locality
Localize
Location
Lockfast
Lock-gate
Lockless
Lock-sill
Locksman
Lock-weir
Loco-foco
Loculate
Loculose
Loculous
Locution
Locutory
Lodesman
Lodestar
Lodgment
Logboard
Log-cabin
Log-glass
Logician
Logicise
Logicize
Logistic
Logogram
Logotype
Log-rolls
Log-slate
Loiterer
Lollards
Lollardy
Lollipop
Lomonite
Londoner
Loneness
Lonesome
Longboat
Longeval
Long-firm

## EIGHT-LETTER WORDS—*continued*

| | | | | | |
|---|---|---|---|---|---|
| Longhand | Lungfish | Magnesia | Mammered | Margaron | Maturate |
| Long-legs | Lungless | Magnetic | Mammifer | Marginal | Maturely |
| Long-moss | Lungwort | Magnific | Mammilla | Margrave | Maturing |
| Long-slip | Luniform | Magnolia | Mammodis | Marigold | Maturity |
| Longsome | Lunulate | Magot-pie | Manchild | Marinade | Maunders |
| Long-spun | Lupercal | Mahadeva | Manciple | Marinate | Maundril |
| Long-stop | Lupinite | Maharaja | Mandaean | Maritime | Maverick |
| Longtail | Luscious | Mahogany | Mandamus | Marjoram | Maxillar |
| Long-togs | Lustless | Mahratta | Mandarin | Markedly | Maxim-gun |
| Long-wise | Lustrate | Maidenly | Mandator | Marksman | Maximise |
| Lonicera | Lustring | Maidhood | Mandelic | Marlined | Maximist |
| Looker-on | Lustrous | Mailable | Mandible | Marlitic | Maximize |
| Loom-gale | Lustwort | Mail-boat | Mandioca | Marmoset | May-apple |
| Loophole | Lutanist | Mailcart | Mandolin | Maronite | May-bloom |
| Loop-line | Lutation | Mailclad | Mandorla | Marooner | Mayoress |
| Loosener | Luteolin | Maildrag | Mandrake | Maroquin | May-queen |
| Lopeared | Lutetian | Main-boom | Mandrill | Marquess | Maziness |
| Lopsided | Lutheran | Main-deck | Man-eater | Marquise | Mazology |
| Lord-like | Luxation | Mainland | Maneless | Marriage | Mazourka |
| Lordling | Luxurist | Mainmast | Manelike | Marrying | Meagrely |
| Lordosis | Lychgate | Mainsail | Manequin | Marsh-gas | Mealpock |
| Lord's-day | Lycopode | Mainstay | Manfully | Marsh-hen | Mealpoke |
| Lordship | Lymphoid | Maintain | Mangabey | Marsh-tit | Mealtime |
| Loricate | Lynch-law | Mainyard | Mangcorn | Martagon | Mealworm |
| Lorikeet | Lyre-bird | Maistery | Mangling | Martello | Meanborn |
| Losingly | Lyricism | Majestic | Mangonel | Martinet | Meanness |
| Lothario | Lyterian | Majolica | Mangrove | Marygold | Meantime |
| Loudness | | Majorate | Manhater | Mary-sole | Measurer |
| Lovebird | | Majority | Maniacal | Marzipan | Meatsafe |
| Loveknot | | Makebate | Manicate | Mascaron | Mechanic |
| Lovelace | **M** | Makeless | Manichee | Masorite | Meconate |
| Loveless | | Makimono | Manicure | Massacre | Meconine |
| Lovelily | Macarian | Malacoid | Manifest | Mass-bell | Meconium |
| Lovelock | Macarise | Malagash | Manifold | Mass-book | Medalist |
| Lovelorn | Macarism | Malagasy | Maniform | Masseter | Medallic |
| Lovesick | Macarize | Malamite | Mannerly | Masseuse | Meddling |
| Lovesome | Macaroni | Malanger | Mannikin | Massicot | Mediator |
| Lovesuit | Macaroon | Malapert | Man-of-War | Massorah | Medicate |
| Lovingly | Macassar | Malarial | Manorial | Masterly | Medicean |
| Lowering | Macerate | Malarian | Mansuete | Masthead | Medicine |
| Lowwater | Machinal | Maledikt | Mansworn | Mastitis | Medieval |
| Loyalist | Machiner | Malefern | Mantelet | Mastless | Mediocre |
| Lubberly | Mackerel | Malefice | Mantilla | Mastodon | Meditate |
| Lucernal | Macropod | Maletote | Mantissa | Matadore | Medjidie |
| Lucidity | Macropus | Maligner | Mantling | Matamata | Medullar |
| Luckless | Maculate | Malleate | Manually | Matchbox | Medullin |
| Luckybag | Maddened | Mallecho | Manucode | Matelote | Meekness |
| Luculent | Madeline | Malmrock | Manurial | Material | Meetness |
| Lukewarm | Madhouse | Malodour | Manutype | Matériel | Megalith |
| Lumberer | Madrigal | Malt-dust | Maori-hen | Maternal | Megapode |
| Luminate | Mæcenas | Malt-kiln | Marabout | Mateship | Meionite |
| Luminant | Maenadic | Malt-mill | Marasmus | Matgrass | Melanism |
| Luminary | Maestoso | Maltreat | Marathon | Mathesis | Melanite |
| Luminous | Maffling | Maltster | Marauder | Matronal | Melanous |
| Lumpfish | Magazine | Maltworm | Maravedi | Matronly | Melanure |
| Lunarian | Magician | Mambrino | Marcando | Mattered | Melibean |
| Lunation | Magirics | Mameluke | Margaric | Mattress | Melinite |
| Luncheon | Magister | Mammalia | Margarin | Maturant | Mellific |

EIGHT-LETTER WORDS—*continued*

| | | | | | |
|---|---|---|---|---|---|
| Mellowly | Metalman | Mimicked | Misquote | Molinist | Moon-eyed |
| Melodeon | Metamere | Mimicker | Misserve | Mollient | Moonface |
| Melodise | Metaphor | Minatory | Misshape | Mollusca | Moonfish |
| Melodist | Metatome | Mincepie | Misspeak | Molybdic | Moonless |
| Melodize | Metayage | Mindless | Misspell | Momently | Moonling |
| Membered | Metazoan | Miniment | Misspelt | Momentum | Moonseed |
| Membrane | Metazoic | Minimize | Misspend | Monachal | Moonshee |
| Memorial | Metazoon | Minister | Misspent | Monandry | Moonwort |
| Memorize | Metecorn | Ministry | Misstate | Monarcho | Moonyear |
| Memphian | Meteoric | Minorite | Mistaken | Monarchy | Moorcock |
| Memphite | Meterage | Minority | Misteach | Monastic | Moorfowl |
| Memsahib | Metewand | Minotaur | Misthink | Monazite | Moorgame |
| Menacing | Meteyard | Minstrel | Mistitle | Mondaine | Moorhawk |
| Mendable | Methinks | Mintmark | Mistrain | Mondayne | Moorland |
| Menhaden | Methodic | Minutely | Mistress | Monetary | Moorwhin |
| Menilite | Methylic | Minutiæ | Mistrial | Monetise | Moorwort |
| Meninges | Methysis | Mire-crow | Mistrust | Monetize | Mootable |
| Meniscal | Metonymy | Miriness | Mistryst | Moneybox | Mootcase |
| Meniscus | Metopism | Mirthful | Mistutor | Mongered | Moothall |
| Menology | Metrical | Misaimed | Misusage | Mongoose | Moothill |
| Menopome | Mezereon | Misapply | Misvouch | Moniment | Mope-eyed |
| Mensural | Miasmata | Misarray | Miswrite | Monistic | Mopishly |
| Mentagra | Microbic | Misbegot | Mitchell | Monition | Moquette |
| Mentally | Microzoa | Miscarry | Mithraic | Monitive | Moralise |
| Mephitic | Middling | Mischief | Mitigant | Monitory | Moralist |
| Mephitis | Midnight | Miscible | Mitigate | Monitrix | Morality |
| Mercable | Midships | Misclaim | Mittimus | Monkeyed | Moralize |
| Merchand | Mightful | Miscount | Mnemonic | Monkfish | Moratory |
| Merchant | Mightily | Miscreed | Mobilise | Monkhood | Moravian |
| Merciful | Migniard | Misdight | Mobility | Monk-seal | Morbidly |
| Mercuric | Migraine | Misdoing | Mobilize | Monocarp | Morbific |
| Mericarp | Migrator | Misdoubt | Mobocrat | Monocrat | Moreland |
| Meridian | Milanese | Misdread | Mobsman | Monodist | Moreover |
| Meringue | Mildness | Misenter | Mocassin | Monogamy | Moresque |
| Meristem | Milepost | Misentry | Moccasin | Monogony | Moribund |
| Merosome | Milesian | Miserere | Modalist | Monogram | Morillon |
| Merryman | Militant | Misfaith | Modality | Monogyny | Mormyrus |
| Merycism | Military | Misfeign | Modeller | Monolith | Moroccan |
| Mesaraic | Militate | Misgraff | Moderate | Monology | Morosely |
| Mesdames | Milk-maid | Misgraft | Moderato | Monomark | Moroxite |
| Mesfaith | Milk-tree | Misguide | Modestly | Monomial | Morphean |
| Meshwork | Milk-walk | Mishmash | Modified | Monophoa | Morpheus |
| Mesitite | Milkwarm | Mishnaic | Modifier | Monopode | Morphews |
| Mesmeree | Milk-weed | Misinfer | Modiolar | Monopoly | Morphine |
| Mesmeric | Milk-wort | Misjudge | Modishly | Monorail | Mortally |
| Mesocarp | Milleped | Mislabel | Modulate | Monotint | Mortgage |
| Mesoderm | Mill-hand | Mislayer | Mofussil | Monotone | Mortling |
| Mesolite | Milliard | Misletoe | Moharram | Monotony | Mortmain |
| Mesotype | Milliare | Mismatch | Mohicans | Monotype | Mortuary |
| Mesozoic | Milliary | Misnomer | Moistful | Monoxide | Moslings |
| Mesprise | Millibar | Misogamy | Moisture | Monsieur | Mosquito |
| Messidor | Milliped | Misogyny | Molasses | Montanic | Mossback |
| Messmate | Milliner | Misplace | Molecast | Monteith | Moss-clad |
| Messroom | Millpond | Misplead | Molecule | Monterus | Mossland |
| Messuage | Millrace | Mispoint | Mole-eyed | Monticle | Moss-pink |
| Metacism | Milltail | Misprint | Mole-hill | Monument | Moss-rose |
| Metairil | Millwork | Misprise | Mole-skin | Moonbeam | Moss-rush |
| Metallic | Miltonic | Misprize | Molester | Mooncalf | Most-what |

### EIGHT-LETTER WORDS—*continued*

| | | | | | |
|---|---|---|---|---|---|
| Motherly | Mungoose | Myositic | Nauplius | Nepotism | Nodosity |
| Motility | Muniment | Myositis | Nauscopy | Nepotist | Nodulose |
| Motioner | Munitiny | Myosotis | Nauseant | Neronean | Nodulous |
| Motivity | Munition | Myriapod | Nauseate | Nescient | Noematic |
| Motor-bus | Murderer | Myriarch | Nauseous | Nescious | Noetical |
| Motor-car | Murexide | Myricine | Nautical | Nestling | Noiseful |
| Motorial | Muriated | Myrmidon | Nautilus | Nethinim | Noisette |
| Motoring | Muriatic | Myrrhine | Navalism | Neuralgy | Nomadise |
| Motorist | Muricate | Mystical | Navarchy | Neuritis | Nomadism |
| Motorman | Muriform | Mytacism | Navicula | Neurosal | Nomadize |
| Mouching | Murksome | Mythical | Navigate | Neurosis | Nomarchy |
| Mouchoir | Murmured | Mytilite | Nazarene | Neurotic | Nominate |
| Moufflon | Murmurer | Mytiloid | Nazarite | Newcomer | Nomistic |
| Mould-box | Murrhine | Myxopoda | Nazirate | New-model | Nomogeny |
| Moulding | Muscadel | | Nazirite | Newsroom | Nomology |
| Moulinet | Muscadin | | Nealogic | Nextness | Non-claim |
| Mountain | Muscatel | | Nearctic | Niceness | Non-elect |
| Mountant | Muscavy | | Nearhand | Nickelic | Nonesuch |
| Mounting | Muscular | | Nearness | Nicknack | Nonjuror |
| Mournful | Museless | | Neatherd | Nickname | Non-moral |
| Mourning | Mushroom | **N** | Neatness | Nicotian | Nonsense |
| Mouse-ear | Musicale | Nacreous | Nebulose | Nicotine | Nonunion |
| Mouthful | Musician | Nailfile | Nebulous | Nidering | Noontide |
| Mouthing | Musingly | Nailwort | Neckatee | Nidorose | Normally |
| Moveless | Music-box | Nainsook | Neckband | Nidorous | Norseman |
| Movement | Musk-ball | Naissant | Neckbeef | Nidulant | Northern |
| Movingly | Musk-duck | Nameable | Necklace | Nidulate | Northing |
| Mucchero | Musketry | Nameless | Necropsy | Niellure | Northman |
| Mucedine | Musk-pear | Namesake | Necrosed | Niffnaff | Norweyan |
| Muchness | Musk-rose | Napiform | Necrosis | Niflheim | Noseband |
| Mucilage | Musk-wood | Napoleon | Necrotic | Niggling | Nose-dive |
| Mucivora | Muslinet | Naporite | Need-fire | Nighness | Noseleaf |
| Muck-heap | Musquash | Narceine | Needless | Night-cap | Noseless |
| Muck-hill | Musquito | Narcosis | Needment | Night-fly | Nosering |
| Muck-rake | Mustache | Narcotic | Negation | Night-hag | Nosology |
| Muck-weed | Mustaiba | Narghile | Negative | Night-jar | Nosonomy |
| Muck-worm | Mustered | Nargileh | Negligee | Night-man | Notalgia |
| Mucosity | Mutacism | Nariform | Negritos | Night-owl | Notandum |
| Muculent | Mutation | Narrator | Negroism | Nihilism | Notarial |
| Mudarine | Mutchkin | Narrower | Neighing | Nihilist | Notation |
| Mudguard | Muteness | Narrowly | Nemaline | Nihility | Notebook |
| Mud-valve | Mutilate | Narthex | Nemalite | Nine-eyes | Noteless |
| Muffetee | Mutineer | Nasality | Nematoid | Ninefold | Notional |
| Mug-house | Mutinous | Nasalize | Nemertea | Ninepins | Notornis |
| Muharram | Mutterer | Nascency | Nemorose | Nineteen | Notturno |
| Mulberry | Mutually | Nasicorn | Nemorous | Ninevite | Notwheat |
| Muledeer | Mycelium | Nasiform | Nenuphar | Nisberry | Noumenal |
| Muleteer | Mycetoma | Natantes | Neocracy | Nitrogen | Noumenon |
| Mulewort | Mycoderm | Natantly | Neo-Latin | Noachian | Novatian |
| Mulishly | Mycology | Natation | Neologic | Nobility | Novation |
| Multeity | Myelitis | Natatory | Neophron | Nobleman | Novelise |
| Multifid | Mylodont | Nathless | Neophyte | Noblesse | Novelist |
| Multiped | Myoblast | Nathmore | Neoplasm | Noctilio | Novelize |
| Multiple | Myograph | National | Neoteric | Noctuary | November |
| Multiply | Myomancy | Natively | Nepalese | Nocturne | Novenary |
| Mumbling | Myonosus | Nativity | Nepenthe | Nocturna | Novercal |
| Mummying | Myopathy | Nattered | Nephrite | Nodecusp | Noverint |
| Munerary | Myoporum | Naumachy | Nephroid | Nodiform | Nowadays |

## EIGHT-LETTER WORDS—*continued*

| | | | | | |
|---|---|---|---|---|---|
| Nubecula | Obliquid | Oiliness | Opopanax | Oscitate | Outslide |
| Nubility | Oblivion | Oil-paper | Oppilate | Osculant | Outspeak |
| Nubilose | Obscurer | Oil-press | Opponent | Osculate | Outspert |
| Nubilous | Observer | Oilskins | Opposing | Osmazome | Outstand |
| Nucament | Obsidian | Oilstone | Opposite | Osnaburg | Outstare |
| Nucellus | Obsolete | Ointment | Oppugner | Ossarium | Outstrip |
| Nuciform | Obstacle | Old-timer | Optative | Ossianic | Outswear |
| Nucleate | Obstruct | Old-world | Optician | Osteozoa | Outswell |
| Nucleole | Obtainer | Oleander | Optimacy | Osterick | Outvalue |
| Nudation | Obtected | Oleaster | Optimise | Ostiolar | Outvenom |
| Nudeness | Obtemper | Olefiant | Optimism | Ouistiti | Outvoter |
| Nugatory | Obtested | Olibanum | Optimist | Outblush | Outwards |
| Nuisance | Obtruder | Oliphant | Optimize | Outboard | Outweary |
| Numberer | Obturate | Olive-oil | Optional | Outbound | Outweigh |
| Numbness | Obtusely | Olivetan | Opulence | Outbrave | Outworth |
| Numerary | Obtusion | Olympiad | Opulency | Outbreak | Ouvriere |
| Numerate | Obvolute | Olympian | Opuscule | Outburst | Ovarious |
| Numerous | Occamist | Omadhaun | Oracular | Outclass | Ovenbird |
| Nummular | Occasion | Omelette | Orangery | Outcross | Overarch |
| Numskull | Occident | Omission | Orangism | Outdoors | Overbear |
| Nuncheon | Occlusor | Omissive | Orangite | Outdwell | Overblow |
| Nundinal | Occulted | Omniform | Oratorio | Outfield | Overbody |
| Nuptials | Occultly | Omohyoid | Oratress | Outflank | Overboil |
| Nursling | Occupant | Omoplate | Orcadian | Outflash | Overbold |
| Nutarian | Occupate | Omphalic | Orchanet | Outfling | Overbrim |
| Nutation | Occupier | Oncidium | Orchesis | Outflush | Overbrow |
| Nut-brown | Oceanian | Oncology | Orchitis | Outfrown | Overbulk |
| Nuthatch | Ocellary | Oncoming | Ordainer | Outgoing | Overburn |
| Nutmeggy | Ocellate | Oncotomy | Ordering | Outgrown | Overbury |
| Nutrient | Ocherous | One-berry | Ordinand | Outguard | Overbusy |
| Nut-screw | Ochlesis | One-blade | Ordinant | Out-herod | Overcame |
| Nutshell | Ochletic | One-horse | Ordinary | Outhouse | Overcast |
| Nymphaea | Ochreate | One-sided | Ordinate | Outlawry | Overcloy |
| Nymphean | Ochreous | Oniscoid | Ordnance | Outlearn | Overcoat |
| Nymphish | Ochroite | Onliness | Ordurous | Outlined | Overcold |
| | Octapody | Onlooker | Organdie | Outliver | Overcome |
| | Octarchy | Onofrite | Organify | Outlying | Overcrow |
| | Octonary | Onomancy | Organise | Outmarch | Overdate |
| | Octoroon | Ontogeny | Organism | Outpower | Overdone |
| | Octuplet | Ontology | Organist | Outprize | Overdose |
| **O** | Ocularly | Onymatic | Organize | Outraged | Overdraw |
| Oak-apple | Odiously | Oologist | Orgastic | Outrance | Overdrew |
| Oakpaper | Odometer | Oosphere | Orichalc | Outrange | Overdrop |
| Oatgrass | Odontoid | Opalesce | Oriental | Outrazed | Overfall |
| Oathable | Œcology | Opalized | Original | Outreach | Overfast |
| Obduracy | Œconomy | Open-eyed | Orillion | Outreign | Overfeed |
| Obdurate | Œnanthe | Openness | Orinasal | Outrider | Overfill |
| Obedient | Œnology | Open-work | Ornament | Outright | Overfish |
| Obeisant | Offender | Opera-hat | Ornately | Outrival | Overflow |
| Oberhaus | Offering | Operatic | Ornithic | Outroper | Overfold |
| Obituary | Official | Operator | Orphaned | Outscold | Overfond |
| Objector | Off-print | Operetta | Orpiment | Outscorn | Overfull |
| Oblation | Offshoot | Ophidian | Orthodox | Outshine | Overgaze |
| Oblatory | Offshore | Ophidion | Orthœpy | Outshone | Overgive |
| Obligant | Offspring | Ophiuran | Orvietan | Outsider | Overgrow |
| Obligate | Ofttimes | Opificer | Oryctics | Outsight | Overhair |
| Obligato | Ohmmeter | Opinable | Oscinian | Outskirt | Overhand |
| Obliging | Oilcloth | Opium-den | Oscitant | Outsleep | Overhang |

## EIGHT-LETTER WORDS—*continued*

| | | | | | |
|---|---|---|---|---|---|
| Overhaul | Overtone | Palamate | Papalize | Parterre | Pearl-eye |
| Overhead | Overtrip | Palatial | Papering | Parthian | Pearlies |
| Overhear | Overture | Palatine | Papillæ | Partible | Pearling |
| Overheat | Overturn | Palebuck | Papillar | Partibus | Pearmain |
| Overhend | Overveil | Pale-eyed | Papisher | Particle | Peasecod |
| Overhold | Overview | Pale-face | Papistic | Partisan | Peastone |
| Overkind | Overwash | Paleness | Papulose | Part-song | Peat-moor |
| Overking | Overwear | Palestra | Papulous | Partyism | Peat-moss |
| Overknee | Overween | Palilogy | Papyrine | Pascuage | Peat-seek |
| Overlade | Overwind | Palinode | Parabema | Pascuous | Peccable |
| Overlaid | Overwork | Palisade | Parabola | Pashalik | Peccancy |
| Overland | Overworn | Palliate | Parabole | Pasilaly | Pectinal |
| Overleaf | Overyear | Pallidly | Paradigm | Passable | Pectoral |
| Overleap | Oviposit | Pall-mall | Paradise | Passably | Peculate |
| Overlive | Owl-glass | Palmetto | Paraffin | Pass-book | Peculiar |
| Overload | Owl-light | Palmiped | Paraffle | Passer-by | Pedagogy |
| Overlock | Oxidable | Palmwine | Paragoge | Passeres | Pedaller |
| Overlook | Oxidator | Palpable | Paragram | Passible | Pedalian |
| Overlord | Oxidiser | Palpably | Parakeet | Passless | Pedality |
| Overmost | Oxidized | Palpifer | Parallax | Passover | Pedantic |
| Overmuch | Oxpecker | Palpless | Parallel | Passport | Pedantry |
| Overname | Ox-tongue | Palstaff | Paralogy | Password | Peddlery |
| Overneat | Oxygonal | Palstave | Paralyse | Pastiche | Peddling |
| Overnice | Oxymoron | Palterer | Paralyze | Pastille | Pederast |
| Overpass | Ozokerit | Paltrily | Paramere | Pastoral | Pederero |
| Overpast | Ozonized | Paludine | Paramour | Pastorly | Pedestal |
| Overplus | | Paludism | Paranœa | Patagium | Pediatry |
| Overpost | | Paludose | Paranoia | Patchbox | Pedicure |
| Overrack | | Pamperer | Paraphia | Patchery | Pedigree |
| Overrake | **P** | Pamphlet | Parapsis | Patellar | Pediment |
| Overrate | | Panaghia | Paraquet | Patentee | Pedipalp |
| Overread | Pabulous | Pancarte | Parasang | Patenter | Pedireme |
| Overrent | Pacation | Pancheon | Paraseve | Patentor | Peduncle |
| Override | Pachalic | Pancreas | Parasite | Paterero | Peep-hole |
| Overripe | Pachyote | Pandamus | Paravail | Paternal | Peep-show |
| Overrule | Pachypod | Pandanus | Paravane | Pathetic | Peerless |
| Overseam | Pacifier | Pandemic | Paravant | Pathless | Peesweep |
| Overseas | Pacifism | Panderly | Parcener | Patience | Peetweet |
| Overseen | Pacifist | Pandowdy | Pardoner | Patoncee | Pegamoid |
| Overseer | Packfong | Panegyry | Parental | Patronal | Pegasean |
| Oversell | Packload | Panelled | Parergon | Pattened | Peignoir |
| Oversewn | Packmule | Paneless | Pargeter | Patterer | Pejorate |
| Overshoe | Padcloth | Panelsaw | Parhelic | Patty-pan | Pelagian |
| Overshot | Paddling | Pangless | Parietal | Patulous | Pelargic |
| Overside | Padelion | Pangolin | Parisian | Pauldron | Pelasgic |
| Oversize | Padishah | Panionic | Parisite | Pavement | Pelemele |
| Overskip | Påduasoy | Pannikel | Parlance | Pavilion | Pelerine |
| Overslip | Paganise | Pannikin | Parmesan | Pavisado | Pellagra |
| Oversman | Paganish | Panochia | Parodist | Pavonine | Pellicle |
| Oversoul | Paganism | Panorama | Paronyme | Pawnshop | Pell-mell |
| Overstay | Paganize | Panotype | Paroquet | Paysheet | Pellucid |
| Overstep | Pagehood | Pansophy | Parosmia | Payclerk | Pelorism |
| Oversway | Pagodite | Pantheon | Paroxysm | Peaceful | Peltated |
| Overtake | Pagurian | Pantofle | Parroter | Peachery | Pelt-wool |
| Overtask | Painless | Panurgic | Parrotry | Peachick | Pemmican |
| Overtilt | Painting | Papalise | Parrying | Peaching | Penalise |
| Overtime | Pair-wise | Papalism | Parsonic | Peagreen | Penalize |
| Overtoil | Paitrick | Papalist | Partaker | Pearlash | Penchant |

EIGHT-LETTER WORDS—*continued*

| | | | | | |
|---|---|---|---|---|---|
| Pencraft | Pertness | Physalis | Pingpong | Planting | Plumiped |
| Pendence | Pertused | Physeter | Piningly | Plantlet | Plumming |
| Pendency | Peruvian | Physical | Pink-eyed | Plantule | Plumping |
| Pendulum | Peruvine | Physique | Pink-root | Planular | Plungeon |
| Penitent | Perverse | Phytosis | Pinmaker | Planuria | Plunging |
| Penknife | Pervious | Phytozoa | Pinmoney | Plashing | Plurally |
| Pennorth | Pestered | Piacular | Pinnacle | Plastron | Plutonic |
| Pennydog | Pesterer | Pianette | Pinniped | Plat-band | Pluvious |
| Penology | Petaline | Piassava | Pinpatch | Plateful | Poaching |
| Penstock | Petalism | Piazzian | Pinpoint | Platform | Pochette |
| Pentacle | Petalite | Picarian | Pinwheel | P'atinic | Pockmark |
| Pentafid | Petaloid | Picaroon | Pipecase | Platinum | Pockwood |
| Pentagon | Petalous | Picayune | Pipeclay | Platonic | Podagral |
| Pentelic | Peterman | Piccadil | Pipefish | Platting | Podagric |
| Pent-roof | Petiolar | Pick-back | Pipe-line | Platypus | Podalgia |
| Penumbra | Petition | Pickerel | Piperine | Plausive | Podargus |
| Penwiper | Petitory | Pick-lock | Piperoll | Playable | Podismus |
| Penwoman | Petrific | Picksome | Pipe-tree | Playbill | Poematic |
| Peperino | Petronel | Picotite | Pipewine | Playbook | Poetical |
| Peptogen | Petrosal | Picromel | Pipewort | Playclub | Poetress |
| Peracute | Pettifog | Piecener | Piquancy | Play-debt | Poignant |
| Perceant | Petulant | Piedness | Pirating | Playgoer | Poignard |
| Perceive | Petuntse | Piercing | Piscator | Playmare | Poinding |
| Perclose | Petworth | Piffling | Piscinal | Playmate | Pointing |
| Perdendo | Pewterer | Pigfaced | Pisiform | Playsome | Poisoned |
| Perforce | Phacitis | Pigeoned | Pisolite | Playtime | Poisoner |
| Perfumer | Phalange | Pigeonry | Pistacia | Pleading | Polarity |
| Perfused | Phantasm | Pigotite | Pistolet | Pleasant | Polarize |
| Periagua | Phantasy | Pigswash | Pitching | Pleasing | Pole-jump |
| Perianth | Pharisee * | Pikehead | Pit-frame | Pleasure | Polemast |
| Pericarp | Pharmacy | Pilaster | Pithball | Plebeian | Polemics |
| Pericope | Pheasant | Pilchard | Pithecus | Plectrum | Pole-star |
| Periderm | Phengite | Pileated | Pithless | Pleiades | Policing |
| Perigeal | Philabeg | Pilework | Pitiable | Plenarty | Polished |
| Perigean | Philibeg | Pileworm | Pitiably | Pleonasm | Polisher |
| Perigone | Philomel | Pilewort | Pitiless | Pleonast | Politely |
| Perilous | Phimosis | Pilferer | Pittacal | Plethora | Politics |
| Perineal | Phlegmon | Piliform | Pittance | Pleurisy | Poll-book |
| Periodic | Phocenic | Pillager | Pituital | Pliantly | Pollical |
| Periotic | Phonetic | Pillared | Pityroid | Plicated | Pollinar |
| Peripety | Phormium | Pillcorn | Pivot gun | Plighter | Polliwig |
| Periplus | Phosgene | Pillwort | Placable | Plimming | Polluter |
| Perished | Phospham | Pilosely | Placeman | Pliocene | Pollywig |
| Perishen | Phosphor | Pilosity | Placenta | Plopping | Polonium |
| Perissad | Photospy | Pilotage | Placidly | Plotting | Poltroon |
| Perjurer | Phrasing | Piloting | Plagiary | Plougher | Polyfoil |
| Perlitic | Phratia | Pimelite | Plaguing | Pluckily | Polygamy |
| Permeate | Phrygian | Pinacoid | Plainant | Plucking | Polyglot |
| Pernancy | Phthalin | Pinafore | Plaister | Plugging | Polygram |
| Peroneal | Phthisis | Pinaster | Plaiting | Plug-ugly | Polygyny |
| Perorate | Phylarch | Pince-nez | Planchet | Plumbago | Polyopia |
| Peroxide | Phyletic | Pinchers | Planetic | Plumb-bob | Polypary |
| Perruque | Phyllite | Pindaree | Plangent | Plumbean | Polypide |
| Persicot | Phyllium | Pindaric | Planking | Plumbery | Polypier |
| Persimon | Phyllode | Pineclad | Plankton | Plumbism | Polypode |
| Personal | Phyllody | Pinecone | Planless | Plum-cake | Polypody |
| Perspire | Phylloid | Pinewood | Planning | Plum-duff | Polypoid |
| Persuade | Physalia | Pinewool | Plantain | Plumelet | Polypous |

### EIGHT-LETTER WORDS—*continued*

| | | | | | |
|---|---|---|---|---|---|
| Polytype | Port-rope | Prankish | Prideful | Pronator | Psittaci |
| Polyzoan | Portuary | Prasites | Priestly | Prong-hoe | Psychism |
| Polyzoic | Posingly | Pratique | Prigging | Prononcé | Psychist |
| Polyzoon | Positing | Prattled | Priggish | Proofing | Pteromys |
| Pomander | Position | Prattler | Priggism | Propense | Pteropod |
| Pomiform | Positive | Preacher | Priggory | Properly | Pterylae |
| Pomology | Posology | Preaches | Primates | Property | Ptilosis |
| Pompeian | Possible | Preamble | Primeval | Prophecy | Ptomaine |
| Ponderal | Possibly | Preceded | Primming | Prophesy | Ptyaline |
| Ponderer | Postable | Precinct | Primness | Proplasm | Ptyalise |
| Pond-lily | Post-bill | Precious | Primrose | Propolis | Ptyalism |
| Pondweed | Post-card | Preclude | Princely | Proposal | Publican |
| Pondwort | Post-date | Predated | Princeps | Proposer | Publicly |
| Pontifex | Post-fact | Predella | Princess | Propound | Pucelage |
| Pontific | Post-free | Pre-elect | Princock | Proppage | Puckball |
| Pontinal | Post-horn | Preening | Prinking | Proprium | Puddling |
| Pooh-pooh | Postiche | Pre-exist | Printing | Propylon | Pudendal |
| Poonspar | Postique | Prefacer | Priorate | Prorogue | Pudicity |
| Poor-John | Postmark | Pregnant | Prioress | Prosaism | Puff-ball |
| Poor-laws | Post-nati | Prehnite | Priority | Prosaist | Puff-bird |
| Poorness | Post-note | Prejudge | Prismoid | Proseman | Pug-faced |
| Poor-rate | Post-paid | Preluder | Prisoned | Prospect | Puggaree |
| Pope-hood | Postpone | Premiant | Prisoner | Prostate | Pugilism |
| Pope-Joan | Post-time | Premiate | Pristine | Prostyle | Pugilist |
| Popeling | Post-town | Premiere | Prizeman | Protases | Puissant |
| Pope-ship | Postural | Premises | Probable | Protatic | Pulingly |
| Pope's-eye | Potation | Premolar | Probably | Protégée | Pullback |
| Popinjay | Potatory | Premorse | Probator | Proteids | Pullover |
| Popishly | Pot-belly | Prenasal | Proceeds | Protense | Pulmonic |
| Poplitic | Potently | Prenatal | Prochein | Protista | Pulpiter |
| Populace | Pot-holes | Prenomen | Procinct | Protocol | Pulsator |
| Populate | Pot-house | Prentice | Proclaim | Protozoa | Pulsific |
| Populine | Pot-metal | Preorder | Procurer | Protract | Pulvinar |
| Populous | Potshard | Prepared | Prodigal | Protrude | Pumicate |
| Porifera | Potsherd | Preparer | Proditor | Provable | Pump-dale |
| Poriform | Pot-stick | Prepense | Prodrome | Provably | Pump-gear |
| Poriness | Pot-still | Presager | Producer | Proviant | Pumphead |
| Poristic | Potstone | Presbyte | Prœmial | Provided | Pump-hood |
| Pork-chop | Pottered | Prescind | Proemion | Provider | Pump-room |
| Porkling | Potterer | Presence | Profaner | Province | Pump-well |
| Porosity | Pottoroo | Preserve | Profiter | Provisor | Puncheon |
| Porotype | Potulent | Press-bed | Profound | Provoker | Punching |
| Porpesse | Pouching | Press-box | Profunder | Provokes | Punctate |
| Porphyry | Poulaine | Pressing | Progress | Prowling | Punctual |
| Porpoise | Pouldred | Pression | Prohibit | Proximal | Puncture |
| Porridge | Poultice | Pressman | Prolapse | Prudence | Pungence |
| Portable | Poundage | Pressure | Prolific | Pruinose | Pungency |
| Porterly | Poupeton | Prestige | Prolixly | Pruinous | Puniness |
| Portesse | Pourtray | Prest-man | Prologue | Prunella | Punisher |
| Portfire | Powdered | Pre-study | Prolonge | Prunello | Punitive |
| Porthole | Powerful | Presumer | Promised | Prurient | Punitory |
| Portiere | Practice | Pretence | Promisee | Prussian | Punjabee |
| Portland. | Practick | Preterit | Promiser | Pryingly | Puntilla |
| Portlast | Practise | Prettify | Promisor | Psalmist | Puntsman |
| Portmote | Practive | Prettily | Promoter | Psalmody | Puparial |
| Portoise | Præcipe | Previous | Prompter | Psaltery | Puparium |
| Portrait | Præfect | Priapean | Promptly | Psammite | Pupation |
| Portress | Prandial | Pricking | Promulge | Psellism | Pupiform |

## EIGHT-LETTER WORDS—*continued*

| | | | | | |
|---|---|---|---|---|---|
| Pupilage | Pyxidium | Quidnunc | Radiator | Rapacity | Reassert |
| Pupilary | | Quietage | Radicant | Rape-cake | Reassess |
| Pupilate | | Quietise | Radicate | Rape-seed | Reassign |
| Pupipara | | Quietism | Radicose | Raphania | Reassume |
| Puppetry | **Q** | Quietist | Radicule | Raphanus | Reassure |
| Puppyish | | Quietive | Radiolus | Raphides | Reattach |
| Puppyism | Quackery | Quietude | Radulate | Rapidity | Reattain |
| Purblind | Quackish | Quilling | Raftduck | Rapparee | Rebeller |
| Purchase | Quackism | Quillnib | Raftport | Raptores | Rebellow |
| Pureness | Quádrant | Quilting | Raftrope | Raptured | Rebuttal |
| Purflier | Quadrans | Quincunx | Raftsman | Rareness | Rebutter |
| Purfling | Quadrate | Quinible | Ragabash | Rareripe | Recanter |
| Purifier | Quadriga | Quintain | Raggedly | Rascally | Recaptor |
| Puriform | Quadroon | Quintile | Ragingly | Rashling | Receiver |
| Purified | Quadrune | Quintole | Ragnarok | Rashness | Recently |
| Puristic | Quæstor | Quippish | Rag-paper | Rasorial | Recessed |
| Purloins | Quagmire | Quirinal | Ragstone | Rataplan | Recessus |
| Purparty | Quagmiry | Quirinus | Rag-wheel | Rateable | Recharge |
| Purplish | Quailing | Quirites | Railhead | Ratebook | Recision |
| Purprise | Quaintly | Quirkish | Raillery | Ratgoose | Reckless |
| Purpuric | Quakerly | Quit-rent | Railroad | Rathripe | Reckling |
| Purseful | Qualmish | Quixotic | Rainband | Ratifier | Reckoner |
| Purse-net | Quandang | Quixotry | Rainbird | Rational | Recliner |
| Purslain | Quandary | Quizzery | Raincoat | Ratitate | Reclothe |
| Purslane | Quantify | Quizzify | Raincrow | Rat's-bane | Recoiler |
| Pursuant | Quantity | Quizzing | Raindrop | Rat-snake | Recoiner |
| Purulent | Quarried | Quotable | Rainfall | Rat's-tail | Recollet |
| Purveyor | Quarrier | Quotient | Rainless | Rattinet | Recolour |
| Puseyism | Quartern | Quotiety | Rainpour | Rattling | Recommit |
| Puseyite | Quartile | | Raintree | Ravehook | Reconvey |
| Pushball | Quartine | | Rainwash | Ravening | Recorder |
| Pushbike | Quassine | | Raisinee | **Ravenous** | Recourse |
| Puss-moth | Quassite | | Raisonne | Ravingly | Recovery |
| Puss-tail | Quateron | **R** | Rakehell | Ravisher | Recreant |
| Pussy-cat | Quatorze | Rabatine | Rakishly | Raw-boned | Recreate |
| Pustular | Quatrain | Rabbinic | Rakshasa | Reabsorb | Rectitic |
| Putanism | Quaverer | Rabbiter | Ramadhan | Reaccess | Rectitis |
| Putation | Quay-wall | Rabbitry | Ramayana | Reaccuse | Rectoral |
| Putative | Queasily | Rabidity | Rambooze | Reaction | Recubant |
| Putchock | Quebrada | Rabietic | Rambutan | Reactive | Recurved |
| Puzzling | Queenbee | Race-card | Ramicorn | Readable | Recusant |
| Pyelitis | Queendom | Racemose | Ramiform | Readably | Redactor |
| Pyogenic | Queening | Racemous | Ramosely | Readjust | Redargue |
| Pyramoid | Queenlet | Racemule | Rampancy | Reaffirm | Red-belly |
| Pyrenons | Queerish | Rachilla | Rampsman | Reagency | Red-cedar |
| Pyrexial | Quellerz | Rachitic | Ramroddy | Realiser | Red-chalk |
| Pyriform | Quencher | Rachitis | Ramshorn | Realledge | Red-coral |
| Pyritise | Quenelle | Racially | Ramulous | Realness | Red-cross |
| Pyritize | Quercite | Raciness | Ranarium | Reanoint | Reddendo |
| Pyritous | Questant | Racketer | Ranchero | Reanswer | Red-earth |
| Pyrogram | Questful | Rackrail | Ranching | Reappear | Redeemer |
| Pyrology | Question | Rack-rent | Ranchman | Rear-line | Redeless |
| Pyrosoma | Questman | Racktail | Rancidly | Rearmost | Redemand |
| Pyrostat | Quibbler | Rackwork | Randomly | Rear-rank | Redemise |
| Pyroxene | Quickset | Racovian | Rangifer | Rear-ward | Redented |
| Pyroxyle | Quiddany | Radially | Raniform | Reascend | Red-faced |
| Pyrrhous | Quiddity | Radiance | Rankness | Reascent | Redigest |
| Pythonic | Quiddler | Radiancy | Ransomer | Reasoner | Redirect |

## EIGHT-LETTER WORDS—*continued*

| | | | | | |
|---|---|---|---|---|---|
| Redition | Regather | Relumine | Reperuse | Resonant | Revisory |
| Redivide | Regicide | Remanent | Repetend | Resonate | Revivify |
| Red-metal | Regiment | Remarker | Replacer | Resorcin | Revolter |
| Rednosed | Regional | Remedial | Repledge | Resorter | Revolute |
| Redolent | Regionic | Remember | Replevin | Resource | Revolver |
| Redouble | Register | Remercie | Replunge | Resperse | Revulsor |
| Redriven | Registry | Remiform | Repolish | Response | Rewarder |
| Redshank | Regnancy | Remigial | Reporter | Rest-cure | Rhabdite |
| Red-short | Regrater | Reminder | Reposure | Restless | Rhabdoid |
| Red-staff | Regrator | Remissly | Repousse | Restorei | Rhabdome |
| Redstart | Regrowth | Remittal | Reprieve | Restrain | Rhabdons |
| Redubber | Regulate | Remittee | Reprimer | Restrict | Rhaetian |
| Reducent | Reguline | Remitter | Reprisal | Restrike | Rhagades |
| Reduvius | Regulise | Remittor | Reproach | Resummon | Rhagodia |
| Red-water | Rehandle | Remoboth | Reproval | Resupine | Rhapsode |
| Reed-band | Rehearse | Remolade | Reprover | Resurvey | Rhapsody |
| Reed-bird | Re-ignite | Remolten | Reptilia | Retailer | Rheocord |
| Reedless | Reimbody | Remotely | Republic | Retaille | Rheostat |
| Reedling | Reimport | Remotion | Repugner | Retainer | Rheotome |
| Reed-mace | Reimpose | Remurmur | Repulpit | Retarder | Rhetoric |
| Reed-pipe | Reincite | Renderer | Repulser | Retentor | Rhinidae |
| Reed-stop | Reindeer | Rendible | Repurify | Retepore | Rhinitis |
| Reed-wren | Reinfect | Renegade | Requirer | Reticent | Rhinodon |
| Reef-band | Reinform | Renegado | Requital | Reticule | Rhizanth |
| Reef-knot | Reinfund | Renegate | Requiter | Retierce | Rhizogen |
| Reef-line | Reinfuse | Renidify | Rerefief | Retifera | Rhizomys |
| Reelable | Reinhook | Reniform | Rereward | Retiform | Rhizopod |
| Reelline | Reinless | Renigate | Resalute | Retinite | Rhodanic |
| Reelrall | Reinsert | Renitent | Rescribe | Retinoid | Rhodeina |
| Reel-seat | Reinsman | Renounce | Rescript | Retinula | Rhodites |
| Re-embark | Reinsure | Renovate | Research | Retiracy | Rhoeadic |
| Re-embody | Reinvent | Renowned | Reseizer | Retirade | Rhomboid |
| Re-emerge | Reinvest | Renowner | Resemble | Retiring | Rhonchal |
| Re-enforce | Reinvite | Rentable | Resenter | Retorque | Rhonchus |
| Re-engage | Rejecter | Renterer | Reserved | Retorter | Rhopalic |
| Re-enlist | Rejector | Rent-free | Reserver | Retraxit | Rhubarby |
| Re-estate | Rejoicer | Rent-roll | Resetter | Retrench | Rhyolite |
| Re-export | Rekindle | Renumber | Resettle | Retrieve | Rhythmic |
| Refasten | Relapser | Renverse | Resiance | Retroact | Rhythmus |
| Referrer | Relation | Reobtain | Resident | Retrorse | Ribaldry |
| Refigure | Relative | Reoccupy | Residual | Returner | Ribaudry |
| Refilled | Relatrix | Reometer | Residuum | Reussite | Ribgrass |
| Refinery | Relaxant | Reoppose | Resignee | Revealer | Rib-nosed |
| Refining | Releasee | Reordain | Resigner | Revehent | Rib-roast |
| Reflexed | Releaser | Reorient | Resinata | Reveille | Ricebird |
| Reflexly | Releasor | Reossify | Resinate | Reveller | Rice-dust |
| Reflower | Relegate | Repacify | Resinify | Revenant | Rice-milk |
| Refluent | Relessee | Repacker | Resinise | Revenger | Rice-glue |
| Reforest | Relessor | Repairer | Resinoid | Reverend | Rice-meal |
| Reforger | Relevant | Repartee | Resinous | Reverent | Rice-soup |
| Reformer | Reliable | Repaster | Resistal | Reverist | Richleft |
| Refreeze | Reliably | Repealer | Resister | Reversal | Richness |
| Refringe | Reliance | Repeated | Resistor | Reversed | Riciniae |
| Refunder | Relicted | Repeater | Resmooth | Reverser | Ricinium |
| Regalian | Reliever | Repeller | Resolder | Reversis | Ricketly |
| Regalism | Religion | Repentent | Resolute | Reviewal | Rickrack |
| Regality | Relisten | Repeople | Resolved | Reviewer | Rickshaw |
| Regarder | Relucent | Repertor | Resolver | Revision | Ricochet |

### EIGHT-LETTER WORDS—*continued*

| | | | | | |
|---|---|---|---|---|---|
| Ricolite | Riverman | Romanism | Rosy-wave | Rufulous | Saccular |
| Riddance | Riverpie | Romanist | Rotalian | Rugbeian | Sacculus |
| Riddling | Rivetter | Romanize | Rotaline | Ruggedly | Sacellum |
| Rideable | Rivulose | Romansch | Rotalite | Rugosely | Sackless |
| Ridicule | Rixation | Romantic | Rotarian | Rugosity | Sackrace |
| Rifeness | Rizzered | Rome-scot | Rotation | Rugulose | Sacredly |
| Riffraff | Road-book | Romeward | Rotative | Ruinable | Sacristy |
| Rifleman | Roadside | Roncador | Rotatory | Rulecase | Saddlery |
| Rifle-pit | Roadsman | Rondache | Rot-grass | Ruleless | Sadducee |
| Rigadoon | Roadster | Rondelet | Rotifera | Rulework | Sadfaced |
| Rigation | Roadweed | Rondelle | Rotiform | Rulingly | Safeness |
| Rightful | Roantree | Roodarch | Rot-steep | Rumanian | Saffrony |
| Rigidity | Roborant | Roodbeam | Rottenly | Rumbarge | Safranin |
| Rigorism | Roburite | Rood-loft | Rottlera | Rumbling | Sagacity |
| Rigorist | Robustly | Roodebok | Roturier | Ruminant | Sagamore |
| Rigorous | Rocaille | Roodtree | Roughage | Ruminate | Sagecock |
| Rill-mark | Roccella | Roofless | Roughdry | Rummager | Sageness |
| Rimiform | Rock-alum | Rooftree | Roughhew | Rumorous | Sagenite |
| Rimosity | Rockaway | Roomsome | Roughish | Rumourer | Sagerose |
| Rimulose | Rockbird | Rootbeer | Roulette | Rumpless | Saginate |
| Rinabout | Rock-cake | Root-crop | Round-all | Rumshrub | Sagittal |
| Rindgall | Rock-cist | Rootfast | Round-arm | Runabout | Sagopalm |
| Ringbark | Rock-cook | Rootform | Rounders | Runagate | Saguinus |
| Ringbill | Rock-cork | Roothair | Rounding | Runner-up | Sahiblog |
| Ringbolt | Rock-crab | Rootknot | Roundish | Runology | Saibling |
| Ringbone | Rock-dove | Root-leaf | Roundlet | Runridge | Saikless |
| Ringdial | Rocketer | Root-less | Roundtop | Rupicola | Sailable |
| Ringdove | Rock-fire | Rope-pump | Roundure | Ruralise | Sailboat |
| Ring-goal | Rock-fish | Rope-ripe | Routcake | Ruralism | Sailfish |
| Ringlety | Rock-goat | Rope-walk | Rovingly | Ruralist | Sailhoop |
| Ringlock | Rock-hawk | Ropeyarn | Rowdy-dow | Rurality | Sailless |
| Ring-mail | Rockhead | Ropiness | Rowdyish | Ruralize | Sailloft |
| Ring-neck | Rock-hewn | Rorulent | Rowdyism | Rush-like | Sailplan |
| Ring-rope | Rocklark | Rosarian | Roxburgh | Rushlily | Sailroom |
| Ringtail | Rockless | Rosarium | Royalise | Rushtoad | Sail-yard |
| Ring-time | Rock-lily | Rosebush | Royalism | Rustless | Sainfoin |
| Ring-wall | Rockling | Rose-drop | Royalist | Rustmite | Saintish |
| Ringwork | Rockmoss | Rose-gall | Royalize | Rustical | Saintism |
| Ring-worm | Rock-rose | Rose-hued | Rubbishy | Rutabaga | Salacity |
| Riparial | Rock-ruby | Rose-knot | Rubeculu | Ruthless | Salading |
| Riparian | Rock-salt | Roselite | Rubedity | Rutilant | Saladoil |
| Ripeness | Rock-soap | Rosemary | Rubellan | Rutilate | Salaried |
| Rippling | Rock-wood | Rose-pink | Rubezahl | Rye-grass | Saleable |
| Riptowel | Rock-work | Rose-rash | Rubianic | Ryot-wari | Saleably |
| Risaldar | Rock-wren | Roseroot | Rubicund | | Sale-room |
| Rise-bush | Rodentia | Rosetree | Rubidium | | Salesman |
| Risewood | Rodomont | Rosetted | Rubiform | **S** | Sale-work |
| Risorial | Roe-stone | Rose-wood | Rubrical | | Salicine |
| Ritually | Rogation | Roseworm | Rubstone | Sabaeans | Salience |
| Rivaless | Rogatory | Roseyard | Rubytail | Sabaeism | Salinity |
| Rivalise | Roisting | Rosiness | Rubywood | Sabbatia | Salitral |
| Rivality | Roitelet | Rosin-oil | Rucervus | Sabbatic | Salivant |
| Riveling | Roll-call | Rosmarus | Rucksack | Sabbaton | Salivary |
| Riverain | Roly-poly | Rosoglio | Rudeness | Sabeline | Salivate |
| Riverbed | Romancer | Rostrate | Rudented | Sabliere | Salivous |
| River-god | Romanese | Rostroid | Rudiment | Sabotage | Salmonet |
| Riverhog | Romanise | Rosulate | Ruefully | Sabotier | Salopian |
| Riverine | Romanish | Rosy-drop | Ruffling | Sabulous | Salpicon |
| | | | | Saccated | |

### EIGHT-LETTER WORDS—*continued*

| | | | | | |
|---|---|---|---|---|---|
| Salsilla | Sand-weld | Satiable | Scampish | Scincoid | Scribism |
| Salt-bush | Sandwich | Satirise | Scandent | Sciolism | Scriggle |
| Salt-cake | Sand-worm | Satirist | Scandium | Sciolist | Scrimply |
| Salt-cote | Sandwort | Satirize | Scansion | Sciolous | Scrivano |
| Salt-foot | Saneness | Satrapal | Scantily | Scioptic | Scroddle |
| Salt-junk | Sangaree | Saturant | Scantlet | Scirrhus | Scrofula |
| Saltless | Sanglant | Saturate | Scapanus | Scissile | Scroggie |
| Salt-lick | Sanglier | Saturday | Scaphism | Scission | Scrouger |
| Salt-mine | Sangraal | Saturnia | Scaphite | Scissors | Scrubber |
| Saltness | Sangrado | Saturnic | Scaphium | Scissura | Scrub-oak |
| Saltwork | Sangreal | Satyrium | Scaphoid | Scissure | Scrupler |
| Saltwort | Sanguify | Saucebox | Scapular | Sciurine | Scrutiny |
| Salutary | Sanguine | Saucepan | Scarabee | Sciuroid | Scuddick |
| Salvable | Sanidine | Saucisse | Scarcely | Sclerite | Scuffler |
| Salvinia | Sanitary | Saufgard | Scarcity | Scleroid | Scullery |
| Samarium | Sanskrit | Saurodon | Scarebug | Scleroma | Sculling |
| Samaroid | Santalic | Saurless | Scarf-pin | Sclerous | Scullion |
| Samaveda | Santalin | Saururus | Scaridae | Scoleina | Sculpsit |
| Sambucus | Santalum | Sauterne | Scarious | Scolopax | Sculptor |
| Sameness | Santonin | Sautoire | Scaritid | Scolytus | Scurrile |
| Samphire | Sap-green | Savagely | Scarless | Scomfish | Scurvily |
| Samplary | Sapidity | Savagery | Scarmage | Scoop-net | Scutcher |
| Sanation | Sapiemic | Savagism | Scarmoge | Scoparia | Scutchin |
| Sanative | Sapience | Savannah | Scarn-bee | Scopeful | Scutella |
| Sanatory | Sapindus | Saveable | Scathold | Scopidae | Scutifer |
| Sanctify | Sapi-utan | Savingly | Scatland | Scopious | Scutiped |
| Sanction | Saponify | Savourly | Scattery | Scopiped | Scuttler |
| Sanctity | Saponine | Savoyard | Scavenge | Scorcher | Scuttock |
| Sandarac | Saporous | Sawbones | Scelerat | Scorious | Scutulum |
| Sandball | Sapphire | Sawflies | Scelides | Scordato | Scythian |
| Sand-band | Sapphism | Sawframe | Scenario | Scornful | Scytodes |
| Sandbank | Sapremia | Sawglass | Sceneman | Scorpion | Sea-acorn |
| Sandbath | Sapucaia | Sawhorse | Scenical | Scot-free | Sea-adder |
| Sandbear | Saraband | Saw-table | Scent-bag | Scotsman | Sea-apron |
| Sandbird | Sarcelle | Saw-wrest | Scent-box | Scottice | Sea-arrow |
| Sandcock | Sarcenet | Saxatile | Scentful | Scottify | Sea-beach |
| Sand-crab | Sarcinic | Saxicava | Sceptral | Scottish | Sea-beast |
| Sand-dart | Sarcitis | Saxicola | Sceptred | Scourage | Seabells |
| Sand-dune | Sarcocol | Saxondom | Schedule | Scourger | Seaboard |
| Sandever | Sarcodic | Saxonise | Schellum | Scouther | Seaborne |
| Sandfish | Sarcosis | Saxonism | Schemist | Scowther | Sea-brant |
| Sandflag | Sarcotic | Saxonist | Scheroma | Scrabble | Sea-bream |
| Sandflea | Sardelle | Scabbard | Schiedam | Scraffle | Sea-chart |
| Sand-heat | Sardonic | Scabiosa | Schiller | Scragged | Sea-coast |
| Sandhill | Sardonyx | Scabious | Schistic | Scraggly | Seacraft |
| Sand-iron | Sargasso | Scabmite | Schlager | Scramble | Sea-daisy |
| Sandiver | Sarplier | Scabrous | Schmelze | Scrannel | Sea-devil |
| Sandlark | Sarrasin | Scaffold | Schnapps | Scrapple | Sea-drake |
| Sandmole | Sarrazin | Scalable | Schoenus | Scratchy | Sea-eagle |
| Sandpeep | Sarsenet | Scalaria | Scholion | Scrattle | Seafarer |
| Sandpump | Sash-door | Scalawag | Scholium | Scrawler | Sea-fight |
| Sandreed | Sassanid | Scaldino | Schooner | Screamer | Sea-front |
| Sandreel | Sassolin | Scalenum | Schuchin | Screechy | Sea-froth |
| Sandroll | Sassoral | Scalenus | Sciatica | Screever | Sea-gates |
| Sandshot | Satanism | Scaliola | Scienter | Screwkey | Sea-gauge |
| Sandstar | Satanity | Scallion | Sciently | Screwpod | Seagoing |
| Sandtrap | Sateless | Scambler | Scilicet | Scribbet | Sea-goose |
| Sand-wasp | Sathanas | Scammony | Scimitar | Scribble | Sea-grape |

## EIGHT-LETTER WORDS—*continued*

| | | | | | |
|---|---|---|---|---|---|
| Sea-grass | Sea-thong | Seir-fish | Sengreen | Serpette | Sheepish |
| Sea-green | Seatlock | Seizable | Senility | Serplath | Sheep-pen |
| Sea-grove | Seatrail | Seizling | Sennight | Serpolet | Sheep-run |
| Sea-heath | Sea-trout | Sejugous | Senonian | Serranus | Sheer-leg |
| Sea-holly | Seatworm | Selamlik | Senorita | Serrated | Sheeting |
| Sea-horse | Sea-water | Selcouth | Senseful | Serratus | Sheiling |
| Sea-hound | Sea-wrack | Seldseen | Sensible | Serriped | Shekarry |
| Sea-jelly | Sebestan | Selected | Sensibly | Servient | Shelduck |
| Sea-leech | Sebesten | Selector | Sensific | Servious | Shell-gun |
| Sea-lemon | Sebundee | Selenate | Sensuism | Servitor | Shell-ice |
| Sea-level | Secamone | Selenide | Sensuist | Sesamoid | Shell-lac |
| Sea-loach | Secesher | Selenite | Sensuous | Sesspool | Sheltery |
| Sea-louse · | Secluded | Selenium | Sentence | Sestette | Shelving |
| Sealpipe | Seconder | Self-born | Sentient | Sestolet | Shemitic |
| Sealskin | Secondly | Self-heal | Sentinel | Sesterce | Shepherd |
| Sea-lungs | Secretly | Self-help | Sentry-go | Setiform | Sheraton |
| Seal-wort | Sectator | Self-hood | Sepaline | Set-piece | Shielder |
| Seamanly | Sectoral | Self-left | Sepalody | Settling | Shieling |
| Sea-marge | Secundum | Selfless | Sepaloid | Setulose | Shiftily |
| Sea-melon | Securely | Self-love | Sepalous | Severely | Shikaree |
| Seamless | Securite | Self-life | Separate | Severity | Shillaly |
| Sea-mouse | Security | Self-like | Sepiacea | Sewerage | Shilling |
| Seam-rent | Sedately | Self-made | Sepiidae | Sewergas | Shinbone |
| Seamster | Sedative | Self-ness | Sepiment | Sexangle | Shingles |
| Seanymph | Sederunt | Self-pity | Septated | Sexagene | Shipless |
| Sea-onion | Sedge-hen | Selfsame | Septaria | Sextette | Shipload |
| Sea-otter | Sedilium | Self-will | Septette | Sextuple | Shipmate |
| Sea-oxeye | Sediment | Selictar | Septfoil | Sexually | Shipment |
| Sea-peach | Sedition | Sellable | Septical | Sforzato | Shipping |
| Sea-perch | Seductor | Selvagee | Septimole | Shabbily | Shiptire |
| Sea-piece | Sedulity | Selvedge | Septuary | Shabrack | Shipworm |
| Sea-plant | Sedulous | Semblant | Septulum | Shadbird | Shipyard |
| Sea-perch · | Seed-bird | Semester | Septuple | Shadbush | Shireman |
| Seapurse | Seed-cake | Semi-acid | Sequence | Shaddock | Shirting |
| Sea-quail | Seed-coat | Semi-bull | Serafile | Shadeful | Shivaree |
| Sea-raven | Seed-corn | Semi-cope | Seraglio | Shadfrog | Shockdog |
| Searcher | Seed-down | Semi-dome | Seraphic | Shagreen | Shocking |
| Sea-reeve | Seed-fish | Semi-flex | Seraphim | Shalloon | Shoebill |
| Searness | Seed-fowl | Semi-mute | Serapias | Shamanic | Shoehorn |
| Sea-robin | Seed-gall | Seminary | Serenade | Shambles | Shoelace |
| Sea-rover | Seed-leaf | Seminate | Serenata | Shameful | Shoeless |
| Searwood | Seed-leap | Seminole | Serenely | Shamrock | Shooting |
| Seascape | Seedless | Semi-nude | Serenise | Shanghai | Shop-bell |
| Sea-shark | Seedling | Semi-opal | Serenity | Shapable | Shopgirl |
| Seashell | Seedlobe | Semi-oval | Sergeant | Sharp-cut | Shopping |
| Sea-shore | Seed-ness | Semi-ring | Sergette | Sharp-set | Shopworn |
| Sea-shrub | Seedplot | Semitaur | Serially | Shatters | Shorling |
| Sea-snake | Seedsman | Semitism | Seriatim | Shattery | Shortage |
| Sea-snail | Seed-tick | Semitist | Sericate | Shauchle | Short-and |
| Sea-snipe | Seedtime | Semitone | Sericite | Shaw-fowl | Short-cut |
| Seasoned | Seed-wool | Semi-vive | Seriform | Sheading | Short-leg |
| Seasoner | Seedy-toe | Semolina | Seringhi | Shealing | Short-rib |
| Sea-squid | Seerfish | Semolino | Serjeant | Shearhog | Shotbelt |
| Sea-stick | Seership | Semplice | Sermoner | Shearman | Shotfree |
| Sea-stock | Segreant | Sempster | Sermonet | Shea-tree | Shot-hole |
| Sea-swine | Seidlitz | Semuncia | Sermonic | Sheeling | Shot-silk |
| Seatback | Seigneur | Senarius | Serosity | Sheepdog | Shoulder |
| Sea-tench | Seignior | Seng-gung | Serotine | Sheepfly | Showbill |

## EIGHT-LETTER WORDS—*continued*

| | | | | | |
|---|---|---|---|---|---|
| Showcard | Siffleur | Sirenize | Sleekily | Smugness | Socially |
| Show-case | Sigmatic | Sirvente | Sleeking | Smutball | Socinian |
| Showroom | Signable | Siscowet | Sleepful | Smuttied | Socketed |
| Showyard | Signally | Siskiwit | Sleepily | Smuttily | Sockless |
| Shrapnel | Signless | Siskowet | Slidable | Smyrniot | Socmanry |
| Shred-pie | Signieur | Sisterly | Sliddery | Smyterie | Socratic |
| Shrewdly | Sign-post | Sisyphus | Slightly | Snagboat | Soda-lime |
| Shrewish | Silencer | Sitology | Slime-pit | Snailery | Sodalite |
| Shrieker | Silently | Situated | Slimness | Snake-eel | Sodality |
| Shrieval | Silicate | Sitz-bath | Slip-dock | Snappish | Soda-salt |
| Shrimper | Silicify | Sixpence | Slip-knot | Snapshot | Softener |
| Shrinker | Silicite | Sixpenny | Slippery | Snap-vote | Soft-eyed |
| Shroving | Silicium | Sixtieth | Slipshod | Snapweed | Softling |
| Shucking | Silicula | Sizeable | Slipslop | Snatcher | Softness |
| Shuffler | Silicule | Siziness | Slithery | Sneak-cup | Soft-soap |
| Shunless | Silk-mill | Skean-dhu | Slop-bowl | Sneaking | Soft-wood |
| Shunpike | Silk-reel | Skeleton | Slop-pail | Sniffler | Soilless |
| Shutdown | Silkworm | Skelloch | Slopshop | Snippety | Soil-pipe |
| Shwanpan | Sillabub | Sketcher | Slop-work | Snip-snap | Solander |
| Siberian | Silladar | Skewback | Slothful | Snitcher | Solanoid |
| Siberite | Sillyhow | Skewbald | Slottery | Snivelly | Solanine |
| Sibilant | Silphium | Skilless | Slovenes | Snobbery | Solarise |
| Sibilate | Silurist | Skilling | Slovenly | Snobbish | Solarism |
| Sibilous | Silurian | Skimitry | Slovenry | Snobbism | Solarist |
| Sibyllic | Silvanus | Skim-milk | Slow-back | Snowball | Solarium |
| Sicanian | Silverly | Skimping | Slowness | Snowbird | Solarize |
| Siceliot | Simaruba | Skin-deep | Slow-worm | Snowboot | Solaster |
| Sicilian | Similise | Skinless | Slugabed | Snowcapt | Solatium |
| Sickener | Similize | Skin-wool | Sluggard | Snow-cold | Soldanel |
| Sick-flag | Simoniac | Skipetar | Sluggish | Snowdrop | Solderer |
| Sicklied | Simperer | Skip-jack | Slughorn | Snow-eyes | Soldiery |
| Sicklily | Simplify | Skipping | Slumbery | Snowfall | Solecism |
| Sick-list | Simplism | Skirling | Sluttery | Snowless | Solecist |
| Sickness | Simplist | Skirmish | Sluttish | Snowlike | Solecise |
| Sick-room | Simulant | Skirting | Sly-boots | Snowline | Solecize |
| Siculian | Simulate | Skittish | Sly-goose | Snowshed | Solemnly |
| Side-arms | Sinaitic | Skittles | Smallage | Snowslip | Soleness |
| Side-beam | Sinapism | Skua-gull | Small-ale | Snubbish | Solenite |
| Sidecomb | Sineater | Skuggery | Smallish | Snub-nose | Solenoid |
| Side-dish | Sinciput | Skull-cap | Small-pox | Snuffbox | Sole-tile |
| Side-drum | Sinecure | Skunkish | Smaltine | Snuffers | Solfaism |
| Side-line | Sinfonia | Skylight | Smaltite | Snuffler | Solfaist |
| Sideling | Sinfully | Sky-pilot | Smectite | Snuggery | Solidism |
| Side-lock | Singable | Skyscape | Smeltery | Snugness | Solidist |
| Sidelong | Singsong | Slabbery | Smelting | Soapball | Solidity |
| Side-note | Singular | Slabline | Smithery | Soap-lock | Solitary |
| Sidereal | Sinicism | Slaister | Smithing | Soapsuds | Solitude |
| Siderite | Sinister | Slangily | Smokable | Soap-test | Solleret |
| Sideseat | Sink-hole | Slap-bang | Smoke-box | Soap-tree | Solonian |
| Side-show | Sinn-fein | Slapdash | Smoke-dry | Soapwork | Solstice |
| Sideslip | Sinology | Slapjack | Smoothen | Soapwort | Solution |
| Sidesman | Sinuated | Slapping | Smoothly | Soberize | Solutive |
| Side-view | Sinusoid | Slashing | Smorzato | Sobranje | Solvable |
| Sidewalk | Siphonal | Slate-axe | Smothery | Sobriety | Solvency |
| Sideways · | Siphonic | Slattern | Smoulder | Sob-stuff | Somatism |
| Side-wind | Sipylite | Slaverer | Smouldry | So-called | Somatist |
| Sidewise | Siraisis | Slavonic | Smug-boat | Sociable | Somatome |
| Siege-gun | Sirenise | Sledding | Smuggler | Sociably | Sombrero |

## EIGHT-LETTER WORDS—*continued*

| | | | | | |
|---|---|---|---|---|---|
| Sombrous | Spacious | Spherics | Sporadic | Squirter | Statuary |
| Somebody | Spadilio | Spheroid | Sporosac | Stabling | Statured |
| Some-deal | Spadille | Spherule | Sportful | Stablish | Stay-bolt |
| Some-dele | Spadroon | Sphragid | Sporting | Staccato | Stay-lace |
| Some-gate | Spagiric | Sphygmic | Sportive | Stag-evil | Staysail |
| Somerset | Spalpeen | Spicated | Spotless | Staggard | Steadily |
| Some-such | Spandrel | Spiccato | Sprachle | Staggers | Steading |
| Sometime | Spandril | Spice-box | Sprackle | Staghorn | Stealthy |
| Somewhat | Spanemia | Spiceful | Spraints | Stagnant | Steam-gun |
| Somewhen | Spangler | Spicknel | Sprawler | Stagnate | Steam-tug |
| Somnific | Spaniard | Spicular | Spreader | Stahlian | Stearate |
| Sonatina | Spanking | Spiculum | Spredden | Stahlism | Stearine |
| Song-bird | Spanless | Spiffing | Springal | Stair-rod | Steatite |
| Song-book | Span-long | Spigelia | Springer | Stairway | Steatoma |
| Songless | Span-roof | Spikelet | Sprinkle | Stake-net | Stedfast |
| Songster | Sparable | Spilikin | Sprinter | Stalking | Steelpen |
| Son-in-law | Spar-deck | Spillway | Sprocket | Stallage | Steepled |
| Sonority | Sparerib | Spilotes | Sprucely | Stall-fed | Steerage |
| Sonorous | Sparhawk | Spinifex | Sprucify | Stallion | Steevely |
| Soothing | Spar-hung | Spinitis | Spuilzie | Stallman | Steeving |
| Soothsay | Sparkful | Spinnery | Spunyarn | Stalwart | Steinbok |
| Sopherim | Sparkish | Spinning | Spur-gall | Stamened | Stellary |
| Sopition | Sparkler | Spinster | Spurgear | Staminal | Stellate |
| Soporous | Sparklet | Spinstry | Spurious | Stampact | Stellion |
| Sorbonne | Sparling | Spirally | Spurless | Stampede | Stem-head |
| Sorcerer | Sparring | Spiracle | Spurling | Stanchel | Stem-leaf |
| Sordidly | Sparsely | Spiricle | Spurrier | Stancher | Stemless |
| Sorehead | Sparsile | Spirifer | Spycraft | Standard | Stenosed |
| Soredium | Spathose | Spirited | Spy-glass | Standing | Stenosis |
| Soredial | Spathous | Spiritus | Spy-money | Standish | Stepdame |
| Soreness | Spathura | Spitcurl | Squabble | Stanhope | Stepgirl |
| Soricine | Spavined | Spiteful | Squab-pie | Stank-hen | Sterling |
| Sororise | Speaking | Spitfire | Squadron | Stannary | Sternage |
| Sorority | Spearman | Spittoon | Squaller | Stannate | Sternite |
| Sorrower | Specific | Spizella | Squaloid | Stannine | Sternway |
| Sortable | Specimen | Splasher | Squamata | Stannous | Stibbler |
| Sortment | Specious | Splatter | Squamate | Stanzaic | Stibnite |
| Sotadean | Speckled | Spleened | Squamoid | Stapelia | Sticcado |
| Soterial | Spectant | Splendid | Squamose | Starcher | Stickler |
| Souchong | Spectral | Splenial | Squamous | Starchly | Stiff-bit |
| Soul-bell | Spectrum | Splenium | Squamula | Stardust | Stiffish |
| Soulless | Specular | Splenius | Squamule | Starfish | Stigmata |
| Soul-scot | Speculum | Splinter | Squander | Starfort | Stilbite |
| Soul-shot | Speedful | Splitter | Squarely | Starless | Stiletto |
| Soul-sick | Speedily | Splotchy | Squarish | Starlike | Stilling |
| Sound-bow | Speedway | Splutter | Squarson | Starling | Stillion |
| Sounding | Spekboom | Spoffish | Squasher | Star-nose | Stimulus |
| Sourdine | Spelding | Spoilful | Squatter | Star-read | Stingily |
| Sour-dock | Speldron | Spoliary | Squattle | Star-reed | Stingray |
| Sour-eyed | Spelling | Spoliate | Squawman | Startful | Stinkard |
| Sourness | Spendall | Spondaic | Squeaker | Starting | Stinkpot |
| Soutache | Sperable | Spondias | Squeegee | Startish | Stippler |
| Southern | Spergula | Spondyle | Squeezer | Startler | Stipular |
| Southing | Spermism | Sponsion | Squiggle | Starwort | Stipuled |
| Southsay | Sperm- il | Spontoon | Squilgee | Stasimon | Stirless |
| Souvenir | Sphagnum | Spookish | Squireen | Statable | Stirring |
| Sow-bread | Sphecius | Spoonful | Squirely | Statedly | Stitchel |
| Sow-drunk | Sphenoid | Spoonily | Squirrel | Statical | Stitcher |

EIGHT-LETTER WORDS—*continued*

| | | | | | |
|---|---|---|---|---|---|
| Stoccade | Striking | Sub-lease | Sultanic | Swadeshi | Symploce |
| Stoccado | Stringed | Sublunar | Sumerian | Swagshop | Synacral |
| Stockade | Stringer | Submerge | Summoner | Swaining | Synalgia |
| Stocking | Strinkle | Submerse | Sumpitan | Swainish | Synancia |
| Stockish | Stripper | Subnasal | Sunburnt | Swamp-oak | Synarchy |
| Stockist | Strobila | Sub-nodal | Sunburst | Swamp-ore | Synastry |
| Stockman | Strobile | Sub-order | Suncrack | Swanherd | Syncline |
| Stockpot | Stroller | Suborner | Sun-dried | Swanking | Syncopal |
| Stoicism | Strombus | Subovate | Sundries | Swanlike | Syndetic |
| Stolzite | Strongly | Subpœna | Sun-light | Swan-neck | Synedral |
| Stomatic | Strontia | Subpolar | Sun-print | Swannery | Syndrome |
| Stone-bow | Strophic | Subprior | Sunproof | Swan-shot | Synechia |
| Stone-fly | Strucken | Sub-pubic | Sunshade | Swan-skin | Syngraph |
| Stone-oil | Struggle | Subrigid | Sunshine | Swartish | Synochal |
| Stonepit | Strumous | Subserve | Sunshiny | Swastica | Synochus |
| Stop-cock | Strumpet | Subsolar | Sun-stone | Swastika | Synodist |
| Stoppage | Struthio | Substage | Superadd | Sweatily | Synomosy |
| Storable | Strutter | Substyle | Superbly | Sweep-net | Synonyme |
| Stormful | Stubborn | Subtense | Superior | Sweet-bay | Synonymy |
| Stowaway | Stub-iron | Subtepid | Superman | Sweet-gum | Synopsis |
| Stowdown | Stub-nail | Subtility | Supernal | Sweetish | Synoptic |
| Straddle | Stuccoed | Sub-title | Supertax | Sweet-oil | Synovial |
| Straggle | Studbolt | Subtlety | Supinate | Sweet-pea | Syntaxis |
| Straight | Stud-book | Subtonic | Supinely | Sweet-sop | Syntexis |
| Strainer | Stud-farm | Subtract | Supplant | Swelldom | Syntonic |
| Straiten | Studious | Sub-tribe | Supplial | Swelling | Syntonin |
| Straitly | Studwork | Sub-trist | Supplier | Swellish | Syriarch |
| Stramash | Stuffing | Sub-tutor | Supposal | Swell-mob | Syrigmus |
| Stranded | Stultify | Subulate | Supposer | Swiftlet | Systasis |
| Stranger | Stumbler | Suburban | Suppress | Swimming | Systemic |
| Strangle | Stunning | Sub-verse | Surbased | Swindler | Systolic |
| Strap-oil | Stundist | Sub-zonal | Surcease | Swine-oat | Syzygant |
| Strapper | Stunsail | Succinct | Surculus | Swinepox | |
| Strategy | Stupeous | Succinic | Sureness | Swine-sty | |
| Stratify | Stupidly | Succubus | Surf-bird | Switchel | **T** |
| Stratula | Stuprate | Suchlike | Surfboat | Swoonded | Tabarder |
| Straught | Sturdily | Sucklers | Surf-duck | Swordarm | Tabashir |
| Straunge | Sturgeon | Sudamina | Surgical | Sword-cut | Tabbinet |
| Stravaig | Sturnoid | Sudation | Suricate | Sword-law | Tabbycat |
| Streamer | Suasible | Sudatory | Surmiser | Sybarite | Tabitude |
| Streight | Subacrid | Suddenly | Surmount | Sybotism | Tableful |
| Strelitz | Subacute | Sufferer | Surmulot | Sycamine | Taboggan |
| Strength | Sub-agent | Suffioni | Surplice | Sycamore | Taborine |
| Strepent | Sub-class | Sufflate | Surprise | Sycomore | Taborite |
| Strepera | Subahdar | Suffrage | Surrebut | Syconium | Tabouret |
| Strephon | Subduing | Suffrago | Surrenal | Syenitic | Tabulate |
| Stretchy | Subduple | Sufistic | Surround | Syllabic | Tacahout |
| Striated | Sub-equal | Suicidal | Sursolid | Syllable | Tac-au-tac |
| Striatum | Suberate | Suilline | Surveyal | Syllabub | Taciturn |
| Stricken | Suberine | Suitable | Surveyor | Syllabus | Tackling |
| Strickle | Suberose | Suitably | Survival | Sylphine | Tacksman |
| Strictly | Suberous | Suitress | Survivor | Sylphish | Tactical |
| Striddle | Sub-flora | Sulcated | Suspense | Symbolic | Tactless |
| Strident | Subgenus | Sullenly | Suspiral | Symmetry | Taenioid |
| Strigate | Sub-grade | Sulphate | Suversed | Symmorph | Tafferel |
| Strigine | Subgroup | Sulphide | Suzerain | Sympathy | Taffrail |
| Strigose | Subhuman | Sulphite | Svastika | Symphony | Tagilite |
| Strigous | Subhyoid | Sulphury | Swaddler | Symphyla | Tailings |

## EIGHT-LETTER WORDS—*continued*

| | | | | | |
|---|---|---|---|---|---|
| Tailless | Tarsiped | Telluric | Testamur | Thlipsis | Tigellum |
| Tailrace | Tartaric | Teloogoo | Testator | Tholepin | Tigellus |
| Tailrope | Tartarin | Telotype | Test-tube | Thomeans | Tiger-cat |
| Tainture | Tartarum | Temerity | Tetanise | Thoracic | Tigerish |
| Takingly | Tartarus | Temerous | Tetanoid | Thornbut | Tigerism |
| Talapoin | Tartness | Temewise | Tetchily | Thornset | Tightens |
| Talented | Tartrate | Tempered | Tethered | Thorough | Tile-kiln |
| Talesman | Tartuffe | Template | Tetradic | Thousand | Tillable |
| Talisman | Tar-water | Temporal | Tetragon | Thowless | Tillered |
| Talkable | Taskwork | Tempting | Tetrapla | Thraldom | Tilt-boat |
| Talliage | Tastable | Temulent | Tetrapod | Thranite | Tilt-yard |
| Talliate | Tasteful | Tenacity | Tetrarch | Thrapple | Timbered |
| Tallness | Tattered | Tenaille | Teutonic | Thrasher | Time-ball |
| Tallower | Tattlery | Tenanted | Text-book | Thrawart | Time-bill |
| Tallyman | Tattling | Tenantry | Text-hand | Threaden | Time-book |
| Talmudic | Tattooes | Tendance | Textrine | Threader | Time-card |
| Talukdar | Taunting | Tendency | Textuary | Threaten | Time-fuse |
| Tamandua | Taurocol | Tenderly | Textuist | Three-ply | Timeless |
| Tamanoer | Tautened | Tendsome | Thalamus | Threnode | Timework |
| Tamarack | Tautness | Tenebrae | Thalline | Threnody | Timeworn |
| Tamarind | Taverner | Tenement | Thallium | Threshel | Timidity |
| Tamarisk | Tawdrily | Tenesmic | Thallose | Thresher | Timonist |
| Tameable | Taxation | Tenesmus | Thalloid | Threstle | Timoneer |
| Tameless | Taxiarch | Tenon-saw | Thanedom | Thridace | Timoroso |
| Tameness | Taxodium | Tenorist | Thankful | Thriller | Timorous |
| Tamperer | Taxology | Tenotomy | Thatched | Thriving | Tincture |
| Tanballs | Taxonomy | Tensible | Thatcher | Thrombus | Tinewald |
| Tancross | Tea-board | Tentacle | Thearchy | Thropple | Tinglish |
| Tangence | Tea-caddy | Tent-work | Theetsee | Throstle | Tingling |
| Tangency | Tea-chest | Tent-wort | Theiform | Throttle | Tinkerly |
| Tangible | Tea-cloth | Tenuious | Thematic | Thrummer | Tinkling |
| Tangibly | Tea-fight | Teocalli | Thentric | Thruster | Tinnitus |
| Tangling | Tea-house | Tepefied | Theocrat | Thuggery | Tinplate |
| Tan-house | Teamster | Tephrite | Theodicy | Thumbpot | Tinselly |
| Tanistry | Tea-plant | Tepidity | Theogony | Thumping | Tinsmith |
| Tannable | Tea-party | Teraphim | Theology | Thundery | Tinstone |
| Tannadur | Tea-table | Terebene | Theorise | Thurible | Tinstuff |
| Tan-stove | Teamwise | Teredine | Theorist | Thurifer | Tintamar |
| Tantalus | Team-work | Tergitic | Theorize | Thursday | Tintless |
| Tanticle | Teardrop | Termatic | Theosoph | Thusness | Tipstaff |
| Tantrism | Tearless | Terminal | Therefor | Thwarter | Tipulary |
| Tantrist | Teaseler | Terminer | Thereout | Thyrsoid | Tireless |
| Tanzimat | Teaspoon | Terminus | Theriaca | Tibialis | Tiresome |
| Tapadera | Technics | Termless | Thespian | Tickbean | Tironian |
| Tape-line | Tectaria | Terrapin | Theurgic | Ticketed | Tirrivie |
| Tapering | Tectonic | Terrible | Thewless | Tickling | Titaness |
| Tapestry | Teemless | Terribly | Thickish | Ticklish | Titanian |
| Tapeworm | Teething | Terrific | Thicknee | Tick-seed | Titanite |
| Tapiroid | Teetotal | Tertiary | Thickset | Tickshop | Tithable |
| Tara-fern | Teetotum | Tertiate | Thievery | Tick-tack | Tithonic |
| Tarboosh | Tegminal | Terzetto | Thieving | Tidegate | Titivate |
| Targeted | Tegument | Tessella | Thievish | Tideless | Titmouse |
| Targumic | Telarian | Tesserae | Thingamy | Tide-lock | Titonium |
| Tarlatin | Telegram | Tesseral | Thinking | Tidemark | Tit-tat-to |
| Tarperan | Teleseme | Tessular | Thinness | Tidemill | Titterel |
| Tarragon | Telestic | Testable | Thinnish | Tidesman | Tittuppy |
| Tarrying | Telltale | Testacea | Thirlage | Tide-wave | Tittubant |
| Tarsipes | Tellural | Testacel | Thirteen | Tidiness | Titubant |

## EIGHT-LETTER WORDS—*continued*

| | | | | | |
|---|---|---|---|---|---|
| Titubate | Toreutic | Tragical | Trewsman | Triplane | Tuberose |
| Titulary | Torentes | Tragopan | Triadist | Triplite | Tuberous |
| Toadfish | Torminal | Trail-net | Trialism | Tripodal | Tubewell |
| Toadflax | Toroidal | Training | Triangle | Trippant | Tubicole |
| Toadpipe | Torosity | Train-oil | Triapsal | Tripping | Tubiform |
| Toad-spit | Tor-ouzel | Traipsed | Triarchy | Trip-slip | Tubipore |
| Toadyish | Torpidly | Trampler | Triarian | Triptote | Tubulate |
| Toadyism | Torquate | Tramroad | Triassic | Triptych | Tubulous |
| Toboggan | Torshent | Tranchle | Triaxial | Trisemic | Tub-wheel |
| Toboggin | Torterer | Trangram | Tribasic | Triskele | Tuckahoe |
| Tocology | Tortilla | Tranquil | Tribelet | Tristful | Tuckshop |
| Toe-piece | Tortious | Transact | Tribonyx | Tritical | Tucotuco |
| Together | Tortoise | Transept | Tribrach | Triticum | Tug-of-war |
| Toilette | Tortuose | Transfer | Tribunal | Triumvir | Tuku-tuku |
| Toilless | Tortuous | Transfix | Tributed | Triunity | Tula-work |
| Toilsome | Torturer | Tranship | Tributer | Trivalve | Tumbling |
| Toilworn | Toruloid | Transire | Trichina | Trochaic | Tumidity |
| Tokology | Torulose | Transmew | Trichite | Trochite | Tumoured |
| Tolbooth | Torulous | Transmit | Trichoda | Trochlea | Tumpline |
| Tolerant | Totalise | Transude | Trichoma | Trochoid | Tumulate |
| Tolerate | Totality | Trap-ball | Trichome | Trollopy | Tumulose |
| Toll-dish | Totalize | Trapdoor | Trichord | Tromblon | Tumulous |
| Tolletan | Totemism | Trapesed | Trickery | Trombone | Tunbelly |
| Toll-gate | Totitive | Trapezia | Trickily | Troopial | Tuneless |
| Toltecan | Touchily | Trap-fall | Tricking | Trophesy | Tungsten |
| Tomahawk | Touching | Trappean | Trickish | Tropical | Tungstic |
| Tomalley | Touchpan | Trappist | Tricksey | Trot-cosy | Tunicary |
| Tombless | Toughens | Trappous | Tricklet | Trottoir | Tunicata |
| Tomentum | Toughish | Trap tufa | Tricolor | Troubler | Tunicate |
| Tommyrot | Tourelle | Trap-tuff | Trictrac | Troupial | Turanian |
| Tomnoddy | Tournure | Trashery | Tricycle | Trousers | Turbaned |
| To-morrow | Towardly | Trashily | Tridacna | Trouting | Turbidly |
| Tomundar | Towering | Trasling | Trifling | Troutlet | Turbinal |
| Tonalite | Town-hall | Traverse | Triglyph | Trouvere | Turcoman |
| Tonality | Townland | Travesty | Trigness | Trowsers | Turf-clad |
| Toneless | Townless | Trawling | Trignia | Truantly | Turf-moss |
| Tonicity | Township | Tray-trip | Trigloid | Truckage | Turgidly |
| Tonsilar | Townsman | Treadler | Trigonal | Truckler | Turkoman |
| Tonsured | Town-talk | Treasure | Trigonic | Truckles | Turlough |
| Toonwood | Toxaemia | Treasury | Trigonon | Trudging | Turmeric |
| Toothful | Toxicant | Treatise | Trigraph | True-blue | Turnagra |
| Tooth-key | Toyishly | Trebling | Trilemma | True-born | Turn-back |
| Toparchy | Tracheal | Trecento | Trillion | True-bred | Turncoat |
| Topazine | Trachean | Tree-calf | Trillium | True-love | Turncock |
| Top-boots | Trachoma | Tree-crab | Trilobed | Trueness | Turndown |
| Top-dress | Trachyte | Tree-dove | Trimeted | Trumpery | Turnover |
| Top-heavy | Trackage | Tree-fern | Trimeter | Truncate | Turnpike |
| Toplofty | Trackman | Tree-frog | Trimming | Trunkful | Turn-sick |
| Toponomy | Trackway | Treeless | Trimness | Trunnion | Turn-skin |
| Toponymy | Tractate | Tree-nail | Trimurti | Trussing | Turnsole |
| Topology | Tractile | Tremando | Tringine | Trustful | Turnspit |
| Top-proud | Traction | Trembler | Tringoid | Trustily | Turreted |
| Top-shell | Tractive | Tremella | Trinodal | Truthful | Tussocky |
| Top-stone | Tractory | Trencher | Triodion | Tryhouse | Tutelage |
| Torchere | Tractrix | Trenches | Trip-book | Tryptone | Tutelary |
| Torching | Tradeful | Trephine | Tripedal | Trysting | Tutorage |
| Toreador | Traditor | Trespass | Tripeman | Tube-form | Tutoress |
| Torcular | Traducer | Tressure | Triphane | Tubercle | Tutorial |

EIGHT-LETTER WORDS—*continued*

| | | | | | |
|---|---|---|---|---|---|
| Tutoring | Umbriere | Unburden | Underbuy | Unfleshy | Unhoused |
| Tutorism | Umpirage | Unburied | Undercut | Unflower | Uniaxial |
| Twaddler | Umquhile | Unburned | Underfed | Unfluent | Unibasal |
| Twangled | Unabased | Unburrow | Underlap | Unfoiled | Unicycle |
| Twattler | Unabated | Unbusied | Underlay | Unfooted | Unideaed |
| Twiddler | Unaching | Unbutton | Underlet | Unforced | Unifying |
| Twigging | Unactive | Uncalled | Underlie | Unforged | Unilobar |
| Twilight | Unadmire | Uncandid | Underman | Unformal | Unilobed |
| Twin-born | Unadored | Uncarted | Undernew | Unformed | Uninvite |
| Twinkler | Unafraid | Uncaught | Underpay | Unfought | Unionism |
| Twinling | Unaiming | Uncaused | Underpin | Unfouled | Unionist |
| Twinship | Unallied | Unchance | Underrun | Unframed | Unionite |
| Twitcher | Unamazed | Unchancy | Undersay | Unfriend | Unipolar |
| Two-edged | Unamused | Uncharge | Underset | Unfrozen | Uniquely |
| Two-faced | Unanchor | Unchaste | Undersky | Unfrugal | Uniquity |
| Two-pence | Unaneled | Uncheery | Undertow | Unfueled | Unisonal |
| Two-penny | Unargued | Unchewed | Undevout | Unfunded | Unitedly |
| Tychonic | Unartful | Unchided | Undimmed | Ungainly | Univalve |
| Tympanic | Unatoned | Unchurch | Undinted | Ungalled | Universe |
| Tympanum | Unattire | Unciatim | Undipped | Ungenial | Univocal |
| Tynewald | Unavowed | Unciform | Undivine | Ungentle | Unjoined |
| Type-high | Unawares | Uncinata | Undoctor | Ungently | Unjoyful |
| Typhlops | Unbacked | Uncinate | Undouble | Ungifted | Unjoyous |
| Typhonic | Unbagged | Unclench | Undraped | Ungilded | Unjudged |
| Typifier | Unbanded | Unclinch | Undreamt | Ungirded | Unjustly |
| Typhoean | Unbarbed | Unclosed | Undriven | Ungiving | Unkenned |
| Typolite | Unbarked | Unclothe | Undrossy | Unglazed | Unkennel |
| Typology | Unbathed | Uncloudy | Undulant | Ungloved | Unkindly |
| Typorama | Unbeaten | Unclutch | Undulate | Uhgoaded | Unkingly |
| Tyrociny | Unbefool | Uncoated | Undulous | Ungorged | Unlacing |
| Tyrolite | Unbeheld | Uncocked | Undulose | Ungotten | Unlading |
| Tyrannus | Unbelief | Uncoifed | Unearned | Ungraced | Unlarded |
| Tyronish | Unbenign | Uncoined | Uneasily | Unground | Unlavish |
| Tyrolese | Unbereft | Uncombed | Unedible | Unguical | Unlawful |
| Tyrranic | Unbeseem | Uncomely | Unelated | Unguided | Unlaying |
| Tyrtaean | Unbiased | Uncommon | Unending | Unguilty | Unlearnt |
| Tyrtoean | Unbidden | Uncooped | Unenvied | Unguinal | Unlicked |
| Tzarevna | Unbishop | Uncostly | Unerring | Ungulata | Unlikely |
| Tzaritsa | Unbitted | Uncouple | Unespied | Ungulate | Unlimber |
| | Unblamed | Uncowled | Unevenly | Ungummed | Unlineal |
| **U** | Unbloody | Uncreate | Unexempt | Unhacked | Unlining |
| | Unbodied | Unctuous | Unexpert | Unhallow | Unlinked |
| Ubiquity | Unboding | Unculled | Unfabled | Unharmed | Unlively |
| Udometer | Unboiled | Uncurbed | Unfading | Unheated | Unlocked |
| Ugliness | Unbolted | Uncurled | Unfairly | Unhedged | Unlooked |
| Ulcerate | Unbonnet | Uncursed | Unfallen | Unheeded | Unloosen |
| Ulcerous | Unbooted | Undamped | Unfasten | Unheired | Unlorded |
| Ulcuscle | Unbought | Undashed | Unfaulty | Unhelmed | Unlordly |
| Ulterior | Unboyish | Undazzle | Unfeared | Unhelmet | Unlovely |
| Ultimata | Unbreech | Undecent | Unfellow | Unhelped | Unloving |
| Ultimate | Unbrewed | Undecked | Unfenced | Unheppen | Unluting |
| Ultimity | Unbribed | Undeeded | Unfences | Unheroic | Unmaimed |
| Ultraism | Unbridle | Undefine | Unfetter, | Unhinged | Unmaking |
| Ultraist | Unbroken | Underact | Unfilial | Unhiving | Unmanned |
| Umbellar | Unbuckle | Underaid | Unfilled | Unhonest | Unmantle |
| Umbonate | Unbudded | Underarm | Unfilmed | Unhooded | Unmarked |
| Umbratic | Unbundle | Underbid | Unflated | Unhooked | Unmarred |
| Umbrella | Unbuoyed | Underbud | Unflawed | Unhorned | Unmartyr |
| Umbrette | | | | | |

## EIGHT-LETTER WORDS—*continued*

| | | | | | |
|---|---|---|---|---|---|
| Unmasked | Unpruned | Unsmoked | Untithed | Upwafted | Vamplate |
| Unmeddle | Unpucker | Unsmooth | Untitled | Upwardly | Vanadate |
| Unmeetly | Unpurged | Unsoaped | Untongue | Uralitic | Vanadium |
| Unmelted | Unracked | Unsocial | Untoward | Uratosis | Vandalic |
| Unmilked | Unraised | Unsocket | Untraced | Urbanity | Vanguard |
| Unmilled | Unranged | Unsoiled | Untraded | Urceolus· | Vanillic |
| Unminded | Unreally | Unsolder | Untruced | Urgently | Vanisher |
| Unmingle | Unreaped | Unsolemn | Untruism | Urochord | Vanquish |
| Unmoaned | Unreason | Unsolved | Untrusty | Urochroa | Vapidity |
| Unmodish | Unreined | Unsoncie | Untufted | Urocissa | Vaporise |
| Un-Mosaic | Unrepaid | Unsonsie | Unuseful | Uromeric | Vaporize |
| Unmoving | Unrepair | Unsorted | Unvalued | Urosleye | Vaporole |
| Unmuddle | Unriddle | Unsought | Unvaried | Urosteon | Vaporose |
| Unmuffle | Unrifled | Unsouled | Unvassal | Urostyle | Vaporous |
| Unmuzzle | Unrigged | Unsoured | Unveiler | Ursiform | Vapourer |
| Un-napped | Unripped | Unspeedy | Unvented | Ursuline | Vaqueria |
| Un-native | Unrobing | Unsphere | Unversed | Urticate | Varanoid |
| Unneeded | Unrolled | Unspoilt | Unvirtue | Usefully | Vargueno |
| Unnerved | Unroofed | Unspoken | Unvizard | Usherdom | Variable |
| Unnetted | Unrooted | Unsquire | Unvoiced | Ustilago | Variably |
| Unnimbed | Unrouted | Unstable | Unvulgar | Ustulate | Variance |
| Unnooked | Unruffle | Unstarch | Unwaited | Usufruct | Variated |
| Un-notify | Unruined | Unstayed | Unwalled | Usurious | Varicorn |
| Unopened | Unrumple | Unsteady | Unwarily | Usurping | Varicose |
| Unpacked | Unsaddle | Unstitch | Unwarmed | Utiliser | Varicous |
| Un-packer | Unsafely | Unstored | Unwarned | Utopiast | Varletal |
| Unpained | Unsafety | Unstring | Unwarped | Utriform | Variform |
| Unpaired | Unsalted | Unstruck | Unwashed | Uttering | Variolar |
| Un-panged | Unsapped | Unstrung | Unwasted | Uxorious | Variorum |
| Unparted | Unsating | Unsucked | Unwedded | | Varietry |
| Unpathed | Unsaying | Unsunned | Unweeded· | **V** | Vartabed |
| Unpawned | Unscared | Unsurely | Unwieldy | | Vartabet |
| Unpeeled | Unsealed | Unswathe | Unwilful | Vacation | Vasalium |
| Unpeople | Unseamed | Unswayed | Unwilled | Vaccinia | Vascular |
| Unpicked | Unseared | Untacked | Unwisdom | Vagabond | Vasculum |
| Unpinion | Unseated | Untackle | Unwisely | Vagarish | Vaseline |
| Unpinned | Unsecret | Untalked | Unwonted | Vaginant | Vasiform |
| Unpinked | Unsecure | Untangle | Unwooded | Vaginate | Vassaled |
| Unpitied | Unseeded | Untasked | Unwormed | Vaginula | Vassalry |
| Unplaced | Unseeing | Untasted | Unworthy | Vaginule | Vastness |
| Unpliant | Unseemly | Untaught | Upcaught | Vagrancy | Vaticide |
| Unpoetic | Unseized | Untenant | Upcoming | Vainness | Vaultage |
| Unpoised | Unserved | Untended | Upgather | Valentia | Vaulting |
| Unpoison | Unsettle | Untender | Upgrowth | Valerian | Vauntery |
| Unpolish | Unsexual | Untented | Upheaval | Valhalla | Vauntful |
| Unpolite· | Unshaded | Untested | Upholder | Valiance | Vaunting |
| Unpolled | Unshaked | Untether | Upmaking | Valiancy | Vauntlay |
| Unposted | Unshaken | Unthawed | Up-plough | Validate | Vavasory |
| Unpraise | Unshamed | Unthorny | Upridged | Validity | Vavasour |
| Unpreach | Unshapen | Unthread | Uprising | Valkyria | Vealskin |
| Unpretty | Unshared | Unthrift | Uprooted | Vallancy | Vedantic |
| Unpriced | Unshaven | Unthrone | Upsnatch | Vallated | Vegative |
| Unpriest | Unshelve | Unthrown | Upstairs | Valorous | Vegetate |
| Unprince | Unshrunk | Untidily | Upstream | Valuable | Vehement |
| Unprised | Unsifted | Untilled | Upstroke | Valuator | Veilless |
| Unprison | Unsinged | Untimely | Upthrust | Valvelet | Veinless II |
| Unproper | Unslaked | Untinged | Uptossed | Valvular | Velarium |
| Unproved | Unsluice | Untiring | Upturned | Vampiric | Velation |

**EIGHT-LETTER WORDS**—*continued*

| | | | | | |
|---|---|---|---|---|---|
| Velatura | Vestment | Virginal | Vomiting | Waltzing | Waterman |
| Velleity | Vestuary | Virginia | Vomition | Wanderer | Waterpot |
| Velloped | Vestural | Viridian | Vomitive | Wanderoo | Water-ram |
| Velocity | Vesturer | Viridity | Vomitory | Wantless | Water-rat |
| Velveret | Vesuvian | Virility | Voracity | Wantonly | Water-rot |
| Velveted | Vexation | Virtuose | Vortical | Wapacut | Water-rug |
| Venality | Vexillar | Virtuoso | Vortices | Wappened | Waterway |
| Venation | Vexillum | Virtuous | Votaress | Warbling | Watt-hour |
| Vendetta | Vexingly | Virulent | Votarist | War-dance | Waveless |
| Vendible | Viameter | Viscacha | Votively | Wardcorn | Wavelike |
| Vendibly | Viaticum | Visceral | Vouching | Wardenry | Wave-line |
| Veneered | Vibrator | Viscount | Voussoir | Wardmote | Wave-loaf |
| Venenate | Vibrissa | Visigoth | Vowelism | Wardrobe | Wavering |
| Venenous | Vibrogen | Visional | Vowelist | Ward-room | Waverous |
| Venerant | Viburnum | Visitant | Vowelled | Wardship | Wave-trap |
| Venerate | Vicarage | Visiting | Voyageur | Wareless | Waveworn |
| Venetian | Vicarial | Vitalise | Vulcanic | Ware-room | Waviness |
| Vengeful | Vicarius | Vitalism | Vulgarly | Warfarer | Waxcloth |
| Veniable | Vice-dean | Vitalist | Vulsella | Warfield | Waxlight |
| Venially | Vice-king | Vitality | | Warhorse | Wax-paper |
| Venomous | Vicenary | Vitalize | | Wariated | Wax-plant |
| Venosity | Vicinage | Vitellin | | Wariness | Way-board |
| Venously | Vicinity | Vitellus | **W** | Warmness | Waybread |
| Vent-plug | Victoria | Vitiator | | Warpaint | Wayfarer |
| Venturer | Victress | Viticide | Wabbling | War-plume | Waygoing |
| Veracity | Victuals | Vitreous | Waddling | Warproof | Way-goose |
| Verandah | Videndum | Vituline | Wafering | Warragal | Waylayer |
| Veratric | Viewable | Vivacity | Wage-fund | Warranty | Wayleave |
| Veratrin | Viewless | Vivarium | Wageless | Warrener | Waymaker |
| Veratrum | Viewsome | Vividity | Wage-work | Warrison | Way-shaft |
| Verbally | Vigilant | Vivisect | Waggling | Wartweed | Waythorn |
| Verbatim | Vigneron | Vixenish | Waggoner | Wartwort | Way-train |
| Verbiage | Vignette | Vizirate | Waggonet | Warwhoop | Waywiser |
| Verdancy | Vigoroso | Vizirial | Wagonage | Washable | Weakener |
| Verderer | Vigorous | Vocalise | Wagonful | Washaway | Weak-eyed |
| Verditer | Vileness | Vocalist | Wagoning | Washball | Weakling |
| Verecund | Vilifier | Vocality | Wagon-lit | Washbowl | Weakness |
| Vergency | Vilipend | Vocalize | Wailment | Washdirt | Wealsman |
| Vergette | Villadom | Vocation | Wainbote | Wasp-bite | Weanling |
| Verifier | Villager | Vocative | Wainrope | Wasteful | Weaponed |
| Verjuice | Villainy | Voidable | Wainscot | Watchbox | Wearable |
| Verminly | Villatic | Voidance | Wait-a-bit | Watchdog | Weariful |
| Vermouth | Vincible | Voidness | Waitress | Watchful | Weed-hook |
| Vernicle | Vinculum | Voigtite | Wakening | Watching | Weedless |
| Veronese | Vine-clad | Volatile | Wakerife | Watch-key | Weetless |
| Veronica | Vine-gall | Volcanic | Waldhorn | Watchman | Weeviled |
| Verrugas | Vine-grub | Volitant | Walhalla | Waterage | Weighage |
| Versable | Vineland | Volition | Walkable | Water-bed | Weissite |
| Verselet | Vineyard | Volitive | Walk-mill | Waterbug | Welcomer |
| Versicle | Vinosity | Volplane | Walk-over | Watercan | Weldable |
| Vertebra | Vintager | Volsungs | Wall-eyed | Water-dog | Weld-iron |
| Vertical | Vintnery | Voltaism | Wall-knot | Waterfly | Welladay |
| Verticil | Violable | Voltzite | Wall-moss | Water-fox | Wellaway |
| Vesicant | Violator | Volubile | Wallnewt | Water-gas | Well-boat |
| Vesicate | Violence | Volulite | Walloper | Water-god | Well-born |
| Vesicula | Viperine | Volumist | Wallower | Waterhen | Well-bred |
| Vespiary | Viperish | Volution | Wallsend | Watering | Wellcurb |
| Vestiary | Viperous | Volvulus | Wall-tree | Waterish | Welldoer |
| | | | Wall-wort | | |

## EIGHT-LETTER WORDS—*continued*

Well-head
Well-hole
Well-knit
Wellnigh
Well-read
Well-room
Well-seen
Well-to-do
Well-worn
Welshman
Weregild
Werewolf
Wesleyan
Westerly
Westward
Wet-nurse
Whacking
Whaleman
Whale-oil
Whanghee
Wharfage
Wharfing
Whatever
What-like
Wheatear
Wheat-eel
Wheat-fly
Wheedler
Wheelage
Wheeling
Wheelman
Wheel-ore
Wheel-tax
Wheezily
Wheezing
Whenever
Whereout
Wherever
Whetting
Whey-face
Whiffing
Whiffler
Whiggery
Whiggish
Whiggism
Whimbrel
Whimpled
Whim-wham
Whinchat
Whinnock
Whinyard
Whipcord
Whiphand
Whipjack
Whiplash
Whipping
Whipster
Whirlbat

Whirling
Whirring
Whisking
Whistler
White-ant
Whiteboy
White-hot
Whitener
Whitepot
Whitling
Whitsour
Whitster
Whittled
Whittret
Whizzing
Whomever
Whopping
Wickedly
Wickered
Wideness
Widening
Widowing
Wielding
Wifehood
Wifeless
Wig-block
Wigmaker
Wild-boar
Wild-born
Wild-duck
Wildfire
Wildfowl
Wild-land
Wildness
Wild-wood
Wiliness
Willowed
Willyard
Winchman
Wind-band
Windfall
Wind-gall
Windlass
Windless
Windmill
Windowed
Windpipe
Wind-pump
Windring
Windrock
Wind-rode
Wind-rose
Windsail
Wind-seed
Windward
Wine-cask
Wineless
Wineskin

Wing-case
Wingless
Wing-shot
Winnower
Winterly
Wiredraw
Wiredrew
Wire-heel
Wire-rope
Wire-work
Wireworm
Wire-wove
Wiriness
Wiseacre
Wiseling
Wiserite
Wishbone
Wish-wand
Wish-wash
Wistaria
Witch-elm
Witchery
Witching
Withdraw
Withered
Withe-rod
Withheld
Withhold
Withwind
Wittolly
Wivehood
Wiveless
Wizardry
Woad-mill
Wobegone
Woefully
Wolf-fish
Womanish
Wonderer
Wondrous
Wontless
Woodacid
Woodbind
Woodbine
Woodbird
Woodborn
Woodchat
Wood-coal
Woodcock
Wood-dove
Wood-evil
Wood-hole
Wood-ibis
Woodland
Woodlark
Woodless
Wood-lily
Wood-lock

Wood-mite
Woodmote
Woodnote
Wood-opal
Wood-pulp
Woodrock
Woodroof
Woodruff
Wood-sere
Wood-shed
Woodskin
Woodsman
Wood-soot
Wood-vine
Wood-wale
Woodwall
Woodward
Woodwork
Wood-worm
Wood-wren
Wooingly
Woolball
Woolding
Wool-dyed
Woolfell
Wool-mill
Woolpack
Woolsack
Woolwork
Word-book
Wordless
Workable
Workaday
Workgirl
Work-room
Workshop
Worksome
Wormcast
Wormgear
Wormhole
Worm-like
Wormseed
Wormwood
Worricow
Worthily
Worthite
Woundily
Wounding
Wrackful
Wracking
Wrangler
Wrannock
Wrappage
Wrapping
Wrathful
Wrathily
Wreakful
Wreathed

Wreathen
Wreckage
Wrecking
Wreckful
Wrestler
Wretched
Wriggler
Wrightia
Wristlet
Wrist-pin
Wrizzled
Wrongous

## X

Xanthate
Xanthein
Xanthian
Xanthine
Xanthite
Xanthium
Xanthoma
Xanthous
Xanthura
Xantippe
Xenogamy
Xenolite
Xenotime
Xenurine
Xeransis
Xerantic
Xiphioid
Xylocarp
Xylonite

## Y

Yachting
Yanolite
Yardwand
Yarwhelp
Yataghan
Yeanling
Year-book
Yearling
Yearlong
Yearnful
Yearning
Yeldring
Yeldrock
Yeomanly
Yeomanry
Yestreen
Yielding
Yokemate
Yoke-toed
Youngish
Yourself

Youthful
Yttrious
Yuletide

## Z

Zalophus
Zambomba
Zamindar
Zampogna
Zantiote
Zaratite
Zarzuela
Zealless
Zealotry
Zelanian
Zemindar
Zenithal
Zeolitic
Zeppelin
Zerumbet
Zeticula
Zibeline
Zinckify
Zingiber
Zionward
Ziphioid
Zirconia
Zizyphus
Zoanthus
Zodiacal
Zoetrope
Zoiatria
Zomboruk
Zoneless
Zooblast
Zoochemy
Zoogenic
Zoogloea
Zoograft
Zoolater
Zoolatry
Zoolitic
Zoometry
Zoonitic
Zoonomia
Zoophaga
Zoophily
Zoophyte
Zooscopy
Zoosperm
Zoospore
Zootomic
Zopilote
Zwieback
Zygadite
Zygodont
Zymology